Martyn Bennett is Professor of Early Modern History at Nottingham Trent University, where he has also served as the university's first graduate school head. His research focuses on the British and Irish civil wars, the military revolution of the seventeenth century and the British Isles in the early modern period. He is the author of *Oliver Cromwell* and the *Historical Dictionary of the British and Irish Civil Wars*.

'This authoritative account of Cromwell's military leadership has a refreshing breadth of approach. Based on long and intelligent reflection, it offers vigorous and enjoyable arguments and is often original in its judgements. It will have the unusual merit of demanding the attention of scholars while appealing to the wide public audience interested in military history.'

Blair Worden, author of *The English Civil Wars 1640–1660*

MARTYN BENNETT

Cromwell at War

The Lord General and his Military Revolution

I.B. TAURIS

LONDON · NEW YORK

Published in 2017 by
I.B.Tauris & Co. Ltd
London • New York
www.ibtauris.com

ISBN: 978 1 78453 511 7
eISBN: 978 1 78672 247 8
ePDF: 978 1 78673 247 7

A full CIP record for this book is available from the British Library
A full CIP record is available from the Library of Congress

Library of Congress Catalog Card Number: available

Typeset in Stone Serif by OKS Prepress Services, Chennai, India
Printed and bound in Sweden by ScandBook AB

For Deborah

CONTENTS

LIST OF PLATES

PLATE 1 Oliver Cromwell, by Robert Walker, *c.*1649. National Portrait Gallery NPG 536.

PLATE 2 Francis Willoughby, 5th Baron Willoughby of Parham, by unknown artist, mid-seventeenth century. National Portrait Gallery NPG D27155.

PLATE 3 A reconstruction of civil war Newark by Simon Fleming.

PLATE 4 Edward Montagu, 2nd Earl of Manchester, by unknown artist, published 1647. National Portrait Gallery NPG D18333.

PLATE 5 Thomas Fairfax, 3rd Lord Fairfax of Cameron, by Wenceslaus Hollar, after Robert Walker etching, 1648. National Portrait Gallery NPG D23416.

PLATE 6 Harquebusier's armour. English, mid-seventeenth century. © Royal Armouries.

PLATE 7 The Battle of Dunbar, 1650. Seventeenth-century plan by Payne Fisher. Lebrecht Music and Arts Photo Library / Alamy Stock Photo.

PLATE 8 The north walls at Clonmel. Part of the town walls which survived Cromwell's assault in May 1650. Design Pics Inc / Alamy Stock Photo.

PLATE 9 Gold Dunbar medal showing Oliver Cromwell, by Peter Blondeau, after an original by Thomas Simon, 1656. National Portrait Gallery NPG 4068.

LIST OF MAPS

All maps created by Sue Sinclair.

ACKNOWLEDGEMENTS

I wish to thank my colleagues at Nottingham Trent University (NTU) for their support whilst I worked on this book. For their unfailing willingness to listen as I pondered over tactics and strategy and conflicting modern interpretations of major battles, I am grateful. I also thank the postgraduate students I have had the pleasure of supervising, who have likewise listened to similar problems and to tales of the delights of battlefield trudging. Thanks also to colleagues outside NTU, David Appleby, Andrew Hopper, Stuart Jennings and David Blackmore, who have been useful sources for queries and so on over the past months. Thanks once again go to the staff members of various libraries, including the British Library, the National Archives, the NTU library and to the archivists at the various records offices who over the years have supported my work. The same thanks go to the staff of the Cromwell Museum and more recently to the staff of the National Civil War Centre at Newark.

My thanks also go to Lester Crook at I.B.Tauris who has supported the work throughout, and from whom the idea for the book originated.

Finally, thanks again go to Deborah for her unfailing tolerance.

PREFACE

In his forty-third year, Oliver Cromwell, with experience of urban government and committee work in the House of Commons, clapped a sword to his side. Whilst this would be nothing unusual for a gentleman, he also donned a buff coat and put on a trooper's metal helmet for the first time in his life. Cromwell had been appointed a captain of horse by parliament, with the authority to raise 80 troopers and appoint junior regimental officers and non-commissioned officers. Cromwell had not served in the military before in any capacity. Other gentlemen charged with creating troops of horse and company's foot had served abroad on the continent, or at least held posts in the county Trained Bands, but Cromwell was a virgin soldier amongst those who had never led men in war or in military training. Unlike the vast majority of others in similar positions during 1642, Cromwell was to rise to colonel and on to lieutenant general, before in 1650 becoming lord general.

This book explores Cromwell in the context of the wars in which he fought, from leading a troop of horse in 1642 to commanding a huge continental-sized army at Worcester nine years later. Most of the book focuses on the fighting, but throughout his military career Cromwell was a political soldier: he had been given command because he was a politician and he used his dual position as an MP and a soldier to attain both political and military goals throughout the 1640s. Because he was such a successful soldier, he became the focus of political and national attention at the end of the 1640s. He was the first president of the republic's Council of State in 1649, and later the man to lead the coup of 20 April 1653, which finally pushed the Long Parliament out of its far-too-comfortable seats in St Stephen's Chapel. However, whilst the first part of this story takes up space in the book, the latter part does not, focussing as it does on Cromwell in the field. The first two chapters present a brief résumé of

Cromwell's early life, firstly to demonstrate the career path from which the middle-aged man veered in 1642, and secondly to chart the route into war, which caused many men's careers to change so wildly in the middle of the century. We follow Cromwell's role in the coming of war, which serves both to highlight his continued unsuitability for the role of a commander and how he came to be placed in the position of command.

As a background to the story of the civil wars in England there were two or perhaps three phenomena which had important consequences for what was experienced across the British Isles between 1637 and 1653, for Cromwell's actions. The first two phenomena, religion and continental war, are related. The Protestant Reformation of the previous century had never gone unchallenged, and an aggressive counter-Reformation had been at least the underlying, if not overt, factor in a series of wars which had important political causes and consequences for several decades, before the British Isles were engulfed in rebellion and war as the Catholic nations and empires sought to destroy the Protestant faiths and the states which had 'adopted them'. Secondly, a war on the continent raged on and off, before and during the period of war and rebellion in Britain and Ireland that would become known as the Thirty Years War. This war had seen many of Cromwell's contemporaries and comrades in arms gain military experience and become veterans. English and Welshmen, Scots and Irishmen had fought in various armies, Protestant and Catholic, sometimes both, and oft-times not according to their own religious preference. This experience they brought back to their home countries at various times between 1638 and 1651, and used their knowledge to advise, train and lead soldiers in various capacities and military ranks during the civil wars.

A third phenomena may well have been less tangible to the participants of any of these wars, as it was labelled only 300 years later as a 'military revolution'. There are various definitions of this revolution, depending upon the perspective taken. These range from the development of fortress or siege defences focussing on the *trace Italienne*, and counter-measures adopted by the besiegers, to battlefield tactics for infantry and cavalry and the size of armies. They include the logistical requirements of armies and the fiscal measures generated, which in turn supported the logistics and the humanist philosophical contribution to command and training. There is no doubt that each of these impacted upon what happened in the run-up to war in the British Isles, as regiments were raised for the first and second Bishops' Wars and beyond, but until August 1642 they had no impact on Cromwell. Mr Oliver

Cromwell Esquire of Huntingdonshire and Cambridgeshire was until that month a civilian. He had, as far as we know and despite speculation, never been abroad, never mind served in the ongoing wars there, and he had not taken on any role in the English militia forces, the Trained Bands, either in the peacetime of his majority, 1620–38, nor in the years of war before the civil war broke out in England, 1639–40. As we shall see, he was technically the wrong man for the job in 1642. Nevertheless, despite this handicap he clearly was the man for this role. As this book will argue, he understood and absorbed what was required of him and conscientiously took on his new role and the facets of the military revolution which affected him. Whilst serving at regimental level he quickly demonstrated the attributes of a field officer, and went on to develop those skills needed by a regimental and brigade commander before being in an official position requiring him to take on these roles. Field command and strategic sense seemed to come easily to him, and although the brevity of his short military career led to gaps in his experience, which showed even as his career came to an end, the balance was firmly tipped the other way and his success far outweighed his shortcomings. We can easily brush aside the speed of his rise through the officer ranks, and point to Wellington or Napoleon a century-and-a-half later making equally speedy leaps through the ranks. However, each of these men and others like them had built up the experience of command slowly over a number of years of training and campaigning before being propelled rapidly through general officer posts. Cromwell did not have the years of training or campaign experience under his baldric: he trained as he fought, learned as he rose from captain to general and outshone his vastly more experienced contemporaries and those with whom he had started on the blocks as a novice.

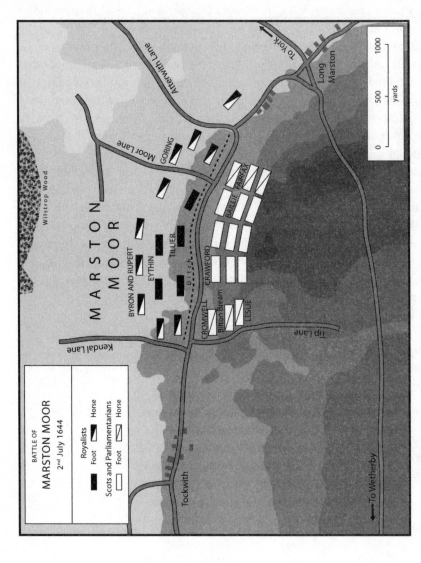

MAP 1   The Battle of Marston Moor.

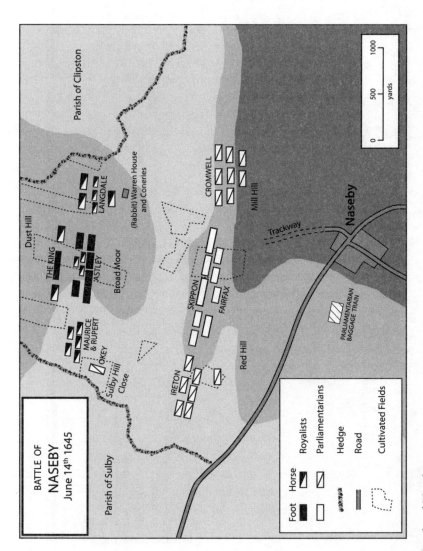

MAP 2   The Battle of Naseby.

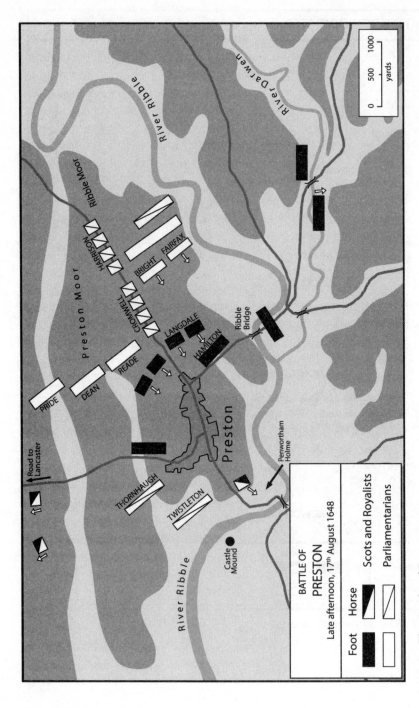

MAP 3   The Battle of Preston.

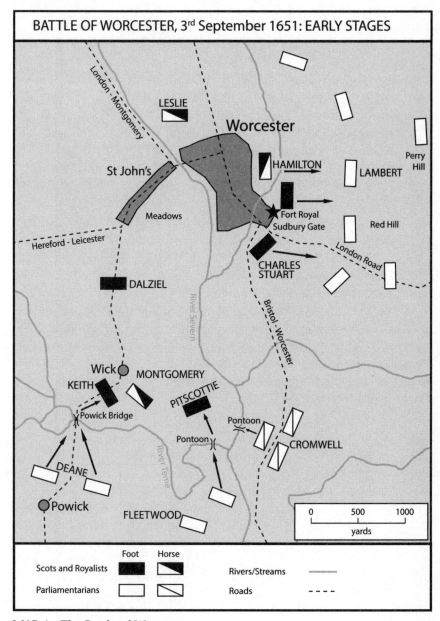

MAP 4 The Battle of Worcester.

1

CROMWELL THE MAN

For most of his life Oliver Cromwell lived away from the public gaze. Not only did he not play any role in military affairs before 1642, for much of his life he held only minor public office and even then this was sporadic rather than constant. Only partly was this due to the social position into which he was born – sometimes it was because of the precarious nature of his status when an adult, and sometimes due to Cromwell's own failings when in office. Looking back on his life, when he was the Lord Protector, Cromwell rightly said of his origins that he was 'by birth a gentleman living neither in any considerable height, nor yet in obscurity'.[1] It was quite an apt description of the station he was born into, and like each social stratum in life his carried certain obligations. Following the death of Cromwell's father and Cromwell reaching the age of 21, and even more so once he was married, there were major family obligations. He had seven sisters and would go on to have a large number of children of his own, and in the 1620s there were the requirements of urban government to attend to. Whilst familial duties remained with Cromwell all of his life, a drop in social status in his early thirties meant a hiatus in socio-political obligations for several years. The rules and regulations of military life were something which did not impinge upon Cromwell until after he was 43 years of age. By then his public and political life had accelerated rapidly beyond the confines of small-town eastern England and even the university town of Cambridge, where he had become an MP at the age of 40. This chapter explores the early years of Cromwell's life from birth until his incorporation into oppositionist politics.

Cromwell was born on 25 April 1599, the second child of Robert and Elizabeth Cromwell of Huntingdon.[2] Their first male child had died during infancy and this, in a society which practiced male primogeniture, made Oliver the son and heir to the majority of the family estate at birth. His family were members of what in England is known as the gentry, that is, they had no aristocratic titles themselves, although they had relatives who were in the nobility, and neither were they were members of the 'middling sort' of yeoman or husbandmen who farmed and still may have worked on their lands themselves. The male members of the family would be entitled to be addressed as Mister (Mr) and the women Mistress (Mrs): and they could have a coat of arms. Cromwell's father was, later in his life, referred to as an esquire, which implied that he was a gentleman of superior status, but this was because of his father's and his brother's social positions rather than an achievement of his own. Cromwell's grandfather, Sir Henry Cromwell, was the wealthy owner of the nearby mansion of Hinchingbrooke and vast estates beside, but Cromwell's father, Robert, was not his eldest son, which meant that he was not in line to inherit the majority of Sir Henry's estate: that would go to Robert's older brother Oliver. Mr Robert Cromwell was Sir Henry's second son and as such his part of the family wealth was relatively small and not enough in itself to justify the rank of esquire. Indeed, an estate of £300 a year could be a gentleman's lot but it would be unlikely to be an esquire's; such an estate could even be enjoyed by a yeoman and his family. However, when Sir Henry died in 1603 and Robert's brother Sir Oliver, after whom young Oliver was presumably named, became the owner of Hinchingbrooke and the majority of the family's other estate, Robert's own status had improved: he had his inheritance from his father, but his uncle's elevation in status through knighthood also dragged Robert in its wake. Whereas at Cromwell's baptism in 1599 Robert had been referred to in the church register as a gentleman, at the baptisms of Oliver's younger siblings he was referred to as esquire.[3] The inheritance Robert received from his father was small for a gentleman, consisting principally of a house opposite St John's Church and an estate which generated an income of £300 a year.[4] The house was a former friary fronting on to the north end of Huntingdon's High Street near its junction with Balms Hole. Three hundred pounds a year was not really an income sufficient for an esquire to fulfil the obligations of the rank, and yet Robert was expected to continue playing a public role because of his membership of the Cromwell family. Robert Cromwell had already been an elected MP back in 1593, he was also a justice of the peace for the county of Huntingdon and served as a town councillor in Huntingdon: in short he was playing the social and political roles expected of one of the Cromwells. Robert's older brother Oliver, whilst still the heir to Sir Henry's lands and property, was also an MP in 1593 but unlike Robert this would not be his only stint in Westminster. Oliver was knighted by Queen Elizabeth in 1598, and at the coronation of King James VI of Scotland as King James I of England he was made a Knight of the Bath. In that same momentous year when Sir Henry died, Sir Oliver succeeded to Hinchingbrooke, Ramsay Abbey and the rest of Sir Henry's estate.

Oliver's mother, Elizabeth, was born a Steward, another gentry family, which farmed the estates of Ely Cathedral. Like the Cromwells, the Steward family had profited from the Reformation, the dissolution of the monasteries and the sales of former church property that followed. For Elizabeth her marriage to Robert was her second: her daughter and first husband had both died in the 1580s, and into her second marriage, to Robert, she took £60 a year and a small brewery. The Reformation had literally made the Cromwell family in more ways than wealth: the Cromwell name was in their case a product of the Reformation. The family had previously been called Williams, and occasionally their original name would appear in legal documents even during Oliver Cromwell's adulthood. In the early sixteenth century the Welsh lawyer Morgan ap William had married Katherine Cromwell, daughter of a blacksmith and the sister of lawyer Thomas Cromwell, who worked for Cardinal Thomas Wolsey. After Wolsey's fall from grace, Thomas Cromwell had served King Henry VIII in various offices until he too fell from grace in 1540. By this time, Katherine and Morgan's son had been adopted by Thomas Cromwell and had taken the surname Cromwell. Richard Cromwell married well: his wife Frances's father had been Lord Mayor of London. Working closely with his uncle Thomas, Richard put the dissolution of the church establishments into effect in the Huntingdonshire and Cambridgeshire region. As monasteries, nunneries, chantries and other religious organisations were wound up, their lands were sold off by the king. Those involved in these financial deals made money and gained lands themselves: thus by such means Richard Cromwell gained Hinchingbrooke Nunnery, Ramsey Abbey, Sawtry Abbey, St Neot's Abbey and Huntingdon's Priory and its friary: these became the core of the Cromwell lands: of which Oliver Cromwell's immediate family inherited a small portion.

Four days after his birth, Cromwell was baptised across the road at St John's Church.[5] He was his mother's sixth child. Elizabeth Cromwell's first daughter Katherine had died and was buried with her father, Elizabeth's first husband, in Ely Cathedral. Her second child, Joan, died before she was ten. Her third child, Elizabeth, was born in 1593, son Henry (born in 1595) died in infancy, Catharine was born in 1597, followed two years later by her brother Oliver.

A sixth Cromwell child and Elizabeth's eighth experience of childbirth, Margaret, was born in 1601. She was followed by Anna (1602), Jane (1605), Robina (1607) and Robert in 1609, who lived for just a few months. In all, Elizabeth gave birth to 12 children, of whom seven survived infancy. Husband Robert himself was one of the ten children of Sir Henry, the 'Golden knight', and the marriages of his siblings and their children would be important in Cromwell's own life, as they married into the Hampden, Whalley and St John families, members of which would become important figures in either the opposition to Charles I, the parliamentarian cause or the protectorate. On the other hand, family marriages would tie the Cromwells into families that would espouse the royalist cause in the ensuing civil war.

Cromwell's parents and his sisters lived in the friary. It was, of course, a perk of the Reformation. The friary was sited next to a common drain on Fryer's Lane on the east side of the town.[6] There is very little evidence of the life of Cromwell as a child and a great deal of speculation – a number of stories exist about his youth, none of them of any substance.[7] When Cromwell was old enough he went to school, just a few yards from his home at Huntingdon Grammar School, another building recycled from the pre-Reformation town – it was the former Hospital of St John the Baptist and thus associated with the church where Cromwell had been baptised. The headmaster there was the minister of the town's main parish, All Saints, Dr Thomas Beard. Much has been made by earlier historians of Beard's influence on the religious development of his charges. He was for many years identified by them as a 'puritan', and it was therefore inferred that he awoke in Cromwell the religious radicalism which marked Cromwell's adult political and religious outlook. This is a good example of reading history backwards when dealing with Cromwell: Beard's religious outlook was as much coloured in the eyes of later observers by his association with Cromwell rather than the other way round. In work by John Morrill, Thomas Beard has been shown to be a trimmer, adopting the appropriate proclivities to suit the diocesan regime. Moreover, although he had critiqued the Pope in *The Theatre of God's Judgement*, Beard was not a radical. Moreover, he was a pluralist – he would hold more than one living or parish: as well as All Saints and the school mastership, he was master of the town's hospital; he held the living of the parish of Kimbolton, and later that of St John's opposite Cromwell's house. Plurality was something frowned upon by the 'puritans' he was supposedly counted amongst, as it meant that the word of God was being inefficiently propagated. As Professor John Morrill has shown, Beard was unlikely to have been much of an influence on the young

Cromwell, and in any case years later Beard would be involved in the painful and humiliating end of Cromwell's life in Huntingdon.[8] We thus know little of what the young Cromwell was like as a schoolboy and whether or not he was a conscientious student; he did not discuss it much as an older man and rarely gave clues as to the sources of his knowledge, beliefs or inspiration – other than the influence of God and interpretations of God's intentions through providence.[9]

On 23 April 1616, just short of his seventeenth birthday, Cromwell was recorded as having matriculated at Sidney Sussex College Cambridge. Matriculation, whilst sounding like some form of qualification, actually means little more than enrolment. That Cromwell progressed to Cambridge does not, in itself, prove that he was a good scholar – attendance at one of Britain's six universities was for many a social rite rather than a career path, as indeed was later progression to one of the Inns of Court for legal training. If we know little of the course of Cromwell's school life, we also little of Cromwell as a student; the master of his college was Dr Samuel Ward, like Beard later identified as a 'puritan' who influenced Cromwell. Ward is more easily assimilated into the milieu of reformers than Beard, yet how much influence he had is difficult to assert.[10] However, he too had establishment credentials, having been one of the team responsible for the Authorised Bible published just four years earlier, and would in two years' time be a member of the delegation to the synod of Dort, part of King James's ecumenical desire to unite the churches of Protestant Europe as a preparatory move towards uniting Christendom.[11] The timing of the synod was unfortunate, coinciding with the continent's descent into a war which would last for most of the remainder of Cromwell's life.[12] Yet the college, with its plain glass-windowed chapel, was noted later by William Laud (who went on to become Archbishop of Canterbury) as a 'hotbed of puritanism'.[13] In any case, how much time does the head of a university's college (even a small one) get to spend with any one undergraduate? In Cromwell's case Ward had little time because Robert Cromwell died in 1617, less than a year after his son and heir had gone to Cambridge. In any case, Abbott's assertion that Cromwell was surrounded by, if not imbued with a puritan ethos can be questioned as the delegation James sent to Dort was not remarkable for its radicalism, and the king had even negated the influence of his home church, the Scottish Kirk, by appointing an Anglican as its representative at the synod.[14] The social aspect of university attendance is underlined by the fact that Sidney Sussex was associated with the Montagus, relatives of the Cromwells and from the same area of the country.

On the other hand, none of Cromwell's contemporaries there played any great role in his later life.

Cromwell's university career was brief; just a year after starting at Cambridge the death of his father meant that he had to leave university and return home. It seems that there was no consideration of him returning after having gone back to Huntingdon for the funeral and settling of affairs. Just as John Morrill has suggested with regard to the schooling under Beard, it seems that the university life that Cromwell was exposed to had little effect on him.

With a lack of money in this rapidly expanding family, it was obvious that Cromwell would have to earn a living, and it is possible that going to Cambridge had been planned as the first stage of getting him an education to suit a gentleman in a business or profession. Attending university in the seventeenth century was not necessarily about getting a degree: there were other facets of university life which were important, although some aspects of undergraduate life, centred on alcohol and dancing, have remained common over the centuries. There was also great emphasis on family links – there was often a strong intergenerational link to particular colleges, and meeting and making socio-economic connections with other undergraduates and their families was important too, although as we have seen, other than the Montagu connection to the college, Cromwell was not able to develop strong links with the families which had sons there at the same time.

After Robert's death there are three years in which Cromwell largely disappears from view.[15] Rumours persist about his having attended one of the four Inns of Court – the 'training colleges' for the legal profession in England. But there is no strong evidence to support that, although there is nothing to rule it out completely. There is speculation that he went to Lincoln's Inn, which given that the Inns like universities had familial and regional links, would not be out of the bounds of possibility.[16] Legal knowledge would be useful to a member of the gentry, especially one who had rural property. Buying, selling and entailing property required legal expertise, and an awareness of the processes involved would enable a gentleman to make the right decisions and lessen his reliance on a paid lawyer's expertise. There was also the same potential to forge friendships and the sort of economic and social ties which a gentleman would find of use later in life regarding land management and government at local and central level. Thus even a man with an incomplete undergraduate education might find his way to one of the four Inns of Court – Gray's, Lincoln's or the Middle or Inner Temple – all clustered north of the Chancery in London. The Inns had regional links too, as students from particular areas of England and

Wales tended to gravitate to particular Inns, and the same was true of families. In the years after Cromwell's estate had been settled, Gray's Inn was, in Abbott's phrase, 'a list of his relatives, friends and later dignitaries'.[17] As the list of associates included the future president of the court that would try Charles I, two of Cromwell's major generals, the speaker of Cromwell's parliament and three members of his Council of State, such a venue would have catered for a convocation of the future protectorate. However, Cromwell was not amongst them, so despite the social introductions which could have potentially smoothed working relationships in Cromwell's future, formally at least Cromwell was not there, even if the Inn did recruit traditionally from East Anglian families.[18] Speculation instead has Cromwell at Lincoln's Inn, and there are similar familial links: his father and two uncles had been there, and three of his later associates were there at the same time as Cromwell could have been there. The second and third of Cromwell's biographers claim that he was there, and both assert that he combined the social skills of a gentlemen on the path to adulthood whilst undertaking the required levels of scholarship.[19] The only issue is that there is no solid evidence: there is no entry in the Inn's documentation and Cromwell himself never referred to having been there, and nor does he ever appear to have mentioned having any legal training. Nor, apart from two early biographers, does anyone else.

During the three 'missing years' of Cromwell's life – those which followed his inheritance and that cover the period when, it is speculated, he attended one of the Inns of Court – Cromwell seems to have made use of his broader family connections in London and the home counties.[20] Possibly through his auntie, Joan Barrington, Cromwell met Elizabeth Bourchier, daughter if the London furrier and former Lord Mayor, Sir James Bourchier, and neighbour of aunt Joan, sister of Cromwell's father. It has been suggested that Cromwell stayed with the Barringtons when in London, but it is possible that he also accompanied them to Essex, where the Bourchiers had a country seat. Whatever the case, the couple met and married in the City of London at the Church of St Giles, Cripplegate, on 22 August 1620.[21] Cromwell, now of age, was able to settle the parsonage of Hartford on his new bride: the estate was now his. The Cromwell family proceeded to grow. Together, Oliver and Elizabeth had nine children between 1621 and 1638; five boys and four girls, most surviving into adulthood, although the first-born, Robert, died in childhood during the 1630s, as did the last son, James. Alongside Cromwell's sisters and his mother, Oliver, wife Elizabeth and their growing family crowded, until 1631 at least, into the old friary.[22]

LOCAL POLITICS AND GOVERNANCE

Like his father, Cromwell served on the town council of Huntingdon and would represent the town in parliament once. We know little of Cromwell's work in town government, but we know because of his fall from grace in Huntingdon that he was not amongst the most powerful men in the town, even though the Cromwell name still had cachet, despite his uncle's decline in wealth and the sale of Hinchingbrooke.[23] There was little to rise to anyway. In terms of population Huntingdon was a small town, but as a county town it was not without importance, and it sat astride England's most important road, the Great North Road, which when Cromwell had been born had been the road from London to the northern shires. Once Cromwell had passed his fourth birthday this had changed somewhat, as the road was more important as the link between the king of Great Britain's principle capital cities, London and Edinburgh. Thus Huntingdon was something of a transport centre. The town was administered by a council of 24 men, called burgesses, who together constituted the common council, and it was an incorporated borough with its own seal: all of this meant that it was a self-governing community. Huntingdon was also a parliamentary borough because it was the county town. Cromwell was one of the burgesses, and with the other 23 comprised the only members of the electorate in the town which chose the two MPs.[24] Cromwell sat on this council, like his father before him, leaving little trace of what he was doing there. In 1628 he was chosen by his fellow councillors to be one of the town's two MPs. He came second in the vote, after James Montagu. Montagu's family was on the rise in the area, and a year earlier Sir Sidney Montagu had bought Hinchingbrooke from Oliver's uncle: nevertheless, the Cromwell name helped Oliver take his seat in the House of Commons. The parliament of 1628 would be contentious in and of itself, but it would be a formative element in the crisis which would develop ten years later. The still-new king, Charles I, was engaged in expensive wars on the continent, simultaneously at war with the old enemy Spain and the regular ally France. To continue the wars he needed money, and his first two parliaments had refused to grant him enough, being suspicious of the king's favourite George Villiers, Duke of Buckingham, who was not only led the king's forces in failed military projects, but supported changes in church governance and liturgy favoured by the king and Bishop William Laud. By 1628 the king had tried extra-parliamentary means of raising cash. First he asked for a benevolence – a request for gifts of money from those able to pay. This had generated very little and was followed by the setting of a forced loan, which obliged the same sort of people who had steadfastly refused to shower the king with cash to lend the money at a fixed rate of interest. Despite it being obligatory the loan was resisted, and so by 1628 Charles decided to brazen it out and face parliament to demand regular taxation.[25]

Cromwell played only a minor role, as befitted a new member of the House of Commons. There is no record of his contribution to discussions of financial matters, but he did contribute to a religious discussion which centred on a two-time convert Dr William Alabaster, who had some years previously preached a sermon outside St Paul's Cathedral which was felt to be too pro-Catholic, and to which Thomas Beard had been commissioned to respond. Beard's response had been prohibited by the Bishop of Lincoln, Richard Neile. However, under orders from the Bishop of Ely, Beard had preached his response only for Neile to charge him with disobedience. Cromwell contributed to the debate by relating the story to the committee. It was in itself of little consequence, but would be another contribution to the image of the king's being surrounded by anti-puritans.[26] The parliament, having generally opened in a conciliatory manner with the king apologising for past behaviour and parliament voting him two subsidies, was to end in acrimony and with great drama. Parliament wanted to ensure that they were not in the same situation again and drew up a Petition of Right, which affirmed that parliament was the sole authority when it came to imposing taxation upon the nation. Whilst the king did in the end assent to the petition after a great degree of prevarication, he determined to dissolve parliament and sent an order to the speaker of the House of Commons, Sir John Finch, to do so on 2 March 1629. As Finch made to rise, several MPs jumped on him and held him down. With the session thereby kept open the Commons made several declarations about the illegality of the Arminian form of worship Laud and the king had determined on and the illegal collection of customs and excise. It is a pity that we do not know what Cromwell did on that momentous day, but it was to be echoed in his return to national politics 11 years later.[27]

Upon his return to Huntingdon, Cromwell took up the role of a councillor again: but there was to be drama in his small political world which dramatic consequences for him. It all began over a bequest, the sort of thing that over many years would increase a town's commonwealth and finance the actions and patronage of its council. Richard Fishbourne, born in the town in the

1580s, left the town £2,000 in his will. He had risen from an apprentice to become a wealthy mercer during his short but profitable life. The town considered its options for three years, trying to decide whether to spend the whole sum on providing employment for the poor or split it between that and endowing a preaching lectureship – the latter was the favoured approach. Thomas Beard, the pluralist preacher and teacher, was happy to add this source of income to his purse. The means by which an endowment would be established involved purchasing land and using the income from renting the land out, but it took years to find a suitable plot. In any case there was opposition to using the money in such a way: some councillors believed that two lectures a week from Beard and the weekly lecture in nearby Godmanchester was enough, and that the whole sum of money, amounting to £100 a year, should be used for employing the poor. This was proposed by councillor Thomas Edwards and possibly supported by Cromwell. Beard and the other councillors argued for a £60–£40 split, with the former going to the town's poor and the latter into Beard's pocket. The Mercers' Company who were overseeing the legacy on behalf of the Fishbourne estate then found out that the council wanted to use the £40 to pay Beard for the lectures he was already giving on Wednesdays and Sundays so that it no longer had to. The Mercers, who had initially liked the idea of a lectureship, but did not want the money spent on existing lectures, then suggested that a new lecture should be set up in the parish (St Mary's), where Fishbourne had lived.[28] Then King Charles I intervened and ordered the town to appoint Beard. The Mercers successfully argued that there should be open competition, and after considering seven candidates, including Beard, they appointed Richard Proctor. At around that point the Bishop of Lincoln, John Williams, intervened, trying to get the decision reversed but have the lectureship shared between Proctor and Beard. The Mercers paid Beard off with £40 and accepted Proctor's appointment. This all took six years: Fishbourne died in 1625, the first Fishbourne lecture was in 1631. The ramifications for Cromwell, who was possibly Edwards's ally in this, played out in parallel.[29]

In February 1630 some of the councillors, who had supported Beard rather than Edwards, petitioned for a new town charter. It was granted in July and the new governance structure consisted no longer of two bailiffs and an annually elected common council, but instead twelve permanent aldermen, able to selected successors to vacancies and chaired by a mayor annually selected from amongst themselves. Below them was a common council of much reduced importance. Neither Edwards, nor Cromwell, were selected as aldermen, although Cromwell, along with Beard and Richard Bernard, was to be a borough justice of the peace or magistrate. Cromwell and another of the former councillors not selected as an alderman, William Kilbourne, the town's postmaster, reacted angrily to the changes and did so publicly. Cromwell was accused of 'disgraceful and unseemly speeches' directed at the newly installed mayor, Lionel Walden.[30] This was an unacceptable attack on legally appointed officials, and Cromwell and Kilbourne were summoned by the Privy Council for investigation. This was serious, and when Kilbourne and Cromwell presented themselves the council kept them in custody for six days. After an initial hearing, the investigation was put into the hands of the Lord Privy Seal, the Earl of Manchester, head of the Montagu family, a near neighbour and distant relative of Cromwell's who held great influence in the town.[31] Manchester's findings on 6 December 1630 were devastating for Cromwell: despite deciding that Cromwell had not attacked the town's constitution as sanctioned by the king per se, and therefore was not a dangerous social or political revolutionary, he had accused the new administration of intending to use powers conveyed by the charter to their own pecuniary advantage. Manchester exonerated the mayor and Richard Barnard from any wrongdoing in obtaining the charter or the potential corruption of which they were accused. This left Cromwell guilty of a personal attack on the mayor and others whom he believed might extort money from the town's property to their own ends without there being a check on their power. Manchester reported that the attempt to turn burgesses against the new charter was 'very indirect and unfit, and such as I could not but much blame them that stirred it'. Cromwell was obliged to make a public apology to the mayor and Barnard there and then, as the two were also in Westminster for the hearing.[32] Cromwell's honour was thus impugned: he was not an alderman, he had refused the position of JP for the town and it was unlikely that he would be able to restore himself to a position of any standing, or get elected as an MP again. The town would know of his humiliation, and so in 1631 he took his family away.[33]

The departure from Huntingdon did not end Cromwell's association with local government entirely. After he left Huntingdon under the cloud of opprobrium generated by the Privy Council case, he moved to nearby St Ives. Whilst John Morrill sees the move as being impelled by the shameful outcome of the charter dispute, Simon Healy thinks that Cromwell sold much of his Huntingdon estate as a move in the direction of Ely, the location of a prospective upturn in the Cromwell fortunes.[34] St Ives was east of Huntingdon, along the fen-bordered River Ouse, on which it nestled on the northern bank, in the direction of the Isle of Ely. St Ives was not a major town like Huntingdon. It had three manors in it – St Ives, Slepe and Bushletters – and by the late seventeenth century 600 acres of arable land, 200 acres of leys or closes and 280 acres of meadow, where Cromwell had ten beasts pastured by October 1634.[35] There were there constables, two for St Ives or the Street and one for Slepe. Cromwell, an experienced urban magistrate, was not called upon to take up this post in his time there. The constables were the top of the town's secular administrative tree and fulfilled the role of overseers of the poor until the late 1660s. Likewise there were three churchwardens also selected on the ratio of two for the Street and one for Slepe. Other officials, apart from the four surveyors of the highways (three for the Street and one for Slepe), were associated with St Ives's role as a market town.[36] Cromwell may simply not have attained one of the offices because he was only in St Ives for a relatively short time: he was, at least at first, on the equivalent of a 'council', the group colloquially know in shire parishes as the vestry simply because it often met in the church vestry – formerly the room where the priest had donned his garments before a service. Cromwell signed vestry documents, although one of his signatures was cut out, apparently by a churchwarden, in 1732 according to Edward Pettis.[37] One of the documents he signed was a minute approving the selection of the churchwardens: practice elsewhere would suggest that such roles were taken by the same people who signed such documents in their turn, and thus Cromwell could expect to hold such an office in time. At this point Cromwell was regarded as one of the inhabitants of St Ives. This was a word used to distinguish the better-off people in the town who filled such offices and functions, and marked them out from parishioners which meant everyone else. In St Ives, Cromwell rented property in the area of the town referred to as Slepe: indeed he rented part and perhaps at first all of the Slepe Hall estate which was owned by one of his relatives, Henry Lawrence, and lived in the estate's farmhouse. The manor of St Ives itself belonged to the Earl of Manchester, whose family had by this time bought Hinchingbrooke from Sir Oliver Cromwell and ironically had been the central figure in Cromwell's downfall.[38] Further decline once Cromwell was settled in St Ives is possible. John Morrill suggested that Cromwell was by then really a yeoman farmer, working the land himself. It is also possible that he had to sublet some of the farm at Slepe Hall too.[39] This might explain Cromwell's absence from subsequent vestry minutes, especially if he did slide from gentry status to that of a yeoman.[40] However, such a slip would only be brief, and Cromwell never officially dropped out of the gentry, because there was to be no heraldic visitation of the county to judge his status officially whilst it was questionable. He remained a gentleman, even an esquire, because he was never recorded as otherwise. In any case, status was often in the eye of the beholder as well as the herald, and the people important to Cromwell did not behold him as anything else, even if the parishioners of St Ives would see someone of declining fortunes. This further decline was brief, for the expectations awaiting Cromwell that Simon Healy outlines came into play.[41]

2

CROMWELL AND THE COMING OF WAR

The flight from Huntingdon was potentially catastrophic. Honour was a central concept in the seventeenth century; it was the core of being for the gentry and others, and holding on to it could transcend other personal catastrophes. A public dressing-down would reflect on Cromwell and upon any dealings he would have – social, economic and potentially political. It may be that he felt that he could no longer hold his head up in Huntingdon; it is certainly the case that he would make no more progress there. Thus as we have seen, Cromwell, his wife and children moved eastwards to St Ives, where on a far more limited scale he took up local government once again. As for his social status, the move did not improve matters. The Cromwells were tenants in a large farmhouse and they may not have had the whole building to themselves. Status amongst those considered to have any was precious, and there was great concern that it should not be abused. Membership of the gentry was restricted to those who could demonstrate that they did not undertake labour themselves to earn a living, or that they were descended from armigerous families. In many ways, looking like and living like a gentleman and being considered such by one's gentry peers conveyed gentility. Officially the status of gentleman was conferred, and continued qualification monitored, by the College of Heralds. Periodic county-based visitations were the process by which fraudulent claimants and those who had fallen in status were weeded out. Had the county of Huntingdonshire been subjected to such a visitation during the period 1631 to 1635 the Cromwell family might have had difficulty hanging on to its coat of arms. John Morrill is not alone in thinking that they may have slipped out of the gentry category, and that Cromwell had become a yeoman farmer in St Ives.[1] Most of the property in Huntingdon, barring 17 acres and the Hartford rectory supposedly settled upon his wife, had been sold in May 1631. Even the family home had been sold, although Elizabeth senior continued to live there as a tenant.[2] The farm belonging to Slepe Hall was rented to Cromwell by Henry Lawrence, and he also knew the new vicar there, Henry Downhall from Cambridge, who had become godfather to young Richard Cromwell in 1626.[3] Much has been made of the push factors which impelled Cromwell to move to St Ives, and when a draw factor has been mentioned it has centred upon Downhall or the availability of Slepe Hall's farm. More recently, Simon Healey has argued that there was one reason more important than any other: Cromwell's great expectations were focussed on Sir Thomas Steward, brother of his mother and thus his uncle.[4]

Sir Thomas Steward was, compared to Cromwell, a wealthy man: he owned freehold estates in Ely, Elme and Emneth in Cambridgeshire. He also leased lands from the church, particularly in Ely. The Stewards had, like the Cromwells, accumulated these estates since the Reformation, aided by having the post-Reformation Dean of Ely in the family.[5] In a break from family tradition, Sir Thomas decided to leave some of his estates to heirs outside the family, and from 1610 Cromwell was referred to in a lease as one of three lives over which the tenancy would run. He would not inherit the lease, but the lease would last at last as long as he was alive, although Sir Thomas had also named his wife and a son of his cousin. Later, Sir Thomas selected Robina, Cromwell's little sister, as one of the named lives for a second lease. In 1625, Sir Thomas took on a lease which he could only transfer upon his death to his direct descendants – he had no children – or to the children of his sisters, and that would therefore include the by this time married Cromwell. Healy speculates that by this point he had been named heir in a will which no longer exists, for although the Stewards had kept their estates within the family, they had never been entailed to 'heirs of the body, male', which would proscribe the limits of inheritance. This would, Healy believes, have given Cromwell the freedom to sell off his own inheritance in Huntingdon. Moving to Ely was thus less of a risky punt, as Cromwell had expectations of far greater estates in Ely and St Ives was therefore more than a geographical step in their direction. What happened next, as accounted by Healy, is not to Cromwell's credit.

It may be that the four years in St Ives had not been an enjoyable time, and that the minor local government roles held no challenge for him, for Cromwell seems to have tried to get hold of his inheritance early by questioning Sir Thomas's state of mind. It remains a suspicion only, but on 30 September 1635, following an inquisition, Sir Thomas was declared not to be a lunatic. As Healy suggests, there would be great shame in even the suggestion that a family member was mentally ill, even if the projected outcome – guardianship of the individual concerned – was the aim. Cromwell falls under suspicion, perhaps with the collusion of Sir Thomas's wife Bridget, of investigating the means by which he could control his uncle's estate early. Whatever the case, it is suggested that Cromwell and his uncle were not on good terms by the mid-thirties.[6]

Such impatience had hardly been necessary, as both Dame Bridget and Sir Thomas died within months, she in December 1635 and he in January the following year. Yet the damage had been done: Cromwell was to receive his inheritance, which comprised part of Sir Thomas's freehold estate and all of his leasehold land, but only once Sir Thomas's debts had been paid. Sir Thomas left his goods to the executor without any responsibility to use them to discharge the debts, as Cromwell would later wrongly claim. The outcome of Sir Thomas's death may well, however, have more than quadrupled Cromwell's income beyond the level it had been in Huntingdon, before his fall from grace, even if it took about two years to settle Sir Thomas's debts. Cromwell was in a much more secure financial position by the last years of the 1630s. He was now far more socially and economically secure.

In the course of Cromwell's life the four nations of the British Isles had undergone great changes, some of which were incomplete and many of them contentious. He had been born into an England which had been ruled by Queen Elizabeth for 41 years. England was united with Wales about 60 years earlier by a series of acts which brought together the means of governance in the two nations, completing a process of absorption lasting half a century. On the other hand, Ireland was an unfinished project. Although it had been subject to English colonisation as long as Wales, whilst there had been extensive settlement in parts of Ulster, Munster and Leinster, there were areas which remained in Gaelic Irish hands. When Cromwell was born the country was wracked by war. The remaining powerful chieftain, Hugh O'Neill (also known as the Earl of Tyrone), had come to the end of his tether as the incomers encroached on his prerogatives; the client clans associated with the O'Neills and his estates and led a rebellion which spread from his Ulster lands throughout Ireland. Meanwhile Scotland was an independent state under King James VI. It was a modernising nation and its king was the heir to Elizabeth's thrones.

As Cromwell turned four, Elizabeth died and the young Scottish king inherited England, Wales and Ireland, where the war came to an end.

The Great North Road became the axis of the king's power. As Cromwell attended the grammar school, the newly united nations underwent great shocks. King James's plans for political union between England and Scotland were blown off course by the gunpowder plot of 1605, which was aimed at destroying the king, his family, the Privy Council and both houses of parliament in one fell swoop. The great rejoicing at the king's (and everyone else's) survival masked the fact that the central political relationship in England and Wales, that of monarch and parliament, was under great strain and riven by mistrust. Parliament believed that the king was trampling on their privileges and trespassing on their rights to determine financial legislation. So by the time there was a plan to settle the question of the king's income (known as the Great Contract) in 1610, the level of mistrust was so high that the plan failed, leaving the king in debt and the state finances mired in inefficiency. As Cromwell approached his twenties, King James's plan to bring together the Protestant churches of Europe was likewise doomed. The synod of Dort where Dr Ward went as a delegate coincided with the beginning of the war in Europe which would become known as the Thirty Years War. James was so ill-prepared that there was no immediate military commitment to the war, even though his daughter Elizabeth and her husband were at the heart of the conflict. The war divided the nation, as there was some consternation at James's failure to support his daughter's cause. Partly this was because the king had advised against the actions of Elizabeth and her husband, Frederick V Elector Palatine. In 1618, angered by constant erosion of religious tolerance in Bohemia, the nobility had revolted, declared the selection of Ferdinand of Styria as king to be null and void, and instead offered the crown to Frederick. Despite several Protestant monarchs, including King James, advising against accepting the crown, Frederick became convinced that he was the vanguard of the Protestant monarchs in the struggle against Roman Catholicism and accepted. His possession of the throne was brief. Ferdinand was elected Holy Roman Emperor and the full force of the empire was turned upon Bohemia. In 1620 the empire's forces had defeated Frederick's army at the Battle of the White Mountain outside Prague, ending the Bohemian adventure. Moreover, the Palatinate electorate itself was invaded, and Frederick displaced from his position of elector. James's second reason for not supporting his son-in-law and daughter's cause was that he thought diplomacy, not war, was the answer to international conflict, and sought to bring about peace through negotiation.

In 1625, when Cromwell seems to have become a potential heir to Sir Thomas's lands, King James died and his son Charles became king. Although

James and the parliament had become steadily estranged, James was a hardworking and quite subtle politician: his son was not. In an attempt to control the king's financial demands, parliament refused to vote for the normal continuous excise and customs taxes. Coupled with this, there were ambitious plans for intervention in the war on the continent and an attempt to support the beleaguered Protestants of France, which pitched Britain simultaneously against two of the great powers of Europe in what turned out to be expensive failures. There followed the search for alternative methods of funding which culminated in the parliament of 1628 of which Cromwell was a member. In England and Wales during the 1630s, Charles ruled without a parliament, and so legitimate political opposition was denied a traditional outlet. For the most part opposition was quite muted. Nevertheless, the king's continued search for alternative sources of funding and his religious policy did provoke opposition. The greatest expression arguably came when ship money was levied across the country from 1635 onwards. Ship money was an emergency tax levied on coastal counties to support sea-borne defence. In 1634 it was levied, with the money supposed to be used to redevelop the navy which had been shown to be in a dreadful state during the wars of the 1620s. In 1635, however, the tax was levied across the whole country for the first time. Opposition grew year after year once it was understood that the tax was to be collected over an extended period: in some inland parts of the country the courts began to fill up with defaulters as the 1630s progressed.[7]

At this point Cromwell paid his tax without complaint when it was levied on Huntingdonshire and Ely. For some years it was thought that Cromwell had defaulted when it came to paying an earlier version of Charles's extraordinary levies, the Distraint of Knighthood, imposed back in the 1620s. Certainly he had not paid the sum of money early, but he did pay it eventually. The Distraint of Knighthood was a fine levied on those men who were deemed to have the financial or other means to be knighted at the coronation of a new monarch, but had not taken up the opportunity. Back in 1625 when the new king was crowned, Cromwell's estate in Huntingdonshire was still sound enough for him technically to bear the honour (it had been set many years before at an income of £40 per annum and had not been adjusted for inflation); he belatedly paid as the Fishbourne case played out. From the evidence of one document where his name had been added later, a whole story about him not paying and his uncle paying on his behalf had been concocted. No such thing had occurred; Cromwell had paid his meagre £10 late, but because of a range of practical reasons, not from any attempt to make a political protest. Even his cousin, John Hampden, who would later make a principled stand against ship money, paid his £30 levy.[8] Similarly with ship money, Cromwell seems to have paid without demur despite Christopher Hill's belief that he had qualms.[9] This was all the more remarkable because his two cousins, Oliver St John and John Hampden, were intimately bound up in the celebrated challenge to the legality of the tax.[10] Hampden withheld a payment of 20 shillings on his Buckinghamshire estate as a test. Appointing St John as his lawyer, Hampden argued that the tax was an emergency tax which could lawfully be levied by the king when parliament was not sitting, but that it should be replaced as soon as possible by a tax levied with the authority of parliament, and that since the tax had been levied in 1634 there had by 1638 been plenty of time to call parliament. The 12 senior judges decided seven to five in favour of the king, the tightest margin possible. This was taken by some as an excuse to challenge the tax further, and there was an escalation in opposition across the country as the decade reached its violent conclusion.[11]

Where Cromwell did object to the vicissitudes of the reign was the religious question. In the later years of King James's life, the king's preference for an Episcopalian church structure, such as that which had survived the Reformation in England, received a fillip. Whilst the Scottish church, the Kirk, had developed a quasi-independent position whereby the king was treated as a member of the church rather than its head, the church in England had retained the monarch as supreme governor. Despite the king's reinforcement of the role and position of bishops in Scotland, many of these men retained a basic belief in the Kirk's structures and interpreted their roles as bishops within those structures rather than subverting them as the king intended. Nevertheless, at the outset of James's reign in England and Ireland in 1603 both the Kirk and the Church of England to a greater or lesser degree rested on Calvinist foundations. However, in England a more 'user-friendly' set of tenets were making headway in the church. At the core of Calvinism was the concept of double predestination: this was the conviction that humankind was divided into the elect and the reprobate, and that this division had happened at the Creation. The elect were destined for salvation and a place in heaven at the side of Jesus; the reprobate was condemned to Hell. It mattered not what sort of godly life a person lived – the decision could not be altered. Neither personal act, nor religious rite would make any difference to a person's fate. The catch was, of course, that no one knew their soul's future and therefore many, especially the godly, sought the truth through an introspective examination of their relationship with God in order to attempt to divine their fate. However, within the Church of England there was a growing number of men influenced by the Dutch theologian Arminius, who rejected predestination and focussed instead upon the ability of the human soul to choose its path by taking up an offer of salvation presented to them by the church, through the undertaking of good works and the acceptance of seven sacraments from baptism to extreme unction. This carried with it other implications, such as shifting emphasis from the pulpit, where the texts which would support the introspective exploration of the potential for grace were preached, to areas of the church where the sacraments were administered. For decades the altars, stripped of their beauty at the Reformation, had been laid out as a meal table. The Roman Catholic sacrament of communion had moved from transubstantiation (the understanding that through the actions of the priest, bread or wafers and wine became the body and blood of Christ, as some believed Jesus had declared to be the case at the Last Supper), through consubstantiation (the understanding that the bread or wafers and wine represented the body and blood of Christ) and even to a belief that communion was just an act of memory (a recreation of the Last Supper where the bread, rather than represented anything, *was* the food that Jesus and the disciples shared). When the communion became one of the sacraments which got a person through the 'pearly gates', then it was to be regarded as more important than the communal sharing of food. The reformers in England therefore believed that the communion table should be restored to its position in the chancel rather than left in the middle of the church, and should even be railed off as ground upon which only the minister could normally tread. Naturally this was not a neutral act. Thus elderly people who could remember the 1550s, those who had travelled in southern Europe and those who knew their religious history, were familiar with such spaces as the fenced-off altars: they knew them to be features of Roman superstition. Thus for some, the Arminians or the supporters of the reforming Bishop William Laud were nothing more than Roman Catholics determined to take England back into the Catholic fold. Cromwell had identified himself as one of those who believed this to be the case back in the 1628 parliament, when he brought up the story of Bishop Neile forbidding Beard from preaching against Alabaster's sermon. By the mid- to late 1630s Cromwell was even more closely associated with such ideas. We are not certain when Cromwell became so thoroughly convinced of a sense of rebirth, which identified him as what might be called a puritan and would certainly identify him as one of the Godly, but there are clues. There was his illness during the sitting of the 1628 parliament during September, when he consulted the celebrity doctor

Theodore Mayerne, one of the late king's physicians. Cromwell presented the symptoms of a black bile in his excessive phlegm, along with a cough and stomach aches after meals. Mayerne diagnosed *valde melancholicus*, and prescribed a series of remedies.[12] This type of illness is associated with personal crisis, but Cromwell was accused of hypochondria by a doctor who treated him in a later decade and Healy is suspicious of the Mayerne story, believing that it might actually have been Cromwell's cousin, the son of Sir Oliver, who had been the patient. He also points out that the diagnosis in any case was a physical, not a mental one, and the in full *valde melancholicus corpus ad modum sici opsius, habere dolorum ventric periodicum* refers specifically to the black bile and may have been a symptom of stomach ulcer, rather than the symptom of a deep personal crisis.[13] Cromwell's religious development may well have been a slow process lasting from before the 1628 parliament into the 1630s, and may have been a reaction to the religious developments in England and his association with the men who opposed them, such as his cousins, the Bourchiers, and the Earl of Warwick's circle, as well as Henry Lawrence, his St Ives landlord.[14] More specifically, John Morrill has identified a series of lecturers and ministers as being formative in Cromwell's religious life. One was Job Tookey, a lecturer in St Ives until 1635 when he was put out of his position by Bishop Williams, and thus there whilst Cromwell was renting Slepe Hall farm, another was Dr Walter Welles, a preacher in Godmanchester and a graduate of Leiden. Welles was a correspondent of Samuel Hartlib and John Dury, a pair of radical thinkers whose ideas ranged from novel ways of teaching to uniting the Protestant churches of Europe. Both men appealed to various other opponents of the king's government, including the likes of Cromwell's cousins, Hampden and St John, the Riches and the Russells. Cromwell was of course associated with the fringes of these families through the Bourchiers and the Barringtons for almost two decades, which cemented his links with Welles and other godly men there, and amongst the Mercers' Company with whom he still had the links forged during the Fishbourne dispute.[15] Moreover, with Sir Thomas's inheritance (even if it took a couple of years to finalise), Cromwell, with his credentials as a gentleman never tested and therefore intact, now had an income which could support a more active social or political role. He also had the right religious credentials: he could be a useful man.

However, even if there were religious fractures in the state – as William Laud rose through the episcopacy from Bishop of London to Archbishop of Canterbury and imposed his liturgical and physical reforms on the Church of

England, and his master the king sought out ever-more controversial financial wheezes – England and Wales were far from breaking into open rebellion. The same was not true of Scotland however. Charles I had begun to anger his home nation shortly after his accession. He interfered with land ownership with proposals to revoke grants of land made during his minority; he reconstructed the Scottish Council with supporters, some of whom were 'new men'; worse still, the king sought to bring the Kirk into line with the Church of England – bearing in mind that this was a church that Laud was vigorously reforming, the way ahead was going to be troubled.[16] This was confirmed in 1633 when the king belatedly went to Scotland to be crowned. He eschewed the traditional site and had an altar built at Holyrood Abbey's east end, and had the ceremony conducted in an English fashion – driving his point home by having the Kirk bishops dress in English style and forcing upon them the indignity of playing second fiddle to the English bishops in utter contempt for the fourteenth-century Declaration of Arbroath, which had asserted the independence of the Scottish church.[17] On 23 July 1637, the pulpits of Scotland gave voice to Charles's religious policy as the various bishops, deans and ministers intoned the new Prayer Book, only to receive an echo of catcalls, angry shouting and the sound of breaking furniture – in St Giles, Edinburgh at least, cutty stools flew through the air in the direction of the pulpit.[18] The Privy Council offered the king advice and suggested withdrawing the book, but the king was incensed and ordered obedience. However, he got more and more opposition; firstly a supplication and then a National Covenant which bound its thousands of signatories to defiance of the king's policy.[19] Despite numerous opportunities to back down, the king remained confrontational and allowed the situation to escalate by refusing to negotiate and beginning to plan for war. The Scottish opposition grew ever-more radical, establishing, over the next months and years, an executive government which borrowed heavily on the pyramidal structure of Kirk management. By the summer of 1639 both sides had geared up for the war: the king calling out the Trained Bands militia funded by coat and conduct money, a further tax levy on a country which was readying its opposition to ship money collection; the Scots with a radical county-by-county assessment which owed something to the organised collection of tax on the continent and an army of Covenanters.

Largely speaking, apart from the king's officers and their reluctant troops, England and Wales stood by as observers. Certainly we do not know what attitude Cromwell took, but as his colleagues and the leading figures of the group upon which fringes he hovered were reading and disseminating Scottish propaganda, we can assume he was keeping informed. Indeed we could go further: he, like his political and religious allies, would have no desire to impose a church structure from which he was increasingly dissenting upon another nation. The first of the conflicts which heralded 16 years of war, and which were eventually to transform Cromwell's life so dramatically, was brief. Known as the First Bishop's War (the Scots and others named the war after Laud), the conflict had consisted of two brief bouts of fighting, one after a truce had been announced. Charles had planned a multi-kingdom approach with an English and Welsh intervention across Scotland's southern border, an attack from Ireland across the North Channel, dividing Ireland from Scotland, and an amphibious attack on the Scottish east coast by loyal Scots. Partly because of the lack of time and money, the ambitious plan gave way to scouting across the border in the direction of Kelso and a rising in Aberdeen by loyalists. Both ended in disaster. The scouting force under the Earl of Holland was driven out of Scotland in a panic after a brief skirmish with the Scottish commander in chief, with Lord Leven's army being reinforced, according to legend, by a herd of cattle it was commandeering for food. This ignominious but ominous event prompted a truce. The Aberdeen loyalists were defeated by another Covenanter general, the Earl of Montrose, outside Aberdeen a few days after the truce had been agreed. The king had no intention of a permanent settlement, and the Pacification of Berwick was understood by neither side to be lasting. Despite advisors suggesting that the war was destructive to the king's reign across Britain and Ireland, and tentative suggestions that a parliament be summoned to Westminster, the king pressed for a renewed war, and Scotland responded by dismantling monarchical rule and developing an efficient war machine. However, the king was soon disabused of one thing: he could not raise sufficient funding through the motley fiscal means he had assembled over the past nine years. Opposition to ship money was growing, to the extent that it was simply not coming in in sufficient amounts, and the disinclination to pay it had spread to the coat and conduct money which funded the Trained Bands in 1639. By early 1640 there appeared to be no alternative to calling a parliament in England and Wales. Sir Thomas Wentworth, formerly one of the king's chief parliamentary opponents, had transformed himself into a loyal servant during the 1630s, and had become the Lord Deputy of Ireland and the Earl of Strafford. In late 1639 he began to formulate a plan based on his own success at managing the 1634 Irish parliament. He believed that he could similarly manage a new parliament in Dublin, and persuade it to approve a financial package for the king. Given such an example, how, he reasoned, could a Westminster parliament refuse to follow suit?[20] And so the plan was laid; a parliament met in Dublin on 16 March and, as hoped, approved the collection of four subsidies. In England and Wales it was all quite different. For a start, as soon as parliament was summoned, large numbers of people simply stopped paying ship money – it was of course an extra-parliamentary levy not to be collected when parliament sat.

In Ireland the elections had been quiet and seemingly well managed, and at least for the time being it did look as if Strafford was fully in control. In England and Wales the king did not manage the elections with the same success. In elections – a problematic word when describing the creation of a parliament in England and Wales – not all the seats were contested; in some cases, as in Huntingdon when Cromwell was chosen as an MP in 1628, only a couple of dozen people actually voted. There was no such thing as a secret ballot and allegiances were thus very public. Much of the competition, if indeed there was any at all, was in the selection of the candidates for the election itself. Here vested interests within the borough seats and between powerful members of the nobility in both rural and urban constituencies exercised influence, and often could simply impose candidates on the electors. During late 1639 and early 1640 this process was set in motion. Aristocrats, with their own seats in the House of Lords secure, set about choosing candidates. The earls of Warwick and Bedford, along with Lord Saye and Sele, began selecting their chosen men. Cromwell's cousins Hampden and St John were supported in their candidacy, and stalwarts of past parliaments were included; John Pym and his half-brother Francis Rous were also in line for seats, as were others associated with the last English and Welsh parliament. By now Cromwell had finally settled the last of the legal issues around his inheritance and was more settled financially. He was now a potential candidate for parliament.

Cromwell had already transformed himself since the death of his uncle. The family were moved again, this time to Sir Thomas's house at Ely where his mother had been born – she moved with them too.[21] Another and final child, Frances, was born in 1638 and was christened in St Mary's Church, Ely: there were now four sons and four daughters. Cromwell had become something of a campaigner too. The area of fenland in which Cromwell had grown up was subject to projects and plans aimed at turning marshy ground into something more productive, through drainage. Such a plan was well supported: it was seen as an improvement which would turn marginal land into profitable arable lands. Wealth would be created and farming improved.

All such schemes tended to ignore that fact that these lands would carry common rights upon which poor labourers would depend in order to supplement income from work, and the very land upon which they had erected their house. Whilst members of the Cromwell family generally supported the prospect, Sir Thomas Steward had rightly understood the difficulties which would beset the poor when the lands were drained. The work was opposed with demonstrations and threats of violence, and Cromwell was associated with such opposition. He later stated that it was not the principle, nor the scheme itself which he opposed. Instead, like his uncle, he believed that the drainers would profit from the scheme and that there would be little left for the poor inhabitants, causing long-term and damaging poverty. He could hardly complain about the project itself – his cousins Hampden and St John were investors.[22] Cromwell was beginning to have a more public role for the first time since the personal catastrophe at Huntingdon in 1631. It was noticed.[23]

Cromwell was already associated with members of the opposition clique. His cousin, John Hampden, with legal representation from another cousin, Oliver St John, had challenged the right to collect ship money as if it were a regular tax. Ever since his late teens he had been at least tangentially associated with the Earl of Warwick, through the Barringtons and Bourchiers. Even if soured by the humiliating sale of Hinchingbrooke and by the 1631 debacle, Cromwell could claim association with the Montagus and their head of family, the Earl of Manchester. The Cromwell boys attended the well thought of Felsted School, which enjoyed the patronage of the Riches, the family of the Earl of Warwick and the Fiennes family, and its head Lord Saye and Sele. Cromwell's connection with the Mercers' Company, which continued long after the Fishbourne incident, simply cemented these connections. Moreover, in other ways Cromwell had shown he was of the 'right stuff': his spiritual conversion – being 'born again' into a more intense and personal faith – made him the sort of man who could be trusted. It is quite risky to place a huge range of interpretations on to a single piece of evidence, especially when it is one amongst so few, but historians have relied heavily on one letter written by Cromwell on 13 October 1638 at his house in Ely. The letter is written to his cousin Elizabeth, the wife of Oliver St John. Sadly it alone remains of what evidently may have been a sequence of letters which meant a lot to the two correspondents, as Cromwell opens by referring to his cousin's comments of his previous 'lines'. By itself the letter can be read as Cromwell's conversion narrative, but in all likelihood is the continuation of one rather than being unique. Cromwell expresses his thankfulness for a God who had never abandoned him and will in time bring him to His tabernacle. He has brought Cromwell to walk in the light, having:

> loved darkness, and hated the light; I was a chief, the chief of sinners. This is true: I hated godliness, yet God had mercy on me. O the riches of his mercy! Praise Him for me, pray for me that He who hath begun a good work would perfect it to the day of Christ.[24]

The letter does contain other elements; there is a slight hint that one of the Cromwell boys had been favoured – possibly a reference to getting him into Felsted. He sends his and his wife's love to the St John family. If ever the St John family needed proof of Cromwell's spirituality and his familiarity with biblical text, for it is replete with references from the bible, this was it. It is problematic having just the one letter, but it is clearly evident that it is part of a sequence, and there is little reason to suspect that the effusiveness and biblical scholarship was unique to this letter.[25]

Despite these credentials, it is not entirely clear how Cromwell's next advancement was secured. On 7 January 1640, he was elected a freeman of the town of Cambridge, a place where, apart from having briefly attended university 23 years earlier, he is not known to have had connections.[26] He was thus in a position to be a candidate in the upcoming elections. Why he was placed there or by whom is unknown. It is not likely that any of his aristocratic connections had put him there; they did not have strong enough links to the town, and had they attempted to place him it may well have been resented – the MPs for Cambridge were usually senior members of the corporation.[27] As to his own merits, W.C. Abbott overstated his case for Cromwell having displayed natural and admirable talents that would have marked him out to the borough; much of what he says is, as Morrill has told us, untrue at that point, or at best arguable.[28] It is a case which Antonia Fraser largely followed.[29] Nor was he a borough man, and nor was he of particularly sound financial standing in terms of MPs who were not men firmly ensconced in borough politics. More recently than either Abbott of Fraser, John Morrill suggested that Cambridge did choose Cromwell in spring 1640 because of his connections to the oppositionist lords – possibly not because of grand national reasons, but for more parochial ones. For example, he might have been able to represent the grievances the town had against the university – particularly its ability to control the town's churches and fill them with Laud's men. Furthermore, the university chancellor was the Earl of Holland, a member of the Rich family and brother to the Earl of Warwick, and Cromwell might have had some encouraging personal influence, for Holland was not a Laudian. James Heath, the author of the early critical biography of Cromwell, *Flagellum*, believed that Cromwell's selection was engineered by an active puritan faction on the council, who knew of Cromwell from one of the local religious meeting in the Isle of Ely, but this cannot be verified.[30] Sir Charles Firth believed that it had been the fen drainage issue which had secured Cromwell's nomination to the seat.[31] Despite some concerns at Cambridge regarding the level of the River Cam, Ian Gentles is certain that Cromwell's interest in fenland projects had nothing to do with his election there.[32] Whatever the case, Cromwell was selected as candidate for the Westminster parliament and duly elected, along with Thomas Meautys esquire, a court candidate who had sat for the town in 1628, to sit in the parliament due to assemble in April. Meautys was the nominee of Lord Keeper Finch, and both men were unopposed in the selection of March 1640.[33]

The parliament which assembled that spring did not last long. The members had no intention of meekly following the example of Dublin. The ire of many of the members would have been sparked as soon as the king departed the opening ceremony, for he left Lord Keeper Finch to outline the business the king wanted transacted. Finch was a bad choice, for he had been the Speaker of the Commons who was held down in his chair at the end of the 1628 parliament, whilst the house by acclaim supported a series of declarations about religion and government. Two of the men imprisoned for that action, Benjamin Valentine and William Strode, still languished in prison, whilst the respected Sir John Eliot had died in prison. More importantly, parliament was not willing to discuss supporting the king's desire for a war, and refused to take seriously his assertion that foreign powers were stirring the Scots to rebellion.[34] John Pym set the agenda with three things that need to be tackled before finance would be discussed: the liberties of parliament – dealing with the dissolution of 1629 and the imprisonment of MPs; religion – the Laudian reforms and the backsliding towards Roman Catholicism; and finally the threat to property posed by the king's extra-parliamentary taxation in contravention of the Petition of Right. The king was furious, and 11 days into parliament's sitting went to the Lords to express his anger and insist that finance be discussed. The king asked the Lords to move the Commons on in their discussion, and the next day they put it to the lower house in a joint session: this incensed the Commons who saw it as breach of privilege.[35] The king, sensing that he was would have to compromise, offered to cease collecting of ship money in return for four subsidies. As the Commons considered ship money to be illegal, and argued that coat and conduct should be abolished too – in short, abolishing an illegal tax was not much of a compromise. This drove the king into a greater fury, and on 5 May he dissolved parliament: it had sat for three weeks. Cromwell hardly had time to get comfortable: there is no record of his activity.

Charles was still determined to go to war against the Scots, who had by this time secured three important things: firstly, their reforms of the Kirk had seen it shorn of bishops and effectively disestablished from the political state machinery, which would allow politicians to interfere in its structure in the future; secondly, they had in some ways disestablished the monarchy, having created an executive government in the Fifth Table which served in the stead of the Privy Council, and had taken charge of the calling of elections and of the process of dissolution of parliaments; thirdly, using these mechanisms they had established a county-focussed structure of wartime management and financing, which was far more effective than any system the king could put in place.[36] Even so, the Trained Bands of England and Wales were summoned northwards once more. There was a lot more opposition this time. Ship money and coat and conduct money were all but impossible to collect, and soldiers smashed church windows and altar rails, opened gaols, mutinied on their way north and in some cases murdered their officers. Others objected that the terms of service in the Trained Bands did not encompass a 'foreign' war, but only home-defence.[37]

Suspecting that the king intended to strike at Edinburgh, a detailed strategy was devised there on 6 May 1640: the decision was to invade the north-east of England.[38] They were aided by the failure of Charles to create an effective and coordinated plan. Many of the Trained Bands were slow in moving north, 8,000 Irish soldiers were never to be shipped over and delays crept in. On 20 August, Alexander Leslie led the Army of the Covenant over the border, and eight days later defeated the king's army at Newburn on the River Tyne, inland from Newcastle.[39] It was a catastrophic defeat, and the king's vanguard forces retreated into the North Riding of Yorkshire. The north-eastern counties of England, Northumberland and Durham, became occupied territory, and the counties west of the Pennines, Cumberland and Westmorland, were threatened with occupation if the king was slow to pay the reparations of £850 per day. The Scots also demanded that any treaty be ratified by a Westminster parliament. The king hoped that the invasion might produce a united front against the Scots and sought to have a council of the peers summoned to York, close to the front line. However, he was now in a very weak position: the Irish parliament had collected one subsidy, but reduced the value of the subsequent ones by over 75 per cent, and in the wake of the Battle of Newburn, the Irish parliament began to question the very nature of government in Ireland. The peers in York were not impressed by the proximity of the Scots, and 12 of the peers, including the future 2nd Earl of Manchester and Lord Saye and Sele, presented the king with a petition calling for a parliament. By 24 September, when he opened the council, Charles announced that he had decided to call a new parliament. In reality he had no choice: backed by the gathering of nobles, the Privy Council had forced him into a corner over the issue.[40]

Once again the king's supporters were unable to manage the elections for the new parliament. In Cambridge, however, there was more of a context than back in March. Cromwell was selected as a candidate again, and so was Meautys. However, this time there was a third candidate, a member of the town's common council and chandler, John Lawry.[41] Cromwell took first place and Lawry the second seat. Meautys, and thereby his supporter Lord Finch, was defeated. Within a week of parliament meeting Cromwell was on his feet. Prisons still had within them the victims of political and religious policy. There were still the heroes of the House of Commons' defiance of Charles and Finch, there were religious opponents of Laud, William Prynne, John Bastwicke and Henry Burton, each mutilated in the stocks – Bastwicke on no less than two occasions – and there were others like John Lilburne, who had protested at the way such opponents were treated and tried to distribute their publications. Cromwell stood up for them one week after parliament met. Petitions from Prynne's wife, Prynne himself, a Scots preacher and John Lilburne were read out. Cromwell was not only one of those MPs appointed to look into the cases of Prynne and Alexander Leighton, he read out Lilburne's himself. Stephen K. Roberts has recently argued that this was part of an orchestrated presentation of petitions, with Leighton's notorious case being so well known that it needed no sponsor; Prynne's was regarded as a very serious issue and so was presented by veteran parliament-man Sir Francis Rous; whilst that of Lilburne, who was something of a supporting cast member, was presented by a relatively new man: Cromwell. New man he may have been, but he was clearly there because he has someone's trust and confidence. Adamson suspects that Rous's half-brother, Pym, might have been behind the selection of Cromwell, leaving something of a distance between himself and the radical Lilburne whilst ensuring that he was supported.[42]

Bringing these petitioners to the attention of the house was just the start. Cromwell, as we have seen, was appointed to a committee to investigate the cases of Prynne and Leighton, and thus he was soon sitting alongside the major players in the opposition camp, including John Pym himself – and he was noticed. Sir Philip Warwick noted that the first time he saw Cromwell was when he was speaking: 'He was very ordinarily apparelled for it was a plaine cloth-sute which seemed to have bin made by an ill country taylor, his linen was plain, and not very clean, and I remember a speck or two of blood upon his little band.' If his appearance was not remarkable, his eloquence was 'full of fervor, for the subject matter could not bear much of reason; it being on behalfe of a servant of Mr Prynn's who had disperst libels against the queen', although Warwick was not being complimentary and he was condemnatory of the house for paying Cromwell's fervour great heed; he was 'very much harkened unto'.[43] Cromwell was quickly appointed to other committees with cousins Hampden and St John, as well as other heroes of past struggle such as Denzil Holles, one of the men imprisoned (although in his case quite briefly) for holding Finch in his speaker's chair back in 1629. This committee, examining Leighton's case, was just one of 22 Cromwell sat on between 1640 and 1641, but historians disagree about what this said of Cromwell's position in parliament. John Morrill sees him as a fringe member of the chief opposition group led by Pym and staffed by his cousins, but J.S.A. Adamson thinks of him as a loner and somewhat of a loose cannon.[44] More recently, Stephen K. Roberts has viewed him as an 'effective and dogged advocate' whose role in committee work accelerated during the second session of the Long Parliament from two committee nominations a month to three. Moreover, he was not the loner of Adamson's essay, but well connected and with an agenda which focussed on the redress of grievances.[45] There were some slips which support Adamson's belief that Cromwell took little care to improve his standing in the house, and in late 1641 he completely misread the temper of the house when it discussed the Grand Remonstrance, believing that what turned out to be a very contentious document would have a smooth passage.

The months between the Long Parliament's assembling in November 1640 and the outbreak of the next war in 1642 were hugely eventful and even revolutionary. The Westminster parliament began to emulate the actions of the Scottish estates, which had reduced the king's role in government by ensuring that he could not dispense with the estates unless it consented, and also removed the king from the process of calling a session: parliament simply adopted the same measures. It also began to examine the Church of England. In the early days of the parliament – alongside political figures such as Finch, targeted after Oliver St John's committee reported on its investigation into ship money, and Stafford, seized because all three of Charles' kingdoms were assembling a case against him – the Archbishop of Canterbury was targeted and arrested.

The religious initiative came from a petition. Whereas some members of parliament would have been content with dismantling William Laud's reform programme, others want a complete overhaul of the church, its liturgy and its structures. A petition signed by 15,000 Londoners was presented to parliament demanding the dismantling of the episcopacy. So far-reaching would the consequences be that it was referred to as the 'root-and-branch' petition. Cromwell was nominated to a committee set up to discuss it. By May 1641 a draft bill had been drawn up by the committee, to a great extent along the lines of the petition, but also following debate and research. This included Cromwell's work in trying to understand the Scots' position on the matter, for they had suggested that uniformity in religion across the British Isles might be a good idea.[46] However, the bill did not progress far after its introduction into the Commons and Lords on 21 May 1641. Instead, months later a much watered-down bill, intended to manage the bishops better, took its place, and even this did not pass the house.

Despite this seeming waste of labours, Cromwell had other successes. He had with William Strode, another of the heroes of 1629, introduced a bill for annual parliaments which was transformed during the debates into the Triennial Act, allowing for regular parliaments to be called automatically rather than at the king's will. As the year progressed Cromwell continued work on a number of grievances, including a further fenland dispute, but religious matters absorbed him despite the failure of both of the reform bills.[47] On 8 August he made a speech in the Commons on removing bishops from the House of Lords – both his failed bills had sought to divorce bishops from secular government as in Scotland. Just before the root-and-branch bill progressed to parliament, the Earl of Strafford had been brought to trial, and following the failure to find convincing evidence of his guilt, had been executed by means of an Act of Attainder which required a far lower standard of evidence. During the trial a plot had been discovered within the army, which was still in existence and facing the Scottish army of occupation. The plot aimed at rescuing Stafford and restoring the king to his traditional powers; it was clear that the king himself was at least tangentially involved. When in the mid-summer the king planned to travel to Scotland to sign the peace treaty, Cromwell was very concerned. If the king were to sign the treaty and give formal assent to several acts of the estates it would be quite humiliating: he was both acknowledging his defeat in the war and his political emasculation. But Charles hoped to do neither. Instead he was planning on creating a royalist party in Scotland and staging a coup d'état in Edinburgh. Although Cromwell and his colleagues did not know this, they suspected that something might happen.[48] Cromwell warned that there would be 'danger in this kingdome if he go'. Even more importantly, Cromwell became interested in military affairs at this point.[49] In June he had argued that they should keep 'all convenience of defence'.[50] In August and October 1641, during the king's absence, Cromwell proposed that the Trained Bands should have an overall commander appointed by parliament: Cromwell nominated the Earl of Essex. On neither occasion did the Commons take Cromwell's advice, but it shows that Cromwell was becoming concerned that the king and or his supporters might be thinking of a military solution to Charles's political emasculation.[51] He was also concerned that men suspected of involvement in the spring Army Plot were communicating with each other, and those on bail were visiting those in the Tower of London; he proposed that they all be incarcerated.[52]

The king's attempted coup in Edinburgh was exposed, and the king had no choice but to accede to his military and political defeat. Just as peace with Scotland was achieved and the armies disbanded, rebellion broke out in Ireland. Once Stafford's grip on government had been loosened, the Dublin parliament began systematically dismantling not only the earl's administration, but the structures of government which had existed for nearly two centuries. However, this reforming work was undertaken largely by the newer men: Protestants who had come into the country during the previous century and not by older Protestant families, and certainly not by the Catholic Old English or old Irish Catholics. As a result, anger within the last two sections of Irish society began to boil over during 1641. By October a plot to seize the chief strongholds of Ulster and Dublin Castle, the seat of government, had been developed. On the night of 22 October the plan had been put into effect, and fortification after fortification fell into rebel hands, although Dublin remained secure. The rebellion spread across Ireland within weeks.[53] News of the rebellion reached Britain as the king made his way south to return to London. Pym and others had constantly used fear of a plot in Ireland as a mean by which to keep up the pressure for further reform. This had been particularly necessary during the summer of 1641, when many people thought that the work of rebalancing power had been done. However, Pym's plot had focussed on an imaginary conspiracy that centred upon the army Stafford had created for the war with Scotland, but he had also suggested that the queen was the centre of a Roman Catholic plot. Neither of these elements had incorporated the realities of the Irish situation.

The rebellion escalated the collapse of Stuart government in England and Wales. Whilst initially king and parliament maintained an impression of unity with regard to Ireland, other issues proved divisive. In order to continue the momentum for further reform and ensure the security of those reforms already made, Pym devised the Grand Remonstrance. This was to be a three-part document: the first part listed the grievances against the king's extra-parliamentary rule which had confronted parliament when it assembled in November 1640; the second part rehearsed the reforms parliament had put in place; whilst the third part outlined unresolved problems which parliament would now address. It was this document which Cromwell had thought would be unproblematic.[54] He was wrong. Debate began at 9.00 am on 22 November and only ended at 2.00 am the following day, the bill passing by only 11 votes. Moreover, the immediate publication angered many people and drove a wedge between the king and parliament, and even more controversially it created a royalist party made up of moderate reformers gathering around the king to inform his responses. Christmastide was violent, as London mobs demanded that bishops be excluded from parliament and forcibly kept them out, eventually achieving by violence what Cromwell had failed to persuade the house to adopt as policy. Sensing that such anarchy was turning many away from supporting parliament, the king attempted a coup d'état. On 5 January he tried to arrest five MPs: Pym, Cromwell's cousin Hampden, 1629 heroes Denzil Holles and William Strode, and Sir Arthur Hesilrige, as well as Lord Mandeville, son of the Earl of Manchester – the man who had investigated the Huntingdon affair in 1631. The attempt failed– the king burst into the Commons chamber with an armed guard peering in from the doorway, but the coup was a badly kept secret and the six men had been smuggled out of parliament and shipped down the Thames to London. As a result of the failure the king found himself in hostile territory as London turned on him. The royal family fled the city, and in the next days and weeks the queen went abroad to buy arms and ammunition, and the king headed north hoping to find support. Parliament began a process which would lead to it taking control of the military. A committee met in January to discuss control of the Trained Bands. By March it had drafted a Militia Bill which empowered parliament to nominate the county lord lieutenants, who had commanded the Trained Bands since the 1570s.[55] When the king would not agree to the bill, parliament put it into effect immediately as an ordinance and began to issue commissions to its nominee lieutenants. By doing so parliament had established the means by which it would undertake executive action for the next eight years: an ordinance was normally used when the monarch was unable to approve a bill through being indisposed through illness or by being abroad, to ensure the continuance of executive government – ordinarily the ordinance would be signed by the monarch upon his or her return to health or to the country. In this case there was little hope that the king would sign later. Once again, Cromwell's unfulfilled suggestions from the previous year had come to pass: in January bishops had been excluded, now the militia was under parliament's command and the Earl of Essex was the Lord General.

In the months which followed, as parliament's lord lieutenants set about mustering the Trained Bands, the king set up alternative machinery, reconstituting the moribund commissions of array which had, until the 1570s, been responsible for the Trained Bands.[56] These two rival mechanisms each attempted to galvanise support as spring turned to summer, sometimes in violent confrontation but more often in the face of sullen apathy. The Trained Bands comprised men of some standing and thus capable of holding political opinions and likely to be politically divided. As a result, apart from the five regiments of the London Trained Bands the attempt to create armies out of the militia failed.[57] Instead the rival sides began to issue individual commissions to men thought capable of raising their own troops, companies and regiments. These regiments had to be funded, and the search for money escalated during the summer months, with the king subverting as much of the £400,000 being raised for the war in Ireland as he could lay his hands on. It was this activity which thrust Cromwell into the war as a soldier. The two sides continued to negotiate whilst assembling their armies, but parliament's Nineteen Propositions, which set out its proposals for a settlement, were unacceptable to the king as parliament probably suspected they would be. At the same time they declared the king to be incapacitated and themselves to be sovereign. With the political lines drawn at this point, the military divisions became open and both sides began openly to assemble armies.

The king requested that the two English universities send to him the silver plate which their colleges had accumulated, intending to melt it down for sale or to make coinage from it. As MP for Cambridge, Cromwell was sent to try and stop the university from complying. To do so he had to assemble armed men to prevent a convoy assembled by the high sheriffs of Cambridgeshire and Huntingdonshire and others from heading towards the king. Assembling troops from west Cambridge, Cromwell, his cousin Valentine Walton and Frances Russell headed to Cambridge only to miss the first convoy to set out to the king at Nottingham. By the time Cromwell got to Cambridge, the county Trained Bands were ready to guard another ammunition train. Cromwell placed men along the Great North Road in the direction of Huntingdon and stopped all traffic. Somehow the convoy was prevented from leaving the town. On 17 August, having seized the county arsenal in the castle at Cambridge, Cromwell was ordered to exercise the county Trained Bands, and was then ordered to prevent people from leaving the region to go to the king. Five days later the king raised the royal standard in the precincts of Nottingham castle. One week later Cromwell was authorised to raise his own troop of horse in Huntingdon.[58]

3

CAPTAIN CROMWELL: THE MAKING OF THE SOLDIER

> The charge of the Captain of horse is of so great importance and qualitie in the army, it should not be given to any, but to men of singular valour and experience.[1]
>
> John Cruso

In the summer of 1642 the rules laid out by one of the most recent military authors, John Cruso, were broken by both parliamentarians and royalists. At the outset of his book, *Militarie Instructions for the Cavallrie*, published at the University of Cambridge in 1632, which he suggested was a digest of several recent authors, Cruso was keen to impress upon his reader the need for experience at all levels. The general must be a 'souldier of extraordinary experience and valour'; the lieutenant general of horse needed to be of 'great experience and valour'; and the captains should be of 'singular valour and experience'.[2] Parliament's cavalry generals were not extensively experienced – indeed the commander of the cavalry at Edgehill had no experience at all – and Cromwell was not alone in being totally unsuited experientially for the job he was given as captain of horse in summer 1642. As well as attempting to suggest that officers should not just be appointed because they were gentlemen, Cruso was also keen to express that experience was crucial and that it should be rewarded over status. Writing of the appointment of cavalry captains by the Spanish court so far distanced from the wars in the Low Countries, Cruso argued 'there are two inconveniencies upon it. First young and inexperienced gentlemen are made Captains. Secondly, many good soldiers are lost, which seeing their hopes of advancement by degrees and merit cut off, abandon the forces'.[3] Parliament and the royalists were not, however, in the midst of a series of wars, and nor was there a standing army in which British soldiers could gain experience, and thus neither side could draw upon a large enough pool of experienced men, although they did have some and employed them as they could. To raise armies in a hurry during the summer of 1642, as England and Wales began to see menacing armed camps develop in and around York and London, both sides had to issue commissions to 'unexperienced gentlemen' like Cromwell. There was no time for these appointed captains to rise through the ranks of cornet and lieutenant, as Cruso implied that they ought to. Such men were going to have to learn the trade as they went about creating the companies, troops and regiments which they were charged with raising, often in very dangerous circumstances and close to where their enemies were doing the same. Copies of Cruso's and other authors' military manuals must have been obtained and read hungrily, and wry smiles may have been generated amongst their readers as they scanned the first pages only to realise that they were exactly the sort of people Cruso was declaring inappropriate for military office.

HORSE REGIMENTS IN THE MID-SEVENTEENTH CENTURY

In the warrant signed by Robert Devereux, Earl of Essex, on 17 December 1643 authorising the payment of half a month's wages, Cromwell's horse troop was referred to as harquebusiers.[4] This was already becoming an outdated and obsolete term during the Thirty Years War, never mind in 1642. Harquebusiers was a term applied to what we might term medium cavalry, although some authors regarded them as light cavalry, and whilst they must not be confused with dragoons, it was the latter arm of the cavalry which a century-and-a-half later was generally thought of as medium cavalry. However, in the mid-seventeenth century, dragoons were not regarded as cavalry at all: they were considered to be infantry with horses. Dragoons very rarely fought on horseback, instead using their horses as a rapid transport system only. Harquebusiers were generally regarded as medium cavalry because they were lightly armoured in comparison with truly heavy cavalry: in some cases their defensive armour was restricted to a very heavy buff coat and a helmet. Confusingly, and this is one of the reason why their name was becoming obsolete, they did not usually carry the harquebus – the short-barrelled musket after which they were named. True heavy cavalry wore three-quarter armour, of the sort sometimes seen on formally sat and posed portraits of civil war commanders, but in Britain, even though the Earl of Essex seems to have initially mounted his lifeguard troopers as cuirassiers, this type of cavalry armament was soon restricted in the field to just small regiments of horse, such as that commanded by Leicestershire MP Sir Arthur Hesilrige (or Hazelrigg) of Noseley, who must have had a store of the expensive suits of armour readily available in 1642. Three-quarter armour consisted of a full-face helmet – which meant that it had a visor which when closed covered the soldiers face completely – back and breast plates, a metal collar or gorget with shoulder pieces or pouldrons, articulated armour for each arm called vambraces, leg armour extending at least down to the knees and articulated gauntlets. The proper term for such cavalry or horse was cuirassier (a term which is derived rather confusingly from the French word for leather) or reiter. Reiters had been armed as lancers or pistoliers: the former charging against an enemy in a line with lances levelled, whilst the latter delivered a sequence of volleys of pistol-shot at close range, rank by rank, in a version of infantry musket firing.[5] Both these types of cuirassier were expensive and required the sort of extensive training that was simply not possible in Britain when the civil wars broke out. Hesilrige's cuirassiers, often referred to as 'lobsters' because of their armour, seem to have fought not as lancers but as pistoliers, but may have conformed to the types of cavalry tactics developed on the continent from 1632 onwards and employed within Britain, as discussed in later chapters.

The expensive nature of cuirassiers or reiters had resulted earlier in the century in the widespread adoption of cheaper cavalry, referred to as harquebusiers in England and on the continent where they had appeared, according to John Cruso, during the wars in Piedmont. More properly in England they would have been arquebusiers, after the type of musket called the arquebus. As the war broke out in England, the arming of the harquebusier was apparently done on the cheap, but generally according to the definition of the harquebusier defined in the United Provinces as wearing an open-face helmet, a gorget and back and breast plates which should be bulletproof.[6] William Barriff, on the other hand, expected harquebusiers to have a simple morion helmet like that worn by pikemen.[7] Ideally such a trooper should have had a barred helmet, a good quality buff coat (they could cost as much as £10 a piece – the same price as a horse), a back and breast plate, gloves (and even an armoured gauntlet to protect the left rein-holding lower arm and hand), a brace of pistols and an arquebus or carbine. It seems that parliamentarian cavalrymen were not always supplied with a buff coat or an arquebus, at least initially.[8] Therefore we can begin to envisage Cromwell's troop at the end of 1642, and perhaps in their dress in the mid- to late summer of that year. They would be mounted on horses about 14 to 15 hands high, and as there seems to have been no guidance on the colour of horses we can assume that the troop would have been of mixed hues. Cromwell would have aimed to have each man armed with a 'pot' – a helmet with a single bar in front of his nose or triple-bars protecting his face and an articulated tail covering the back of his neck – rather than an open morion. The troopers would have had a 'proofed' back and breastplate fastened together at the shoulder and just above the waist, a few inches above the bottom of the armour and just above the small skirt on its lower edge. Proofed armour would have had a carbine shot fired at it to prove that it was bulletproof, and thus on the front plate there would be a bullet-shaped dent. Captain Cromwell's men should have had two flintlock or wheel-lock pistols with barrels about 14 to 15 inches long, carried in holsters on the front of the horse's saddle, and a sword, perhaps either a basket-hilted sword or one referred to now by a later name – the mortuary sword. As for the colour of Cromwell's men's jackets, we cannot be sure. Uniform colours were often decided by the use of the field or background colour of the colonel's heraldic design. However, Cromwell later referred to russet-coated gentlemen at one stage; whilst this might simply be a reference to country clothing in general, it may suggest that even before the creation of the New Model Army and its standard red-brown jacket colour, Cromwell's men were dressed in a shade of brownish red. The troop would have a cornet – the most junior commissioned rank – in Cromwell's case John Waterhouse, who would carry a small square or swallow-tailed guidon, also referred to, like its carrier, as a cornet. The cornet would normally have been in the captain's heraldic field colour with a painted motto and device of some form. Troops of horse would normally have had around 60 or perhaps more troopers, and Cromwell was given an allowance of £1,104 'mounting money' which parliament paid to each captain raising a troop of horse. Conversely, the royalists commissioned colonels to raise regiments from their own resources and those of the men they recruited as troop captains. If Cromwell aimed initially to raise 60 men, that allowed him about £18-8s-0d per man. With a horse costing up to £10 it only left about eight pounds each for the equipment, which probably precluded buying expensive buff coats. Swords and belts could be a little as five shillings each wholesale, carbines as little as 12s-9d wholesale, and a pair of pistols 18/-. Armour for harquebusiers consisting of the helmet, back and breastplates could be bought for about a pound a set. Thus for as little as £12-12s-9d, Cromwell could arm each of his troopers.[9] This meant that Cromwell could have provided for the 80 men he apparently had in his troop just within the mounting money he had been given. The costs of coats and boots would have to be added and possibly bought at the troopers' own expense, something that might have depended on the level of Captain Cromwell's desire for uniformity at this stage of the war.

HORSE TACTICS IN 1642

The wars on the continent during the late sixteenth and the first half of the seventeenth century – particularly, but not exclusively, that series of interlinked conflicts collectively known as the Thirty Years War – had a series of dramatic impacts on Britain, even though for much of the time the British nations avoided direct involvement which went beyond military experience and knowledge. The significant religious overtones to the wars abroad shaped the way men and women viewed the political and religious developments in Britain and Ireland. Indeed, the way the wars in Britain and Ireland between 1639 and 1653 were understood owed a lot to the ongoing war in Europe: for some people they were considered part of the same conflict. At the same time, warfare in Europe was changing and developing too, and by 1639 continental strategy and tactics was ingrained in the minds of the British and Irish who had served in armies abroad, but in different ways. The decline in the dominance of cuirassiers, whether chiefly armed with lances or pistols, and their respective battlefield tactics, could have created almost a fully formed format for cavalry warfare in Britain, where if not for the fact that the soldiers who returned to Britain and Ireland from 1639 onwards brought their experiences of being in different armies and the preferences they had derived. For the most part, as the war developed mounted action was waged by medium cavalry. Hesilrige's lobsters were almost unique and did not shape the nature of mounted combat; similarly the lancers found in the Scottish armies, who were in any case light cavalry rather than armoured as cuirassiers, did not shape battlefield tactics to any great extent either. Instead it was to be the harquebusiers such as those raised by Captain Cromwell which had the most decisive and likely continuing impact on battlefield warfare in Britain.

By the turn of the sixteenth century, cavalry or horse regiments fought in lines: if lancers, contemporary illustrations show them in three lines; if pistoliers, then in dense columns of five or six lines. With lancers, who required a great deal of training as well as being expensive, becoming largely redundant by the seventeenth century, the armies ranged against each other on the continent by the seventeenth century were formed initially into the dense six-deep columns common to pistoliers. Pistoliers were used for their firepower rather than as the shock troops which carried out the dramatic charges associated with cavalry in popular imagination. A unit of horse would advance towards the enemy and halt within pistol-shot range. The front rank would then fire and retire to the rear of the unit to reload whilst the next rank moved forward to fire and then retire, and so on, until they had made so significant an impact on their enemies as to force them to retreat or until they themselves were similarly forced back. By the 1630s the Swedish army had refined the use of harquebusiers, including depriving them of the harquebus. Swedish cavalry was ranged in three ranks, only the first two of which would draw their pistols (when they could see the whites of their opponents' eyes) and fire. The third rank would draw their swords. When the first two ranks had fired they too would draw their swords and advance on the enemy, generally at a trot rather than a gallop. This innovation was firmly in the minds of many British and Irish soldiers by the time of the wars in Britain. One cavalry general at least, Prince Rupert, was to refine this still further, ruling out the preliminary pistol firefight and speeding up the contact velocity of his cavalry. Nevertheless, some parliamentarian cavalry tactics continued to rely upon the initial pistol fire for a while, and it would probably be this tactic which Cromwell would have picked up as he began constructing his troop.

CROMWELL'S REGIMENT OF HORSE

In the same warrant which called Captain Cromwell's troopers harquebusiers, the number of his soldiers was listed as 80. This was a good sized troop at a time when many troops of horse were much smaller than the regulation size. However, when raised, and for the initial months of the war, it was just a troop, not a regiment – troop number 67 in Essex's army as a whole.[10] When it was required to play a part in the field, Cromwell's troop was detailed to join a much larger unit – a regiment. Armies on the continent were similarly composed of small units marshalled into larger fighting units by a field marshal, or in the Spanish armies a sergeant major – a general officer not, as in later armies, a non-commissioned rank. Cromwell's initial eighty-strong troop was assigned to the Earl of Essex's own regiment (note this was not the cuirassier-armed lifeguard, but in all likelihood a harquebusier regiment commanded in the field by Yorkshireman Sir Phillip Stapleton).[11] Assembling forces in this way was standard practice in the seventeenth century, although the Spanish practice of creating massive bodies of both horse and foot – but particularly *tercios* or *tertias* which had been modelled originally on

Macedonian phalanxes – had largely been superseded by the Dutch practice of having smaller units which were more manoeuvrable based on Roman maniples. Assembling Essex's regiment did not it seem to mean that every one of the troops assigned to it was always acting together. The job of cavalry during campaigns was manifold, and included some element of scouting (although this was not achieved well during the initial months of Cromwell's military service) and searching out forage for its own needs and the army as a whole. This manifold practice may explain why, although Sir Phillip Stapleton and Essex's regiment was present at the Battle of Edgehill, Cromwell's troop and its captain probably was not.

We do not know exactly how Cromwell prepared his men for battle, but we do know that he had a considerable amount of time to do it, for the troop and then regiment was not involved in a real battle for over six months from its foundation. We do not know how the basic and more sophisticated drill was arranged, and who was responsible under Captain Cromwell for executing it. There were plenty of drill books available, including John Cruso's *Militarie Instructions for the Cavallrie*, published by Cambridge University in 1632. Cromwell may have read this work or become familiar with it, although it was based on Dutch practices and thus somewhat dated by comparison with the example set by King Gustavus Adolphus's Swedish army just as Cruso's work went to press. As General Sir Frank Kitson pointed out in his biography of Cromwell, bits of the book were made redundant because of the generally heterogenic nature of the parliamentarian (and royalist) cavalry, which thus did not need the complexities of coordinating lancers, reiters and harquebusiers. The cavalry commanders above Cromwell, Stapleton and the Earl of Bedford, who had been given command of the parliamentarian cavalry, would also have been getting familiar with military texts and relying heavily upon the experience of those men who had served on the continent. Essex had served in Europe at field level of regimental command as he had been a colonel of foot. Bedford, the cavalry general, was young and had no military experience at all. Sir Philip Skippon, the sergeant major general of foot, was a veteran of the continental wars.

There is a legend, which in part inspired the idea that Cromwell was influenced by what he saw of the Battle of Edgehill, that whilst he may not have been present on the battlefield he was in the vicinity, perhaps as Kitson suggests at Kineton, about a mile-and-a-half north-west of the field.[12] Some accounts, including scurrilous ones, had Captain Cromwell observe the battle from a nearby steeple. Certainly towards the end of his life Cromwell hinted that he had observed something of the fight when he referred to a conversation he had had with his cousin John Hampden, whose units also missed the battle.[13]

In the weeks that followed the battle, we may assume only that Cromwell's troop marched with Essex's field army on its journey to London, and that somehow it was involved in the great stand-off at Turnham Green in mid-November after the king's army had barged through Brentford. Even if troop number 67 was one that was ranged as part of Stapleton's regiment that day, it saw no action, for the outnumbered king's army withdrew from the field. It was after that that Cromwell was sent back to Cambridgeshire, where he was based from early 1643. It was during this period, when his troop was carrying out policing duties, that Captain Cromwell was in effect empowered to create a full regiment of horse. A regiment of horse in England comprised six troops in both parliamentarian and royalist armies. For parliament that entailed a colonel's own troop, a major's troop and four troops commanded by captains. Royalists had, in addition, a lieutenant colonel, which meant that there would only be three troops commanded by captains. The ranks of colonel, lieutenant colonel and major were known as field ranks of commands, whilst lower ranks, starting at captain, were considered regimental ranks or commands. All troops would have a lieutenant; Cromwell's original troop had a man called Cuthbert Baildon in this position, according to Cruso, 'nourished and educated in Cavallrie'. The lieutenant should usually have served as a cornet and possibly even as a corporal before being elevated to the rank of lieutenant – we do not know if Baildon had done so, but it would have been useful to Cromwell if he had, as he could have tapped into his experience. Lieutenants often had to do the hard work, Cruso acknowledged, because the captain might be a social appointment, although in this case it was political one. Either way, Cromwell was a novice, and his lieutenant had to ensure the company was trained and equipped. In battle the captain was at the front of the troop whilst the lieutenant was at the back with his sword drawn, encouraging the soldiers to follow the captain and 'killing any that shall offer to flee or disband'.[14] When the captain was absent, the lieutenant was in charge. As mentioned earlier, Cromwell would have appointed a cornet who had to be courageous. He carried the cornet – the small troop colour – and rode behind the captain, between him and the front rank of the troop in battle. During a charge the harquebusier cornet was probably within the body of the troop, as was the case with cuirassiers, rather than having the ritualised role of charging alongside the captain, breaking his cornet-bearing lance on the armour of the enemy and leaving the colours lying on the ground as incumbent upon the cornet of a regiment of lancers. Cornets would command the troop in the absence of the lieutenant and the captain, and were responsible for mounting the guard. The non-commissioned officers, quartermasters and corporals, would be 'useful'. Quartermasters were the fourth in command of a regiment and would be in charge of billeting the troopers. On the march, and as part of an army, the quartermaster would be with the army's quartermaster to assist in billet allocation. Corporals should be literate and, in the still-developing role of the harquebusiers, which Cruso still wrote of as if they were light cavalry, corporals were responsible for leading commanded detachments of troopers on scouting missions.[15] As Cromwell's troop became part of a regiment and he became a field officer, he would not have been expected to command his own troop any more. Instead he as colonel – like the other field officers, majors in parliament's armies, and lieutenant colonels and majors in royalists regiments – would have captain lieutenants undertaking those duties, but there would be no lieutenant yet there would of course be a cornet. A colonel of a regiment of horse would draw half his pay as a captain and half as a colonel, and the same would be true of majors and lieutenant colonels. By 26 January Cromwell was a colonel: he had been a captain just a week earlier. This entitled him to raise five more troops. By early March 1643 he had five troops, totalling about 400 men. He had achieved this partly by recruitment and partly by absorption. James Berry now became Cromwell's captain lieutenant to command his own troop once he held field rank. Cromwell had brought in a cousin, Edward Whalley, a Midlander, as major – he would command the second troop and employ a captain lieutenant too. His brother-in-law, John Desborough, formerly the quartermaster of the original troop, had been promoted to captain's rank and had a troop of his own – troop number three, gaining his own quartermaster, Coxe Tooke, in April 1643.[16] Oliver Cromwell junior, originally a cornet in Lord St John's regiment of horse, was likewise promoted to captain and brought into the regiment with troop number four. Troop number five was another relative, nephew Valentine Walton junior, formerly of his father's regiment of horse. A sixth troop was added in the summer under Captain Ayres, and that should have been it; a full complement of six troops. However, by the end of summer there were ten troops, and it did not stop there as by the end of the year it would seem that Cromwell's regiment had as many as 14 troops.[17] This makes Cromwell's regiment very unusual at a time when many regiments on both sides were undersized at troop and regimental level. It may be that we are viewing the regiment, at least at this stage, in the wrong way. We know that during 1643 Cromwell had a number of infantry or foot companies under his command whilst undertaking the policing duties in and around Cambridgeshire, yet no one refers to anything known as Cromwell's regiment of foot. There may be another way of looking at it. The clue may be the way that two troops were 'absorbed' in the course of 1643. One, that of Captain Ralph Margery, was originally raised in Suffolk by the parliamentarian county committee, who then questioned the troop's behaviour in levying horses. Cromwell then offered to have Margery's troop from them for service in the region, but it does not necessarily mean that at that point they became part of Cromwell's regiment.[18] The second troop acquired in such a way came from Nottinghamshire. It was led by Captain Henry Ireton of Attenborough and was part of Colonel Sir Francis Thornhaugh's regiment of horse stationed in Nottingham. By mid-1643 Cromwell had served alongside the Nottingham-shire horse in attempts to capture Newark, or to interrupt communications and supply routes between the royalist Earl of Newcastle's command in the North of England and the king in Oxford, and this is how he met Ireton. During the summer, Nottingham had become ever-more isolated and royalist attacks on the town had threatened the security of the garrison's ability to hold on to territory in which to station cavalry. It may have been this declining situation which enabled or forced Ireton to move into East Anglia and take up garrison duties in Ely. Again, at this point this troop was not necessarily part of Cromwell's regiment. Whilst in European terms raising a double-sized regiment of horse was not unknown (Albrecht Wallenstein, the future imperial general, had raised a double cuirassier regiment in 1618–19), it may be that here we are looking at assembling troops of horse into a brigade rather than creating a single regiment under one colonel.[19] At the very least this was the same system as adopted by parliament as it assembled Essex's army in 1642, building artificial regiments of horse from individual disparate troops for the purpose of creating a field army. The system was very different from that adopted by the royalists, who commissioned individuals to raise entire regiments rather than individual troops. Their system, borrowed from continental Europe, was highly problematic as the nominated colonels then passed the task of raising the troops to men they had in turn nominated which, as these were often being raised within a small geographical space, meant that some of these captains were competing for manpower.[20] Thus some royalist troops were undersized from the start, and regiments became top-heavy with officers, in turn meaning that a disproportionate amount of money was being spent on officers' pay.

COMMAND AND THE MILITARY REVOLUTION

The military revolution was perhaps in part inspired by the technological leaps in weapons production. Firearms, pistols and the variety of longer-barrelled guns – heavy muskets, carbines and the harquebus, with their equally varied firing mechanisms ranging from the relatively cheap matchlock to the flintlock, snaphance and wheel-lock – became cheaper and more reliable. Both these factors meant that it was feasible for them to be used in increasing numbers on the battlefield, even if some cavalry still carried lances and a proportion of all infantry regiments carried 18-foot-long pikes. This had in turn influenced the tactical use of such forces over the 70 years before the civil wars in Britain and Ireland began, as first Spanish, then Dutch, and later German and Swedish developments in battlefield tactics influenced those Englishmen, Scotsmen, Irishmen and Welshmen who served in the competing European armies and came to admire their commanders.

However, there was another type of change which was impinging on armies. The desire to document, illustrate and understand warfare was part of the increasing desire to understand the universe by detecting patterns in the physical world. The need for self-discipline at individual and state level was considered by academic Justus Lipsius, from the University of Leiden. Lipsius considered that the point of government was to protect the individual from both external threats and from the sorts of personal incivility which led to (often religious) violence. Passions had to be controlled through self-discipline. Although Lipsius was concerned with political and civil government, he turned his mind to warfare, and studied the history of the Roman Empire. This became the basis for his four-fold philosophy of discipline and thus linked into military lore. Drill was the basis of victory and had two core purposes: firstly, it was essential for the perfect execution of the means of loading and firing weapons; and secondly, it conditioned the soldier to accept orders. In other words, it conditioned soldiers to accept their subordination within a larger military unit. Together this forced the individual soldier to forego individualism and accept self-control. Finally, Lipsius's ideals ensured standardised wage structures and terms of service. This all impinged upon the minds of some of the commanders of the English civil war through their experience of war abroad, which had to a greater or lesser degree adapted to Lipsius's notions which were transmitted during the Dutch Revolt through Prince Maurice's army, and through the books of military discipline which began to be printed by Dutch presses and were quickly translated. This was not of course simply a military doctrine, for it coincided with the civil aims of society regarding discipline, order and decency that were often labelled as puritan, but were equally sought by less radical Protestants and Catholics alike. We know from his later pronouncements that Cromwell was essentially a political conservative, even if his religious attitudes were more radical, and so we could expect that there may be a mixture of this in Captain Cromwell's early military career. Discipline was clearly part of his military perspective: the lessons he learned from his observations upon, or his understanding of, the Battle of Edgehill suggest that he saw room for improvement in the discipline of both sides. Yet even so, Cromwell was looking for something else in his troopers. The evidence of Cromwell's desire for something special about his soldiers comes from a variety of sources over the period of his life, but there is a good deal that is contemporary or near contemporary with his recruitment and early campaigns. Cromwell claimed to have discussed the battle with John Hampden shortly after Edgehill. Cromwell was talking about how he had risen to positions of importance after first becoming a captain. This was naturally associated in his mind with working towards God's end or plan: 'and God blessed me as it pleased him', but then he added, 'And I did truly and plainly – and then in a way of foolish simplicity, as it was judged by very great and wise men and good men too – desired to make my instruments help me in that work'. It seems that Cromwell was, some 15 years after the event, claiming that he chose men as 'his instruments' who were working to the same ends as he was. He went on to say that other methods were not working: 'At my first going into this engagement, I saw our men were beaten at every hand. I did indeed.' Cromwell then gave advice to his older relative Hampden, suggesting that he raise new 'additions' or regiments to Essex's army, and that he would bring him 'such men in as I thought had a spirit that would do something in that work'. He then criticised Hampden's own regiments, some of the first volunteers to be assembled to fight the king and thus supposedly ardent in the struggle against Charles I. 'Your troopers', he is claimed to have said, 'are most of them old decayed servingmen and tapsters and such kind of fellows'. Perhaps strangely he compared them to the royalist cavalry, who he saw as men of a certain élan, being men of 'honour and courage and resolution'.

Cromwell then told Hampden he needed men of spirit, 'and take it not ill what I say – I know you will not – of a spirit that is likely to go on as far as gentlemen will go, or else I am sure you will be beaten still'.[21] Some of this has to be read carefully, as in 1657, when he made the speech, Cromwell was in the middle of the political discussions following the offer of the crown made to him by the Protectorate Parliament, and he was keen to explain why he was in such a position. He may also have been aiming to salve the wounds which the recent 'rule of the major generals' had caused, along with the concomitant decimation tax which had so angered the former royalists upon whom it had been levied, in contravention of the longer-term aim of healing the nation. It was thus no time to make enemies, and instead time to play up the honourable nature of the royalists. Yet this theme was not a new one. It does fit with what critics said of him. The Earl of Manchester – a distant relative whose family had bought uncle Oliver Cromwell's Hinchingbrooke estates – was Cromwell's commander from 1643 until the beginning of 1645, and had by the end of their working relationship become an enemy of Cromwell's, as will be shown later. Some three years after the event he said:

> Col. Cromwell raysing of his regiment makes choice of his officers not such as weare souldiers or men of estate, but such as were common men, pore and of meane parentage, onely he would give them the title of godly, pretious men [...] I have heard him oftentimes say that it must not be souldiers nor scots that must doe this worke, but it must be the godly to this purpose [...] If you look at his owne regiment of horse, see what a swarm ether is of thos that call themselves the godly; some of them profess they have sene visions and had revallations[22]

Manchester, like Cromwell, was talking within a different context, and thus the reference to the Scots was to the later opposition from Cromwell and the political group to which he belonged regarding parliament's alliance with Scotland. Nevertheless, even without the class prejudice we can understand that outsiders saw something unique and socially challenging about Cromwell's men. The lawyer, politician and diarist Bulstrode Whitelocke wrote:

> He had a brave regiment of horse of his countrymen, most of them freeholders and freeholder's sons and who upon matter of conscience engaged in this quarrel, and under Cromwell.
>
> And thus being well armed within, by the satisfaction of their own consciences and without, by good iron arms, they would as one men stand firmly and charge desperately.[23]

Here there is less of the implied social fears expressed by Manchester, for the troopers that Whitelocke is referring to are the very people that we would expect: freeholders – men who, depending upon where they lived, might yet be part of the franchised rural classes, possessed of some land and probably able to provide their own horse for the service at first. Their inner strength is what impressed Whitelocke at this point in time, or as he later recalled it. Presbyterian Richard Baxter also recalled this later:

> At his first entrance into the wars, being but a captain of horse, he took special care to get religious men into his troop. These men were of greater understanding than commons soldiers and therefore more apprehensive of the importance and consequence of war and making not money but that which they took for public felicity to be their end, they were more engaged to be valiant [...] these things it's probable that Cromwell understood, and that none would be such engaged valiant men as the religious yet I conjecture that at his first choosing such men into his troop, it was the very esteem and love of religious men that principally moved him; and the avoiding of those disorders, mutinies plunderings and grievances of the country which deboist men in armies are commonly guilty of, By this means he indeed sped better than he expected. Aires, Desborough, Berry, Evanson and the rest of that troop did prove so valiant that as far as I could learn they never once ran away before an enemy.[24]

Baxter was clearly well informed about the first recruits, for he names some of the men who became the captains of the troops in the larger regiment, including Ayres, who led troop number six. Yet here there is nothing truly extraordinary. He does not think Cromwell fully understood the importance of conviction, suggesting that it was more for the reason of order that the religious men were enlisted. This sort of claim could be made by many social leaders in the post-Lipsius world, where the desire for social order was common across religious divides, and where the point of the modern world was to be less violent because of the element of social control which Lipsius thought was at the core of the relation between drill, discipline and victory.

In any case, Cromwell belied the suspicion that Baxter held about the relationship between religious conviction and victory in what is probably the most famous quotation from him. It relates to his men at this time, and is a reference to his officers that chimed well with Whitelocke's remarks and Cromwell's remarks to Hampden recalled in 1657. In a letter to the Suffolk County Committee at the end of August 1643 on matters relating to county defence and the raising of more troops within the county, Cromwell sought to lecture them on what sort of person to recruit:

> I beseech you be careful what captains of horse you choose, what men be mounted; a few honest men are better than numbers, Sometime they must have

for exercise. If you choose godly honest men to be captains of horse honest men will follow them, and they will be careful to mount such.

The King is exceedingly strong in the West. If you be able to foil a force at the first coming of it, you will have reputation; and that is of great advantage in our affairs. God hath given it to our handful; let us endeavour to keep it. I had rather have a plain russet-coated captain that knows what he fights for and loves what he knows, than that which you call a gentleman and is nothing else. I honour a gentleman that is so indeed.[25]

As I have written elsewhere, this is only a limited social challenge, for Cromwell seems to makes it clear that if the russet-coated captain is a gentleman then it is all the better.[26] Yet whilst we often read this letter as being a general statement of Cromwell's social beliefs, it probably is not, for the letter then moves on to discuss Captain Margery, who is the epitome of the russet-coated man of the letter: 'I understand Mr Margery hath honest men will follow him: if so, be pleased to make use of him. It much concerns your good to have conscientious men.'[27] Margery had raised a troop of horse in Suffolk, but the committee appears to have fallen out with him about a month later over the way he was requisitioning horses in the county. As a result, Cromwell welcomed Margery and his troop into the regiment, presumably convinced by his honesty.

Cromwell had written to his cousin, Oliver St John, during September when Margery was making himself unpopular in Suffolk: 'I have a lovely company; you would respect them, did you know them. They are no Anabaptists, they are honest, sober Christians; they expect to be used as men.'[28] Cromwell's respect for his soldiers comes over clearly here: he may have been acutely aware that even at this early stage – it was 11 September 1643 – he was being associated with religious if not social radicalism. However, it is possible that this is a joke between him and his cousin about the reference the king had made a year previously regarding the nature of Essex's army: 'You shall meet no enemy but traitors and most of them Brownists, Anabaptists and atheists, such as desire to destroy both Church and State.'[29]

However, a sense of élan and conviction are not enough, and even the armour and horses Cromwell had provided for his men would not stand up to the royalist mounted gentlemen, which they would encounter. As Lipsius well-knew, drill was essential. However, it may be quite simply that Cromwell was referring to the courage shown by the royalists at Edgehill, when they charged headlong into the parliamentarian cavalry without pausing to fire their pistols first, as they may have been expected to. By comparison he appears to have asserted Hampden's men were not yet ready to take that risk or make that leap.

FINANCING THE REGIMENT

One thing which marked out service in home-raised and employed regiments like that of Cromwell, and those raised by cavalry colonels abroad like Albrecht Wallenstein, was the ability to turn them into profit-making businesses. Potentially Wallenstein would have made money as a colonel of a double regiment once he had personally invested in its creation, in Wallenstein's case it is possible that the profits of the first regiment paid the initial outlay of the second regiment, itself potentially double-sized resulting in Wallenstein being effect in command of what in 1640s England would be a brigade.[30] What both colonels would have agreed on would have been that regular pay led to good discipline and made civil/military relationships calmer. Cruso was explicit on the point: pay should be fair and regular – it was one of the chief reasons why soldiers were soldiers, and discipline depended upon it. We can see echoes of Cruso in Cromwell's letters to the county committees and others asking for money due, which may imply that he was familiar with the text of the 1632 edition. He knew that without regular or even irregular pay, soldiers would go home, plunder the vicinity and mutiny. Whilst the colonels' employers – parliament for Cromwell, the Holy Roman Emperor for Wallenstein – were responsible for funding the regiments raised at their behest, day-to-day pay often fell behind. On the continent, colonels could raise local taxes known as contribution (a term adopted by the royalists in England and Wales) directly: they could equally well adopt collections with menaces such as *brandschatzung* or 'burning money'.[31] Cromwell was dependent upon the local county committees established in late 1643 by parliament for money. County committees had been established to organise the war effort and were responsible for the collection of the weekly tax – an income and property tax levied upon a broad cross-section of the population. Cromwell was luckier than many in his position, for the counties around him had been associated into what turned out to be probably the most effective of parliament's associations: the Eastern Association. However, obtaining money for his officers and men was always a problem. In March 1643 he wrote to the deputy lieutenants of Suffolk:

> I am sorry I should so often trouble you about the business of money: it's no pleasant subject to be too frequent upon. But such is captain Nelson's occasion for the want therof, that he hath not wherewith to satisfy for the billet of his soldiers [...] Truly he hath borrowed from me else he could not have paid to discharge this town at his departure.
>
> It's a pity that a gentleman of his affections should be discouraged! Wherefore I earnestly beseech you to consider him and the cause. It's honourable that you to

do so. What you can help him to, be pleased to send into Norfolk; he hath not
wherewith to pay a troop one day, as he tells me.[32]

A couple of months later, whilst in Nottingham, he told the mayor of Colchester
in a letter:

> I beseech you, hasten the supply to us; forget not money; I press not hard, though I
> do so need that I assure you, the foot and dragooners are ready to mutiny. Lay not
> too much on the back of a poor gentleman, who desires, without much noise to lay
> down his life, and bleed the last drop to serve the Cause and you. I ask not for your
> money for myself; if that were my end hope (viz the pay of my place) I would not
> open my mouth at this time. I desire to deny myself that others will not be satisfied.[33]

In August, after requesting money from Essex to repay a debt incurred in
Nottingham to cover billeting, clothing, shoes and wages for three companies
of the county's foot, he noted: 'I think it is not expected that I should pay your
soldiers out of my own purse.'[34] Essex was not alone – the Cambridgeshire
committee was also slow in sending Cromwell money that summer:

> The money I brought with me is so poor a pittance when it comes to be distributed
> amongst all my troops that, considering their necessity, it will not half clothe
> them, they were so far behind. If we have not more money speedily they will be
> exceedingly discouraged. I am sorry you put me to it to write thus often. It makes it
> seem a needless importunity in me; whereas, in truth, it is a constant neglect of
> those that should provide for us. Gentlemen, make them able to live and subsist
> that are willing to spend their blood for you.[35]

The Suffolk Committee also had to be reminded of their duty in the letter
already cited about Captain Margery's raising of a troop of horse. And in the
letter to Oliver St John, in which Cromwell told him of his 'lovely company',
he was writing to urge him to get the monies due to him forwarded by all the
counties in the association, because 'I have little money of my own to help my
soldiers. My estate is little, I tell you the business of Ireland and England hath
had of me, in money, between eleven hundred and twelve hundred pounds;
therefore my private can do little to help the public.'[36]

The first civil war was a drain on the Cromwell family resources and, unlike
their continental contemporaries, war was not profitable in the early stages.
Providing for wages, and stabling at 8d per trooper and vastly more for the non-
commissioned and commissioned officers, cost about £50 a day.

TRAINING THE REGIMENT

General Frank Kitson was right to point out that Cromwell had the luxury of a
secure area in which to train his first troop and those which joined him.

Cromwell's first military exploits were not on the battlefield. He had first been called upon to prevent the University of Cambridge from sending its plate to the king in July 1642. This predated the raising of the first troop and involved arming volunteer foot soldiers with muskets to try and prevent the second convoy of plate from leaving the town. He next took over the county magazine in the castle and exercised the county's Trained Bands during August. The raising of the original troop followed these incidents, but the nature of the work before Cromwell hardly changed. Even though troop 67 was ordered to march with Essex's army it was not present at the Battle of Edgehill and there is no record of it being engaged at either the Battle of Brentford or the stand-off at Turnham Green. At the end of the year Cromwell returned northwards to Cambridgeshire as part of the programme of gaining control of local governance and financial and other resources, launched by both sides as winter approached. This gave Cromwell's troop, which had so far not been exposed to battle, let alone defeat on the battlefield – a fate that had been inflicted upon so many of the equally new parliamentarian troops of horse at Edgehill – the opportunity to undertake training. We cannot be sure how the training was conducted and by whom specifically. Cromwell was not a major landowner like the other parliamentarian cavalry general of note, Sir Thomas Fairfax, and would not have stable employees to work with him.

We do not know (we may never know) how Cromwell moved from being the 'unexperienced' captain supported by men of experience like Cruso's 'gentlemen of singular valour and experience'. There must have been an element of experience from those appointed in the original troop, but academic study probably also played a part. There are some hints in what Cromwell said about his soldiers which echo contemporary books, even if sometimes they appear to be dressed up or interpreted as religious inferences. Cruso spent some time defining how the cavalry should behave. Soldiers should not be allowed to gamble or blaspheme, but they should also be paid regularly, and where there was booty to be had it should be distributed fairly and publicly. A soldier should ideally be aged between 20 and 40 years and be keen to 'addict himself to that profession and [have] a desire to learn it'. In common with Cromwell's predilection, a soldier in a regiment of horse should have 'Above all the feare of God, which will direct him to virtuous actions, and to abhorre vices'.[37]

As for training, Cromwell regarded this as a virtue: he wrote approvingly of Captain Dodsworth: 'He hath diligently attended the service, and much improved his men in their exercise', and his soldiers 'brought into as good order as most companies in the army.'[38] Training or exercising was of course essential. Horses must be ridden in a ring or circle of varying diameters, in a figure of eight at a walk, trot, gallop and career, as well as moving sideways without turning its head in the direction of movement.[39] But the rider too had to be taught. We can only presume that, at least in the first troop, all of Cromwell's 80 men were able to ride before they enlisted. Troopers have been reckoned by historians to be husbandmen or men of equivalent status, which implies that they may have owned a horse that was not used for heavy farm labour but for riding, and in Cromwell's case hunting. Even so, this would not have enabled the troopers to become soldiers immediately. William Barriff, in *Military Discipline or the Younge Artillery Man*, was equally in favour of experience. He thought that a trooper should serve as a harquebusier – which he thought were the 'worst sort' of horseman – before becoming a hargoletier or mounted scout for as long again, and then as a light cavalryman, before becoming a heavy cavalryman, or as he termed it, a man at arms. Barriff was trying to encourage the development of a professional or perhaps a 'professionalised' army, in which soldiers might serve for 15 years in the manner of ancient armies. In terms of the civil war it was impractical, but it does point up the general opinion that experience was central to a successful cavalry force.[40] It also needs to be pointed out that Barriff was somewhat out of step with some contemporaries, as he advocated the use of bows and crossbows, and had a very low opinion of the harquebus as a weapon and harquebusiers as troops in general. Only in the stables of the great houses, such as that of the Earl of Newcastle (a renowned horse trainer), would the riders have been used to the more subtle requirements of a drilled horse; to be able to control its movements precisely with hands, legs and voice. Cruso suggested that a horse should be able to be turned by simply using the finger or wrist, not the whole arm. Of course, the horse had to be used to battle conditions too: the smell of gunpowder, the sight of armour and the noise of muskets, cannon fire, drums and trumpets all needed to be introduced gradually. For instance, 'When he is at his oats (at a good distance from him) a little powder may be fired, and so nearer to him by degrees.'[41] Armour could be set upon a stake and the horse ridden up to and into it so as to knock it to the ground as is attacking an armed man. Horses should also be taught to leap, use difficult pathways and swim. Yet Cruso acknowledged that this guidance was just a start, for whole books had been written on horse training, and he recommended several. Nevertheless, Cromwell would have had to undertake this training at the same time as conducting his early policing duties around Cambridge.

Cruso's manual was, as has been argued, getting dated or at least not wholly appropriate for the wars which broke out in England and Wales in 1642, and naturally he included a great deal about cuirassiers and devoted much space to illustrations for these heavily armoured men. Even so, although often conflating the harquebusier and carbine (later on the continent referred to as carabineers), Cruso did spend time discussing their training. Cruso, however, was still dealing with harquebusiers as chiefly light or medium cavalry, and treated them as if their harquebus was the primary weapon. Unlike cuirassiers, the harquebusier was supposed to fight the man to his front and left, rather than his front and right, because the harquebus or carbine was hanging to his right on the march, and when brought into use it was aimed and fired by the right hand using the bridle hand as a support or rest. Therefore most of the instructions are about firing the harquebus, with which the soldier was to be an exquisite marksman. There follow 20 instructions regarding firing, with only the last line of chapter 30 dealing with the sword: 'For the use of the sword, he is to demean himself as the Cuirasier.'[42] As for the cuirassier's use of the sword, it was a last resort dealt with in chapter 29, only once the cuirassier's pistols had been fired. The sword is drawn and rested on the pommel on the horse's saddle until raised for use. The sword should be aimed at the opponent's belly, throat or armpits – in other words, where there is a join between two parts of the suit of armour. The blow, if not causing a piercing injury, should knock a rider from his horse. If the enemy made it past the cuirassier, then a backwards blow should be made to sever the connections between parts of the armour as much as to cause physical injury. It is a mark of how quickly cavalry battle tactics changed that even though Gustavus Adolphus died before the end of 1632, the year of Cruso's publication, the Swedish king's use of harquebusiers, and cavalry in particular, had not had an impact on Cruso or indeed upon Barriff. Neither envisaged a charge as being anything like that used by the royalists at the very first formal battle of the civil wars. Even fully armoured heavy cavalry was seen as most useful in boot-to-boot formation when standing still to receive an attack, rather than as a type of shock troop attacking at a gallop: it was certainly not the role of the harquebusier. Gustavus had his horse regiments ranged in three ranks whereas Cruso still recommended eight ranks by eight files for harquebusiers, who of course, it will be remembered, were expected to be shooting not charging. Thus there would be eight files of eight men, making eight ranks, or a formation of eight ranks of eight men and eight files – in other words, a square. This formation allowed for the troop of 64 men to fire by ranks, moving forward or backwards. There was debate over how far apart the horses were, and Cruso fell firmly in favour of having six feet between each horse – in the form referred to as open order, to allow for manoeuvring the soldiers and their horses easily. Cruso set out a series of 14 simple diagrams and instructions to get the troop commander through the motions of facing forward, right, left, to the rear and so on.[43] Whilst we can assume that Cromwell, Lieutenant Baildon and Quartermaster Desborough put their troop through these paces, we do not know how. We know that to familiarise themselves with the motion later soldiers used 'model soldiers', but we do not know if Captain Cromwell used physical markers to practice, or just lined up his sixty-odd men to start the training from scratch.

However, getting 64 men to turn their horses in various directions in unison, whilst static or on the move, was just the start. Troops and regiments of horse had to march. Maps may, said Cruso, be of some use, but they were too general, meaning that they were largely blank when it came to much of the kind of topography a cavalry officer would need. The lie of the land was, on many contemporary maps, blank or white space between iconographic representations of towns, houses and some natural features like woodland, although rivers, bridges and roads might be more realistic. Wagonmasters were a fund of knowledge, and they should in turn use local knowledge of roads, bridges and lodgings. Moreover, the cavalry officer needed to know where the enemy was, and so intelligence-gathering by commanded units was recommended. As Cruso's harquebusiers were still considered light cavalry, it was they who should have borne the burden of scouting ahead for the enemy.

For a man like Cromwell the basics of managing a number of horses at one time must have been another set of lessons to be learned. Men with large stables would have stable officers who would understand the needs of a large number of horses, but Cromwell would not have such knowledge to draw on as a matter of course. Whilst encampments needed to be made in such a way as to render them defensible, the first requisite was water and the second shelter, for as Cruso wrote: 'one cold or rainie night might ruine the Cavallrie'.[44] Foraging was especially important. Collecting forage was recommended at least twice a week, in convoys escorted by horse and foot soldiers and led by a captain at least and escorted by harquebusiers.

On the field of battle Cruso was to prove of less value than the experience of the soldiers influenced by the tactic used by Gustavus Adolphus, and Cromwell did not participate in anything like a formal battle until the spring of 1643: it is his experience of or understanding of what happened at Edgehill which was important. In Cruso's work, cavalry fighting remains formal and was conducted slowly. A charge, for example, can be met by a regiment dividing into half ranks, that is into two down the centre, with the right half of the eight files turning first 90° to the right and the left-hand eight files turning to the left as the enemy approached, and then both halves turning 180° to face inwards towards the attacking cavalry on both flanks. Cruso knew this to be impractical and suggested a better method might be to turn secondly through 240° and attack him in the rear as he passed through the position whereupon your force once stood. Harquebusiers should give fire by ranks. The first rank should fire, wheel left and retire to the rear to reload; the second rank should then fire, wheel left and likewise retire, and so on until all eight ranks had fired. In an attack the first rank should advance 30 paces at the gallop or career, fire, and then the second rank do the same and so forth. However, by the time of the Battle of Edgehill cavalry commanders in the royalist army had eschewed these techniques. The royalist horse commander, Prince Rupert, whose cavalry experience was in part theoretical, had adapted techniques from the Dutch and imperial forces on the continent, but also was served by a chaplain, Dr Watts, who was a military observer and had written extensively about the Swedish cavalry techniques. The horse regiments were drawn up in three ranks, not eight, and they did not fire their pistols of harquebuses but charged at the gallop or career straight into the Earl of Essex's cavalry, which stood ready to meet them and fired their harquebuses and pistols very much as Cruso instructed, only to be swept away by the onrush of Rupert's horse. It was this which Cromwell either observed from the steeple he was supposed to have witnessed the fight from, or more realistically understood from what he was told. Edgehill was not disastrous for all of the parliamentarian horse regiments – in the combined arms operations against the royalist foot, the regiments of horse which had not been driven from the field by royalist charges were successful, and Cruso's instructions on attacking foot regiments was largely followed.

However, at Cromwell's first battle, to which we will turn later in more detail, it was shown that the royalists were not all converts to Prince Rupert's adaptation of Gustavus Adolphus's headlong charge – but Cromwell was. In this unnamed skirmish, the royalist horse stood to receive Cromwell's charge, and were defeated. Such tactics not only caused an enemy which stood still to lose the fight, but could exacerbate the disproportionate outcome by enhancing the level of casualties amongst the defeated. Cromwell demonstrated during this small battle that he was just as much a scholar of the ways of

Gustavus Adolphus as Prince Rupert, a man half his age but with more than double his experience of warfare at first- and second-hand. In an exceedingly short time Cromwell's regiment had been formed from nothing, drilled according to the best instructions available and its horse accustomed to the sounds of battle during which men and horses had stood still as required without shying away from the sound of constant gunfire. In the end they were trained to attack in a controlled manner which led to a full charge into an enemy which had chosen to stand still to receive them, in a manner which would not have been out of place a few years earlier, but which was now outmoded and dangerous. In short, Cromwell commanded a trained and disciplined modern cavalry regiment, and he had achieved it in about six months. His men had learned their trade and the up-to-date means of exercising it in half a year, not the six years advocated by William Barriff.

4

CROMWELL THE TACTICIAN: EDGEHILL TO WINCEBY

Cromwell's troop of horse was one of at least ten which could have been with the Earl of Essex's field army at the Battle of Edgehill, but instead had been dispatched from the army by the earl on a variety of missions – the most significant of which was a regiment under the command of Sir John Hampden, which was attached to the slow-moving artillery train en route from Worcester. This dispersal of vital troops was an error of judgement given that Essex knew that the king was moving on London and the route that the king was taking.[1] There was little need to secure other garrisons; even if the king had intended to attack Banbury the earl could still have advanced upon him as he did. Eight regiments of foot had also been detached from the field army to man or bolster garrisons. With Essex ordered to destroy the king's army, not to establish a chain of garrisons, it was, as Malcolm Wanklyn has pointed out, a great error, leaving the earl short of troops when he needed them and just when they would have provided him with overwhelming numbers for the forthcoming battle. If battle had taken place on 24 October rather than the day before, many of the dispatched units, especially that under Hampden, would have returned to the field army. Essex would not be the only commander to be obsessed with the notion of establishing garrisons during the first civil war: on both sides there were conflicting interpretations of modern warfare, pitching advocates of entrenched garrisons against supporters of large and mobile field armies.

Thus, as the two armies in training clashed at the Battle of Edgehill on Sunday 23 October, neither Cromwell nor his cousin Hampden were present. Instead they were both, to a greater or lesser degree, observers. What they saw was instructive. The two armies had adopted formations that were standard practice on the continent, and would be in Britain in battles fought in open country. The foot regiments were brigaded, the parliamentarians in three and the royalists possibly in five, and placed in the centre of the armies, with horse regiments placed on each flank. Dragoons – which in the mid-seventeenth century were always used as mounted infantry – were also placed by the Earl of Essex on his flanks, to prevent any attempt by the king's army to outflank him. As a result of a break from long-established practice, the king's army had an initial advantage, as charges drove off the opposition horse regiments on both wings after a brief fight. The cavalry charge was the innovation – more typically, cavalry forces advanced on one another and engaged in a pistol or carbine firefight, and then may have advanced upon one another and engaged in hand-to-hand combat. However, Prince Rupert had introduced the notion of an all-out charge without even drawing pistols: an even more aggressive attack than Gustavus Adolphus had employed a decade earlier. For Rupert it was still a theoretical exercise, as he had not until this point led several regiments of horse in a battle, but he had been exposed to the notion whilst serving abroad. It had worked, and the parliamentarian regiments preparing to receive the royalists at a stand were overwhelmed. Moreover, in a state of panic, and possibly before there was any contact between the foot regiments, Essex's parliamentarian brigade ran from the field. Yet inexperience played into Essex's hand. All the royalist horse regiments had joined in the charges – the reserve horse had attacked the remaining brigade in Essex's front line, instead of some remaining in reserve, and this left royalist brigades of foot exposed. Essex had retained a brigade in reserve and this was quickly led into place in the front line whilst Essex's reserve horse regiments were able to attack the royalist centre and artillery, causing confusion.[2] The royalists withdrew, but the exhaustion of his soldiers and the threat posed by the gradual return of the royalist horse prevented Essex from taking further action. Nevertheless, on the day Essex had, as Wanklyn says, gained a 'modest victory'.[3] On the day after he engineered to turn it into a defeat by retreating to Warwick, leaving the road to London open. The king moved slowly via Banbury and Oxford, but there was no doubt that he was heading to London.[4]

We do not know exactly where Cromwell was for sure, but legend has filled in the gap by placing him in a church tower behind Essex's lines: he was most likely in Kineton, a mile-and-a-half to Essex's left and rear, from where he witnessed the aftermath of the collapse of Essex's left-wing battlefield.[5] We know he did comment on the battle and had the conversation with cousin Hampden about the royalist horse's *esprit de corps*. He judged them to be 'gentlemen's sons, younger sons and persons of quality'. However, they could be matched by 'men of spirit' who would 'go on as far as gentlemen will go' even if, as Cromwell suspected, cousin Hampden thought it was impractical.[6] No one knows if that conversation followed hard on the heels if the Battle of Edgehill, but it may well be likely that it was conducted in the early weeks of the war. Cromwell is presumed to have rejoined Essex's army immediately after Edgehill and marched on the earl's convoluted journey via Warwick towards the capital. The king marched on London within days of Essex's arrival, and attacked down the Great Western Road at Brentford, pushing back the parliamentarians to Turnham Green where they were joined by the rest of Essex's army. Essex outfaced the king's army and Charles withdrew to Oxford, where his forces were sent into winter quarters.

Both sides sent some officers and their regiments and troops to secure their home territories. Cromwell was amongst them. At the same time parliament grouped its counties into associations. Cromwell's forces could well have served in two of them, the Midlands Association led by Lord Grey of Groby, which contained Huntingdonshire, and the Eastern Association under Lord Grey of Wark, which contained Cambridgeshire, each commander being appointed major general under Essex. It was at this point that Cromwell received the pay for his troop of 80 'Harquebuziers'.[7] Cromwell personally became part of the two associations, as he was appointed to each of the committees in the two counties, Cambridgeshire and Huntingdonshire, reflecting his residence in one and being an MP in the other. By January 1643, Cromwell was in Cambridge and appointed as recipient of money raised for the war in Ireland. It was in his capacity as an administrator that he began to question Robert Bernard's loyalty. Bernard had been one of those men whom Cromwell had crossed over the charter affair, and he suspected that Bernard, although a Huntingdonshire committeeman, seemed to be lacking in zeal. At some point Cromwell's status changed. It is first noticeable at Norwich, where he was referred to as Colonel Cromwell on 26 January (only eight days earlier parliament had referred to him as captain when sending him to Cambridge). On 6 February, Major General Lord Grey of Wark also called Cromwell colonel.[8]

For a few weeks, it was anticipated that the royalists might target East Anglia, and Cromwell with the committees began to consolidate the region's troops. The Norfolk committee was asked to send horse and foot to Cambridge to answer a threat from Prince Rupert, rumoured to be at Wellingborough in Northamptonshire.[9] However, Rupert had been on his way towards

Leicestershire to rescue Henry Hastings and his nascent army headquarters, which in the end proved unnecessary, and royalist attention soon turned to the West Midlands.[10]

CROMWELL THE COLONEL

As his troops moved into Cambridge, Cromwell began to be a colonel in more than just name. His original troop had been joined by others. By the beginning of the month he had five troops in his regiment and a total of 400 men. He was doing well in recruiting – only a few regiments had been recruited to full strength, and he had already gathered what seems to be five full-strength troops: his own (the original troop), Major Whalley's, Captain Desborough's, Captain Walton's and Captain Oliver Cromwell junior's troops were based at Cambridge, with possibly as many as 400 foot soldiers too.[11]

Cromwell now had new responsibilities. He had a regiment to command, and was, in Vernon's words, in charge of a 'small army' and should be a 'Souldier of extraordinary experience & valour'. Moreover, a colonel should have experience of 'imbattailing of the cavalrie for the actions of one regiment of horse could win a battle'.[12] Cromwell of course still had nothing of this: he had missed the only battles fought by the field army he had been a part of; still less had he experience of 'imbattailing' a regiment, by which Vernon probably meant the marshalling of a whole regiment on the battlefield and organising the regiment's individual troops in a charge, rather than handling just one troop. A colonel should watch over his major and his four captains, ensuring that they in turn were making certain each of their troopers had everything they needed. Cruso, unlike Vernon, did not give a specific description of the role of a colonel. His litany of job descriptions jumps from commissary general to captain, upon whom he imposed the most onerous burdens. This was somewhat similar to the command structure of Essex's cavalry before Edgehill, which was initially organised into troops and more loosely banded into regiments once they were gathered into the army itself. Cromwell was now of course in charge of the major and the three captains. Together they had to train the regiment, and in theory at least 'inbattail' it. This training would have to have been whilst the regiment was based around Cambridge, and may have followed the patterns laid out in Chapter 3, but now would have expanded to training the regiment to act as a body of horse. This is what Vernon referred to as 'inbattailing', that is working as a unit as on the battlefield. Cromwell had little time to gain this still 'theoretical' experience.

March was a very busy month, as the campaign season got underway. The East Midlands Association had tried to capture Newark with help from Lincolnshire forces. Newark bordered both the East Midlands and the Eastern Association and blocked access to the Great North Road on both associations. The siege at the end of February had ended in failure and acrimony, and in the meantime the royalists had strengthened their hold on the East Midlands with a number of large and small garrisons ringing the counties and making it difficult for Lord Grey of Groby to mobilise his region's resources. It was an event on the north-east coast which united Grey's and Cromwell's interests that spring. On 23 February, parliamentarian ships chased a small flotilla into Bridlington Bay. The ships made for the small port of Bridlington Quay, and there the most precious of cargoes disembarked. It was the queen, Henrietta Maria, and as the cannon balls of her pursuers landed about her she sheltered by the Gypsy Race, before her Dutch escort vessels interposed themselves between the quay and the parliamentarian ships. Then the rest of the cargo was unloaded, and arms and ammunition for the king's army were escorted with the queen to the Earl of Newcastle's base at York. The earl extracted some of the supplies for his own army, and the queen used yet more to raise troops of her own who would in turn become an escort to accompany her and the ammunition southwards to join the king.

During this activity in the north, Cromwell had been active in the south of Lincolnshire, where the royalists were making inroads into the county both to secure resources and block the routes between East Anglia and the north. A garrison had been established at Crowland, about half way between Stamford and Wisbeach, after Willoughby and Ballard's failed attack on Newark. Leaving his base at Huntingdon, Cromwell marched to attack the small royalist garrison at Crowland. He took his growing regiment and was joined by foot from Norfolk and local Lincolnshire troops. It was, however, according to Clive Holmes, a three-day bombardment which persuaded the garrison to surrender.[13] It was an early example of Cromwell working with a combined force.

The queen sent one convoy south under the command of Sir Charles Lucas, who was joined at Newark by General Hastings, who then aided the convoy on its journey to join Charles at Oxford. There was little in the way of an attempt to stop this convoy, despite royalist preparations in the belief that this was likely. Grey had failed to leave his county, leaving Cromwell and Sir John Hotham at Sleaford in Lincolnshire without sufficient forces to make a move; by the time they all rendezvoused there the ammunition was in Banbury.[14] Even so, this was momentous for Cromwell. He and Hotham drew their forces towards Newark and faced the garrison. The Newark regiments drove them off and chased them towards Grantham. Near there, Cromwell turned to face them:

> For after we had stood a little above musket-shot the one body from another and the dragooners having fired on both sides for the space of half an hour or more, they not advancing towards us, we agreed to charge them, and advancing the body after many shots on both sides, came on with our troops a pretty round trot, they standing firm to receive us; and our men charging fiercely upon them, by God's providence they were immediately routed, and ran all away, we had the execution of them for two or three miles.
>
> The true number of men slain we are not certain of, but by a credible report and estimate of our soldiers, and by what I myself saw, there were little less than a hundred slain and mortally wounded, and we lost but two men at the most on our side. We took forty five prisoners beside divers of their horses and arms [...] and we took 4 or 5 colours.[15]

This demonstrates that whatever training Cromwell had both received and given, it was learned thoroughly. It was he that, in this instance, charged as Rupert had at Edgehill, at speed and with the same success. There are several clues to Cromwell's training and learning here. He used his dragoons to fire on the royalist forces before his attack. This, it would be hoped, could disrupt enemy formations by causing casualties amongst the ranks, and if well aimed might kill enemy officers, disrupting command and control – just what Essex had intended at Edgehill. Moreover, Cromwell had been a consultative leader, for as Vernon recommended, the decision to attack was not taken solely by Cromwell: he had clearly consulted 'with one or more of his faithfullest and most experienced Captains' for as he reported 'we agreed to charge'.[16] Then he charged at full speed, advancing at a 'full trot' which then built into 'charging fiercely'. His forces hit the royalists standing and broke his enemy just as effectively as Rupert had at Edgehill. After the fight he then ensured the royalists remained in a state of confusion by pursuing them for two or three miles. That this was effective was amply shown by the disparity in casualties, even if Cromwell overestimated them, and the amount of prisoners taken. It was a minor fight in many ways, and the parliamentarians continued their retreat to Lincoln despite it. But it remains important from a learning perspective. S.R. Gardiner hailed the skirmish as hugely important, even if some historians have sought to minimise it.[17] Its importance lay not in its strategic consequences, as it is quite right to note that the campaign had failed. It is important because it shows that Cromwell had learned his lessons well and put them into effect successfully the first time around: this would be useful both from a developmental point of view, but also from the standpoint of building a cohesion in his regiment based on high morale and success.

However, it was known that the queen wished not only to send the bulk of the ammunition but to escort it herself. She had raised troops and called herself the She Majesty Generalisima in preparation for the attempt. With her own troops and some lent by the Earl of Newcastle, the queen set off from York, again making use of the Great North Road which would take it through Newark, the most powerful single royalist garrison in the Midlands. The parliamentarians in the surrounding area once again targeted the town.

Newark had been garrisoned by the Nottinghamshire county high sheriff, Sir John Digby, and a Scottish veteran, Sir John Henderson, at the tail end of 1642 under the orders of the Earl of Newcastle, who had assumed command of the north and east of England.[18] This offset the seizure of Nottingham by John Hutchison and Sir John Gell, who had seized Derby and begun to garrison Derbyshire. The Newark garrison had, by the early summer of 1643, already seen off one siege, a fairly half-hearted affair led by the forces of Lord Willoughby and Major General Sir Thomas Ballard, and as a result had begun redeveloping the defences.[19] The garrison was in the region commanded by Mr Henry Hastings, second son of the Earl of Huntingdon, who in February had been appointed colonel general of all the royalist forces in Leicestershire, Nottinghamshire, Staffordshire, Rutland, Derbyshire and Lincolnshire (which was later passed to Lord Widdrington). Although the garrison, having been directly established on Newcastle's orders, maintained a distance from the general, he was still expected to support it if necessary.

Lord Grey of Wark was no longer in the region, having been commanded to join his forces to those of Lord General Essex, and most of the Eastern Association forces were involved in the earl's Reading campaign in April (they were to remain with Essex until July).[20] Grey of Wark's absence allowed Cromwell to develop his strategic understanding, and Newark was central to this. By 24 May, Cromwell and Captain John Hotham had joined Lord Grey of Groby at Hutchinson's base at Nottingham.[21] There was little action, but Hotham and his father were attempting to switch sides – their actions became increasingly suspicious and Lord Grey of Groby was nervous of venturing far from his home county of Leicestershire; his one attack on the royalist outpost at Wiverton was driven off.[22] In any case there were already large numbers of royalist forces in the vicinity of Newark, and according to Hotham 'we could not come to them without great disadvantage'.[23] The queen left York on 4 June with 4,500 men, having asked Hastings to join her for the journey beyond

Newark.[24] It took two weeks for her army to reach Newark, which she entered without interference and joined Hastings there. The assembled parliamentarians claimed that they had prepared to fight the royalists, which they supposed to be solely drawn from Newcastle's army, but otherwise they made no attempt to stop the queen.[25] They then remained at Nottingham, where they were attacked by the queen and Hastings a few days later. The parliamentarians were paralysed, and Hastings and the queen took over the town, trapping the parliamentarians in the seemingly impregnable castle, before moving on to attack the parliamentarian garrison at Burton on Trent. Cromwell and Grey of Groby then left Nottingham, the latter's reputation in tatters. Hotham had been exposed as a would-be turncoat: Essex ordered his arrest and he was held at Nottingham before escaping and claiming that his accusers were men without honour or status. Cromwell, he claimed, was associated with religious radicals and both he and Nottingham colonel Charles White were iconoclasts.[26] Hotham made his way to Hull, where he and his father were arrested by the mayor and sent to London. Cromwell's activities were still dependent on commanders who were social superiors like Grey of Groby and the absent Grey of Wark, and he could exercise little initiative off the battlefield, but he was showing a keen interest in strategic matters, trying to ensure that his home territory was protected against the queen's army even when he was serving away.[27] Grey of Groby was half Cromwell's age, and his lack of experience was telling. After the debacle with the queen, Grey of Groby too set off to join the Earl of Essex's army. Cromwell had returned eastwards, where he was soon to become part of the attempt to ensure a route northwards free from the interference of the Newark garrison and its satellites.

Sir John Meldrum had been sent by Essex to assemble troops from Nottinghamshire and Lincolnshire to capture the inland port of Gainsborough, with the assistance of Eastern Association forces. Gainsborough was north of Newark, seated on an alternative route north from Lincoln towards Rotherham and Doncaster via a ferry over the Trent, but also with access to the Humber estuary crossing to Hull, which was useful to parliamentarians because the Great North Road had been held by royalists since January. The Lincolnshire parliamentarian commander, Lord Willoughby of Parham, had defeated his counterpart, the Earl of Kingston, and captured Gainsborough on 20 July, but had in turn become trapped in the town by Newark forces under Sir Charles Cavendish. Other sections of the Newark-based royalists had been collecting their taxes – called contribution – from across Lincolnshire, and on 22 July had reached as far as Peterborough. They retired to Stamford, which although it was on the Great North Road, was not fortified, and rather than attempt to hold the town they shut themselves up in nearby Burleigh House and its park. After waiting for the arrival of some foot and artillery, for he had six of seven troops of horse only, Cromwell attacked Burleigh Hall. After a hard fight, Cromwell forced the garrison into surrendering on 24 July. He then marched through the town to Grantham, pushing aside some hastily gathered royalist forces en route, and from there he set off to join Sir John Meldrum.[28]

THE BATTLE OF GAINSBOROUGH

Gainsborough was not as strongly fortified or defended as was Newark, yet holding it secured a major routes northwards, the line of the present A156 and A159, thus cutting communications between Lincoln and the north, in particular the parliamentarian garrison at Hull. Willoughby of Parham's success in taking the town from Kingston's forces had to be challenged, and the Newark garrison had responded quickly, putting the town under siege. Meldrum assembled local forces on 27 July at North Scarle, west of Lincoln, in order to relieve the town. Meldrum had about 300 horse and Cromwell brought another six or seven troops of horse and dragoons. These forces marched on Gainsborough from North Scarle via Lea and pushing back a royalist reconnaissance party once they were close to the town.

Royalist horse under Sir Charles Cavendish were formed into four sections or brigades, three of which were in the front line, and he had clearly read Vernon for Sir Charles's own regiment was placed in the rear as a reserve and in the fighting it played a textbook role: 'you must always appoint troops of Reserve, which are not by any means to engage themselves in the fight till the First troops have given the charge and reassembled behind them to make readie again for the second charge'.[29]

The royalists had drawn up on a flat-topped hill one mile from the town, on part of which the town's coney warren was situated. This hill, known as Foxby Hill, is to the south of Gainsborough with, nowadays, Warren Wood to the south of it and several modern copses on the top, new-build housing on its western fringes and nineteenth-century developments between it and the town. Cavendish had chosen his position well: he had placed his brigades at the top of the hill, the very steeply rising ground in front of them on both the western and southern side facing the parliamentarians' approach was covered by the rabbit holes of the warren. The steepness of the rise from the Lea Road would make it difficult for Meldrum to approach. Cavendish's right flank was protected by a meadow and marshy ground, extending from the River Trent almost to the base of the hill even today.

Meldrum marched from North Scarle on 28 July, possibly via Laugherton and Torksy, which would mean they would have arrived, via Lea, towards the south of the town on the present-day Lea Road, which skirts the hill and proceeds into the town centre. Cavendish had sent a 'good party' of a hundred horse to watch their approach from Lea, and these were driven back after a struggle by mounted dragoons as Meldrum approached. Undaunted by Cavendish's position, Meldrum pressed on 'under the Coney Warren' which was on the side of the hill, and then began to advance across the ground broken by the rabbit holes. Meldrum organised his regiments into three 'brigades' and placed Lincolnshire troops in the front or vanguard of his army, Northampton (two troops) and Nottingham (three troops) regiments in the 'battle' or centre of his army and Cromwell's regiment of four or five troops in the rear.

There are three accounts of the battle, which, despite all being signed by Cromwell, contain slightly different accounts of what happened at Gainsborough, and by doing so leave some doubt as to the full story of Cromwell's handling of his men that day. The most detailed of these, certainly regarding Cromwell's activities, is the third account written on 31 July to the Suffolk Committee. The vanguard began a slow advance up the hill, picking its way amongst the warrens, above what is now Sandsfield Lane.[30] It is possible that the dragoons which had first encountered Cavendish's men were employed on foot, as there was clearly musket or carbine fire directed at the royalist horse on the hill. Royalist John Hussey was struck by a ball in the chest that ripped into and through the upper seam of his cuirass and through his buff coat, suggesting a fairly close-range shot.[31] The royalists, possibly using dragoons, tried to slow them down or stop the parliamentarian advance; although it is not clear precisely what attempts were made to impede the parliamentarians' progress up the hill; but it was clearly insufficient. Cavendish's position was strong. He could arrange his brigades on the flat top of Foxby Hill and could have possibly held the hill with a sufficient number of dragoons or commanded musketeers as a forlorn hope. Even then, a well-timed charge could have caught the parliamentarians as they topped the hill even if there was not a sufficient forlorn hope. The Lincolnshire troops got up the hill and were followed by the rest of the horse who together pushed the royalists' 'forlorn hope' back upon their main body, the line held by the three regiments Cavendish had brought out of Newark. As the parliamentarian horse arrived near the top of the hill they began to dress their lines seemingly unimpeded, and Cromwell took command of the right wing (the place of honour usually led by the senior commander of the horse), the royalist front line advanced upon them. It is not known at what speed they were advancing when they made contact, as one parliamentarian report written that evening states only that the parliamentarians charged, and just one of Cromwell's accounts, written a few days later, says that the royalists met the parliamentarians at the charge. The royalist forces, or at least some of them, were possibly caught moving more slowly than the parliamentarians, but put up a strong fight. Cromwell said that neither side could break the order of the other, but it was noted that 'they a little shrinking', perhaps referring to their resolve or frontage. The latter would have allowed the parliamentarians to press 'in on them', which saw the royalist front line break and flee. They left the field, dividing both to the right and left of Cavendish's reserve. Some of the parliamentarians followed the fleeing royalists, including Cromwell's regiment, which may itself have pursued the defeated royalists via both sides of Cavendish's reserve. Foxby Hill to the north and east is less steep than on its southern and western edges, making such a retreat possible. The royalists fled as far as six miles from the battlefield, although the parliamentarian regiments may not have all followed that far; according to the joint account, Cromwell's regiment as a whole probably did not get swept away in the pursuit, and some of his troops certainly remained closer to the hill. Back on the hilltop, Cavendish charged those parliamentarian troops which had not followed the retreating royalists; it may have been that they had been held as a reserve by Meldrum, just as Vernon recommended, although initially it was Cromwell's regiment which had formed the reserve so this may have been more of an ad hoc group of Lincolnshire horse held together by one of the senior officers. As this second fight developed, Cromwell had clearly remained close enough to the action to be able see what was happening on the hill behind him, and see that Cavendish's rear was dangerously exposed, possibly because the royalist trusted that all the other parliamentarians were involved in the pursuit. However, some of the pursuers were still near enough to have a view of the southern edge of the hill top. Cromwell began to gather three of his troops: his own; Whalley's, which should have been to the immediate left of his own; and one other, perhaps that of the senior captain John Desborough with troop number three, immediately to the left of Whalley's. The joint account, written on the day after the fight, says:

> Cromwell and his major Whalley and one or two other troops were following the chase, and, were in the rear of that regiment. When they saw the regiment unbroken endeavoured, with much ado to get into a body those three or four troops which were divided.

Whilst the third account, Cromwell's letter to the Suffolk Committee, makes it clear that only three troops were brought back under orders: '[I] kept back my major, Whaley, from the chase, and with my own troop and another of my regiment, in all being three troops, we got into a body'.[32]

Cavendish had by this time succeeded in defeating the two or three troops of Lincolnshire horse and pushing them from the hill. Then Cromwell charged into Cavendish's rear, scattering the regiment and probably sending it down the almost precipitous western edge of Foxby Hill, towards Lea Road and across into the Summer Gangs – the meadows only usable in the summer, marked today by Summer Gangs Lane, and into the marshy meadow ground to the south-west of the hill between it and the river. There Cavendish was trapped in a bog, which suggests that not all of the meadow land had drained by July that year. It is now known locally as Candish (Cavendish) Bog. Cavendish was knocked from his horse and mortally wounded by Captain Lieutenant James Berry (confirming that Cromwell's own troop was involved), after, according to John Aubrey, he had surrendered, although there is no corroboration suggesting that Berry had defied the rules of war.[33] The royalist regiments had now all left the field, leaving Meldrum able to resupply Willoughby's garrison.[34]

Reports of the battle give a confused and potentially mixed picture of Cromwell's performance in the battle. The letter sent to William Lenthall from Lincoln that night, written by Cromwell and the two Lincolnshire committee-men, Sir Edward Ayscough and John Broxholme, placed Cromwell and his troop on centre stage once the fight had begun. Abbott suggested that the letter was not written by Cromwell – it is not in his hand – but it is unclear whether or not he had any part in drafting it. It is interesting that Meldrum is not referred to in this letter's account, after the references to the rendezvous he initially organised. According to this account, Cromwell was able to halt his forces during the pursuit of the royalist front line. It was no mean feat to achieve this because his troops had become separated; moreover, he was able to get them in order and bring them back to the centre of the field, attack and defeat Cavendish, and thus cement Meldrum's victory. However, we have to ask what Cromwell's regiment was doing in the pursuit as they may not, according to this joint account, have been involved in the attack on the front line, because it refers only to the Lincolnshire troops forcing their way up the hill and attacking the royalists, seconded by the 'battle' (the Northamptonshire and Nottinghamshire troops). In Cromwell's own account, sent to Sir John Wray from Stamford two days after the battle, he did not mention his own role very much at all, but he did refer to the disorder that the parliamentarians were in after the defeat of the royalist front line.[35] It is possible that having done the hard work of forcing the passage up the hill the Lincolnshire troops were rested and the next stage of the attack undertaken by the Nottinghamshire and Northamptonshire horse and Cromwell's Eastern Association regiment. This scenario would explain why the Lincolnshire horse were still on the hill when Cavendish launched his reserve forces. It is possible that the confusion lies only in these first two sources, because the third account makes it clear that Cromwell's regiment was involved in the attack on Cavendish's front line and thus was legitimately part of the pursuit. If so then Cromwell's control of part of his regiment was praiseworthy, although there remains a question over his inability to hold back all of his regiment. It could be that it was considered necessary to send his remaining troops after the fleeing royalists to keep them from rallying, but not it is more likely that the regiment was not yet so well disciplined that all troops behaved as if the colonel was present. Nevertheless, the propaganda effort was effective – Cromwell's own success on the field was highlighted, whilst Meldrum the commander of the relief attempt was almost forgotten in the description of the fighting.[36]

That Cromwell was not yet in command of his own destiny was underlined by the lack of control he had over the aftermath of the battle of Gainsborough. Once again he was obliged to retreat to Lincoln following a personal triumph on the battlefield. After the fighting on Foxby Hill was over, and whilst Cromwell was in Gainsborough delivering the supplies needed by the garrison, it was heard that some six troops of the royalists had rallied north of the town and had joined with about 300 foot and two cannon. Cromwell was given command of a party of horse sent out of the town to meet them, along with 600 foot from the garrison. The royalists were 'driven' back from the windmill hill near Morton, on which they stood. Then a great shock hit the parliamentarians as they reached the summit of Spital hill: there was another whole regiment with the royalists: 'after that another and another and another and as some counted about fifty colours of foot, with a great body of horse, which was indeed my Lord Newcastle's army'.[37]

Upon seeing the parliamentarian forces, Newcastle's army chased them and Cromwell was only just able bring his force off in any order. The garrison troops ran back into the town and the horse was only reorganised with difficulty. Whilst the town was shut up quickly Meldrum's horse army was sent off towards Lincoln, pursued by part of Newcastle's Northern Horse. Despite the pursuit Meldrum got the horse away without loss. Within days,

Willoughby had been forced to surrender and the royalists reoccupied Gainsborough, once again ensuring the control of the two main routes between the north and the south on the eastern side of the country, making it difficult for the parliamentarians to communicate with their forces under Lord Fairfax in the north. Parliamentarian attempts to secure the routes north had been unsuccessful, and the great resources offered by the huge county of Lincolnshire could not be harvested, as the royalist garrison at Newark and its satellite outposts (which comprised a chain of small garrisons) at times stretched as far as the coast. Catastrophe followed on from the recapture of Gainsborough. As part of the surrender terms, Newcastle allowed Willoughby and his garrison to withdraw to Lincoln, but then pursued them quickly and closely, forcing them to abandon the county town almost immediately and obliging the earl to leave behind the parliamentarian artillery as the garrison melted away, leaving Willoughby to withdraw to Boston.[38] Something had to be done to improve the level of leadership in the region, as two commanders had failed: Lord Grey of Wark and Lord Willoughby of Parham. East Anglia had only been secured largely because of its distance from any large royalist force and because there had been few royalist strategic plans of any consequence which focussed on its heartlands, despite Cromwell's fears, but its resources too needed to be harnessed more carefully. However, this had changed more recently with Newcastle in the region: he of course was the titular royalist commander of East Anglia and he had an experienced army with a victorious record with which he could turn his title to reality.

MANCHESTER TAKES COMMAND

Since mid-July, Lord Grey of Wark was in disgrace for having refused to act as a commissioner in a mission to Scotland aimed at bringing about an alliance between parliament and the estates.[39] The new plan was not long in coming and it involved one of Cromwell's distant relatives, Edward Montagu, Earl of Manchester, son of the man who had conducted the inquiry into Cromwell's behaviour in Huntingdon over a decade before. Manchester's task was to bring the region into a single command and develop the army which would be supplied by the region's resources. The opening of the route to the north was one of the priorities for the new army. First, however, the army needed to be created, and Oliver Cromwell would be involved in this; on 28 July he was appointed governor of the Isle of Ely, which gave him command of a small but central defensive point on the north–south route through East Anglia. At the beginning of August, as Cromwell and Willoughby attempted to build a barrier to protect East Anglia, parliament turned its attention to the region. On 8 August, Cromwell was forced to abandon his recent conquest, Stamford, and march eastward to Peterborough, but he 'dare not go into Holland with my horse, lest the enemy should advance with his whole body of horse this way into your association, but am ready endeavouring to get Lord Gray's and the Northamptonshire horse to me, that so, if we be able we may fight the enemy, or retreat to you with our whole strength'.[40] On 10 August the association was reorganised, with Manchester as sergeant major general. Cromwell was named as one of the four colonels of horse in the army and retained his membership of the two county committees, Cambridge and Huntingdon. By the end of the month, Cromwell, with Manchester's backing, summoned the horse and dragoons from Essex and Suffolk to join him at Huntingdon: it was at this point that he absorbed Captain Ralph Margery's troop into his regiment.[41] Manchester wanted these forces for a campaign in Lincolnshire to restore control in the county in the wake of Newcastle's arrival, and to prevent the earl moving southwards to Essex where Lord Fairfax thought, based on an order he claimed to have seen, he was heading.[42] However, Newcastle sought to delay his march southwards and turned north again to tackle Fairfax's garrison at Hull, which threatened his rear and his access to the resources of Yorkshire. Manchester took on the job of capturing the small port of King's Lynn, whilst Cromwell went further north along the coast to Boston, where Willoughby remained hemmed in.[43] From there he headed north.

The Earl of Newcastle had, upon returning northwards, besieged Hull. The great port of Kingston upon Hull was in itself important. It was a gateway through which parliament could supply its northern forces and in return received resources from the north, and within Hull lay the forces of Lord Fairfax. Originally strong in the West Riding of Yorkshire, and with the important garrison of Scarborough on the east coast, the Yorkshire parliamentarians had challenged Newcastle's control over the county. Scarborough's governor, Sir Hugh Cholmeley, had handed the town and castle to the queen when she arrived at Bridlington, and the cause in Yorkshire had been damaged when Sir John Hotham and his son tried to betray parliament. Furthermore, the earl's offensive in the West Riding saw the defeat of Fairfax at the Battle of Adwalton Moor on 30 June 1643 and the capture of Leeds and Bradford. The parliamentarian cause was effectively confined to Hull, but even so Fairfax's army remained a potent threat in the minds of Newcastle's soldiers, and it was this which drew Newcastle out of the Midlands and back to Hull to a siege which was to drain his force's moral and physical strength. In the meantime Lord Fairfax had realised that his horse was both useless under siege and a drain on resources. So as Cromwell moved north from Boston, Lord Fairfax's son, Sir Thomas Fairfax, led the horse across the River Humber into Lincolnshire.[44] This allowed Manchester to launch an offensive in the county, which in turn brought together for the first time the two men who were to dominate the later history of the first civil war, both at this time trusted – if still untested – lieutenants. Cromwell and Fairfax were to cooperate closely over the next few months. On 20 September 1643, Lord Willoughby's command in Lincolnshire was further undermined when the county was absorbed into the Eastern Association, thus placing him under Manchester's authority rather than directly under the Lord General Essex's command.[45] This remained a point of contention as Willoughby's command was not definitively terminated until the new year. In the meantime Manchester had appointed Colonel Edward King to command Holland and Boston. In the subsequent months, King steadily undermined Willoughby, and in January Cromwell excoriated the Lincolnshire commander in parliament, bringing about the end of Willoughby's career.[46] In the meantime, Manchester followed up Newcastle's departure with a military offensive using the support sent to him from Lord Fairfax which had accompanied Cromwell to Boston, where they joined Manchester after his capture of King's Lynn on 15 September.

HORNCASTLE AND WINCEBY

On 9 October the Eastern Association Army left Boston and drove the royalists from Wainfleet where they had been placed by Newcastle, and then moved to besiege Bolingbroke Castle, another of Newcastle's recent establishments, camping at Kirkby on 10 October. Royalist forces, led by General Henry Hastings (including those from the separate command at Newark and its satellite at Gainsborough, led by Sir John Henderson), quickly marched from Lincoln on 11 October towards Manchester's army; so quickly that it caught him unawares, even though he had intended to draw royalists into the county. The chief account suggest that the royalist forces numbered 80 colours of horse and dragoon. Each colour should consist of 60 troopers, and thus what should have been approaching 5,000 men, but was likely far fewer as Hastings's army consisted of undersized troops. Henderson drove into Horncastle, pushing parliamentarian horse back upon Manchester himself and some, but not all, of his horse. Overnight the earl blocked the route from Horncastle to

Bolingbroke and at a council of war decided to fight. Cromwell urged caution, thinking that the horse was exhausted from a long series of marches, but he was overruled.[47] On the following morning the earl drew his army up in battle order on Bolingbroke Hill. At noon on 12 October the royalist forces approached – Manchester marched towards them and they met at Winceby. The earl's forces was clearly a full army of horse, foot and artillery, although the foot were slower in arriving on the field. The nature of Henderson's force is less clear and it may have comprised only of brigaded horse, under Henderson, Lord Widdrington and Sir George Saville, Saville's forces having been part of Newcastle's army. There is reference to both sides having a forlorn hope, the commanded body of musketeer skirmishers sent out ahead to both annoy the enemy and break up any charge before it reached the main army, but we know that the royalists had dragoons who had dismounted to fill this role. The rival forlorn hopes battled it out for about an hour. Manchester then launched his own and Cromwell's horse regiments in 'such a charge as they would not abode a second'. At this point it went wrong for Cromwell: for some reason he had got ahead of his regiment when his horse was killed by royalist dragoons, who were able to get off two volleys before Cromwell hit home. The horse fell on top of him and had to get himself out from under it, but as soon as he did so he was 'again knocked down', before getting a 'poor horse' from a trooper.[48] Whilst both the author of *An Exact Relation* and John Vicars assert that the royalists could not stand another charge, the parliamentarians did have to launch at least one more. Cromwell's regiment was supported to its rear by that of Sir Thomas Fairfax, and as Cromwell's regiment engaged the royalists to their front Fairfax was able to manoeuvre around it and attack the royalists in the left flank, creating chaos amongst their line and breaking them. Sir Miles Hobart's regiment then charged and the royalist horse was comprehensively defeated and chased some five miles. Twenty-six colours were taken, and as at Grantham the casualty ratio reflected the victory, with many parliamentarians wounded but few killed, which would be representative of the face-to-face fighting. More royalists (1,200 it was claimed) were killed, wounded and captured, reflecting the fact that they turned their backs on their enemy, and suffered more casualties in their rout. More were drowned in the river at Horncastle too; local sources reporting to the complier of *An Exact Relation of the Victory Obtained by the Forces Under the Command of the Earl of Manchester, Against the Earl of Newcastle's Forces in Lincolnshire Under the Command of Sir John Henderson*, suggested more than a hundred.[49] Cromwell was not able to give a good account of himself at Winceby, although no one doubted his bravery, for he would have been badly shaken by the fall with his dead horse and by the fact that he was knocked over possibly by another horse rather than a sword-wielding royalist; he evidently was able to carry on the fight. There is a question over his position on the field – Manchester did not lead his regiment, as the commander in chief cedes regimental command in order to command the army overall – but Cromwell was at the head of the brigade that included his and the earl's regiments. He should have not been so far in front as to be vulnerable to the accurate dragoon musket fire as it was suggested he was. On the other hand, the positioning of the regiments seems to be sound, with Fairfax to the rear and possibly to the flank. It is not clear whether Fairfax was to the left rear or right rear of Cromwell's regiment. But he may have been to the right. It might be supposed that if Cromwell's and Manchester's horse were the front line, then Cromwell's would be to the left of Manchester's, which as the commander's regiment would be in the position of honour to the right of the line; this was a battle line which had been drawn up overnight, and Winceby was not an encounter battle where troops were fed in as they arrived or became available, allowing for precise positioning. This may suggest that Fairfax was to the left rear of Cromwell's regiment and to the right rear of Manchester's. Thus he would be able to attack the royalists on their left from between Cromwell's and Manchester's regiments, if the battle positions were laid out on chequer-board formation and Fairfax was able to move into the gap between Manchester's and Cromwell's regiments having been placed to their rear. This type of cavalry formation would have been found in the Dutch armies of the period in which many Englishmen and Scotsmen had served, and given that the battle had been planned as a 'sett battle' by Manchester there had been time to give consideration to the placing of the regiments. The position of Cromwell ahead of his regiment may give a clue as to what happened to him during the fight.[50]

LATE AUTUMN 1644

Lincoln fell to Manchester shortly afterwards, and the North Midland royalists were briefly more closely constrained than before. Henderson was replaced as the governor of Newark by a local man, Sir Richard Byron, brother of Lord John Byron, the field marshal appointed to oversee the arrival of troops from Ireland; the regiments sent there a year-and-a-half earlier to fight the rebels, but now during the uneasy peace following the Cessation of September 1643, expected to return to join the king. Henry Hastings was promoted to lieutenant general and ennobled as Lord Loughborough. Newcastle became a marquis. Whilst this may seem strange following the failure to secure the southern gateway of the marquis's command, the situation in the rest of the North Midlands had never looked better. The county towns were hemmed in and deprived of the ability to support themselves from the counties they had been intended to control, and Lord Loughborough now commanded fortress Midlands.

On the other hand, Lincolnshire still had to be dealt with, and therefore Cromwell and Manchester coordinated a military and political solution to cement Lincolnshire to the Eastern Association, just as Willoughby began to reorganise the county administration and garner the fruits of being able to tax the county's resources more fully. Manchester initially placed Colonel Edward King into the governorship of Boston and Holland, but within a month of the fall of Lincoln on 20 October, King was appointed governor of the ancient city and county high sheriff. This gave him administrative powers including that of raising a hue and cry, which was used by the royalist high sheriff of Staffordshire, Sir Thomas Leveson, to raise a *posse comitatus* and challenge the other appointed authorities in the county; in this case (if necessary) King could challenge Willoughby. King, a Presbyterian like his new commander, believed his former commander, Willoughby (he had served under the earl until captured at the fall of Grantham), to be ineffective. For his part Willoughby regarded King as an example of Manchester's interference.[51] King used his powers in the county to deny Willoughby the supplies, money and men he needed, even though technically Willoughby was the county's commander in chief, with a warrant which predated Manchester's incorporation of the county. King was the very willing tool which Manchester was using to prise control from Willoughby. King also encouraged a petition from the county calling for Manchester to be given full control. As the rival forces settled into winter quarters, the political battles began. With the Lincolnshire petition before it, parliament turned to the county situation. Cromwell had remained in Ely as winter got underway and was concerned with the civil duties of a governor during those months, even though he had by now appointed a deputy for the Isle – his recently absorbed captain of horse Henry Ireton from Nottinghamshire, formerly of the Nottingham garrison. On 10 January 1644, Cromwell warned the cathedral minister not to continue with his choir services in case 'soldiers should in any tumultuous or disorderly manner attempt the reformation of your Cathedral Church'.[52] Nine days later, on Friday 19 January, Cromwell was in London, but still attending to administrative duties in the Isle of Ely, ordering the Wisbeach treasurer to pay £600 to Major Dodgson. Monday's business was not parochial. On 22 January the attack on Willoughby began. Cromwell accused Willoughby of quitting:

> Gainsborough, when [Cromwell] was not far off, with forces to relieve him. That he quitted the city of Lincoln etc., left powder, match, and arms there, and seven great pieces, mounted with all the carriages, which the enemy made use of. That he had low and profane commanders under him of the conduct of one of them he gave instances.[53]

Willoughby was ousted despite being defended by one of the very commanders Cromwell alluded to, Sir Christopher Wray.[54] Manchester was given undisputed command of the county forces and Cromwell was promoted.

GENERAL CROMWELL

On the same day that Cromwell made the attack on Willoughby in the Commons he became a lieutenant general. There is some speculation about this rise, for there is no direct reference to Cromwell having been a sergeant major general as might be expected. The ranks of general involved a reverse order of military rank prefaces; thus the lowest level general was a colonel general, followed by major or sergeant major general and then lieutenant general: bizarrely, captain general (usually referred to as a lord general) is a higher rank than lieutenant general, but that would appear to be a reversion to the actual meaning of lieutenant as someone serving in lieu of the office holder, thus a lieutenant general would serve in lieu of a captain general if required. Therefore it might be considered that Cromwell should have had a general officer rank previous to the role of lieutenant general, which accorded him the status of second in command at army level: most immediately that of major general. However, it does not necessarily follow, for Colonel General Henry Hastings, the royalist commander, had leapt from the rank he had been appointed to in February 1643 to lieutenant general in October without, it seems, having been a major general. On the other hand, Cromwell may have been briefly appointed to the rank of major general under Manchester. Manchester's own rank was lieutenant general according to his commission, even through he and other commanders in his position on both sides were actually operating as captain generals. Officially there was only one parliamentarian captain general until April 1645 and that was the Earl of Essex.[55] Sir Charles Firth discovered that he had received a major general's commission during the first three weeks of 1644, immediately prior to becoming a lieutenant general on 22 January.[56] This does not necessarily suggest that Cromwell served in such a post for only three weeks, and there had been speculation that he had been so promoted in November or December. There may be another way of looking at this conundrum, and that would be at his activities during the year, especially in terms of his battlefield actions at Gainsborough and Winceby. On both occasions, Cromwell was placed honorifically and practically in the role of a general. At Gainsborough, Cromwell was clearly on the right of the line with his regiment. Whilst Meldrum gets little mention in the coverage of the battle, he was the commander in the field and would be expected to be in a position where he could see as much of the whole field as possible. This left Cromwell in the position of a lieutenant general when he was in the lieutenant general's place with the horse on the right wing. Similarly at Winceby, he held the same place – he was clearly with the van of the army, which along with the battle was where the senior regiments were placed (which included his double regiment, and the Earl of Manchester's). As Manchester was in command and should have been in a central position with a clear view, but was possibly directing the arrival and positioning of the foot on the field, Cromwell naturally stood in the place of the lieutenant general on the right. This may account for why he was ahead of his regiment and such an excellent target for the royalist forlorn hope. The placing of Oliver Cromwell on the battlefields after May 1643 suggests that even if not on the general officer payroll, he was acting as the colonel general and then at least as a major general.

Manchester and Cromwell had concluded 1643 successfully. After more than six months they had secured control of Lincolnshire, both militarily and administratively. The royalists had been driven out of the county and so had the man they considered incompetent.

There has been a great deal of speculation about the relationship between the two men, centring very much on their religious difference – Cromwell was a Congregationalist or Independent whereas Manchester was a Presbyterian. By the end of 1644 they were at loggerheads, locked in a dispute that could well have derailed the parliamentarian cause, so deep did it run, yet a year earlier the relationship was fruitful despite the difficult family background. Cromwell was demonstrating his ability to think inclusively with regards to religion, becoming convinced that God favoured the parliamentarian cause because of the string of victories in Lincolnshire which he saw firsthand: the failure of Newcastle to capture Hull, of which he had close knowledge and reports from further afield received as third-hand news; the salvation of Gloucester; and the

Earl of Essex's victory at the first Battle of Newbury. He seems not to have believed that God was favouring any particular religious clique. With the collapse of the Church of England's hegemony in 1640–2, the numerous and previously and necessarily secretive underground religious congregations and sects began to appear publicly. The greater single number were initially drawn to the Presbyterian church as favoured in Scotland, and whilst thoroughly hierarchical in some ways it was founded on a form of representative democracy. Manchester and Edward King, for example, were adherents of this movement, and they were in favour of the alliance with the Scots which John Pym engineered in autumn 1643. This entailed serious discussion around creating a Presbyterian church in England, which many wanted and which the Scots saw as the only sure defence for their Kirk against interference from England and the monarch. On the other hand, others were drawn to a variety of minority sects, collectively known as Independents or Congregationalists because they were very much focussed on local congregations that were not centrally or officially bound into a national organisation. Cromwell was of the latter, although he never explicitly said which one of the Independent or Congregationalist groups he had opted for. Within years these two groupings became (often deadly) enemies, and by the end of 1644 Cromwell was labelled by Manchester and Essex as a dangerous sectarian. For now Cromwell did not feature in the consciousness of the Presbyterians as he was loyal to Manchester and promoted King's work; he even signed the Solemn League and Covenant, which all but mandated the establishment of a Presbyterian church in England, Wales and by extension Ireland. There was certainly no barrier to his working with Manchester, even if some people were collecting evidence of his radical religious views.

But by the end of January 1644, Cromwell was a lieutenant general. Before considering how Cromwell worked at this central officer rank and in this important role, what did a lieutenant general do? According to commentators such as Cruso, the lieutenant general would usually be associated with the horse, as was the case in England, where the lieutenant general or second in command led the horse and a major general led the foot, even if, as in Cromwell's case, he was appointed a lieutenant general of horse and foot.[57] Such a general should be of great experience and valour, and by now Cromwell had demonstrated the latter and was developing the former, a very different picture than that of the man whom a year-and-a-half earlier had none of the qualifications required of a captain of horse. In a practical sense a general would have to be constantly aware of how an enemy might advance upon him and attack his forces. The general should be able to marshal regiments on the march and think ahead about lodging, quarters and fodder for an entire army wing. This takes us back to the nature of Cromwell's work during 1643, when he was constantly on the lookout for incursions into Lincolnshire and the association counties from the Newark forces, and latterly the Earl of Newcastle during the summer months. He demonstrated his capacity to know when to attack, such as the seizure of Stamford, and when to retreat, for example abandoning the same town and moving to Peterborough. In terms of logistics, during those same fraught months Cromwell commanded a growing regiment of his own, which by the end of the year had grown to double size and thus required the attention of a brigade. Moreover, he had led it and other regiments on the field at Grantham, Gainsborough and Winceby, and guided large forces on marches to Gainsborough in July 1643, from Huntingdon to Goole in October 1643, and back again this time with a force enlarged by the inclusion of the Northern Association Horse. Indeed his qualms about fighting at Winceby were based on the condition of the horses of the entire army, not just his own regiment. Cruso considered these things to be of great importance, in particular when the lieutenant general and the horse were operating without infantry support, as was often the case with Cromwell, as at Belton and Gainsborough and temporarily at Winceby, as well as in the campaigns on the borders of Lincolnshire. A general of horse had regard for the training and discipline of the whole of the regiments of horse, and as he was second in command he had to have knowledge of how to lead the foot. In this latter aspect Cromwell had less experience than of the horse, but he had commanded units of foot right from the beginning of the war and had been responsible for raising a foot regiment in the later stages of the Lincolnshire campaign.[58] Lincolnshire and the East Midlands as a whole had indeed been the proving ground of Lieutenant General Oliver Cromwell.

5

CROMWELL THE GENERAL, 1644

In many ways the war had reached something of a stalemate at the point Cromwell became a lieutenant general. Neither parliament nor the king held the initiative, but new offensives were about to take place, both using troops from elsewhere in the British Isles. In 1643, both sides had battled it out for control over regions and their resources: the king held the north-east and parliament had secured East Anglia. The king also held the south-west and much of Wales, but Essex's success in securing the safety of Gloucester disrupted communications with Oxford, and it also had something of a limiting effect on the importance of the royalist capture of Bristol that year. Parliament likewise was blocking access between the king's garrisons and North Wales due to the successes of Sir William Brereton in Lancashire and Cheshire. Whilst Lord Loughborough held on to the North Midlands, despite the loss of Lincolnshire, his forces were tied up in garrison duty because the region still contained potent parliamentarian forces which it would be unwise to turn one's back on. Of course England and Wales were not alone in being at war. The war in Ireland, which had begun in the wake of the October 1641 rebellion, had raged on for over two years. The situation had been complicated by the outbreak of war in England and Wales and affected loyalties. The rebels, known later as the Catholic Confederation of Kilkenny, had consolidated their governmental structure and set up a form of parliament called the General Assembly in Kilkenny, with provincial governments, armies and commanders in all four of the provinces. The effect had been to confine 'loyalist' forces to the fringes: the north-east of Ulster, around Dublin in Leinster, the south-west coast of Munster and pockets of territory in Connacht. Loyal to whom was a good question. In the north-east this was less difficult on the face of it, as many of the troops there were Scots originally led by Lord Leven, victor of the Bishops' Wars, and their first loyalty was of course to Edinburgh. The others of course were English and Welsh, and whilst theoretically having been sent there by king and parliament they were loyal to the Westminster government. However, whilst the Marquis of Ormond in Dublin, the Earl of Clanricarde at Galway and Lord Inchiquin in Munster had remained loyal to the king, there were as many swathes of political position in Ireland as there were in England and Wales. During the summer of 1643, as Cromwell was struggling to keep the royalists under control in Lincolnshire, the king's chief representative in Ireland, Ormond, had secured a cessation of fighting in much of Ireland (the Scots did not feel necessarily obliged by it) as preparation for a full set of negotiations. This meant that the regiments sent there in 1641–2 from England and Wales could return home, and the king planned to incorporate them into his army regardless of the mix of loyalties within. Many of these were to be brought in via the ports of Chester, the nearby North Welsh coast and Bristol.[1]

Over in England, to combat this potentially massive allocation of new resources, parliament scaled up its discussions with the Scots. Scotland had remained, on the face of it, studiedly neutral, although naturally it feared an outright victory for the king would leave them and their Kirk exposed to a rematch of 1639–40. A negotiated settlement would be a more positive outcome and Scottish politicians had talked to all sides, but the king was less than welcoming, partly because he regarded the Scots as rebels and because in the spring and summer of 1643 he appeared to be winning the war.[2] John Pym took advantage of the situation and alerted the Scots to the dangers posed by the cessation in freeing Irish confederation soldiers for service in Scotland, either at the king's bidding or the confederation's. By the time Pym had died of cancer the alliance was all but in place: the Scots would send an army into northern England paid for by the English and Welsh people, and a grand assembly would be set up at Westminster to debate the future structure of the church in England and Wales. Everyone in England and Wales, but most importantly the politicians and army officers, would have to sign up to the treaty – the Solemn League and Covenant.[3] Cromwell, despite not being in favour of a Presbyterian state church, had signed too as he took up his role as lieutenant general.[4]

Thus, five days before Cromwell opened his attack on Willoughby in the House of Commons, a large Scottish army marched across the eastern border into Northumberland for the second time in four years. In 1640, Lord Leven (then still called Sir Alexander Leslie) had led the Army of the Covenant with the tacit and covert support of Charles I's political opponents south of the border. Now he commanded the Army of the Solemn League and Covenant into England at the express wish of the English and Welsh parliament; well, at least one of them.[5] Another parliament had assembled at Oxford, with about half of the members of the Lords and a third of the MPs actually sitting or on military duty associated with it, and it immediately condemned the Scottish invasion.[6] The intervention of the Scots and the veteran regiments from Ireland potentially changed the situation dramatically. Royalists drew resources northwards to support the Marquis of Newcastle in holding back Leven. In the North Welsh marches the royalist commander Lord Byron sought to clear Cheshire and the routes into England of Brereton's garrisons: it was to be a very active off-season for all the armies involved.[7]

Cromwell stayed in London for several days after the attack on Willoughby, taking part in crucial discussions between the Lords and Commons over the king's secret approaches to Sir Henry Vane, and was involved in a discussion setting up a joint English, Welsh and Scottish executive – the Committee of Both Kingdoms, on which he was appointed to sit.[8] The following month brought personal tragedy to Oliver and Elizabeth Cromwell. As the Eastern Association continued to secure its territory, a garrison was established at Newport Pagnell in Northamptonshire, utilising part of Cromwell's regiment. Cromwell's attention had firmly switched from the north of the association to the south and west, for that month he was busy tackling the outposts of the royalist capital, Oxford, stealing cattle from under its very nose in early March and capturing an outpost, Hillesdon House, on 4 March. However, smallpox had broken out in the Newport garrison, and later that month Captain Oliver Cromwell died of the disease.[9] He was replaced as captain of the fourth troop by John Browne.

With Lincolnshire under parliamentarian control and the siege of Hull ended, Sir Thomas Fairfax had returned northwards to Yorkshire. Tension in the south of the county was further eased as the Marquis of Newcastle's attention turned to strengthening the north of the country in order to resist in various ways the Scottish invasion. Sir Thomas was thus able to lend assistance to Sir William Brereton over in Cheshire. Brereton was under sustained pressure from Lord Byron, who was clearing the way for the influx of troops from Ireland who were landing in the Dee Estuary and either marching by land into England or being shipped to the inland port of Chester by small river-craft. Brereton had, in 1643, hemmed in Chester with garrisons at Beeston Castle and

Nantwich, and Byron was trying to push them out. Nantwich was besieged in early January by Byron's local forces and substantial numbers of veterans from Ireland. Brereton had requested that Fairfax come to help him break the siege, and the young cavalry commander struggled across the snow-laden Pennines to his aid. On 25 January, together they defeated Byron and scattered his forces. For the first time some of the veterans from Ireland had a choice regarding whom they fought for, and some, officers like George Monck amongst them, took up the offer of service with parliament and chose to join their conquerors. This one victory disrupted the royalist plans for reinforcement so much that even though over 17,000 troops crossed to Wales and England by March 1644, they failed to make a significant contribution to royalist strategy that year.[10]

The Scottish invasion was, on the other hand, to have a significant effect and would soon sweep Cromwell up in its fallout. As Newcastle prepared the port of Newcastle to withstand isolation and siege, and built up defensive points on the River Tyne having decided to abandon Northumberland, troops from his southern territories were drawn northwards, to support his field army in the Palatinate county of Durham and strengthen those garrisons further south which would undoubtedly face attack from the newly enlarged Fairfaxes. The consequences of this were the removal of some of the troops in Newark, and from Lord Loughborough's command. As these troops left the North Midlands, a new plan was hatched to capture Newark. Sir John Meldrum returned to the area to command the Midlands forces and Willoughby left Westminster, where his previous activities had been subject to scrutiny, and led those troops still under his command to join Meldrum in the attack on Newark, just as Cromwell was taunting the garrison in Oxford with cattle raids.[11] The siege was a close one, and even though Lord Loughborough's regiments tested the leaguer it was clear that the forces under Meldrum were too large for an attack by the local royalists alone. Loughborough appealed to Prince Rupert for help.[12] The prince was to Loughborough's west, reorganising the royalist war effort on the Welsh borders following the disaster at Nantwich. On 20 March the prince joined Loughborough, and they barged their way across the River Soar at Cotes and made a lightening march on Newark. Meldrum and Willoughby were caught by surprise when the combined royalist armies appeared east of the garrison between them and Lincolnshire. In the early hours of 21 March, Rupert and Loughborough attacked Meldrum. They defeated him, drove him on to the island in the Trent west of Newark, and cut off his retreat north having already closed down the route to Lincoln. Meldrum surrendered his army and weapons.[13] Within days Lincoln fell to the royalists and the county was exposed to their tax levies again.[14] Cromwell's work was soon undone; he and Manchester were too busy in the south of the region to take immediate action.

However, attention was generally directed towards the northern sector. Newcastle spent March trying to bring Leven to battle, but in vain; he was out-manoeuvred and Leven steadily marched southwards, but the Scots were now diminished by the need to secure a line of communications to the border and to besiege the town and port of Newcastle. For the Marquis of Newcastle, disaster struck further south when his commander in Yorkshire, Sir John Belasyse, was defeated at Selby by the Fairfaxes on 11 April. In order to protect York, the marquis abandoned Durham and marched to his base, sending the Northern Horse to join Lord Loughborough in the North Midlands. The Scots filled the vacuum in the north-east and marched into Yorkshire, where they joined the Fairfaxes and began preparing a siege. The Earl of Manchester soon began to turn his attention to the state of Lincolnshire, and moved the weight of his forces from Northamptonshire to the Vale of Belvoir on the Leicestershire–Lincolnshire border, near to the garrison of Belvoir Castle.[15] Lincoln was recaptured on 6 May by Manchester, as Cromwell kept an eye on the Newark horse regiments and those of the Earl of Newcastle's Northern Horse which had joined them. The Eastern Association Army then progressed northwards through Lincolnshire into Yorkshire, and headed towards York to join Lords Leven and Fairfax in the great leaguer surrounding the city.

THE GREAT AND CLOSE SIEGE OF YORK

From 23 April 1644, the Marquis of Newcastle was holed up in York, a mediaeval walled city ringed with earthwork defences on the major approach roads. It was not by any means a modern fortification; rather it was a city, as Geoffrey Parker wrote, 'enclosed (rather than defended) by outdated mediaeval walls susceptible to artillery bombardment'.[16] Nevertheless, a ring of earthworks had been established around the old walls. Sconces had been erected around the city: three to the west, with associated works, and one each to the north, south and east. There was, no doubt, a line of earthworks and trenches between the sconces and gun positions.[17] This was to be Cromwell's first taste of a fully developed siege, although his role in it is obscure and he probably spent most of his time leading the Eastern Association Horse in screening activities designed to keep the royalists in and supplies and support out. By contrast, most attention in the press and elsewhere focussed on the walls, and the earthworks of each side rather than on the essential work of hemming in the garrison in the fields and roads of the Vale of York. Cromwell would experience siege warfare more closely a year later.

Newcastle had evacuated the horse regiments to Nottinghamshire leaving the foot regiments and artillery to defend the city. On 18 April the Scots had been joined by the Fairfaxes with their northern forces, and together they had marched on York, but the city was large and the leaguer proved incapable of completely hemming the marquis' army.[18] The Scots tried to seal York's southern approaches and camped immediately south. The Fairfaxes positioned themselves to the Scots' right hand and sealed off the south-eastern and eastern approaches to the city, but although the northern approaches lay along the Scottish army's lines of communication this proved of little value in keeping Newcastle's forces quiescent, and supplies could still be brought into the city with some ease. This changed on 3 June when the Eastern Association Army arrived and took up station to the north and west. Large gun batteries were constructed opposite the southern side of the city at Lamel Hill and St Lawrence's churchyard. Attempts were made to undermine the nearby gate, Palmate Bar, but Manchester's main contribution having closed the northern routes to the city was to undermine an outwork. The outwork concerned was the walled grounds of the King's Manor, seat of the Council of the North, and had formerly been part of the building complex of St Mary's Abbey. The walls of the manor were not of the same standard as the city defences, but they abutted the western city walls and Bootham Bar and thus had to be defended. Their weakness proved a tempting target for Manchester's engineers and they tunnelled under the corner tower, known as St Mary's Tower, at the junction of Bootham and Marygate. It was just under a fortnight before they were ready to spring the mine. A bombardment of the precinct walls preceded the explosion of the mine on 16 June, which may have been delayed by negotiations conducted between 12 and 14 June. The attack was a job for foot soldiers under Major General Lawrence Crawford's command, rather than Cromwell's. There was a hand-to-hand fight in the precinct, and the King's Manor buildings were reached before the garrison troops were able to push the parliamentarian attackers back, killing 40 and capturing 216 of the Eastern Association Army soldiers.[19] The close work of sieges was normally designated to foot and dragoons, and so it would seem that the horse under Cromwell and the other second in commands, Sir Thomas Fairfax and David Leslie, were patrolling the vicinity of the city throughout the siege, collecting levies of food and money in lieu of formal taxes, preventing royalist sallies and watching for the approach of relief forces. They certainly spent some time near Wakefield and then nearer to York at Wetherby.[20]

THE RELIEF OF YORK AND THE ROAD TO MARSTON MOOR

The three commanders, Fairfax, Leven and Manchester, knew that their siege would not go unchallenged. Prince Rupert had assembled a force in late May comprising his West Midlands troops, and sections of Lord Loughborough's army, the Newark Horse under Major General Porter and Newcastle's own Northern Horse. These he had led through Cheshire and Lancashire, where he stormed Liverpool and relieved the siege of Lathom House.[21] The ensuing two weeks of the siege of York were spent waiting for the prince's arrival, and possibly hoping that the 4,000 troops in York could be starved out. Prince Rupert crossed the Pennines via Ribchester, Clitheroe and Gisburne, arriving at the royalist garrison of Skipton on 26 June. On 29 June the prince's army quartered around Lord Fairfax's house at Denton. The parliamentarian forces had been taken by surprise, as they had expected Rupert to take one of the southerly routes across the Pennines, which is why Cromwell spent so much time in the vicinity of Wakefield. Occupying Wetherby had been a waste of time, even though the most direct route from Knaresborough, where the prince had arrived on 30 June, was via that town. But Rupert had instead crossed to the north bank of the Ouse and marched via Boroughbridge to relieve the city. The leaguer broke up as the prince approached, and the three armies' foot regiments joined the horse at Hessay Moor. However, with the prince so near York they decided to move southwards towards Tadcaster, facing in the direction they had expected the prince to come. There was a possibility that Sir John Meldrum, who had gathered parliamentarian forces in Lancashire and then crossed the Pennines via one of the southern routes, could join them. There has also been some speculation the Earl of Denbigh was on his way north too.[22] However, Denbigh was well to the south. He had besieged Dudley Castle for over a week in early June, probably because he knew that part of the garrison had gone north with Rupert. Thereafter Denbigh had worked with the Earl of Essex as his army pursued the king to Worcester, and after several skirmishes with the king's forces had marched north to join Sir Thomas Mytton in Shropshire and south Cheshire, but just after the middle of the month had suddenly returned to London.[23] Meldrum's forces, however, were in Yorkshire, but they could not possibly reach the Wakefield area before 3 July, whereas it had become clear to the Scots and parliamentarian allies that Prince Rupert was not going to rest on his laurels and seemed determined to fight them near York. In a similar vein, the Marquis of Newcastle too would have preferred to await reinforcements that were on their way and, like Meldrum, just a few days away.

On 30 June, Cromwell's horse was south-west of York at a village called Long Marston watching the royalists approaching from the north, but Rupert's royalist horse that had debouched from Knaresborough in that direction was simply a decoy. Rupert had moved the majority of his army across the Ouse and the River Ure at Boroughbridge before finally crossing the River Swale at Thornton Bridge, and reached York from the east.[24] Over the two days the allied commanders discussed their options, which included waiting for Meldrum. It was argued later that Leven was in favour of the latter, and it may still have been the case that all of the commanders both knew that Newcastle was expecting reinforcements and that they had earlier overestimated the size of Rupert's army. Peter Newman argued that there may not have been a real and disruptive reluctance to fight, as has been traditionally thought to be the case, although it was probably the second in commands who were the keenest to go into battle whilst the oldest and most experienced, Leven, considered it to be very risky.[25] In the end, on 1 July the decision was taken to move away from York to beyond Tadcaster, where they expected to meet with reinforcements on or around 3 June. Newcastle believed that the three armies were about to break apart, and he urged Rupert to await events rather than attack straight away. However, it was not likely that the allies were going to disband imminently, given that they expected to be reinforced.

To some extent the decision just one day later, to reverse the resolution made on 1 July to move into the West Riding of Yorkshire, was forced upon the three commanders, as Rupert moved his army across the River Ouse and requested Newcastle to join him with the garrison. As the allied forces had begun to march towards Tadcaster the three lieutenant generals of horse, Cromwell, David Leslie and Sir Thomas Fairfax, had remained near Long Marston with a section of the horse watching the rear. It was thus they who became aware that Rupert had crossed the river using their own bridge of boats at Cawood and was approaching them. The commanders, well on their way south-west, were informed, and the army turned around and marched back towards Long Marston. During 2 July, the opposing forces were marshalled in the fields and moorland between Long Marston to the east and Tockwith to the west.

'STUBBLE TO OUR SWORDS'

The Battle of Marston Moor marks a sea change in Cromwell's career, both militarily and politically. Importantly for this book, it marks Cromwell's debut as a field commander in a large-scale battle – it was in fact to be the largest battle of the 1640s. Even if he had played an important role at Gainsborough and Winceby, Marston Moor was his first as a real general, not as a stand-in for a general in a small-scale battle. It was also where he truly became a controversial figure in the political arena, and the arguments about his contribution on the battlefield were used to reflect upon his political and religious stances.

The Battle of Marston Moor has attracted a great deal of attention from historians, reflecting the importance accorded to it by contemporaries in terms of the apparently complete nature of the victory. The first modern study was by Peter Young, and came after years of research into the armies and the battlefield itself. Young's exhaustive study of the sources remains a crucially important work, but it is not the last word. Peter Newman improved on Young's findings from the 1970s onwards by incorporating fieldwork undertaken by him and his students on the battlefield. Newman produced a full-length study of the battle in 1981, which was regarded as a major advance on Young. Newman worked on a series of projects thereafter, but then returned to work on the battle with Peter Roberts. Others also worked on the battle, Stuart Reid amongst them, but in 2003, following the death of Peter Newman, the book he and Roberts had been working on was published: it developed points Newman had written about over 20 years earlier and revised other of his findings. Some of the results of that study, which made extensive use of recent fieldwork, remained controversial, and some of its conclusions have been challenged, notably by Malcolm Wanklyn, although the confused ending of the battle posited by Newman and Roberts remains largely unchallenged, even if the positions of some of the royalist forces differs from study to study.[26] This analysis is focussed on Cromwell's contribution, which is less controversial than it was in the 1640s and 1650s: most historians recognise his crucial role in the battle. The course of the battle given here follows the Newman and Roberts argument to a very great extent, but not uncritically – it makes use of a large-scale analysis of the sources and the site and presents a convincing if challenging interpretation.

The fields, woodland and moorland which comprise the locale of the Battle of Marston Moor were situated in the four parishes of Long Marston, Bilton-in-Ainsty, Kirk Hammerton and Moor Monckton. It is a floodplain dominated by a ridge on the southern edge of the battlefield in one of Long Marston's open fields. Towards the west and the boundary between Long Marston and Bilton-in-Ainsty, parishes where the village of Tockwith was situated, the ridge took the form of a series of hummocks known as Bramhan or Bilton Bream: these are lower than the main part of the ridge and still fairly irregular.[27] They are now traversed by the lane known locally as Tip Lane, which once led to the village tip and beyond to Bilton. This lane's precursor may, according to Peter Newman, have marked the extreme western edge of the parliamentarian line, because to have straddled it and the ditches either side of it would have disrupted the organisation of the parliamentarian left wing. Similarly the lane now built up across the Long Marston Road and further west than Tip Lane is Kendal Lane; this too may follow an older field boundary or track, and could equally have formed the western edge of the royalists' right wing. The site of the tip on the eastern side of the lane is now overgrown with spindly trees that change the perspective of this end of the field, the opposite side of the lane is occupied by allotments. It was here that the first fighting took place on 2 July: despite being a fairly small clash compared with the fighting later in the day, it was to have important implications for the way the battle was fought. Stewart noted:

> In the mean while the Enemy perceiving that our cavalry had possessed themselves of a cornhill, and having discovered neer unto that hill a place of great advantage, where, they might have advantage of both sun and wind of us advanced thither with a regiment of Redcoats, and party of horse; but we understanding well their intentions and how prejudiciall it would be unto us if they should keep that ground, we sent out a party which beat them off and there planted our left wing of Horse; having gained this place, Generall Lesley gave order for the drawing up of the Battell[28]

Whereas the author who identified himself as W.H. noted:

> no sooner we looking about us the enemy with displayed colours entered the same place, bending towards the left hand by reason of some advantage they had perceived there, which we striving to prevent made for it, before they could possess themselves of it.[29]

Lionel Watson, the scout master of the Eastern Association Army – surprisingly, as his knowledge would be second hand at worst, but who demonstrated himself throughout the battle to have a keen eye for what was happening – makes only oblique reference to the success of his army's cavalry: 'we were put to draw up our men in a Corne-Field close to the Moore making way by our Pioners to get ground to extend the wings of our army to such a distance that wee might conveniently fight.'[30]

Cromwell acted positively. It seems clear that he understood the danger of royalists holding the end of the ridge, as it could precipitate the rolling up of the allied armies' left flank, and he attacked. Cromwell was at the heart of this first action and it is probably the fighting to which Cromwell referred in the opening section of the letter he wrote to Valentine Walton senior concerning the death of Valentine junior, and according to Newman and Roberts it was probably where Captain Walton was mortally wounded by a cannon ball that shattered one of his legs.[31] The death of one of his earliest lieutenants must has shaken Cromwell and his regiment, particularly those who had served with him since the regiment was created, and it illustrates the effect the artillery fire was supposed to have on the morale of a combatant as well as its deadly effect.[32] Rupert had placed the guns near to the Bream, possibly, according to one account, on Rye Hill. It is not known where that hill was or why, given that the whole of Bramham Hill was covered in rye, it was singled out as a unique feature. Of course it is possible that it was a generic name for the whole area, its use mangled in the Chinese whispers which provided Edmund Ludlow with the information. On the other hand, it might have been one of the hummocks on the Tockwith edge of Bramham Hill. Recent discussions with inhabitants have not given any more information than Peter Newman was able to gain in the 1970s about its location.[33] This had been a risky move in the face of royalist artillery and Rupert's experienced horse regiments, and the death of a trusted captain and relative was the price to pay. Nevertheless, the bold response worked – the royalist were driven off the ridge's west end and the flank was secured. The Eastern Association Horse occupied the Bream.[34] The significance of the action was not lost on the authors of several pamphlets dealing with the battle. Although Cromwell was not specifically named in relation to the action and details were generally scant, the need to seize the ground was well understood. One thing that Cromwell was able to do now was order his command. He was in charge of the left wing of horse. It is possible that this was due to the circumstances of arrival on the field, or it may have been that he was reckoned to be lower in status Sir Thomas Fairfax, who had the command of honour on the right flank. Although there is currently no record of Sir Thomas's being commissioned as lieutenant general to his father, it may have been the case that he was so commissioned as a general officer before Cromwell.[35] The position of Lieutenant General David Leslie is likewise confusing. He would have been commissioned in the rank before Cromwell, in autumn of 1643 when the Army of the Solemn League and Covenant was established, but clearly, and despite his own commander, Lord Leven, being the commander in chief of the allied army, he was subordinate to Oliver Cromwell on the day, perhaps because of the practicality of him being in command of a smaller number of troops of horse. Cromwell, probably in consultation with Leslie and the regimental colonels, drew up his regiments in three lines. His own regiment and the Earl of Manchester's regiments probably formed the front line as at Winceby, and given the order of precedence it may have been Manchester's which took up position on the right of this line with Cromwell's to their left again. The other regiments of the Eastern Association formed the second line and David Leslie's Scottish regiments the third. Dragoons were attached to this flank and probably ranged to the left of the horse regiments, as Lionel Watson, author of *A More Exact Relation*, makes it clear that the allied flanks were secured by dragoons.[36]

As a result of the action on Bilton Bream, the royalists were pushed back on to the moorland beyond the rabbit warren and the cultivated land north of the ridge, and Rupert established his right flank there consisting of experienced horse regiments protected by commanded musketeers to their front. It was an inferior position to the one he had contended for that morning; the prince was firmly on the defensive, even if he was able to use the broken ground in the form of rabbit warrens to his front as protection for his outnumbered horse regiments. The prince, according to Peter Newman, had attempted to offset some of his difficulties by placing the Duke of York's veteran regiment, commanded by Sir Samuel Tuke, in a position to charge into the flank of any regiment attacking the royalist right wing.

Cromwell and the allied right flank were in the dominant position on the field, being uphill of the royalists and outnumbering them 4,000 to 2,600. Moreover, the first two lines of his flank came from one army and had been serving together since the previous autumn, some for even longer. The royalist right commanded by Field Marshal John, Lord Byron, was not only smaller, it was less homogenous. Some regiments had served with the prince for some time, others only since the journey from the West Midlands to York. Tuke's was one of the marquis' regiments and could be counted amongst them, along with Sir Thomas Leveson's regiment of horse which was part of Lord Loughborough's army, if reluctantly so. Nonetheless, Leveson had served with Rupert in the Newark campaign, even if some historians have dismissed his regiment as a garrison force. Newman has argued that these royalist regiments were all an estimable enemy for Cromwell, and that he would be aware of who they were, and of their character, possibly more so than they were of him, but there was no denying that in numerical terms, cohesiveness and tactical position Cromwell held the advantage. The first of these circumstances, the composition of the royalist wing, was the result of a series of strategic decisions made on both sides that were for the most part beyond Cromwell's control. The second was something he held at least partly within his grasp and was certainly able to exploit. But the third, the seizure of Bilton Bream, was wholly his doing.

Much of the day of 2 July passed with neither side able to begin the fighting. The prince had lost the initiative at Bilton Bream and was firmly on the defensive, possibly because he realised that his horse was outnumbered. Nevertheless, all of his horse regiments, whether from the prince's marching army or from the Northern Horse, were on the field. Likewise the foot regiments he had brought with him were arranged on the field, but the Earl of Newcastle's foot regiments, so recently confined to garrison duties in York, were slow to leave the city for reasons which remain unclear, and only began arriving on the moor after midday. On the ridge the story was similar: the horse regiments were mostly present; having been guarding the army's rear as it retreated towards Tadcaster, but the foot was making its way back and on to the ridge. On both sides of what was to become the battlefield, the armies drew up in open country formations with the foot in the centre, the horse regiments massed on both flanks and, at least in the case of the allied Scots and parliamentarians, with dragoons covering the exposed flanks.

Sometime in the afternoon the artillery of both sides began to open fire, and the fire of the allied artillery was so intense upon the royalist left that it forced the withdrawal of the horse on that flank. It was not all in the allies' favour as it seems that royalist fire too was effective, and at least on one part of the field silenced the opposition.[37]

For much of the afternoon the two armies watched each other as they both grew in size, and the late-coming regiments were marshalled into the positions the generals had laid out for them. By early evening the fine weather had turned to rain as the last regiments joined the lines. As the final regiments of the Marquis of Newcastle's Northern Army settled into place the royalists stood down. Rupert and the marquis had decided that there would be no action that day. The allied generals had decided differently and had probably been preparing to attack for much of the day, just awaiting their latecomers. Although for days the allies had overestimated the size of Rupert's army, by now, with the royalists laid before them on the lower ground, experienced observers must have noticed the disparity in numbers. Whilst both flanks of horse outnumbered the royalists it was in the centre were the disparity was greatest: the allies had over double the number of royalist foot soldiers. At about 7.30 pm the allied army advanced down the hill and into the dip which temporarily hid them from the royalists, singing psalms as they marched. The royalists struggled to ready themselves. Some had been cooking and most had been resting, and time was short on the flanks, although for the foot there was a little more notice to get ready.

To the west the Scottish dragoons of Colonel Hugh Fraser assaulted the royalists foot that Rupert had placed ahead of the royalists horse on that flank, and pushed them from the their positions.[38] In the wake of this success, Cromwell led the three lines of horse forward, quickly forcing the royalist flank commander, Lord Byron, to take rapid action. The intention on that flank had been to let Cromwell's men advance into the broken ground where the rabbit warren made movement difficult, and then attack them at that point to try and use the temporary disorder caused by passage over this ground to offset the disparity in numbers. However, large numbers of the royalist horse were probably dismounted and may even have removed saddle and tack from their horses. Byron's own regiment, possibly because it was the front line and nearest to the enemy, was not in such a state of unreadiness, and he led it forward to protect the other regiments and give them time to saddle up and remount. This precipitous if necessary action of course meant that Byron's regiment reached the rabbit warrens first, and there his regiment was caught by Cromwell's front line and defeated, disordered by the very ground which was supposed to protect them.

Even so, this may have bought the time that the royalists needed, for the other regiments now joined the counter-attack. They engaged Cromwell's second line, as the front line may have been assailed and halted by Tuke's regiment as it tried to smash into the flank of Cromwell's attack. Seconded by Leslie, the second line, consisting of the rest of the Eastern Association regiments, now engaged the second line of royalists, including Rupert's own horse.[39] The weight of numbers told, and the confusion caused by the defeat and rout of Byron's front line hampered the royalists in their attempt to stem the tide of advancing allied regiments, who drove then backwards after stiff fighting lasting up to an hour. Cromwell had written: 'We never charged but we routed the enemy [...] God made them as stubble to our swords'; the latter part of the assertion being more appropriately a description of the phase following the initial victory.[40]

In the centre of the field the story was far more mixed. Whilst the regiments of foot nearest to Cromwell's successful flank met with similar success when in contact with the royalist front line, the same was not true all along the line and the royalists were able to make significant progress in holding back the parliamentarian and Scots' attack on the right of the parliamentarian line.[41] Furthermore, when Sir William Blakiston's brigade of horse stationed in the left rear of the royalist foot joined in the counter-attack, the allied foot were driven back in confusion.[42] At the eastern edge of the battlefield things were even worse for the allied commanders. The royalists' horse in this flank had also made good use of the land between them and the Northern Association Horse, and the three regiments of Scots ranged behind them. The allied commander on that wing, Sir Thomas Fairfax, advanced to the attack but became caught up in the road and track system which he had followed down from the hill on to the moorland. As he became entangled, the royalists under Lord Goring counter-attacked. Although Fairfax's own regiment reputedly did well and chased off the royalists regiments it faced and pursued them towards York, the commander became separated and the rest of the wing collapsed and routed towards the ridge.[43] The view from the little clump of trees from where the three allied commanders, Leven, Fairfax and Manchester, were gathered looked bleak. Only the left wing had had any success, and it had now to some extent come to a standstill after its victory. The rest of the allied army appeared to have been defeated and was fleeing the field. The three commanders concluded that the day was lost and turned their horses towards Tadcaster for the second time that day and fled.[44] It was not as bleak as they thought: Blakiston's attack was halted and not all of their horse on the right wing had fled the field.[45] Moreover, the royalists' defeated right wing had raced towards York and some of its victorious left wing had left the field in search of plunder in the wake of the routed parliamentarians. The royalist foot, despite its success on the eastern flank, remained outnumbered and there was a limit to what training, experience and initial success could do in such a situation. Once Blakiston's had reached the slopes of Bramham Hill he was halted by the third line of the parliamentarian foot and some horse, possibly led by Manchester himself, who, according to Robert Douglas, had been persuaded not to flee and instead to rally some of the routed horse.[46] A second royalist attack on the extreme eastern end of the parliamentarian foot had been launched by Sir Charles Lucas and Sir Richard Dacre, who together commanded the rear lines of Goring's wing. They, like Blakiston, had made some headway in a series of three charges, the last of which almost broke the Scottish regiments of the Earl of Lindsey and

Lord Maitland, which bore the brunt. Despite the combined assault on the Scottish regiments by royalist foot and Lucas and Dacre, the attempt to break the line failed when the allies' reserves joined the fray. Lucas's horse was killed and he was captured.[47]

Sir Thomas Fairfax could do nothing to further the cause from where he was as the majority of his wing had left the field. As Lionel Watson said:

> there was not a man left standing before them, most of the Horse and Foot of that wing, and our main battle retreating in haste towards Todcaster and Cawood thinking the day lost as the enemies right wing did towards York. The enemy in pursuit and chase of retreating men, followed them to our carriages, but had slain few of them: for indeed they ran away before the enemy had charged them.[48]

Fairfax, according to his own account, tore off his field signal – a white scarf – and seems to have circumnavigated the fighting in the centre of the field and made his way to Cromwell over to the west and rear of the royalist centre.[49] He then urged Cromwell to action, as Watson reported:

> Just then came our horse and foot from the chase of their right wing and seeing the business not well in our right came in a very good order to a second charge with all the enemies Horse and Foot that had disordered our right wing and main battle. And here came the business of the day (nay nearly the whole kingdome) to be disputed upon this second charge.[50]

Before this 'second' charge, Cromwell had, in the later stages of his first offensive, been wounded and left the field briefly to have the wound dressed. By that time, however, victory was his and Leslie was able to take over and use the Scottish light cavalry to pursue the retreating royalists towards York. Fairfax, if his story is true, arrived on Cromwell's flank during this pause as Cromwell's men redressed their ranks and the commander had his bleeding neck wound staunched. Fairfax enjoined Cromwell to attack the royalists in the rear, and it is probable that Cromwell intended to do this anyway once ready. The result was devastating, for the wavering royalist infantry left on the field and sealed the defeat of Rupert's and Newcastle's armies. Goring's forces, which returned to the field, could do little to rescue the situation and they made their way to York as darkness fell, as did the other elements of royalist horse left on the field on their blown horses. The royalist foot was not so lucky. Attacked on all sides by horse and foot, thousands were killed and many taken prisoner. The Earl of Newcastle's own regiments attempted to hold back the tide of attacking allied forces and secured themselves a strong defensive position, but were assailed from all sides and large numbers of them died on the spot.[51]

The final stages of the battle were confused, and recently historians, particularly Newman, Roberts and Wanklyn, have advanced very different end-game scenarios. Newman and Roberts have suggested that there remained significant numbers of royalist horse on both ends of the field ranged on the very ridge where the allied forces had started the battle, after the defeat of the royalist centre.[52] Wanklyn believes that any such force was concentrated in the east. In either scenario these forces or single force was in no position to rescue the day, defeated or exhausted and also leaderless, and so made their desultory way to York.[53] The war was over as far as Newcastle was concerned. He continued on from York to Scarborough and from there took a ship for the continent fearing that the court at Oxford would treat him as a laughing stock. Rupert gathered what forces he could and retired westward. Other royalists made their way to York or other smaller garrisons, and some of the Midland regiments edged their way home, avoiding the victorious parliamentarians and those who had been marching to their assistance. York surrendered a fortnight later and the royalist hold on the north fragmented. Despite there being several garrisons remaining in the northern counties, as a result of this battle the royalists lost a huge army; there were estimated to be 4,150 dead on the field, most of them royalists. Others were prisoners and yet more simply left their colours. The royalist foot was hurt most and Newcastle's infantry never again comprised an important force, although Goring was able to gather something of his horse and lead it for the next year or so as a composite body. More importantly perhaps, the royalists lost the vast resources of the northern counties and the network which exploited them, making them available to the parliamentarian Northern Association.

That this was the case was largely due to Cromwell. Whilst he was only the commander of one albeit significant flank of the allied army, he had both made victory possible by seizing Bilton Bream, and had seen the job through by crashing into Byron's regiment, forcing the royalist's flank attack off the field and driving Rupert's best horse regiments into a rout. All of this was achieved in such a way as to leave his own forces capable of rescuing the parliamentarian and Scots regiments which needed help, and assisting those which had held their own and turned the tables on the erstwhile successful royalists on other parts of the field. Cromwell had demonstrated his strengths as a general, exercising expert command and control, and using his forces piecemeal as required to ensure the defeat of several brigades of royalist horse and foot, without committing his entire force to each task. Perhaps most importantly, despite this being his first major battle, he demonstrated mastery over the geography at Marston Moor. He spotted that Bilton Bream simultaneously posed a major threat to the allied left wing and presented an opportunity for allied possession that could make the royalist right virtually untenable, forcing them on to the defensive. That one insight handed parliament and the Scots northern England.

DOLDRUMS IN THE MIDLANDS

In the wake of Marston Moor, Cromwell and Manchester were, like Leven and Fairfax, presented with a favourable situation in the North Midlands. Lord Loughborough and the Newark garrison had committed a good deal of men and materiel to the war in the north since the beginning of the year, and with good reason; their safety and security depended upon saving the north. Not only did Marston Moor expose the northern borders of the Midlands to invasions from the Scots, the Fairfaxes and Manchester, but vital regiments had been scattered and some had been the stubble to Cromwell's swords. Loughborough had seen four regiments of horse and three regiments of foot join Rupert in the summer, but detachments from these and other regiments had gone north at the beginning of the year, and of course Major General George Porter had led the Newark horse northwards with Lord Goring and the Northern Horse.[54] There had already been attacks on southern Staffordshire that had resulted in the loss of a Staffordshire garrison, and Loughborough would soon lose a crossing point on the Trent in Derbyshire. The door was apparently wide open for the Earl and his Eastern Association Army. On 1 August, Manchester summoned the Nottinghamshire garrison at Welbeck, and a day later he received its surrender.[55]

The Eastern Association moved across the border into Derbyshire and besieged another of the Marquis of Newcastle's houses at Bolsover. Ten days later the Bolsover and Staveley garrisons surrendered to Manchester.[56] The central Derbyshire garrison of Wingfield surrendered to local Derbyshire and Nottinghamshire forces on 17 August. A sustained attack on the remaining garrisons could have cleared the Midlands, but rather than turn on Loughborough's headquarters at Ashby-de-la-Zouch or Newark, Manchester led his army to Lincoln. A great opportunity had been lost.

FAILURE TO WIN

Marston Moor had handed parliament the north's vast resources, but there was work to be done there, just as there was in the Midlands. There were strong royalist garrisons to be dealt with: Skipton, Scarborough and Newcastle. Just as they seemed on the point of doing so when Rupert relieved York, the allies divided themselves into their three armies once York had been captured and established as Lord Fairfax's base. Manchester had gone south, Fairfax with the aid of Meldrum took on the garrisons in Yorkshire, and the Scots marched all the way north to try and conclude the siege of Newcastle to secure their supply lines and open the port to Scottish and parliamentarian shipping. There was no hope of bringing the victorious armies down from the north to take on the king's main army in the south. The bleak outlook facing the royalists was misted over by the astonishing success in the South Midlands and the south-west. In late June the king, having been hounded out of Oxford by the combined forces of the Earl of Essex and Sir William Waller, had heard that the two generals had split their forces and turned on one of the hunters. Whilst Essex marched off into the south-west believing that the erstwhile royalist stronghold was about to undergo a sea change in loyalties, the king attacked Waller as the two armies shadowed each other through Oxfordshire. At Cropredy Bridge the king observed Waller's army become over extended as it marched, and launched an attack which split it in two and succeeded in comprehensively destroying the parliamentarian army. With parliament's Midland forces in disarray the king then pursued Essex into the south-west. By the beginning of September the parliamentarian commander in chief was trapped beside the River Fowey and its estuary. Despite managing to get the cavalry past the royalists in the night and personally escaping by boat, Essex lost all of the veteran foot regiments and the artillery to the king at the Battle of Lostwithiel. If it had not been for the tradition of releasing common soldiers, Essex's defeat would have been catastrophic. As it was the foot were released on a bond not to take up arms until they reached Portsmouth. There they would be able to join the horse regiments and the defeated earl.

Parliament was faced with rebuilding Waller's army and rearming Essex's. Nevertheless, it was determined to continue an offensive war in the south which would see a steady encroachment on the king's headquarters at Oxford. To do this they need the support of the Easter Association army which had been summoned from comparative inactivity in late August. They were facing the king, who was concerned to ensure the safety of his capital by reinforcing three beleaguered garrisons: Basing House, Donnington Castle and Banbury. There had been talk of an ambitious plan to march into and conquer the Eastern Association territory before winter set in, but essentially this had been abandoned in favour of resupplying the three garrisons using the materiel captured at Lostwithiel. Parliament, whilst carrying out its work on Waller's and Essex's armies, had placed a cavalry screen between Oxford and London, using Cromwell's and Essex's horse. Royalist attempts to defeat the three parliamentarian forces before they could conjoin failed because of poor timing, and the three commanders assembled their large army at Basingstoke. The three generals disliked and distrusted each other and Waller and Manchester bridled under the official seniority of Essex. To solve the problem of command, parliament created a council of war consisting of the three generals and two civilians chosen by the Committee of Both Kingdoms. Decisions of the committee were then issued under Essex's name. Almost immediately upon the assembly of the three armies, Essex took to his bed with an illness.

THE SECOND BATTLE OF NEWBURY

The king's army, which was combination of his own Oxford Field Army and Prince Maurice's army from the west, relieved Donnington Castle and assembled in and around Newbury, determined to relieve Basing House. The horse regiments were sent to raise the siege of Banbury, as Wanklyn suggests, underlining the royalists' confidence that they were safe from attack.[57] However, the parliamentarian generals had decided otherwise and moved on Newbury, cutting the king off from Basing House and forcing him back across the River Kennett to a position south of Donnington Castle. This was a very strong position and the parliamentarians were going to have to come up with a very imaginative plan to defeat the king, even though his army of 9,000 was much smaller than their own. The strength of the king's position related to the placement within the elongated V formed by the rivers Kennet on the southern line of his position and the Lambourne, which formed a line running from the east to the point south-east where it joined the Kennet. The northern approaches were guarded by the castle itself to the north, and to the east by Shaw House and the west by fortifications around the village of Speen. To deal with this strong position the parliamentarians decided to send a force around to the rear of the royalist forces and attack them from the east and west simultaneously. The forces chosen for the expedition were led by Sir William Waller and comprised Essex's infantry, the London Trained Bands, the Eastern Association Horse and a good proportion of the rest of the parliamentarian horse led, as reckoned by some, by a combination of the two most imaginative parliamentarian generals present: Waller and Cromwell. The parliamentarians drew up in the Lambourne valley on 26 October and began probing royalist defences. It was the realisation of the strength of the king's position as a result of these explorations which determined their course of action. Waller was to lead the detachment north to cross the Lambourne at Boxford and then moved southwards towards Church Speen. The royalists were not taken by surprise by this dramatic strategy: Waller had moved northwards in full view making it seem as if he was intending to block any potential for a royalist retreat towards Oxford via Wallingford. However, Waller's change of direction was noticed possibly because the royalist had suspected an attack from the west from the outset.

The plan was for Waller first to open fire with the bulk of the parliamentarian artillery on the royalist western face, and thereby give Manchester the signal to make a diversionary attack on the royalist forces in Shaw House, as Waller then launched his attack from the west. During the night Prince Maurice, posted on the royalists' west flank, had built a series of fortifications to make the approach as difficult as possible; it was already constricted by an enclosed field which would make Cromwell's work harder. On 27 October, Manchester's forces made an attack on the royalists at Shaw House and Shaw village, using a pontoon footbridge to cross the Lambourne, It was a short-lived attack, for royalist reserves drove Manchester's men back across the river. On the opposite flank Waller's men approached the royalists' barricades facing little resistance. As they got nearer Waller's forces had adopted the traditional open field line of foot regiments in the centre and horse regiments on the flanks, but because the battle itself received little press coverage, there is scant detail beyond this broad description, other than knowing that in the centre Essex's regiment of foot was in the position of honour on the right with two regiments of the London Trained Bands, Colonel Barclay's brigade to the left and Colonel Aldridge's brigade in reserve. Sir William Balfour, the senior cavalry commander, led the right flank and again had the Earl of Essex's regiment alongside one of the Earl of Manchester's regiments; the remainder of the Eastern Association were under Cromwell on the left wing. Wanklyn suggests that the open fields were small and that Waller's regiments must have had a short frontage and great depth.[58] When it came sometime after 3.30 pm following the artillery barrage, the initial attack cleared the royalist forward barricade and drove back Cornish regiments and the Earl of Cleveland's cavalry after heavy fighting, as the right wing of Waller's army made progress between Speen village and the river Kennet to the south. The royalists were pushed back towards the hedges which separated Speenhamland from fields east of Speen. Waller did not press on further before George, Lord Goring exacted his revenge for Marston Moor and led

Cleveland's cavalry in a devastating attack on Cromwell's horse, catching them as they crossed a ditch. Cromwell then attempted a counter-charge, but he was pushed back and thereafter appears to have become inactive for the rest of the battle. Whilst the right wing of Waller's force was initially more successful, it too was brought to a halt before the royalists' centre was put under serious pressure. In the meantime there had been little action on the Earl of Manchester's side of the field. Only once the fighting had come to an end in the west did Manchester launch another attack on Shaw House, from where they were again repulsed. The battle faded out completely in the early evening. The following night saw the king's army pull away towards Oxford, leaving its artillery and supply wagons in Donnington Castle. Even if the battle had not quite seen the parliamentarian army defeated, their ambitious plan had failed to deliver and the poor performance of the left wing of Waller's force had seriously impeded the attack on Prince Maurice.

Cromwell's role in the battle was, compared with the triumph at Marston Moor, lamentable. If he was actively involved in the advance of his wing towards Speenhamland then he had made the mistake of being caught crossing a ditch when he was attacked, leading to defeat and inactivity. Whilst Cromwell's performance as a general in the two battles could not be more different, there was one thing which united his performances in 1644: his actions and inaction were not just discussed in military circles, they became hot political topics.

6

THE POLITICS OF WAR, 1644−7

By the end of 1644, parliament had seemingly thrown away their major victory in the north by losing an entire army in Cornwall and failing to defeat the king when they seemed to have him cornered at Newbury. The collapse in fortunes led to acrimonious debates, which thrust Cromwell into centre stage and almost cost him his military career when the New Model Army was created and the Self-Denying Ordinance forbade sitting members of parliament from holding command in the armed forces.

CROMWELL AND GOD

The Battle of Marston Moor, and to a less positive extent the Battle of Newbury, had made a national figure of Cromwell. His minor success at Belton and his role at Gainsborough had attracted press attention, but the spectacular success at Marston Moor gave him a truly national profile. By the end of the year, not only had he acquired a number of supporters, he had also inspired distrust and had accumulated a number of powerful enemies. Cromwell had dealt with Marston Moor in the now famous letter to Valentine Walton senior, which for the most part had concerned the death of Captain Walton following the smashing of his leg in the attack on Bilton Bream before the battle.[1] However, there was one sentence which betrayed the political nature of wartime reportage. Cromwell, after an opening sentence which presaged the bad news which the letter contained ('we may praise the Lord together in chastisements and trials'), had opened by praising God's role in the great victory at Marston Moor: 'England and the Church of God hath had a great favour from the Lord, in this great victory given unto us, such as the like never was since this war began'. He focussed on his role chiefly: 'we never charged but we routed the enemy. The left wing which I commanded, being our own horse, saving a few Scots in our rear, beat all the Prince's horse.' There had of course been three regiments of Scottish horse in the third line, commanded by Lieutenant General David Leslie: a few Scots was not an adequate way of describing them or their role in the defeat of the royalist right. But the next sentence demonstrated a degree of general callousness when Cromwell dehumanised his enemies: 'God made them as stubble to our swords'. The press on the other hand made it clear that Cromwell 'was a great agent in this victory'; Lionel Watson too was convinced of this 'fact'.[2] Religion was bound intimately into the accounts of the battle, and Cromwell's reference to a few Scots may be seen as something of a slight aimed at Presbyterians were it not for his broader references: he attributed the victory to God above all, but saw it as a blessing upon what he referred to as the 'Godly Party', usually an exclusive term by which 'puritans' referred to themselves. So if Cromwell was using the term in such a way, he was suggesting the battle had been won by a few men whom God had chosen and not the 'few Scots in our rear' or the Scottish foot which had held the line on the right of the field, or even the majority of the Fairfax's Northern Army, and perhaps not even parts of Manchester's army, those who were associated with the Presbyterian Major General Lawrence Crawford. Yet in doing so God had granted victory to the many – the largest army to take the field during the civil war. By the time Cromwell wrote he had had three days to think over the battle and talk to others, and would have had time to understand the course of the whole battle and the roles played in the allied victory by a diverse range of Protestants: Scots Presbyterians like Leslie, English Presbyterians like Crawford and Independents or Congregationalists like John Lilburne.

It may be that Cromwell, at this point in time, saw all the parliamentarians and Scots at Marston Moor as comprising the 'Godly Party': the officers at least had one thing in common: all had sworn to defend the Protestant faith and they were signatories to the Solemn League and Covenant, fighting for a parliament and the Scottish nation currently engaged in the greatest discussions of the future of the church in England since the seventh century. Cromwell was not alone: the inclusive nature of the allies had been noted by many commentators, Captain W.F., the author of *A elation*, for one. Thomas Stockdale, whose letter to John Rushworth was read in parliament, showed how the three armies coordinated their dispositions according to the instructions of 'General Lesley' – Lord Leven. The author of *The Glorious and Miraculous Battell at York* had likewise referred to the variety of forces involved, which it 'hath pleased God to bestow on us far above our deserts': God was rewarding a multifarious army. To argue differently, Cromwell's God would have rejected many people, including Sir Thomas Fairfax, with whom Oliver had worked closely. This was an important issue. In the years preceding the war in England and Wales, the establishment of the Church of England had been under attack. The Archbishop of Canterbury, William Laud, had been arrested and held in the Tower, and by the end of 1644 his trial was imminent, the Court of High Commission had been abolished and the high-level management of the church had been frozen. Individual ministers in areas where parliament had control were subject to investigation. Since September 1643 and the alliance with Scotland, England, Wales and (because it was an adjunct of the English crown) Ireland had promised to at least consider adopting a Presbyterian system like the Kirk. Discussions over the future of the church were ongoing in Westminster, where an invited group of divines were meeting. There had been some unity of purpose over what in the Church of England the king's opponents did not like, but far less common resolve even before the war over what should replace it, as the failure of the root and branch bill which Cromwell had been involved with showed – now there was possibly even less. Presbyterianism, which enjoyed strong support in the House of Commons, if not the House of Lords, was not universally popular and in the absence of a strong church authority many congregations or groups of individuals had 'gone it alone', wanting far less central direction and management than a renewed, if Presbyterian, Church of England would allow. These groups were referred to as sectaries by their bitter opponents, but also were referred to as Independents or Congregationalists. Cromwell was numbered amongst these people, but Manchester, Essex and others were in the Presbyterian camp.

The failure at Newbury caused a rancorous argument which spilled out of military circles into the religious and political arena. Cromwell came under scrutiny, especially as he had had a poor campaign in the south, and it could be claimed that he had failed to obey Manchester's order to attack the king upon his return to Donnington, in order to reclaim the artillery he had left there after the battle in the face of an apparently impotent enemy. Moreover, Cromwell's character was called to account. Naturally, as commander in the field during Essex's absence, Manchester was the focus of criticism after the Newbury campaign, and perhaps to deflect this he sought to put the blame on others. The relationship between the earl and his lieutenant general had declined rapidly and Major General Crawford had played a part in this. It has been argued that the quarrel dated back to the affair of Lieutenant Packer and

Cromwell's defence of him back in March that year, when he found the lieutenant under arrest on the orders of Crawford (who was also his colonel), accused of being an Anabaptist. Anabaptists were seen as radicals for their rejection of infant baptism and their argument that entry to the fellowship of the church could only be voluntary, by someone capable of understanding such a commitment. Although they were amongst the newly burgeoning groups, there had been Anabaptists in the country since 1570. Parker was contravening the Orders of Parliament relating to the Solemn League and Covenant which he was obliged to sign. Crawford reported him to Manchester, who could have been expected to sympathise with Crawford. Instead, Manchester was busy reforming Cambridge University and left the matter to Cromwell. Cromwell contacted Lawrence and questioned the wisdom of removing Parker from his command, and affirmed Parker's commitment to his regiment and his desire to join it in the field, effectively discounting the question of Parker's religiosity: 'Ay but the man "is an Anabaptist" Are you sure of that? Admit he be, shall that render him incapable to serve the Public? "He is indiscreet" It may be so, in some things, we all have human infirmities.'[3]

Parker may not have been an Anabaptist and Crawford may have used a convenient detrimental label, whilst Cromwell seemed to question Crawford's assertion whilst not himself enquiring too deeply into Parker's affiliations. Parker's opposition to the Solemn League and Covenant may have been the source of the accusation, and his opposition was known to others – it was this that may have forced Crawford's hand. Cromwell had no doubts about Parker's military commitment and his argument seems to have won Crawford over at this point. Moreover, the opening of the campaigning season meant that a committed and experienced lieutenant was needed in the field, especially after the fall of Lincoln in March.[4] From at least this point onwards, Cromwell's enemies had turned their attention to him and gathered information about alleged financial peculation and religious misconduct. Now, in the wake of Newbury, parliament demanded an explanation, and MPs Cromwell and Sir William Waller returned to present their testimony. On 25 November, Cromwell went further and launched a scathing attack on Manchester's actions both at Newbury and earlier. Manchester had, Cromwell argued, 'some principal unwillingness [...] to have this war prosecuted to a full victory, and a design or desire to have it ended by accommodation (and that) on some terms to which it might be disadvantageous to bring the king so low'.[5]

Cromwell had launched a three-pronged attack on the earl, questioning Manchester as his commander, Manchester as an aristocrat and Manchester as a member of the House of Lords.[6] Cromwell's attack also went beyond Manchester and also questioned the behaviour of the Earl of Essex. Diarist and MP Bulstrode Whitelocke, one of Essex's supporters, thought the earl was the main target, writing that Cromwell 'seemed (but cautiously enough) to lay more blame on the officers of the lord-general's army than upon any other'.[7] The potential scandal was so great that a committee, under the Presbyterian MP Zouch Tate, was established to examine the accusations and counter-accusations.

Manchester went on the offensive, and a large number of members of the House of Lords were angry that the two earls had been attacked in the Commons, but it was Cromwell's commander who led the attack in early December. Manchester focussed Cromwell's performance during the New-bury campaign, both in failing to prosecute the attack on Maurice on the battlefield and his inability to intercept the king's return to Donnington when he retrieved his artillery from the castle.[8] But the attack went further: evidence of Cromwell's activities had been collated throughout much of the past few months, ranging from the misuse of a financial allowance supposedly paid to his wife Elizabeth to allegations that he had embezzled funds collected for the defence of Ely. There was yet more: Manchester accused the lieutenant general of being a social revolutionary who wanted to abolish the aristocracy and reject Presbyterianism. Much of the evidence for this had come from the same source, for Manchester had an informant who had provided information, which also included an assertion that after the capture of Crowland, Cromwell had been told that several members of the nobility were amongst the casualties and he had responded: 'God fought ag[ains]t them [lords] for god would have noe lording over his people & he verily believed that god would sweep away that lord in power out of this nation.'[9]

When some of Cromwell's officers had tried to get Manchester's informant to support a petition asking for freedom of worship he had identified himself as a Presbyterian, saying that 'if any nation in the world were in the ready way to heaven it was the Scots'. Cromwell's officers allegedly replied: 'but now they perceive what I was & went away ever after Coll Cromwell did sleight me'. Cromwell was also accused of celebrating the defeat of Essex at Lostwithiel 'with joy as if they had won a victory'.[10] Meanwhile Essex too had turned on Cromwell, and sought potential allies for the attack. Whitelocke was summoned to Essex's home on 3 December 1644 for a meeting with the lord general and the Earl of Loudon, Lord Chancellor of Scotland and five

Presbyterian MPs, including Denzil Holles, who had planned to get rid of Cromwell because 'since the advance of our army into England he hath used all underhand and cunning means to take off from our honour and merit of this kingdom; an evil requital of all our hazards and services'.[11]

They added, somewhat unnecessarily given the public nature of Cromwell's attack, that 'he is no well-willer to his excellency'. The meeting was to seek Whitelocke's and Sir John Maynard's advice as to whether Cromwell could be accused of being an incendiary having the intention of 'kindling of a fire of contention betwixt the two nations'. Whitelocke argued that it was a dangerous strategy because if the lords failed to make it stick, having made what could turn out to be a false accusation, it would reflect upon their honour. Cromwell, Whitelocke said, had a lot of supporters in the army and called upon 'some honourable persons here present, his excellency's officers [...] to inform your lordships'.[12] As for parliament, Whitelocke told the meeting:

> I take lieutenant general Cromwell to be a gentleman of quick and subtle parts, and one who hath (especially of late) gained no small interest in the house of commons, nor is he wanting of friends in the house of peers, nor of abilities in himself to manage his own part or defence to the best advantage.

To which Maynard added:

> Lieutenant General Cromwell is a person of great favour and interest with the house of commons, and with some of the house of peers likewise, and therefore there must be proofs, and the more clear and evident against him, to prevail with the parliament to adjudge him to be an incendiary.[13]

Even Manchester's informant could not provide any proof other than Oliver's antipathy to Presbyterianism. Holles and Sir Philip Stapleton countered that Cromwell was not so popular in the Commons as Maynard and Whitelocke believed, because the power of the familial base which had got him into parliament and into the army in the first place was on the wane. Hampden was dead, and although Oliver St John was now able to hold the balance of power between the War Party and the Peace Party, he remained personally overshadowed by Presbyterian Denzil Holles, by now an inveterate opponent of Cromwell. It was Holles who attacked Cromwell in the Commons on 4 December, countering the charges against Manchester.[14] Whitelocke's comment about Essex's own army was important, and he suspected that some of the men in Essex's house that night supported Cromwell and would no doubt inform the lieutenant general of the meeting.

Cromwell's testimony to Tate's committee stretched back to the days after the siege of York. He claimed that the Earl of Manchester was 'most in fault for most of those miscarriages and ill consequences of them' during the campaign.[15] More specifically, he claimed that the earl had scorned 'both in words and actions' instructions from parliament and the Committee of Both Kingdoms: he had failed to attack Newark, instead staying around Doncaster and then Lincoln instead of tackling the garrison or its satellites.[16] No doubt for Cromwell, who had spent a good proportion of 1643 in ultimately futile attempts to curtail the activities of the Newark and North Midland garrisons, this was a frustrating failure on his commander's part. Cromwell also returned to the Donnington debacle, having castigated the earl for his dilatory march southwards: 'At St Albans he caused the army to lie still for 8 or 9 days, and then marched slowly to Reading' and then contrary to orders failed to rendezvous with Sir William Waller.[17] Manchester was held responsible for the defeat at Newbury because he had delayed the attack on Shaw House until it was dark, and thus failed either to capture it or relieve pressure on Waller's side of the field. To compound this the earl had let the king's army slip away from under his army's nose.[18] Other evidence included versions of a meeting during the Newbury campaign at which Manchester expressed his frustration with waging a war against a lawful king: 'if we beat the King 99 times he would be King still, and his posterity, and we subjects still; but if he beats us but once we should be hanged, and our posterity undone'.[19] Cromwell was reportedly exasperated and responded: 'My lord, if this be so, why did we take up arms at first? This is against fighting ever hereafter.'[20] There were minor differences in several versions of this conversation, from Waller and Crawford amongst others, but all emphasised the divisions which in parliament formed the basis of arguments between the War Party and the Peace Party over the way the war was to be pursued to a conclusion: the former desired an all-out military victory, the latter preferred a negotiated peace. Cromwell wanted all-out victory. The weight of the other evidence coming from army officers bore our Cromwell's charges: Manchester seemed unwilling to prosecute an all-out victory, and even Major General Lawrence Crawford's evidence, whilst attacking Cromwell, tended to support the main thrust of his case.

THE SELF-DENYING ORDINANCE AND CROMWELL'S CAREER

After receiving such corroboration, it appeared that Cromwell had managed to turn the tables on Manchester. He then stopped his attack on the earls and announced that the quarrels of individuals was less important that the cause for which they were fighting: 'no less than to save a Nation out of a bleeding, nay almost dying, condition, which the long continuance of this War hath already brought it', adding, 'I am far from reflecting on any [...] if the Army be not put into another method, and the War more vigorously prosecuted, the People can bear the War no longer, and will enforce you to a dishonourable Peace'.[21] This followed a report from Tate's committee which had laid the blame on pride and covetousness. Cromwell now proposed that 'Members of either House will scruple to deny themselves, and their own private interests for the public good'.[22] This statement was then honed by Zouch Tate into the Self-Denying Ordinance, whereby members of either the Commons or Lords were to be prohibited from holding military office. It was not universally accepted, although many saw it as a way out of the damaging introspection parliament had been forced into. Manchester for instance did not wish to call off his attack and the committee investigations continued until the end of the month, whilst the House of Lords rejected the Self-Denying Ordinance on 13 January 1645. A week later the house pressed the Committee of Both Kingdoms into continuing the investigation into Cromwell's behaviour. Cromwell had created enemies amongst the Scots, and Manchester's collection of evidence seemed to show antipathy towards Presbyterianism, but Cromwell was probably not seeking a settlement which only encompassed small associations of congregated churches and precluded others: his use of the word 'Godly' after Marston Moor can still be read as embracing Independents like Parker and Scots Presbyterians like Leslie and Crawford, as well as English Presbyterians like Fairfax. In the same way we need to accept that Cromwell meant what he said about self-denial in December 1644, for he could not read the future and the logical outcome of such self-denial would have excluded him from command as well. However, it also needs to be remembered that, at that point, whereas a member of the Commons could resign his seat, a member of the Lords could not, although this changed when the Commons proposed to the Lords in 1645 the possibility of reappointment to command. It was this change which was to save Cromwell's military career. However, it did not save those of Manchester or Essex.[23]

The quarrel was greater than just the careers of Cromwell, Essex and Manchester – at one point it threatened to divide parliament. When Cromwell's evidence was heard in the Commons and Manchester's in the Lords, it effectively created two camps. Nevertheless, having the impending negotiations with the king, later known as the Treaty of Uxbridge, on the horizon was enough to present a united face. Moreover, the need to reorganise the army was recognised across the divide and presented a challenge for both houses. The common effect was to ensure that the controversy fizzled out. A bill creating a new army was passed by the Commons on 21 January, accompanied by the new Self-Denying Ordinance draft which kept silent on the issue of reappointment to military command.

THE NEW MODEL ARMY

The bill which created the new army became an Ordinance on 11 February. It established a centralised army or, as Ian Gentles has it, a 'southern army', to be free of local and even regional constraints which had hampered the use of even the Eastern Association Army in theatres of war outside East Anglia and its 'marches'.[24] It did not get rid of some the other armies still in existence; the Western Army, the Northern Association Army and the forces under Sir William Brereton and in the Midlands under Sir Richard Browne, but it did dissolve Essex's army, Waller's army and the Eastern Association Army, draining them of officers, men and income.[25] The regiments from these latter three armies were either incorporated wholesale under their existing colonels, or forged into new, more uniformly structured regiments. In what was perhaps the South-Eastern Army, if not really a Southern Army, were to be 12 regiments of foot, still of ten companies and 1,200 strong, 11 regiments of horse, still of six troops but now with each supposed to comprise 100 troopers rather than 60 or 80, and most unusually of all just one single regiment of dragoons of ten companies, to replace all of the smaller units which had sometimes been attached to small regiments of horse piecemeal.[26] There was likewise to be just the one train of artillery. Lieutenant General and Colonel Oliver Cromwell was of course, because of the Self-Denying Ordinance and due to his seat in the Commons as MP for Cambridge, not in the original line-up of officers named by Sir Thomas Fairfax in the new army. Therefore his old double-sized regiment was divided up into two normal-sized regiments and placed under new colonels: six troops of the old regiment were passed to the commander in chief Fairfax, with John Desborough as the major. It included several of the longest serving members of the regiment, amongst them James Berry who was now a captain in his own right, as well as the troops formally commanded by the dead captains, Oliver Cromwell junior and Valentine Walton. The other six troops now constituted Edward Whalley's regiment. Whalley, a cousin of Cromwell, had been a captain in the original regiment, as had others including William Evanson.[27] The Eastern Association Horse provided several complete troops for the new regiments in the army, but others were drawn too from Waller's army and Essex's.[28] The foot regiments were a different matter: some were based wholly upon companies from one or other of the old armies, if not from a single old regiment. Others, like Thomas Rainborough's, comprised units from several different regiments, in his case three different regiments from the Eastern Association.[29] The dragoons, under Colonel Thomas Okey, comprised men from all dragoon regiments and companies, as well as some cavalry captains, from all three old armies.[30]

The new army was soon named the New Model Army, and assembled in the south Midlands under its new commander, Sir Thomas Fairfax, and its major general, Phillip Skippon. The command of the horse was as yet undecided, but the army was at first directed from London. Cromwell and Waller were closely involved in the selection of officers and the design of the new force, especially during December 1644 and the ensuing January. The Committee of Both Kingdoms, with Manchester and Essex sitting on it, was deciding the army's priorities. The continuing work on assembling the army left much of the initiative to the royalists. By May the king determined on a course of action which would lead him into conflict with the New Model Army.

CROMWELL'S DETACHMENT

On 4 March 1645, Cromwell and Waller were sent into the west to deal with a royalist resurgence with Goring at its head. During this campaign, Cromwell impressed his commander in a way which he had not done at Newbury, where his support for Waller's attack had been lacklustre: 'As an officer he was obedient, and never did dispute my orders, nor argue upon them. He did indeed seem to have great cunning'[31] – a judgement very different to Manchester's accusations the previous year. The campaign comprised a number of minor successes against isolated royalist forces, before moving on Bath and Bristol via Salisbury. However, they achieved little during March, and in any case Waller's commission was coming to an end. He had been allowed 40 days' grace only, and under the terms of the Self-Denying Ordinance he was summoned to hand his commission to Sir Thomas Fairfax on 17 April. Cromwell should have also stepped down from army command at this point. However, before he could do so he was ordered to take his regiments into the marcher counties to block communications between Oxford and Wales. After a small fight at Islip against the young Earl of Northampton, he captured

Bletchingdon House which the young and inexperienced governor surrendered to him precipitously, for which he was court martialled and shot at Oxford.[32] Cromwell's brief campaign prevented the king from marching westwards and thus forced the royalists into a reconsideration of their strategy. To conclude his expedition Cromwell harried the royalist quarters around Oxford. However, in these latter days Cromwell was unsuccessful: his attack on Farringdon was repulsed with loss and Goring beat up his quarters outside the garrison during the night of 2 May. He did the same again at Burford less than a week later. By this point the king was marching northwards towards Chester with the Oxford Field Army and Prince Rupert's forces which had united at Stow-on-the-Wold. At first Cromwell was sent after the king, but was then redirected to the Isle of Ely as it was feared that the king was heading for East Anglia as he had planned the previous year. In the wake of the king's and Cromwell's departures, Fairfax and the New Model Army moved into position and besieged Oxford. The siege of Chester was called off by Brereton once he realised that the king was heading in his direction. Charles then debated attacking Sir John Gell in Derby and made his way to Lord Loughborough's headquarters at Ashby-de-la-Zouch. Instead of Derby, the king determined on Leicester and moved from Ashby to besiege the county town. The original move to Ashby had been mistaken in London for the start of an easterly route via Newark towards the Eastern Association counties, which had, since the disbandment of its army, been made far more vulnerable than at any time since 1643. Cromwell was sent to Ely – he was still the governor – and he had received a second temporary extension to his commission, again for 40 days, much against the wishes of his former commanders; it would expire on 22 June.[33] At Ely all local forces were gathered in and money and gunpowder sent to him. Whilst this was all going on the king attacked and stormed Leicester, entering the town by force in the early hours of May 31. It was a bloody storm and over relatively quickly, given that alongside the small garrison, townsmen and women had fought off the attackers side by side. It was to be a profound shock to parliament's system and it furthered the vulnerability of East Anglia. However, the king failed to capitalise on his success: instead of continuing his offensive he turned southwards, determined to drive Fairfax from Oxford.

Cromwell bemoaned his situation in a letter to Fairfax, but optimistically believed that Colonel Vermuyden and a section of the New Model Horse would join with Gell and slow the king's progress; he did not know about Leicester when he wrote of Ely: 'it is yet but weak, without works, ammunition or men considerable, and of money least'. After hearing of Leicester, he elaborated in a letter to the Suffolk deputy lieutenants on 6 June: 'the cloud of the enemy's army hanging still upon the aim at the Association. In regard whereof, we are having information that the army about Oxford was not yesterday advanced albeit it was ordered to do so.'[34]

He was not long disappointed, as he was wrong. The Committee of Both Kingdoms gave Fairfax the freedom to decide his own strategy: he would no longer be directed centrally, and he broke up the siege on 5 June, the day Cromwell had expected. The king had by this time begun his southward drift and as Cromwell wrote, was at Market Harborough about to enter Northamptonshire rather than Rutland or the eastern counties. On 7 June the king had reached Daventry; the following day Fairfax set out to meet him there. The king's strategy was somewhat confused; he had no clear design, and his options included heading northwards through Yorkshire and the north to join the Marquis of Montrose who had all but conquered Scotland in the past few months in the absence of Leven and the army, or head to the fertile resources of East Anglia. Instead of either the king had been swayed by the pleas of the courtiers left in Oxford who perceived themselves as being in a perilous situation and by the courtiers in the army who had received similar messages from their wives. In truth Fairfax posed no real threat, he had insufficient numbers and no heavy artillery; moreover Oxford's governor Sir William Legge had thoroughly prepared the town for a long siege. The same day that Fairfax moved away from the city his council of war wrote:

> The general esteem and affection which he hath both with the officers and soldiers of the whole army, his own personal worth and ability for the employment, his great care, diligence and courage, and faithfulness in the service you have already employed him in, with the constant presence and blessing of God that has accompanied him make us look upon it as a duty we owe you and the public to make our suit.[35]

It was Cromwell they wrote of, with the aim of persuading parliament to appoint him to the still-vacant lieutenant generalship.[36] The House of Commons agreed and Fairfax, without waiting for the Lords to concur, summoned Cromwell to take up the post of lieutenant general of horse and second in command. Ireton, the deputy governor of Ely, was soon to be appointed the fourth member of the leadership team as commissary general. Cromwell set out for Northamptonshire. The king got no further than Daventry before realising that the New Model Army was moving towards him, and that the reserves he had called in were not likely to get to him in time – Goring had been sent back to the south-west, and part of the Newark Horse had also been sent back home. The elements of the Northern Horse that remained with the king, having been promised a march into Yorkshire, were becoming discontented and threatened to leave the king's army. The army lingered in Daventry for five days and sent provisions to Oxford. Fairfax was not content to have an army without a commander for the horse; a lieutenant general was usually the second in command and he had supported his council of war's request to have Cromwell on, at least, temporary commissions. With the appointment in the bag, Cromwell was summoned: with 600 horse and dragoons he arrived at Kislingbury in Northamptonshire at 6.00 am on 13 June as a council of war began to meet in the early morning summertime light. This ensured that he was present on the morning of 14 June when the New Model Army watched the king's army moving towards it from the direction of Market Harborough. In the hours before he arrived, Fairfax and Lionel Watson had actually watched as the royalist army had upped-sticks and headed in the reverse direction, back towards Market Harborough via Kilsby and Husbands Bosworth.

THE BATTLE OF NASEBY

The Battle of Naseby has, like Marston Moor, received attention from a number of historians over the years. The former Northamptonshire county archaeologist Glenn Foard produced an important study, based, like Peter Newman and Peter Roberts's study of Marston Moor, not only on close documentary study but upon an archaeological study of the site, inspired in part by the building of the A1–M1 motorway link in the 1990s. This roadwork inspired a great deal more than the book, for it also prompted the creation of the Battlefield Trust which is intended to give an organised voice to consultations on future building projects which impinge on British battlefield sites. Foard is not alone: Martin Marix Evans has contributed a study for Osprey with some controversial suggestions about the aftermath of the fighting, and Malcolm Wanklyn has also contributed to the debate with his recent studies of generalship.[37] The battlefield has been looked at more closely in recent years, but Austin Woolrych made headway in the 1960s when he was alerted to an estate map that had been drawn just 15 years before the battle, which captured most of the ground over which the battle had been fought.[38] Whilst Woolrych made only generalised comments about the nature of the ground, his reference to the map has made subsequent work possible. But this map was not the only seventeenth-century illustration of the battlefield, for Joshua Sprigge's *Anglia Rediviva: England's Recovery*, published in 1647, contained a pull-out map by Robert Streeter which displays the layout of both armies in a bird's-eye style. The precise meaning of each of these near contemporary maps and their relationship to each other has been the subject of discussions over the last 50 years. Use of the 1630 map enabled the present author some 30 years ago to make adjustments to the traditional positioning of Colonel Okey's dragoons with regard to Sulby Hedges, which seems to have been accepted by others.[39]

Cromwell made a major contribution to the planning at Naseby, and it is probable that it underlines why he was instrumental in the victory at Marston Moor but not at Newbury, for he was involved in the selection of the ground on which to fight at both the first two; this was not the case with Newbury. On the morning of 14 June the two armies were aware of each other's presence and, despite advice to the contrary, the king had decided to offer battle. Whilst neither side was fully cognisant of each other's strength – the parliamentarians were convinced that the royalists had higher numbers – some of the royalists certainly knew that they would better off if they could reunite their forces. Goring had been ordered to leave the south-west even before the storming of Leicester, Sir Charles Gerard's forces were expected to march from South Wales, and sections of the Newark horse, which had returned home on 4 June, could be brought in again. Rupert had tried to persuade the king not to move on Oxford, and now he and Lord Astley argued for a continued move north in contrast to the civilian courtiers, led by Lord Digby, who were determined to attack the New Model Army for which they had little but contempt, and about which they and the king believed ridiculous rumours, despite now having a far more realistic understanding of the size of Fairfax's army.[40] There were some genuine reasons for not continuing the retreat: Fairfax had shown a capacity for outmanoeuvring the king's army in the past few days, and the royalist baggage train was massive and would be difficult to get away during a pursuit. There was also an issue of morale to consider – the royalists knew that Fairfax had failed to make any impression on Oxford and therefore why should they retreat? To do so would have an adverse effect on the soldiers' morale and confidence in their leaders. At the council of war in the early hours of 14 June at Market Harborough, based at least partially on such arguments, the decision to turn and face Fairfax was taken: the king followed the advice of his courtiers over that of his soldiers. The royalist army was roused from its encampments in and around

Market Harborough and set on a course towards the villages of north Northamptonshire.

Cromwell, now reunited with Fairfax, watched from their vantage point on the Naseby to Clipston road as the royalists began to leave the town, and saw it begin to draw together on the road south of East Farndon between there and Clipston, west of Great Oxendon. Fairfax and Cromwell had ranged their forces on a ridge north of Naseby on the same road but between Naseby and Clipston, a couple of miles south of the royalist forces. It was a well-chosen site if an army was attempting to avoid being attacked, for the slope of the ridge upon which Fairfax had begun drawing his army into battle formation was quite steep and covered in the front by clumps of furze. The valley between it and Clipston was clay soil, well-watered by numerous small streams which would after the recent rain have made the ground boggy and difficult to pass. According to some commentators it was Cromwell who realised that the position was too strong. W.G., in a tract whose purpose was to portray the New Model Army as a manifestation of God's will, wrote:

> I must never forget the behaviour of that servant of the Lord Lieutenant General Cromwel, who as if he had received direction from God himselfe, where to pitch the battell; did advise that the battalia might stand on such a ground, although it was being drawn up on another place, saying *Let us, I beseach you draw back to yonder hill, which will encourage the enemy to charge us, which they cannot do in that place, without their absolute ruine.* This he spake with so much cheerful resolution and confidence, as though he had foreseen the victory, and therefore he was condiscended too, and with an houre and halfe after the effect fell out accordingly.[41]

Of course, this was written some time after the event, and moreover after several accounts of the battle had already been published, and we must remember that other accounts had circumscribed Cromwell's influence:

> The General, [Fairfax] together with the Major-General [Skippon], put the severall Brigades of Foot into order: having committed the Ordering of the Horse to Lieutenant General Cromwel, who did obtain them from the general, That seeing the Horse were more neere 6000 and were to bee fought in two wings; His Excellency would please to make col. Ireton Commissary gen. of horse and appoint him to command the Left Wing that day, the command of the Right wing being as much as the Lieutenant General could apply himself too.[42]

The decision to move to the new position was credited to Fairfax alone. Whatever the case, the New Model Army did shift south and westwards to a position more squarely north of the village of Naseby, along a ridge line which led to Mill Hill. From there it moved forward to a plateau called Closter on the edge of Broadmoor. Rupert had roughly shadowed this move with some of the royalist horse, and then selected Dust Hill across the Broadmoor from the parliamentarians as the ground on which to draw up the royalist army into battle formation. As Rupert moved, Fairfax drew back from the front of the Closter plateau to move his army out of sight. It is possible that Rupert mistook either Fairfax's slight southward move to Mill Hill or the subsequent withdrawal from the ridge line as a retreat. Equally possible is that Rupert, despite having opposed the strategy decided upon at Market Harborough, wished to seize the initiative by launching an attack as quickly as possible. By withdrawing the army about 100 paces Fairfax denied the royalists an opportunity to form up in response to the way he, Skippon and Cromwell had drawn up their army.[43] It also protected the new recruits from the disturbing sight of the royalist army in all its battle array, expanding from the restrictions of the parish hedges of Sulby and Clipston as they approached the front of Dust Hill. The battlefield was bounded to the west by thick hedges bordering the Naseby and Sulby parishes and to the east by the sort of impassable ground which had once fronted the New Model Army as it was drawn into battle formation earlier in the morning: furze-covered boggy ground. Fairfax's left wing crowded up against the Sulby Hedges. This was champagne country (largely open land), and so Fairfax had his foot drawn up in the centre in three lines. The horse on Sulby Hill on the left was led by the recently promoted Henry Ireton, deputy governor of the Isle of Ely and now commissary general of horse. In the centre it was Skippon as major general of foot who commanded, and Fairfax remained with the foot. On the right, in the place of honour regarding the horse, was Cromwell as lieutenant general. The move westwards had placed Cromwell in a very strong position, protected by the broken ground of Naseby's rabbit warren. The warren had a house in the centre and would have been bounded by an earthwork bank. Inside the ground was pitted with burrow holes which threatened to break the legs of any horses which tried to negotiate the warren at speed. Most of Cromwell's cavalry was positioned in the warren, with Edward Whalley's brigade outside on the right of the rest of his colleagues. The royalist forces ranged opposite Fairfax's army were also were formed in open country order, with the horse on the flanks and the foot in the centre. Prince Maurice commanded in the position of honour on the right, Lord Astley in the centre with the foot and Sir Marmaduke Langdale commanded on the left. The king remained with the reserve and Rupert was at the outset towards the right.

In some histories, the chief reason for the parliamentarian victory is firmly laid at the feet of numbers. The royalist army has been regarded as being half the size of the army it marched uphill to attack. Naturally the numbers have been assessed and reassessed in recent years. Austin Woolrych suggested that the king had 'no more than 9,000', of which about 4,500 were horse, pitched against 'nearly 14,000', of which 6,500 were horse. Peter Young suggested that there were 10,000 royalists pitched against 15,000 parliamentarians.[44] More recent and thorough studies are reconstructed from a wider range of sources. Ian Gentles believed the New Model Army to be no smaller than 15,000, and possibly it was as large as 17,000, where the king had no more than 10,200 and more likely nearer to 9,000.[45] Foard settled upon 15,000 for the New Model Army as well, some 6,600 horse and 7,500 foot, and Okey's dragoons, about 500 strong. As for the royalists, he estimates that there may have been as few as 9,500.[46] Martin Marix Evans, using David Blackmore's statistics, put the New Model Army at 15,222 (5,478 horse, 8,624 foot and 676 dragoons) and the royalists at 10,200 (5,590 horse, 4,600 foot).[47] The disparity in the size of the two armies is significant, for in all these cases the parliamentarians had the advantage of somewhere between 5:3 and 3:2. Not everything was stacked against the royalists. Their ranks were packed with veterans, and significant numbers had fought side by side for some years in the Oxford Field Army, the Northern Army and the North Midlands and Newark forces. The numbers of royalist horse may have been roughly equal to the parliamentarians, and they were experienced troops. Moreover, the parliamentarian army, whilst not the fractious and argumentative collation Charles and his courtiers believed it to be, was a new organisation with officers and men who were in some cases relative strangers to each other.

The battle began at about 10.00 am, shortly after Cromwell ordered Okey to take up the position (according to *England's Recovery*, and despite the suggestion that the right wing was as much as he could manage). Okey himself had no doubt: 'I was halfe a mile behinde in a Medow giving my men Ammunition, and had not the Lieutenant Gen. come presently, & caused me with all speed to mount my men, & flank our left Wing, which was the King's right wing of horse; where was Prince Maurice.'[48]

Cromwell had instructed Okey to move from his encampment to the western side of the Sulby Hedges, which could be accessed from the road between Naseby and Welford. Okey took his men up the western side to Archwong Close, which abutted from the parish hedges into the field through which Prince Maurice's men would become stationed as they moved into position. Okey went too far initially and musketeers Rupert had stationed with the horse on that flank were able to fire through the lighter hedging of the close on to Okey's men, driving them backwards until they could get better cover from the parish hedge: from there they opened fire on Maurice's troopers.[49] It was this second round of firing which precipitated the fighting on the western flank: Maurice's men could not stand long under the fire and moved forward to avoid it. This looked from Sulby Hill as if they were moving into attack and Ireton's wing of two lines of horse advanced to meet the challenge, only to see the royalists suddenly stand still once out of Okey's way; they then realigned themselves ready to begin their advance proper. Ireton's men halted likewise, before once more moving to meet the attack.[50] Cromwell meantime squeezed Edward Rossiter's late arrivals into his lines of horse regiments on the right. This flank was drawn up as at Marston Moor in three lines; possibly only because of the strictures of the ground. Nevertheless, it was again to prove a winning formula for the general. It was shortly after this that both armies began to move towards each other – Fairfax moved the foot forward towards the edge of the ridge and for the first time the armies saw each other and began to cheer. Rupert, possibly drawn to the right wing by the premature fighting, seems to have joined his brother's command and become involved in the charge on that wing, whereas he probably should have remained in a central commanding view from where he could see the field.

Maurice's wing, led in this first attack by his brother, the commander in chief, charged at Ireton's men who, as was now almost obligatory, had also advanced with the troopers' legs interlocked – their right legs pushed hard behind the left leg of the man to their right – and gradually increasing in speed to meet them. Finally both sides smashed into each other at the charge, swords pointing at their opponents' throats. Out of his six divisions of horse, Ireton's own division, partly made up of his own regiment on the right-hand end of his front line, was not confronted by charging royalists and thus escaped the shock of impact. On the left of Ireton's line Colonel Butler's regiment, divided into two divisions, was severely mauled, possibly because the ground upon which it met the royalists was broken and difficult to traverse at the point of contact: Butler himself was seriously wounded and taken from the field.[51] On the other hand, the three division to Butler's right succeeded in defeating the royalists who attacked them and drove them backwards. Following their victory, but somewhat impetuously, Ireton turned his unengaged right-hand regiment into the flanks of the advancing royalist foot regiments which were by now driving back the parliamentarian regiments to his right, only to find himself out of his depth when faced with the royalist veteran forces. His regiment was driven off, his horse shot dead from under him: he was wounded with a pike head to the thigh and a halberd in the face and taken prisoner.[52] Rupert and Maurice charged a second time, breaking through what had been Ireton's wing, at which point the centre regiments seem to have fled the field. However, not all of the left wing did flee ahead of the pursuing royalists, and Foard suspects that the majority were left on the field, disordered but not pursued in the confusion which marked the end of perhaps half an hour's fighting.[53] It was on this wing that the New Model Army suffered most; Foard shows that the casualty rates for horse and Skippon's regiment of foot were the highest in the army. The foot regiments in the centre of each army had met shortly after the horse regiments on the west of the field clashed for the first time. Skippon had led his foot regiments forward to the edge of the ridge in time to meet the royalist advance, and possibly this momentum carried them forward and gave them the advantage on the first attack. Rupert had, however, interlaced his second line with horse and these helped push in a second attempt: Foard speculates that this may have been learned in Germany by Rupert, and he had also used the tactic at Leicester successfully a fortnight earlier. The second royalist attack saw Skippon lose the advantage, and at this point so harshly was his regiment being mauled that Ireton turned his regiment inwards to take on the Duke of York's regiment and perhaps Sir Richard Page's, which seconded it. Notwithstanding, the royalists bore down on the New Model Army and pushed the first line back on the second. Skippon, like Ireton, was wounded but stayed upright on his horse and led the fightback as the royalists became exhausted and the weight of numbers began to tell. Even so, the left flank of Fairfax's army was in disorder and pushed back from its starting point, perhaps as far as Mill Hill. However, the New Model reserves soon made their presence felt and 'repelled the Enemy, forcing them to a disorderly retreat'.[54] The simple mathematical equation of numbers now came into play once the shock tactic of the attack failed to break the will of the parliamentarians behind the ridge line.

As royalist Sir Henry Slingsby wrote: 'Had our left Wing but at this time done as half as well as either the Foot or right Wing we had got in a few minutes a glorious Victory'.[55] Slingsby had seen parliamentarian colours fall, but his optimism was ill-founded, possibly because he could not see that beyond the ridgeline the parliamentarian reserves were bearing down on the hitherto successful royalists. The author of the plan of attack, Prince Rupert's work on the royalist right flank was long done by this time, and he returned to his place at the centre. No doubt he intended to coordinate the results of the attack in the west with the outcome to the east, but he soon had to tackle the near catastrophic result of the fighting on the eastern side of the battlefield.

Cromwell, on the parliamentarian right as befitting the lieutenant general, had chosen his ground well, but despite this his wing was cramped with the late-coming regiment – Rossiter's from Lincolnshire crammed on the right-hand end of the second and third lines. The front line comprised Cromwell's double regiment, now divided between Fairfax and Whalley with the former on the right and the latter on the left, with Sir Robert Pye's regiment placed between them. There is something reminiscent of the front line at Marston Moor and even Winceby, as Pye's regiment had within it the former lieutenant colonel of the Earl of Manchester's horse and two of its captains. Two further captains, Ireton and Margery, had of course been in Cromwell's own regiment.[56] Behind them were two further lines of regiments which emphasised the larger numbers at Cromwell's command. The royalist wing comprising forces from the north and Midlands were led by Sir Marmaduke Langdale. They advanced through the constricted ground available, given that much of their frontage was covered by the rabbit warren. More of a disadvantage was the fact that Cromwell's front line was longer and stretched to the east beyond Langdale's left flank. When the two sides met at the charge Cromwell overlapped the royalists, although his right wing was slower at reaching the front. Nevertheless, the royalists fought a tough battle: they 'did as well as the Place and their Numbers would admit'; once again they were experienced soldiers who would not have been overawed by their enemies.[57] Even so, as the eastern flank was overlapped and Cromwell's second line moved into the attack, the royalists began to waver.[58] This seems to have occurred at the time Rupert reached his position at the reserve line. The front two regiments of Langdale's line broke and retreated towards the reserve, driven back by Whalley's regiment.[59] To Whalley's right rear the parliamentarian reserves fell on the remaining royalist front line. *England's Recovery* suggests that the terrain moulded Cromwell's tactics, saying that: 'In the mean time, the rest of the Divisions of the Right wing, being straightened by Furzes on the right hand, advanced with great difficulty'.[60] Marix Evans supports this, believing that the reserves came on in an orderly fashion because of the terrain they had to cross: 'terrain rather than discipline held the horse in check so that part of the second line could be ordered to wheel left'.[61] Foard thinks that the use of reserves was planned and that only the regiments supporting Whalley and Pye needed to be committed to the attack on Langdale, and for him it was the discipline of the New Model Horse, both the ex-Eastern Association men like Whalley's and the Lord General's, as well as Pye's one of Essex's former army. With Cromwell's eye for terrain and his advice to Fairfax that day, it is unlikely that the terrain was a barrier rather than a tool of the general's plan. It was for Foard a matter of quality and quantity. Langdale's wing was matched in numbers by Fairfax/Cromwell's, Whalley's, Pye's and Colonel Sheffield's regiment from Cromwell's second line; every man in the rest of Cromwell's second line and everyone in the third was a man Langdale could not pitch a trooper against; he simply did not have enough soldiers. Slingsby was right about their performance; the Northern Horse did as well as it could. It was possible anyway that the prince had only wanted them to hold Cromwell in check whilst the crushing demoralising blow to the west delivered victory and the resources to tackle the eastern flank. Unfortunately, whatever Langdale was supposed to achieve, Cromwell was the master of the timed release of resources in these circumstances: he had done it at Gainsborough and Marston Moor, and now he did it again at Naseby. As the second and third line of Cromwell's wing moved in to attack the royalist second or third line (and perhaps both), Fairfax seems to have taken charge there leaving the lieutenant general to rescue the disordered left flank, which, although there were perhaps a thousand New Model cavalry men brought under orders by their regimental officers, had no commander.

Cromwell's description of the battle is brief and he left no details about his part in it:

> He drew out to meet us; both armies engaged. We, after three hours fight very doubtful, at last routed his army; killed and took about 5,000, very many officers [...] We took also about 200 carriages, all he had; and all his guns [...] we pursued the enemy from three miles short of [Market] Harborough to nine beyond, even to the sight of Leicester whither the king fled.

Cromwell gave all the credit to God again, 'this is none other than the hand of God; and to him alone belongs the glory, wherein none are to share with him'. On the other hand, he identified Fairfax's role in his letter to Speaker Lenthall:

> the General served you with all faithfulness and honor; and the best commendation I can give him is, That I daresay he attributes all to God and would rather perish than assume to himself which is an honest and thriving way, and yet as much for bravery may be given to him in this action as to a man.[62]

Fairfax, in his account, referred to both Skippon and Ireton but not to Cromwell. Parliament's commissioners, Lieutenant Colonel Harcourt Leighton and Colonel Thomas Herbert, wrote: 'The general, Lieut. Gen. Cromwell, and Major Gen. Skippon did beyond expression gallantly; so did all the other commanders and soldiers', and Colonel John Okey's account too saw the victory was due to God and identified Cromwell as central to the godly plan.[63] Joshua Sprigge later made the point in *Anglia Rediviva*:

> The great share Lieutenant General Cromwell had in this action, who commanded the Right wing of Horse (which did such service, carrying the field before them as they did at Marston Moor) is so well acknowledged, that envy itself can neither detract nor deny.[64]

Cromwell had used the landscape north of Naseby in a way reminiscent of his approach to the Bilton Bream end of the ridge at Marston Moor, and the victory at Naseby was no less emphatic than that at Marston Moor. Observers saw similarities between the two battles when contemplating Cromwell's military reputation, and the 11 months since July 1644 marked a major shift in Cromwell's military career: it was his military successes which made him of political importance and to a great extent ensured that he had survived Manchester's and Essex's attack upon him and then shielded him from the Self-Denying Ordinance. Cromwell's attitude towards religion was also of importance: he had been urging religious toleration and it was this that had largely drawn Manchester's attack on Cromwell, determined as the earl and the Scots were to establish a single and therefore intolerant Presbyterian Church of England. In his letter, which had given all the glory to God, Cromwell referred not just to Fairfax:

> Honest men served you faithfully in this action, Sir they are trusty, I beseech you in the name of God, not to discourage them, I wish this action may begat thankfulnesse and humility in all that are concerned in it he that ventures his life for the liberty of the country I wish he trust God for the liberty of his conscience, and you for the liberty he fights for.[65]

The House of Commons that Cromwell addressed was, however, still dominated by a coordinated clique of Presbyterians, led by Denzil Holles, whose dominance ensured that that the printed version of the letter was edited and the plea for tolerance excised from first version. However, the House of Lords was less dominated by Presbyterians, allowing Cromwell's ally Lord Saye and Sele to reprint the letter with the call for toleration reinstated.

But what of Cromwell's contribution to the victory? As shown earlier, one account portrayed him as a direct agent of God who through choosing the ground upon which they would fight had given the parliamentarians victory before the first shots had been exchanged. There is something to be said for this rather direct assertion: the ridge upon which the foot was ranged did keep Fairfax's centre free from the cloying mud which would hinder everyone crossing the moor. Okey's position, chosen personally by Cromwell, did allow the New Model dragoons to disrupt Prince Maurice's wing and possibly force it to move to the attack earlier than intended. Whether or not it was discipline, or the strictures of the ground, Cromwell's right wing behaved impeccably, attacking and defeating Langdale's horse and retaining a reserve which could then be used flexibly. The balance must be in Cromwell's favour, and he would have been very aware of the chicane effect of the warren – he had dealt with coneries at Marston Moor and as a huntsman would have been very aware of the dangers of such ground to horses. He would have had a clear view of the ground ahead of him before the battle began and would have been able to ask villagers if unsure. As a commander on the wing, he had performed well, ensuring the defeat of the enemy on his flank. He was moreover confident of the leadership of his lieutenants, many of them fellow veterans and men from his own regiment, and as such he was able to give his attention to rescuing Ireton's wing by bringing it back under command and leading it forward to join Fairfax as he confronted the king's reserve forces that were forming up or continuing their retreat across Wadborough Hill, north of the battlefield.[66] If we agree with Foard and others that the New Model Army was capable of being reformed into battalia by the time they reached Wadborough Hill, then Fairfax had achieved a great deal. He had defeated a veteran army comprising the king's best troops and arguably his best generals, taken between 40 per cent and 50 per cent of the enemy prisoner, and reformed his still-new army within a short distance in time and space of the hard-won victory. True, he did have numerical superiority in overall terms, but Rupert had managed to bring superior numbers to bear at particular points: the attack on Ireton's wing and the initial engagement between the foot regiments too. In both case initial tactical victories had been won by the royalists, but in the circumstances they needed to have such a devastating effect on the first, second and third lines of the New Model Army as to cause a complete rout. That simply did not happen, and the numerical imbalance played a significant part. However, the high levels of experience in the New Model command and the backbone of veterans within each regiment was responsible for Ireton's wing and Skippon's west flank of foot eventually withstanding the assault. Had it not, then there would have been little point in Cromwell switching his attention from right to left.

PLATE 1   Oliver Cromwell, by Robert Walker, *c*.1649.

The liuelie Effigies of that noble
Lord Willoughbie de Parham..

PLATE 2 Francis Willoughby, 5th Baron Willoughby of Parham, by unknown
artist, mid-seventeenth century.

PLATE 3   A reconstruction of civil war Newark by Simon Fleming.

The right Hon:ble Edward Earle of
Manchester &c: major Generall of
the Association

PLATE 4   Edward Montagu, 2nd Earl of Manchester, by unknown artist,
published 1647.

S. THOMAS FAIRFAX
Generael van de Armee van de Parliament van Engellandt, A° 1648.

W. Hollar fe,   E.V. Wyngae, excudit Antuerpiæ.

PLATE 5   Thomas Fairfax, 3rd Lord Fairfax of Cameron, by Wenceslaus Hollar,
after Robert Walker etching, 1648.

PLATE 6   Harquebusier's armour. English, mid-seventeenth century.

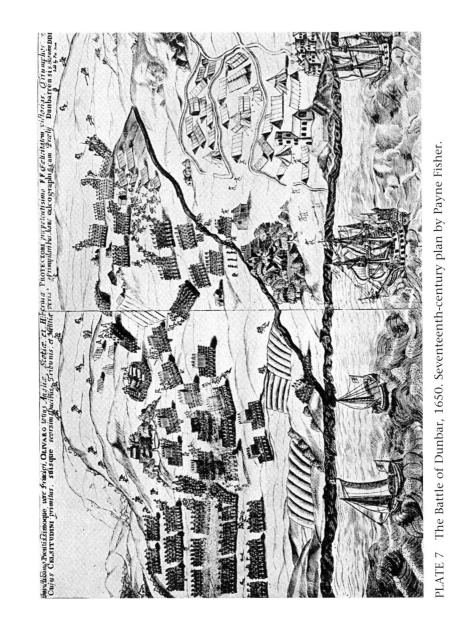

PLATE 7 The Battle of Dunbar, 1650. Seventeenth-century plan by Payne Fisher.

PLATE 8   The north walls at Clonmel. Part of the town walls which survived Cromwell's assault in May 1650.

PLATE 9 Gold Dunbar medal showing Oliver Cromwell, by Peter Blondeau, after an original by Thomas Simon, 1656.

Naseby was a complete victory. The loss of about 4,000 of his veteran experienced foot, some of whom had been with him since the autumn of 1642, was a blow from which the king would never recover. Whilst around the country there were foot soldiers as experienced in general terms as these, they were in garrisons and were veterans of small-scale skirmish-based warfare, useful in many ways but not of immediate service in a field army. Moreover, they were scattered about the country and would be difficult to gather. Leicester fell within days, for defeat at Naseby let down Lord Loughborough's hopes of redeveloping his command. Taking the broad view, Loughborough reneged on part of the generous terms of surrender granted to him and the governor of Leicester, Sir Matthew Appleyard, by Fairfax and Loughborough's old adversary Cromwell, by evacuating as many as 500 horse from the town the night before they were supposed to march out in front of the New Model Army.[67] It did not prevent his being arrested briefly on the king's orders a few days later at Lichfield.

Of more consequence was the capture of the king's cabinet of letters, which proved that he was negotiating with the Catholic Confederation of Kilkenny and showed that he despised the enemies at home with whom he was negotiating. It was a diplomatic blunder which would be difficult to set right. Once again we might surmise that Cromwell was disappointed, for again he was within miles of Newark following a victory which had seriously undermined the prowess of the garrison, but his commander had other priorities: this time the defeat of Lord Goring and his small army down in the south-west.

LANGPORT

After capturing Leicester, Fairfax pressed on to the south-west, targeting Lord Goring who was assembling a new army of 7,000 or 8,000 that he intended to unite with the king who was expecting to cross the Bristol Channel from South Wales with newly recruited regiments. Goring's intention was to avoid battle and preserve his forces until the new regiments arrived, but he had considered attacking either Edward Massey's Western Army or even Fairfax before the two armies could unite. In the event he could do little more than harass them, especially after 3 July when Fairfax and Massey joined forces. Nevertheless, Goring did hold the line of the River Yeo and protected the important garrison at Bridgewater with Major General Porter and two brigades at North Curry. However, on 9 July Massey surprised Porter's men feeding and watering their horses and routed them.[68]

This defeat obliged Goring to abandon Ilchester, and on 10 July Fairfax approached Goring's army at Langport where the royalist had chosen a strong position to the west of a small brook which had just one crossing, a ford (some historians, including myself, have suggested that this was a bridge, but it was certainly a ford at this time), and was protected by marshy ground which the New Model Army would have to traverse. Goring was intending nothing more than securing a safe retreat towards Bridgewater, confident that he could get his army to safety, and had sent the artillery and wagons on towards Bridgewater, certain that his position was one which would protect him from attack. Maybe a few months earlier he would have been right, but the New Model Army and its two most important commanders, Fairfax and Cromwell, had, less than a month before, won an emphatic victory because their skills and the morale and confidence of their army was extraordinary. With this confidence behind them, and reinforced by the knowledge that their horse regiments were superb, Fairfax devised an ambitious strategy of which he would always remain proud, confident that Cromwell as commander of the horse could deliver – particularly as the attack was launched using the two regiments which had once formed the lieutenant general's own regiment.[69] Using their superiority in artillery the New Model Army quickly silenced the three guns which Goring had held back from the train heading to Bridgewater, and then they pushed commanded musketeers to the riverbank to tackle the royalists guarding the crossing. Overwhelming musket fire silenced the royalist musketeers and cleared them away from the ford. Cromwell next sent six troops of horse to the ford, so narrow that only two riders abreast could cross it. Nevertheless, three troops, at most 300 men (probably substantially fewer) got across before Goring's horse were ready to attempt to prevent them. Cromwell's leading men attacked straight away on a narrow frontage without manoeuvring into line, and almost reached the main royalist force before being pushed back by weight of numbers to the crossing. However, by this time they were joined by another three troops which crossed the ford more easily, because the initial attack had prevented the royalist horse from engaging them at the stream whilst the presence of horse had stopped the musketeers from trying to interrupt the river crossing (in any case, the musketeers were being fired on from across the stream). Cromwell had now got six troops across the river and together they advanced on the three royalist horse regiments, which they succeeded in driving back. The effect of the daring advance had shattered royalist morale and Goring ordered a withdrawal, possibly a prearranged plan, but this precipitated the disintegration of his horse and, as was often the case in such circumstances, the rout was potentially bloodier than the initial fight – half of the royalist casualties were killed during the flight. The foot regiments managed to withdraw more successfully, crossed the Yeo and burned the bridges behind them.

Cromwell was elated, believing that God's divine plan was evident and even clearer than ever:

> Thus you see what the lord hath wrought for us. Can any creature ascribe anything to itself? Now we can give all the Glory to God, and desire that all may do so, for it is due unto Him Thus you have Long Sutton mercy added to Naseby mercy. And to see this, is it not to see the face of God! You have heard of Naseby; it was a happy victory. As in this so that, God was pleased to use his servants.[70]

Victory was only achieved 'through the goodness of God, who still appears with us'.[71] He was not alone: several officers and soldiers in the New Model Army also believed that God was demonstrating his unequivocal approval. Cromwell was absolutely convinced: 'I cannot better tell you than write, that god will go on.'[72]

The year from July 1644 to July 1645 was a remarkable year for Cromwell. He can be credited with being the architect of two major victories: Marston Moor and Naseby. In both cases he was recognised by contemporaries as having controlled the ground upon which the fight was to take place, directly at Marston Moor and at Naseby. There is a great deal to support this in both cases. Clearly at Marston Moor he had seen the importance of Bilton Bream to both the royalists and to parliament and its allies. He had not only sealed the potentially open end of the allies' western flank, but simultaneously provided his wing of the army with a platform from which to launch a devastating attack on the royalists. At Naseby he had at least done the same for his wing, but may have influenced Fairfax's choice of the field of battle. Cromwell's mastery of his own wing at both battles was superb. Even if we allow Marix Evans's suggestion that the ground, not discipline, forged the action on the New Model Army's eastern wing some credence, then we would not be being out of line to suggest that Cromwell knew this would happen because he understood the ground. In any case Fairfax was so convinced of Cromwell's mastery of the horse that he confidently built his daring plan at Langport around it, and was crowned with success. Naseby underlined the fact that Cromwell, as a commander of horse, was formidable, dependable and successful. It also underlined that if he had a hand in the selection of the field of battle he had a superb eye, just as Newbury had shown that if he did not, then there was little he could do, even with his superb ability in command and control, to control the outcome.

7

CROMWELL IN COMMAND

In 1648 the Scottish political position shifted from neutrality towards supporting the king, and a series of rebellions broke out across England and Wales. Whilst the commander in chief, Lord Fairfax, tackled the rebellions in the south-east of England, Cromwell led part of the New Model Army into South Wales to tackle the rebellion there, and later marched into Lancashire to defeat the Scottish invasion force and its royalist allies. This was Cromwell's first experience of leading a major detached force and provides insights into his role as an independent commander. But first the civil war in England and Wales had to be concluded: it is alright for historians such as Foard to say that the war was won at Naseby, but the end of a war needs a consensus amongst the protagonists, with both sides recognising that one side or other has won and that the situation as it stands cannot, for the time being at least, be overturned. That consensus was nearly a year away as Cromwell and Fairfax turned their horses south-westwards. Even they, it is clear, did not see the victory which the 20:20 vision of tail-gunner historians has made perfectly clear to students and readers. There was work to be done even after they had overwhelmed Goring at Langport and seen the face of God. The king's view of the situation was different. Whilst he had lost much of his veteran foot, he still had veteran horse regiments at his command, even though there had been losses amongst the Northern Horse during and after Langport. There were recruitment drives afoot in Wales. He still held on to the south-west and there were, at Chester and Bristol, bridgeheads to Ireland. In Scotland the Marquis of Montrose was continuing to win a string of stunning victories which might yet bring the government in Edinburgh to its knees and draw Lord Leven and the Army of the Solemn League and Covenant from the north of England, thus opening it and its resources up for recapture. Negotiations with Ireland were continuing and might yet have yielded a new army to be shipped into England and Wales. All was not yet lost.

Langport had destroyed the potential for recruitment in the south-west as far as the king was concerned, but Goring was to some extent an outsider to the region and there were plenty of local royalists ensconced in garrisons in the south: the three which had played a part in the defeat of Manchester, Essex and Waller – Donnington, Basing and Banbury – were still in operation, and further west there were significant royalist garrisons at Sherborne, Bristol, Bath and Exeter. It was these at first to which Fairfax turned the attention of the New Model Army, and it brought them into contact with the region's clubmen.

Immediately after the victory at Langport, the New Model Army was confronted by the garrison at Bridgewater, with its strong walls and connection to the Bristol Channel, which not only provided a supply route but supplied a wet moat. The town would provide a threat to the rear and to the supply lines of any army which bypassed it en route to the south-west. Preparations for a storm, including the building of a small fleet of boats, were made and an attack scheduled for 22 July. The New Model Army had allied itself with Sir Edward Massey's Western Association forces, and units from the two armies combined in a brigade to the west of the town: two regiments of Massey's and four New Model regiments were placed under Massey's command. However, it was a New Model commander, Colonel Hewson, who led the attack on the north-east side at 2.00 am. This assault drove through the outer works and captured the guns within, which were then turned on the town. The drawbridge was seized and let down, allowing the eastern half of the town to fall into parliamentarian hands; a fire then broke out and burned furiously. The New Model Army then turned its guns on the western half of Bridgewater, setting it alight too. With the town ablaze around him, the governor, Sir Edward Wyndham, surrendered.[1] The fall of Bridgewater effectively isolated royalist forces in Devon and Cornwall, severing connections between them, Bristol, the West Midlands and the Welsh borders. But there were still the garrisons of Bath and Sherborne in Fairfax's rear: Bath was to his north and east serving as a satellite of the major garrison at Bristol, whereas Sherborne was to his south and east. His council of war thought that pushing Goring's disintegrating force further west should be a priority. Fairfax disagreed and overruled them, marching instead to Wells, from where he sent forces to tackle both Bath and Sherborne.[2] It is possible that Cromwell was not involved much in these discussions as he was reportedly ill.[3] Taking Bath would have a major impact on the garrison of Bristol, currently under the command of Prince Rupert. Moreover, Bath's royalist governor was having difficulty keeping the town under control. Fairfax sent a brigade of horse and some of Okey's dragoons to the town intending it to act as a force of observation.[4] Instead, Okey and Colonel Rich summoned the town and launched an immediate attack, causing disproportionate panic amongst the garrison during the night of 18–19 July. Governor Sir Thomas Bridges surrendered the town the following day, assuming that he was surrounded, whereas the New Model regiments of horse had remained to the south and west because of their relatively small numbers.[5] Bath was refortified and parts of the New Model Army stationed there to hem in the garrison at Bristol.[6]

Fairfax turned on Sherborne whilst Cromwell led the horse into Wiltshire to confront the clubmen of that county, and Dorset and Hampshire, which Fairfax saw as a threat.[7] The New Model Army began firing heavy artillery at Sherborne Castle on 14 August, whilst civilian miners constructed earthworks around the site and undermined the walls. Fairfax was short of ammunition and fell into the practice of recycling, paying soldiers a reward for crawling out and retrieving the used cannon balls which had bounced back off the 12 foot-thick walls, for further use. By the evening of 14 August there was a breach in the walls because of the repeated bombardment, possible only because of the reuse of the scarce cannon balls. On the following day, before the mine could be exploded, an attack drove the defenders from the walls and brought about the surrender of Sherborne.[8]

Fairfax and Cromwell faced another problem in the south-west: clubmen. There had been several attempts by people across the country to resist the onset of war back in 1642. Some of these had been gentry-led, others were spontaneous reactions to incursions by soldiers of one party or another. By the later years of the war these movements had become more sophisticated and had consolidated around a series of political and practical propositions. On a political level they had often focussed on the broad demands for a settlement first mooted back in 1642: the rule of law and the governance of king and parliament working together with the church as established by law. Some clubmen organisations opposed the war completely; others, like that in Worcestershire, were prepared to accept the presence of soldiers and the necessities of a war effort so long as collections were legal and orderly. However, there were growing signs that the clubmen were not strictly neutral: those besieging Hereford in the spring of 1645 opposed the royalists there, but they steadfastly refused to side with parliament. Those in the south-west began to appear in late May 1645 in Dorset and Wiltshire, and, within weeks, Somerset. Their aims were to present petitions to both king and parliament, and to do this they developed parish-based structures to defend their localities and raise money to support that aim. John Wroughton portrays the clubmen of the south-east and west of the region as having 'slight leanings towards the royalists'.[9] Those north of Bristol, on the other hand, were predominantly supporters of parliament.

Fairfax seems to have felt himself freed by the collapse of the main royalist outposts, and it also seemed to justify the validity of his approach to securing the rear of his army, and the next council of war agreed with his desire to attack Bristol. In the meantime Cromwell had marched to Shaftsbury, where he would confront the clubmen there. He met Mr Newman, with whom he discussed several matters, including the arrest of 40 clubmen at Shaftsbury on Fairfax's orders on 3 August and the forthcoming meeting of the clubmen of Dorset and Wiltshire.[10] The men arrested had only been in arms to protect their property from being plundered, Newman argued. Cromwell was reticent in discussing the matter: 'no account was due to them' because he clearly did not recognise them as holding any form of authority, but was probably wary of their numbers. He did go as far as assuring them that they would not be plundered by the New Model Army, and if the men had only assembled to defend themselves they would not be punished.[11] This seemed to satisfy Newman, and Cromwell proceeded to the town. However, not all were satisfied, and at an iron age fort near to Shaftsbury, Hambledon Hill, 2,000 clubmen had assembled. When Cromwell sent what he described as a 'forlorn hope' on a reconnaissance mission the clubmen fired upon the soldiers – it may have been a warning shot for there appear to have been no casualties. They then demanded a meeting with Cromwell. Cromwell refused to go to them but offered to meet representatives elsewhere and discuss their intentions, but the violence began to escalate. Cromwell seems to have sent his former regiment, indeed his former troop, to deal with the clubmen, as he informed Fairfax that he had ordered his captain lieutenant to prepare to attack. Fairfax's regiment of horse of course comprised half of Cromwell's old regiment, and Fairfax's own troop would be led in the field by a captain lieutenant as stand-in troop commander. At one time this would have been James Berry, but after Berry became a captain (he had succeeded William Ayres the previous year) it was John Gladman who held the post.[12] Even as the troop prepared to attack, Cromwell continued to be conciliatory, stressing to Gladman: 'if upon his falling on they would lay down Armes, he was to accept them, and spare them'.[13] However, as the troop approached, the clubmen began firing and killed two of the troopers and four horses. The clubmen were seemingly making some use of the fort's ramparts and were able to keep the regiment out of what may have been one of the fort's three gateways. Certainly they had got themselves the protection of a passageway that was only wide enough for three troopers abreast: all the entrances were indirect, involving negotiating a series of enclosed approaches. However, the amateur clubmen were faced with a hardened veteran, John Desborough, now Fairfax's major and effectively the regiment's commander in the field. Desborough may have feigned a retreat, which had drawn some of the inexperienced but enthusiastic clubmen out of their fortified position, or he may just have got in between the clubmen and the fort's defences; either way he wheeled about, got amongst his attackers and entered the fort mingled with them, killing about a dozen, wounding many more and taking 300 prisoners. Despite the violence Cromwell was willing to let the prisoners go home, convinced that they would pose no further trouble. His men in the field had been able to identify the leaders and two 'vile ministers' – these had been seized and the rest of the clubmen disarmed. Cromwell believed that these clubmen favoured the royalists and had wanted the now retired royalist general Ralph Lord Hopton to lead them, however from this point onwards the region's clubmen came to see the New Model Army as the means by which the war would be ended soonest and lent 'clout' if not political sympathy to Fairfax's men.[14]

With the clubmen contained, and possibly won over to some extent (at least temporarily), Fairfax and Cromwell were able to concentrate upon Bristol. The capture of Bath had had the desired effect and there was fear in the town. Rupert had been confident of being able to hold Bristol, but the cold light of dawn had shown this to be based on false premises. The city, Rupert now argued, was too large for his garrison to defend and he now, in a reversal of fortunes, found himself in the position Sir Nathaniel Fiennes had been in in 1643 when the prince had besieged the town himself. Fiennes's surrender had nearly cost him his life, and in the end it did cost him his seat in the Commons and his reputation. Rupert had more men than Fiennes had had, but Bristol, despite its importance as a port, had not been fortified extensively like Hull, Plymouth or Berwick, and its defences were mediaeval like York. Early in the war the city had been encircled by earthworks, which like York linked a series of forts. Like many of the newly built forts they were viewed by observers as 'incomplete' – this probably does not mean that they were unfinished as intended by their builders at the time (there had been plenty of time to complete them as planned), but that they were not up to the standards of modern European fortifications witnessed by the veterans of continental siege warfare. Rupert argued that there should have been over 3,000 in the garrison but that he never got the number above 2,300, and in reality he thought 1,500 was the real number of effective soldiers.[15] The breastworks were four miles in circumference and weakly constructed, and the 1643 siege part of the wall between Brandon Hill Fort and Windmill Fort had proved of no use at all in keeping the attackers out.[16] Moreover, even now the chief fortress – the 'Great Fort' – was overlooked by Brandon Hill Fort, and if the latter fell it would become vulnerable to cannon fire. Rupert had strengthened the works, with the aim of keeping an attacker as far from the walls as possible, and he began to produce ammunition as fast as he could for the 100 cannon defending the walls and to supplement the musket balls, which on his arrival he had estimated would be expended in three hours. He also built up stores of food in the town for the garrison and the inhabitants, subsidising the poor particularly, which he believed numbered 1,500 families out of the 2,500 the living in Bristol.[17] Whilst the food was enough to last a long siege, the state of the walls and the numbers of troops meant that at the council of war and he agreed on a straightforward plan: one assault could be driven off, hopefully with the attackers suffering a high casualty rate that would cause a severe loss of morale, allowing for a pause before a second attempt would be made – the coming of autumn might yet save Bristol. It was a bleak summation and entirely dependent upon fighting off the New Model Army's first attack. The alternative was to have all the garrison's foot soldiers crowd into the castle precinct and hold just this part of the town as a kind of citadel, with the prince and the horse breaking out before Bristol was tightly besieged and leaving it to its fate. The idea had been rejected as both dishonourable and because the proposed citadel was too small to contain even the foot.

On 21 August the New Model Army moved close enough to Bristol for Fairfax and Cromwell to get a look at the town from Bedminster. This provoked the defenders into making a sally to disrupt the besiegers; a practice that was to become common over the next few days.[18] Bedminster, Clifton and other outlying villages had been destroyed to prevent them being used as fortifications and lodgings for the New Model Army as it approached. Notwithstanding, the New Model Horse began to ring Bristol's Pile Hill, to the south and within a musket-shot (about 300 yards), occupying it with a brigade of horse which could overlook, and potentially fire into, the town.[19] Ireton led horse and dragoons across the River Avon to the north of the city to close off the escape routes and approaches. Over the next two days foot brigades began to arrive and were allocated places in the developing ring around the town. To prevent Goring making a relief attempt, Massey's Western Army was based in Taunton ready to intercept him. Earthworks were begun and a battery erected opposite Temple Gate, and the road out of the town severed by a ditch.[20] At the same time Fairfax and Cromwell began to send propaganda into Bristol to try and convince the townspeople to force Rupert to surrender the town. This probably had no effect, and elicited Cromwell's comments about the promise of support from within Bristol 'that did not answer expectation'.[21]

If Bristol's fortifications were stretching Rupert's forces inside the town, then ringing them was equally stretching for the New Model Army: 'our horse were forced to be on exceeding great duty, to stand by the foot, lest the foot, being so weak in all their posts, might receive an affront'.[22] For the next few days the weather was unseasonably bad and the army outside Bristol suffered from the cold and wet. On 2 September the weather improved, and the fort at Portishead and its commander, Sir Bernard Astley, was captured, opening the Avon to parliamentarian traffic.[23] Fairfax and Cromwell had by this time scouted the entire line and then called a council of war to decide upon the course of action. The council considered the options, but what seems to have weighed heavily on their minds was the possibility that they could be attacked by Goring or royalist-inclined clubmen if they stayed too long. Thereby, they decided to storm the town. They hoped to carry all before them, but decided that if they captured some of the forts and part of the walls and drove the garrison into the castle, they could keep the garrison in check using supportive clubmen and just part of the army, leaving the rest of the New Model Army free to deal with Goring and any other royalist forces.[24] Cromwell thought that there was an unwillingness amongst the officers to carry out the storm; but this may have been during the early days of the leaguer when the weather was poor and when the expectations of support inside Bristol were dashed. However, these deliberations were 'no sooner concluded but difficulties were removed' and the doubters changed their minds and resolved on an attack.[25] Once the decision was made, Fairfax asked Prince Rupert to surrender and Rupert, to play for time, asked if he could contact the king before answering. When he was told no, the prince suggested terms which were in turn refused. The date for the storm had in any case been set – Wednesday 10 September.

The plan of attack involved Weldon's brigade attacking the town from the Somersetshire or south-eastern side with 600 men from four Taunton regiments. These men would storm the walls with ladders, get into the town and let down the drawbridge and allow in the horse regiments which had been seconding them for the past week or so. To their right and the eastern side of the city, a second brigade of four New Model regiments under Colonel Montague would attack the walls on either side of Lawford's Gate. To Montague's right, Colonel Rainsborough, again with four New Model regiments, would attack the walls near Prior's Fort. Over to the west of Bristol, Colonel Pride's brigade of one regiment each of horse and foot was stationed in the closes outside the town to occupy the attention of the garrison in the royal fort. In each case the storm was to consist of specialist troop, pioneers or engineers carrying ladders, supported by engineers and gunners who would spearhead the assault on the gates themselves with the aim of throwing them open to let in the horse regiments. A waterborne assault was also planned, but Rupert had covered the riverside with cannon.[26]

The assault began at either 2.00 am, according to *A True Relation of the Taking of Bristol*, or 3.00 am, according to *A True Relation of the Taking of Bristol by Sir Thomas Fairfax*, on Wednesday 10 September, although Cromwell suggested that it was supposed to start at 1.00 am.[27] Rupert also thought it about 2.00 am.[28] All points were attacked simultaneously to prevent Rupert concentrating his forces at any point. The attack on Lawford's Gate was carried out quickly despite there apparently being a strong force in the works there. This enabled Desborough and the horse to enter via the gate, followed by the foot which occupied the inner gate on Castle Street, giving them access to Bristol Castle. Waller's regiment breached the wall south of Lawford's Gate, and thus the section of the city between the rivers Frome and Avon was in the hands of the New Model Army.[29] Rainsborough's attack on Prior's Hill Fort, which according to one account was supported by clubmen, may have been the next to meet with success, and the fort entered after three hours' fighting. This in turn gave Fairfax control of the whole eastern side of Bristol north of the Avon, and on both banks of the Frome.[30] However, according to the same eyewitness account Weldon's assault on the south-east did not succeed in getting inside the walls, something explained by *A True Relation*, partly because they had underestimated the height of the walls and had made their ladders too short, and also because the moat was deeper than expected.[31] The shortness of the ladders had also affected, though less seriously, the attack on Prior's Hill Fort.[32] The fighting was hardest and bloodiest here, and when the New Model regiments forced their way in they were in no mood to issue quarter to the defenders. As everyone agreed on the fact that it took three hours to capture the fort (two of them at the 'push of pike') and that daylight was breaking, it suggests that the fighting had begun between 2.00 am and 3.00 am rather than nearer to 1.00 am. This attack had been a coordinated action, with Colonel Riche's horse driving a wedge between the attacking foot regiments and royalist horse which had been placed to challenge any such incursion. The taking of the fort had been a high priority, as it dominated the whole eastern line down to the Frome. Cromwell argued that even if the whole eastern wall line had fallen, but the fort remained in royalist hands, any New Model Army regiments inside would have been vulnerable: 'neither horse nor foot would have stood in all that way, in any manner of security, had not the fort been taken'.[33]

Nevertheless, as day broke the eastern defences were in parliamentarian hands. In the end little had been done on the western side – the attacks there had been diversions designed to keep the soldiers on that side of the town from supporting those on the eastern side where the chief attacks were. In spite of this, and Weldon's failure, Rupert was in a difficult position and the troops driven in from the east gathered in the city. True, the western forts were all still well manned, but there was a dangerous wedge appearing between the troops in the city and those in the castle, whose defences had already been pierced in the follow-up to the attack on Lawford's Gate. Furthermore, there was no hope of outside help. Rupert opened negotiations.[34] Cromwell was ecstatic:

> It may be thought that some praises may be due to these gallant men, of whose valour so much mention is made; their humble suit to you nd all that have an interest in this blessing, is, that in the remembrance of god's praises they may be forgotten. It is their joy that they are instruments to God's glory, and their country's good; it's their honour that God vouchsafes to use them. Sir they that have been employed in this service know that faith and prayer obtained this city for you I do not say ours only, but of the people of God with you and all England over, who have wrestled with God for a Blessing in this very thing.[35]

Faith and Prayer had produced a clear strategy and a series of tactics which had achieved the required goal: seizure of a sufficient section of the city's walls, two gates and a major fort. The use of the horse had been a particular success, but it is likely that Cromwell was not wholly responsible for devising this tactic. Rupert had used the same technique at Leicester, back in May. It is also clear that the prince had expected it, for no doubt he had seen that horse regiments backed up each of the brigades of foot during the run-up to the storm. Horse regiments had been stationed inside the defences near Prior's Hill Fort and these had attempted to force Hammond's and Rainsborough's men back until defeated by Riche's regiment. The ground was suitable in places for the use of horse: they certainly were not engaged in street fighting once inside the defences, for there were fields between the walls and Bristol itself, although some of them were enclosed by hedges and others possibly by boundaries such as ditches. However, Cromwell was really making a religious and political point, indicating as he had after Marston Moor and Naseby that God was favouring a wide spectrum of Protestant believers within the New Model Army: 'Presbyterians, Independents, all had here have the same spirit of faith and prayer the same pretence and answer; they agree here, know no names of difference: pity it is it should be otherwise anywhere. All that believe have the real unity.'[36] Again, he was making the point that there should be a liberty of conscience because it was clear that God favoured it and showed that favour by making the New Model Army, composed of men of different strands of Protestantism, collectively successful. However, within a short space of time he drew a very clear distinction between these strands of Protestant faith and Catholicism.[37]

Fairfax and Cromwell did not rest long. The headquarters were moved into Bristol as soon as Rupert's defeated forces moved out towards Oxford on Thursday 11 September, but because there had been an outbreak of plague in the city, most of the army was kept out. On 15 October, Cromwell led four regiments – some of those which met with most successful on 10 October – towards Devizes, whilst another brigade set off to capture Berkeley Castle. Devizes fell once Cromwell's artillery was in place on 21 October following a brief bombardment. Three days later, Laycock House surrendered, and Berkley surrendered to Rainsborough a couple of days after that. Fairfax then divided his forces, assured that the royalists had been rendered almost impotent between Worcester and the gateway to the south-west. He himself decided to go after Goring, and sent Cromwell off through the southern counties towards the scene of the previous year's humiliation, the nexus of royalist garrisons in and around Berkshire. En route, Cromwell took Winchester after a brief but destructive attack on the castle garrisoned by Lord Ogle, on 4 October.[38] He then marched to Basing.

Basing House, the seat of the Marquis of Winchester, had been turned into a formidable garrison despite it being a relatively modern country seat rather than a castle, but it was not a thoroughly modern fortress by any means. After the siege, Hugh Peters reviewed the siegeworks and reported to parliament was that they: 'were many though not finished, and of too great a compass [...] the circumvallation being aboue mile and a halfe about'.[39] The word unfinished is important here, as it suggests that despite the series of sieges and alarms suffered by the garrison at Basing House the defences were not completed by the builders. It may, however, be a comment on their technical completeness rather than them having been 'finished' in the eyes of the builders. Certainly there was not what would be recognised as *trace Italienne*, by veterans of the wars on the continent. What surrounded Basing was at best a partial *enceinte*, comprising a breastwork and ditch behind which defenders could shelter rather than the massive flat-topped low earthworks on which guns could be mounted. Guns at Basing, as elsewhere, would be behind the breastwork firing through embrasures. The Paulet family were Roman Catholics and the house, as well as being a garrison, had become a refuge for several Catholic families who saw it as a sanctuary. The garrison was something of an anomaly, containing a larger number of Catholics than was normal in the south – there were larger numbers in the forces in the Midlands and the north than were generally found in royalist forces in southern England.[40] The author of *More Sulfure for Basing*, a minister with the army, had likened Basing to Babylon in a sermon preached on 21 September. A 'day of Wrath' was coming and those in this new Babylon would perish: 'let their joynts loosen for feare, and their knees smite together for horror, for as true and God is in Heaven, they shall perish, I say unlesse they repent, they shall assuredly *perish, and come to a fearful end'*.[41]

The garrison was well prepared and on the face of it confident, at least in the report of Hugh Peters. Peters knew the governor (they had been near neighbours), and so by the time he gave his post-siege report to parliament, he had had a conversation with the chief prisoners, Governor Sir Robert Peake and the Marquis of Winchester himself. Whilst the marquis seemed to believe that Basing would be last place in the kingdom to fall to parliament, Peake had been less confident, telling Peters that he had only about 300 effectives to man the wall a mile-and-a-half in circumference. On the other hand, Peters commented that the food stores could have lasted years. Rooms were hung with meat and live cattle were kept in underground rooms.[42] It was probably because he had an inkling that this was the case that Cromwell decided upon a storm rather than repeat the earlier attempts to capture the garrison through a lengthy siege. There was another factor which was to make Basing a different experience: whilst the confessional element explained why the New Model Army soldiers and their commander behaved as they did once they had got into the fortress, their entry was made possible because Cromwell was able to employ siege artillery. Siege batteries were slow and vulnerable as the moved across country; they involved hundreds of wagons, men, horse and oxen to support the slow-moving guns, which were best shipped by means of water transport than by land. The Earl of Essex had lost all of his in the disastrous Lostwithiel campaign, and right until the end of the war royalists succeeded in capturing parliamentarian guns en route to sieges. It was really only safe to move these lumbering convoys through territory which was under tight control.

The parliamentarian guns at Basing made short work of the old tall buildings and smashed the 'not finished' works. The damage was so great that Cromwell wrote: 'we took the two houses without considerable loss to ourselves'. After that, however, the fighting could have ended, but when the royalists called for a parley the parliamentarians continued to fight them, killing about a third of the royalists troops and some civilians, including at least one woman. It was not a massacre on the scale of the slaughter of civilians after Naseby, nor of the butchery which followed the capture of the Abbey Cwm Hir in Wales or of Shelford in Nottinghamshire. Nevertheless, it was a very different ending to a siege than those Cromwell and Fairfax had been involved with in recent weeks, even if to some extent Peters's image of the aftermath of the killing conveys a sense of civility in the discussions he had with Winchester and Peake. There is a clear sense that Cromwell had identified the garrison as something 'other' – a Catholic nest to which the normal rules of warfare he had hitherto applied were not appropriate. And it was true that Harrison had killed three men during the siege, one of whom was allegedly disarmed and at the major's mercy apparently shouting 'cursed is he that doeth the Lord's work negligently'.[43] Although the latter accusation is dramatic, and made a decade-and-a-half later, nevertheless Peters noted that Harrison had killed Majors Cuffe and Robinson (the man whose death was supposed to have prompted the fanatical expostulation). He also noted that some '8 or 9 Gentlewomen of some ranke running forth together were entertained by the common soldiers somwhat coursly though not uncivilly'. He added that 'they left them with some clothes upon them'. He also noted that the daughter of a Catholic priest had been killed.[44] However, the outcome at Basing was not outside the bounds set elsewhere. The garrison at Abbey Cwm Hir had been massacred during and after the siege there, the garrison at Shelford in Nottinghamshire was likewise been wiped out during and following a storm, and neither of these had been a nest of papists. Moreover, despite being stripped and one of their number killed during the storm, the women at Basing were not treated as savagely as those found with the royalist baggage train during the pursuit after Naseby.

The year's campaign season was drawing to a close and Cromwell, having received the surrender of Langford House, returned westwards to join Fairfax and the rest of the army. Together the generals established winter quarters in the vicinity of Exeter. The army was struck with influenza and campaigning only resumed in the following January, and even then with skirmishing and raids which nevertheless wore down the royalist opposition and secured the region for parliament. In the early hours of 17 February, the last royalist army of any significance in the west was defeated at Torrington. By the end of March the west was in parliamentarian hands and Prince Charles, the king's heir, has fled for the Scilly Isles. From there the army returned eastwards with the aim of besieging Oxford once again, as parliament sought to negotiate an end to the war with the king.

The king surrendered to Lord Leven in his section of the leaguer before Newark in early May 1645, and the last two great royalist garrisons, Newark itself and Oxford, were surrendered on the king's orders not because they had fallen to their besiegers. The anvil upon which Cromwell had forged his career at the expense of three noble generals was finally surrendered to the parliamentarians on 8 May, but none of them would go in for fear of the plague. Even the demolition of its defences was abruptly halted by the need to pen the disease in, which mirrored the enveloping of the troublesome royalist forces within. In March the last royalist field army had been destroyed in the Midlands, not by Fairfax and the New Model Army but by Sir William Brereton's experienced and long-established regional army. Following the king's meddlesome surrender to Leven at Newark – which he had intended to prolong the struggle by selecting the one faction of his opponents which by then had a significant propensity for antagonising other factions – the remaining royalist strongholds began to make their peace with parliament's leaguers and commanders, and the first civil war in England and Wales sputtered to a close.

ARMY POLITICS AND THE REVOLUTIONARY IMPETUS

By the middle of 1646, as the war ended, the political situation had changed dramatically since even the end of 1644, never mind mid-1642 when Cromwell strapped on his sword for the first time as a soldier. The consensus of opposition to Charles I which had driven the country to the edge of war in

1642 had of course collapsed when war began to seize hold of the England and Wales. Even so, the initial drive to restrain or control the role of the monarchy within the established political structures of governance had remained at the core of the parliamentarian 'cause', even if there was no single agreed means of doing so. As some moderate opponents of the king had drifted to the royalist cause, parliament could at least concentrate upon several tenets in its push for change. The need to defeat the king, however, served to cloud the picture, as the means of political change depended upon how strong a position parliament wanted to occupy in any victory. To maintain any appearance of an agreed settlement, the defeat of the king needed to be one which could be seen as persuasive rather than compulsive. Thus there was great store set upon the discussions at Oxford in early 1643, as this, if successful, could have been presented as an agreement between both sides. However, parliament had identified people it regarded as incendiaries upon whom the king had depended since the previous year, which might have provided a set of scapegoats on whom to heap opprobrium to avoid blaming Charles himself for the war, had not the king been rightly grateful to them. The context of the war, which at that point the king considered himself to be winning, drove two sides apart the and thereafter they both took on allies – the king the Irish, and parliament the Scots – which effectively drove an enormous wedge between the political positions of the two sides, ensuring that a negotiated peace was less and less likely. As parliamentarians began to debate the need to move to a position in which they had to destroy the king's side rather than simply convince him to return voluntarily to negotiating, the war itself began to change the broader political views held of it. Parliament's insistence on mobilising the understanding of its cause amongst its soldiers by such means as *The Souldiers Pocket Bible*, which used selected biblical quotations to justify a war against a lawful monarch, and the *Souldiers Catechisme*, which utilised the church's method of inculcating the understanding of religious tenets and principles, seems to have played a role in getting soldiers to feel that parliament's cause really was their own cause. Moreover, amongst the wider population the infringements of property rights which were necessitated by the need to fund the various armies had continued to foreground the very discussions of taxation, billeting and property which had been current since at least 1610, and ever more so since Charles I had come to the throne. In short, several vocal if not necessarily large sections of the population had had their political consciousness raised.

Whilst on the one hand, this inspired rumblings and outright riots targeting tax collection, on the other hand, parliament's determination to negotiate with the king as if it were still 1642, and at the same time disband the army without ensuring legal protection for the soldiers or that they received back pay, provoked rebellion within the army. Against the background of the king's continued mischief, which made negotiating a settlement difficult, parliament provoked its soldiers into a virtual state of mutiny over pay and protection. It is not surprising that Cromwell (and indeed his commander) sided with the soldiers, for he had always attempted to use his muscle to ensure that they were paid and treated with respect by their political masters. Nor is it surprising that he sought to use his position in parliament to do so. It is perhaps more surprising that he was prepared to accept the degree of self-determination which the troops adopted in presenting their demands through elected officials, rather than simply through their officers. Matters became even more advanced when a section of soldiers seized the king in June 1647. Charles had surrendered to Leven in order, he hoped, to drive a wedge between the Scots and the faction in parliament which opposed the threatened imposition of a Presbyterian state church, and perhaps even to try and get Scotland to change sides. The plan had met with some limited success, as Leven had taken the king with him when marching his army homeward, thus continuing to allow the king to play the Scots and parliament off against one another during the ensuing negotiations, known as the Treaty of Newcastle. By the end of 1646 his captors became tired of the game and sold Charles for the price of the back pay due to the Army of the Solemn League and Covenant, and duly dispatched parliament's purchase southwards. The king was lodged in various large houses en route, and by the beginning of June 1647 he was at Holdenby House in Northamptonshire. Cornet George Joyce and almost half a regiment of horse rode to Holdenby, seized the king from parliament's jailors and took him to the army headquarters at Newmarket, four days after the date parliament had set for the disbanding of the army. Fairfax, despite being in possession of a major bargaining chip, persuaded the army to remain loyal to parliament in spite of having avoided being replaced as commander in chief by just 12 votes in the Commons. Parliament had strengthened and manned the defences of London, established forces to combat the New Model Army and appealed to the Scots for help against what it saw as a rebellious army. The army was developing a radical political platform at least partly in conjunction with a new and important political group in London: the Levellers. Levellers and allied representatives in the army known as agitators had developed a political programme which went beyond any political platform advanced in the war so far: it not only supported the rights of the soldiers to their service dues and access to state-wide pensions for widows and orphans, it actually demanded a level of democracy not currently witnessed in the world, based on the entitlements and freedoms of 'birthright' rather than inheritance. Fairfax and Cromwell were in tune only with the service-based demands for their soldiers, but nevertheless realised that the achievement of these required them to at least give the impression of being in sympathy with the army as a whole. Therefore they led the army to London, with the king in their 'baggage train' forcing parliament to back down somewhat, find the cash for back pay and drive leading anti-army figureheads into self-imposed exile from the House of Commons. Fairfax was able to view this as a victory and drew the army back to Bedford, but a reactionary rising in London strengthened the resolve of the conservative Presbyterian group. With the return of the 'exiled' members, this group turned on the army despite its planned use of the Northern Association Army falling apart when the soldiers arrested General Sydenham Pointz and turned up near Bedford to support Fairfax with Pointz as a prisoner. The army once again advanced on London, camped on Hounslow Heath and with a show of force drove parliament into submission, having taken over the city's defensive works in early August. In the meantime the army leaders had presented a treaty of their own to the king, called the Heads of the Proposals, by which they not only distanced themselves from parliament but also from the army rank and file, whom they had not consulted during the drafting process and as a result created a fairly liberal set of proposals with no room for the sort of radicalism displayed within the army as a whole. The king continued to play off his suitors one against the other, letting Presbyterians north and south of the border know that the army treaty was not to his liking and indicating that it did not favour Presbyterianism. In the end he rejected the treaty proposals.

With London and parliament under control, in late October at Putney Church the army began one of the greatest experiments hitherto attempted in democratic discussions. The army command and representative agitators discussed the nature of the political settlement in the light of failing to bring the king to terms in the months since the fighting in England and Wales had ended. It was not a completely open discussion as there were certain things which the commanders present (Cromwell was in the chair in lieu of Fairfax, and Ireton, now Cromwell's son-in-law, did much of the talking) could not conceive of – such as ending property qualifications for voting and the overriding need for loyalty to parliament – but nevertheless for the first time in such an arena concepts like universal male suffrage and the rights of people who were governed by a regime to consent to that regime were debated. As the discussions were coming to some form of consensus about the rights of veteran soldiers to have a vote, and the difficult subject of bringing the king to trial was raised, the conference broke up upon news of the king's escape from captivity at Hampton Court. In order to ensure unity in the face of potential chaos, Fairfax and Cromwell prohibited the planned rendezvous of the regiments at Corkbush Field which had been arranged to discuss the army's radical document, *The Case of the Army Truly Stated*, and the Levellers' constitutional draft, *The Agreement of the People*. Furthermore, when several regiments ignored the prohibition, Fairfax and Cromwell angrily berated the regiments assembled on Corkbush Field and had perceived ringleaders tried and shot. The king's escape proved to be more of an alarm than a crisis, and he was soon incarcerated in Carisbrooke Castle on the Isle of Wight in the care of the governor, New Model Army Colonel Robert Hammond. Nevertheless, the king remained determined to turn the tables, and whilst parliament submitted a quick-fix set of preliminary proposals, the Four Bills, to him, Charles negotiated with the Scots and signed the Engagement with them guaranteeing military aid should the English and Welsh parliament fail to restore him to his former position and dignity. Amongst many others, Cromwell's attitudes towards the king were hardening and he supported the Vote of No Addresses, making it a treasonable offence to negotiate with the king.

In the meantime, as the Scots began to construct an army and war effort to support an intervention south of the border, rebellion was breaking out in South Wales and eastern England. The commander of the garrison at Pembroke, Colonel John Powell, resented his planned replacement by New Model officers and led the garrison in a rebellion against parliament. The rebellion spread when Major General Laugharne joined them and gathered a rag-tag army of royalists and Presbyterians to a total of around 8,000 opponents of the regime.[45] The trials of rioters in Norfolk who had defied the prohibition on Christmas convened in April 1648 and led immediately to more riots. The royalist Earl of Norwich led rioters in Kent in defiance of the county committee and government, and likewise in Essex there were royalist-led riots against the government. Royalists seized Pontefract and Scarborough castles, and the navy mutinied: the scene seemed set for a Scottish invasion with a coordinated series of rebellions in England and Wales in support.

It did not work out that way. The seizure of Pembroke did not set all of South Wales alight and nor did it persuade the Scots to act hurriedly, In any case, the royalist Scots, known as the Engagers after the Engagement signed with the king, were finding it hard to create an army in the first place and were equally taxed in trying to find commanders for it. The lack of coordination gave the New Model Army the time and Fairfax the confidence needed to divide his forces. The lord general took the bulk of the army into Kent, where Sandwich, Deal and Walmer had fallen into rebel hands, to tackle a gathering at Maidstone. Cromwell set off for South Wales with around 5,000 men from the New Model Army, and John Lambert took three regiments of horse and two foot regiments north to tackle the royalists there. Kent had become a hotbed of rebellion following the release of those arrested for celebrating the previous Christmas, but it was not alone: in the south-east, Essex, Suffolk and Surrey were now in revolt. It was here that Fairfax directed his attention, as 10,000 people gathered in Kent to elect the Earl of Norwich as their leader. Fairfax went straight to the heart of the rebellion, putting a watch on the occupied ports and the garrison at Rochester whilst attacking the gathering near Maidstone and focussing on those under Norwich's orders. Three days after Norwich had been elected leader, on 1 June, Fairfax defeated the rebels and the heart went out of the Kentish rebellion, Norwich retreated northwards via Canterbury and on to Gravesend. From there the hardy royalists crossed the Thames and joined the Essex rebels under Cromwell's old adversary Henry Hastings, Lord Loughborough and Arthur, Lord Capel. Fairfax was on to them, quickly marching into Essex and driving the rebels into Colchester, thus beginning a long siege. The royalists hoped to receive support from the mutinous fleet, but the situation at sea was even more complex than on land, and since the initial rebellion some of the ships had returned to their loyalty towards parliament and others with some reluctance sailed to the United Provinces to join Prince Charles.[46]

CROMWELL IN COMMAND

Cromwell left London on 3 May 1648 with his detachment of the army, and reached Gloucester on 8 May. He told his regiments that they were again facing a potent enemy and exhorted them to arm themselves with the same 'resolution as formerly'.[47] What he and they did not know at this point was that Colonel John Horton and advance units of the army had defeated Rowland Laugharne's combined forces at the Battle of St Fagans near Cardiff on that very day: a victory so emphatic that it confined the rebellion to Pembrokeshire.[48] Cromwell marched to Monmouth, and there on 10 May heard of the victory at St Fagans. In the meantime he asked Fairfax to get parliament to put a garrison into Bristol. Doing so would further confine the rebels and make it harder for their supporters from the west of England to get across the Bristol Channel to South Wales. Cromwell's men stormed Chepstow Castle on 25 May, the lieutenant general himself having left the siege to Colonel Isaac Ewer whilst he moved to Cardiff. With less of a threat ahead of him, Cromwell dispatched five troops of horse and dragoons to the northern marches, only to have Fairfax send them on to Lancashire where there was a possibility of a Scottish invasion force.[49] Cromwell moved next to Swansea, reaching the town by the 19 May, which like Chepstow was partly his own property, having been granted both manors by parliament seeking to reward him for his role in the first civil war. On 24 May Cromwell arrived at Pembroke – the other rebel stronghold, Tenby, was under siege from Horton's forces. Chepstow Castle fell on 25 May and Horton received Tenby's submission on 31 May. Cromwell sent some units, Ewer's regiment and two troops from Francis Thornhaugh's regiment, back to England. Of more use to him was a train of siege artillery but for now he did not have one, although he did have some field artillery supplied from Milford Haven, but he needed ammunition for these, especially the $14\frac{3}{4}$-inch mortar.[50] Cromwell, however, was optimistic and felt able to accede to requests for troops sent to him from Fairfax, who needed men in Essex, and parliament, which urged him to send more men northwards and suggested perhaps that he went himself. Nevertheless, Cromwell focussed on Pembroke. St Fagans had ended the rebellion and concentrated its remnants in the castle at Pembroke, but Cromwell was confident that this would be an affair of days, not weeks. On 14 June he reported that the garrison in the castle was mutinous and had threatened to kill Poyer, and that somehow Cromwell had heard that Poyer had promised that they would shortly be relieved. He also heard that they were short of food. Even so, much of this seems to have been wishful thinking to compensate for the lack of a practical means of battering the garrison into submission. In the same letter Cromwell referred to establishing a small battery of guns, no doubt those from Milford Haven, but they would not be ready until 16 June, and even then their calibre was so slight that they could only be used on the mills supplying the castle, not the castle itself. He had set fire to parts of the town to cause panic, possibly using the mortar to do so, but there was no suggestion of an attack on the castle. An attempted storm ten days earlier had failed because they could not make a large enough breach in the walls and their ladders were too short.[51] So instead Cromwell referred to the siege train which was supposes do be on its way to supplement the guns 'we have scraped up'. The great guns referred to in *A Dangerous Fight* would simply have been the field artillery sent from Milford Haven, as the real great guns did not arrive for another fortnight after the pamphlet went on sale.[52] The fortnight following Cromwell's letter to the Derby House Committee passed without the castle surrendering, and his own difficulties mounting. He told Fairfax that the country was poor and exhausted, and that it was difficult to get food and fodder through requisitioning as he had no money to buy any. Moreover, there were a few small-scale insurrections which had to be put down, and the country controlled through billeting the horse regiments around the outskirts of the leaguer. Worse still, the siege train had been ditched at Berkeley on the Bristol Channel and had needed to be hauled out of the mud. Yet Cromwell still believed that the garrison was on the verge of surrender. Someone was feeding him misinformation about either the state of morale in the garrison or about the level of command and control Poyer and Laugharne were still able to exercise, or both.[53] Nearly a week went by before the siege artillery finally arrived, but once there the threat they presented effectively ended the siege, and Poyer and Cromwell negotiated. The terms appear generous: only the high command, Major General Laugharne, Colonels Poyer, Matthews Captain Bower and David Poyer were to surrender to the mercy of parliament; 17 officers and gentlemen were to emigrate; the rest of the officers and men were allowed to go home unmolested. However, Cromwell had taken a firm line and one he would continue to hold over the forthcoming months. In his letter to Speaker Lenthall he explained that he singled out

> those who have formerly served you in a very good cause, but, being not apostatised I did rather make election of them than of those who had always been for the king, judging their iniquity double, because they have sinned against so much light, and against so many evidences of Divine Presence going along with and prospering a righteous cause, in the management of which they themselves had a share. [54]

Cromwell could now turn his attention elsewhere; he had wasted time at Pembroke, blind sided by false information. One thing mitigates Cromwell's apparent carelessness in remaining at the siege of Pembroke until after the surrender on 11 July, when he might have been expected to go into the north of England where the Scottish army was daily expected to cross the border. It may be that Cromwell genuinely believed the information he was getting from the castle, and thought that the garrison was so riven that surrender was imminent. However, from a strategic position it seems extraordinary that after his letter to Derby House on 14 June he still waited four weeks, until Poyer surrendered, instead of leaving one of his colonels in charge. The point about the danger in the north was of course constantly being put before him by parliament and Fairfax when they requested that he send troops and regiments northward. Cromwell's decision might have been partly based on the tardiness of the Engager forces which constantly delayed their invasion. It was 8 July before the Engager Army crossed the border, and the siege of Pembroke was in its final stages by this point. Within three days Cromwell was in a position to consider his options. He had dispatched forces northward already, and began to prepare his tired and hungry men for the long march to the north-east of England. Thirty troops went ahead and the foot followed on 14 July as Lambert skirmished with the invaders.

Major General John Lambert had been sent north to command the Northern Association Army by Fairfax in May. Small royalist forces had captured the border fortresses of Carlisle and Berwick-upon-Tweed in late April, and royalist supporters had drifted towards these embryonic garrisons in the intervening weeks, to a total of about 3,500 men. Lambert's forces were smaller and so he shadowed royalist movements on the east side of the Pennines. By mid-June, Lambert still had fewer men than the royalists, but reinforcements were on their way. Cromwell had dispatched five troops and some dragoons before he had invested Pembroke on or around 10 May which were directed towards Lancashire, and by 30 May he had sent Colonel Ewer's regiment and two troops of horse from Colonel Thornhaugh's regiment towards Coventry, en route to the north-east. The units Cromwell sent after the siege took just under a fortnight to reach Lambert, so the reinforcements could have been expected to get to him by the end of May and the middle of June respectively. Recent historians have not fully addressed the reasons for Cromwell's remaining at Pembroke. Alan Marshal simply refers to him being 'delayed', whilst General Kitson does not pass comment at all other than to say that Cromwell was tied down.[55] There is no question that the decision to sit out a siege was the correct one, certainly after the failure of the earlier attempt at a storm. The artillery to hand before early July was simply insufficient to damage 20-foot-thick walls. Any questions relate to Cromwell feeling the need to remain in situ, when he could have delegated the siege to one of his subordinates as he did at Chepstow. It may be that Cromwell saw the position as a dangerous one. His army was ill-supported: food and money were short and that would affect moral. At Gloucester Cromwell had promised 'to live and die with them', and his men had affirmed that they would 'venture their lives and fortunes under his conduct and command'.[56] Also, the siege had required the forces under Cromwell to maintain order in the county when there was a consistent threat of insurrection. This combination of promise and complexity may well have led Cromwell to conclude that in the immediate absence of a Scottish invasion, Lambert could watch the relatively small royalist forces in Berwick and Carlisle as long as reinforcements could be sent regularly, and that he was better placed to command the campaign in South Wales. Of course, his commander in chief, Sir Thomas, now Lord Fairfax, was in the process of doing exactly the same thing over at Colchester, where he remained in command of the siege there until 29 August.

Cromwell returned to England and reached Gloucester before marching towards Warwick, thence to Leicester where he met with a supply of shoes from Northampton and stockings from Coventry. Whilst there on 1 August he was appointed commander in chief of the forces in the north, incorporating the Northern Association forces under Lambert, to whom he wrote ordering him to 'forebear engaging before he came up'.[57] From thence to Nottingham where Poyer and Laugharne were lodged prisoner in the castle. From Nottingham Cromwell marched north via Mansfield and Rotherham to Doncaster in Yorkshire, where he received ammunition from Hull. Cromwell left Doncaster and marched via the siege of the royalist garrison at Pontefract, where he drove the garrison into the castle. Cromwell withdrew experienced men from the leaguer and left behind some of the new recruits who had joined him in the Midlands.

The horse troops Cromwell had sent from Pembroke had reached Lambert on 27 July, and he had shadowed royalist incursions southwards since the beginning of the month and had skirmished with the royalists on 14 and 17 July. Cromwell's instructions at the beginning of August meant that Lambert remained shadowing the Scots without endangering his small army. Meanwhile, the Engager Army under the Duke of Hamilton advanced only slowly into north-west England. Hamilton had remained at Carlisle for six days before advancing as far south as Penrith, where more forces joined him on 14 July, but then after proceeding to Kendal he waited for another week before moving southwards again to Hornby, where a council of war was held on 13 August which finally decided on the route to be taken. An argument occurred between the commander of the horse, Sir James Turner, who favoured crossing the Pennines to Yorkshire where his horse would be able to operate more freely, and Sir William Baillie, who favoured the enclosed countryside of Lancashire to protect his foot against parliamentarian horse. Hamilton sided with Baillie. It was too late. By this time Cromwell had reached Lambert between Wetherby and Knaresborough a day earlier. All of the potential problems caused by the delay Cromwell had played out in June and July were now gone. Cromwell stowed the baggage train in Knaresborough, marched to Skipton and prepared to cross the Pennines. Hamilton's army had grown to about 20,000, including the royalists led by Langdale. There were another 6,000 troops in his rear brought from Ireland by Sir Robert Monro. Cromwell on the other hand had as few as 10,000, including New Model troops, the Northern Association Army and local militias. Nevertheless, Cromwell now opted to attack.

THE BATTLE OF PRESTON

Cromwell and Lambert moved to Otley on the 13 August, and a day later they were at Skipton with scouts probing the valley of the River Ribble on the other side of the Pennines.[58] Langdale, in the van of the invading army, received reports that there were forces moving to his east, but there were also rumours about parliamentarian moves in other parts of the region, including south of the advancing forces, and so no specific action was taken by the army as a whole. Later that day, Langdale moved his forces nearer to the Scots – by this time the parliamentarian advance units were getting closer to him. On 15 August, Cromwell was himself closing in, and his advance units were skirmishing with the enemy. Insufficient notice was being taken of the rumours and initial contacts. Bull and Seed think that Hamilton and the high command simply did not believe that Cromwell was in the area, and certainly would have found it difficult to accept that he would attempt to attack them with so small a force and having marched all that way: he had covered 400 miles before meeting Lambert, and another 60 since.[59] It was not an illogical decision: Cromwell was bold in contrast to his apparent torpor over the past months. In any case, Hamilton's army behaved as if it were moving in friendly territory: the reserves under Monro remained north of Lancaster, the foot were on their way to Preston and north of the River Ribble. The horse were ahead south of the Ribble and heading towards Wigan.

Cromwell held a council of war near Clitheroe at Hodder Bridge. The choices the leaders discussed was to cross into Lancashire ahead of the Scots and bar their route south, or cross and head for Preston and attack them there.[60] The decision was influenced by the belief that Hamilton would stand at Preston and in expectation that Monro was approaching from the north, thus Hamilton might expect more support to join him farther south.

The decision was taken to cross the Hodder Bridge and the army camped at Stoney Hurst Hall nine miles from Preston.[61]

Hamilton's army had about 3,200 troopers in as many as 23 small horse regiments: each should have been 180-men strong in three troops. There were 21 regiments supposedly comprising a minimum of 800 men, with some being larger, but all were undersized and there were probably no more than 11,500 in total. There may have been 20 field artillery pieces. With them was Langdale's forces of English royalists, of about 3,000 foot in nine undersized regiments, and 600 horse. Sir Phillip Musgrave, who had seized Carlisle, also led a small royalist force of no more than 500 horse and 1,500 foot in a number of undersized units.[62] The total allied Scots and royalist forces would have been impressive had the army been enthusiastic and well trained. Moreover, it would have been more so had it not been spread out on a seemingly leisurely march. Nevertheless, at somewhat over 20,000 men the total invasion force still represented a challenge for Cromwell's 11,200 available men in the region.

Cromwell was determined to 'attend the enemies motion' and had already parked the supply train in Knaresborough because it would slow progress through the Pennines. Leaving Stoney Hurst early the following day Cromwell moved towards Preston. He seems to have believed that Hamilton may have heard they were approaching, as he thought that his 'out quarters' were being drawn in to the main army. A forlorn hope of 220 horse and 400 foot was created and the horse sent to within a mile of Preston, where they met with the enemy in 'inclosed ground' on the north and east side of the town and skirmished on a moor with scouts and out (or advance) guards forcing them back before being joined by the forlorn hope foot. This skirmishing was not simply to drive in the outposts, it served to hold the Engager Army in place whilst Cromwell's forces moved up, ensuring that the battle determined on by the Hodder Bridge Council of War would happen. However, the ground matched what Sir James Turner had stressed as his preferred choice. Cromwell described it thus: 'totally inconvenient for our Horse, being all inclosure, and myerye ground'. The road leading to Preston was 'deep and ill', meaning that any soldiers or troopers on it would be below the level of the surrounding ground, which would divide them from the files on either side of the road if a regiment marched down it in a formation broader than the road width and thus would become disordered. If they marched down a sunken road in a column their limited frontage would likewise be vulnerable front and flank and become separated from any flanking regiments.

Two regiments of horse, Harrison's first followed by Cromwell's own (this was now the regiment which had once been Vermuyden's, not part of Cromwell's own regiments which remained with Whalley and Fairfax), were sent down the lane. On the right or north side of the lane were the foot regiments of Reade, Deane and Pride, and to the left or south, were Bright's and Fairfax's. Two foot regiments formed the reserve, the Lancashire militia and Colonel Ashton's. Despite this being enclosed country, there was an attempt to form something approximating an open field battle order, with two regiments of horse arrayed on the right – Thornhaugh's and Twistleton's – and what Cromwell referred to as the remaining horse to the left. There was a further regiment in reserve on the lane. In this formation the army advanced on the invader foot between it and Preston. This was a creative use of the ground: Cromwell mentions the difficulties of the terrain, which had been exacerbated by the appalling weather of the past few weeks that had turned much of the ground into mud. Yet once again Cromwell demonstrated his mastery of the terrain. The sunken lane presented a real problem and would have dangerously divided his foot regiments and exposed them to attack in detail – that is, the possibility of an enemy attack concentrating on one of them with a holding action, making the other unable to offer support without endangering itself by fragmentation when crossing the road. Instead Cromwell was able to use the road for a spearhead of horse in the centre, which would put pressure on the foot ranged against them when pushing down the road into the town when resistance collapsed. It was not easy work, and it must have taken its toll on Harrison's regiment in the four-hour battle to defeat Langdale – Cromwell makes it clear that Harrison's regiment led the attack down the lane, but when the attack on the town took place later, it played the supporting role to Cromwell's regiment which had been seconding Harrison in the initial fighting.[63]

The regiments Cromwell was facing on the morning of 17 August were those commanded by Langdale, which by now was covering the rear of Hamilton's foot, having progressively moved closer to it since running into Cromwell's scouts a day or so earlier. A fairly small rearguard of Scottish horse regiments was approaching Langdale's left, but there were no horse units available on his right flank to oppose Cromwell's horse. Moreover, the bulk of the Scottish foot were south of Langdale and facing away from him crossing the Ribble via the bridge in Preston and still, at the point of Cromwell's contact with Langdale, intent on marching southwards. Even after some discussion, Hamilton was convinced that only skirmishers from Cromwell's advance guard and not his whole army were involved in the fighting.[64] Because of the misapprehension, the Engager foot continued to cross the bridge to the south bank of the Ribble, and it would take some time to get them turned around. Once it became clear that the attack was serious, the Engager commanders decided that Lambert could firstly hold off the attacking New Model Army in a fighting withdrawal which would bring his forces towards the bridge and unite them with the Scots and hold the line of the river.[65]

According to Cromwell's published account, the fighting in the opening stages of the battle was most intense in the centre both on the lane and to each side of it as well as on the left of Cromwell's army, clearly taking its toll on Harrison's horse. For a time it must have seemed that the plan to hold Cromwell back and withdraw to the line of the Ribble was working: the author of *A Letter from Holland* considered that 'Sir Marmaduke his soldiers assisted with some of the Scottish Horse, seemed hard enough for the enemy, who severall times were glad to retreat'.[66] It took four hours for the foot regiments, facing 'stiff and sturdy resistance', to press Langdale back. As the afternoon drew to a close, Langdale had reached the outer edge of Preston and was in a good defensive position with the small stream called Eves Brook, where he established a line three-quarters of a mile long between Pope Lane and Hope Slack. The right flank was somewhat in the air and was outflanked as the fighting developed. Nevertheless, the relentless pressure of Cromwell's spearheaded attack line told, and Langdale was pushed back on to Preston itself.

When Cromwell reached Preston four troops of his regiment, now supported by Thomas Harrison's, pushed into the town where they cleared the streets. The hard fighting en route to the town seems to have resulted in Cromwell's horse supplanting Harrison's regiment at the head of the column. Cromwell later commented that Langdale made skilful use of reserve forces as he retreated and constantly threatened Cromwell's right, ensuring that to secure himself Cromwell could not bring all of his forces to bear on the royalists as they headed for the bridge.[67] However, it is probable that Cromwell was mistaking confusion for good management and saw it as a planned introduction of Scottish regiments into the fight. Cromwell himself hardly mentioned Scottish regiments in his description of the fighting at Preston, and others mentioned only lancers when talking about the Scottish horse, so it would seem that the regiments on Langdale's left may have been light cavalry who had been part of the scouting and covering forces in the rear of the advancing army. After describing the close-quarter fight by the Lancashire Trained Bands and Fairfax's foot regiment who forced the bridge,

Cromwell did refer to Hamilton retreating southwards from the town and the events of the ensuing evening in which Hamilton continued southwards. However, the entry into the town and the capture of the bridge there had been so swift that the Scottish command had been cut off on the north bank of the river, and with some horse, possibly Hamilton's lifeguard, had to charge the advancing parliamentarians three times to get the necessary space to find a safe point to ford the swollen Ribble. It was not just Hamilton who was endangered, for the Scottish foot which had been belatedly and reluctantly sent to support Langdale were also trapped and unable to cross the river or attempt to follow the Scottish horse in their march north towards Lancaster to try and join Monro. Many of them were, alongside their royalist allies, captured where they stood.

The fighting had been so hard that Cromwell acknowledged he failed to pursue the duke as closely as he might.[68] The forces sent after Hamilton were led by Colonel John Thornhaugh, formerly of the Nottingham garrison, who was killed in the pursuit, but they succeeded in slowing the Scots down near Wigan, only to see them retreat into the town without offering battle (although a few skirmishes occurred in the vicinity of Wigan). The following day Cromwell pursued the enemy southwards towards Warrington. There the final major fight of the campaign was at Winnick Pass, where the Scots held back Cromwell's horse vanguard for some time and at some point even pushed back the foot when it arrived. It was in vain, for the New Model Army overcame the opposition and drove the Scottish foot back into Warrington. There Sir William Baillie surrendered the foot with the agreement of the officers and because the foot soldiers, 'tired with an incessant March', would not obey orders.[69] Just over 3,000 survivors who had stayed with their colours, of no less than 20 of the 21 foot regiments Hamilton had led into England, surrendered. Only Hamilton's lifeguard were there, the rest of the horse regiments were scattered to the south and north of Warrington.

As Alan Marshall argued in 2004, the battle of Preston allows us to judge Cromwell's generalship in the round. General Kitson plays up Cromwell's luck in the campaign, especially in coming into contact with Langdale's forces first because they were the most formidable forces in the invading army and defeating them may have sealed the fate of the invasion as a whole. But both he and Marshall think that the decision to attack and destroy Hamilton's army in detail taken at Hodder Bridge was masterly.[70] Kitson's overall conclusion is that Cromwell's campaign and battle lacked finesse, but that he capitalised on the experience and training of his forces. Marshall is more generous, seeing

Cromwell as being able simultaneously to manage a battle and keep the wider strategic issues in mind, as shown by his attempts and efforts to keep parts of Hamilton's forces from going north to join Monro.[71] It is clear that Cromwell had shown great skill in the campaign and in the battle. Pembroke and Preston could not be divided. From the information Cromwell received he calculated that Lambert could deal initially with any situation in the north which arose in the short term. This confidence was, however, tempered by drip-feeding regiments, which he did not need for the developing siege, northwards to support Lambert's operations. Cromwell made the right decision; it is possible that had anyone else who was available in mid-July 1648 tried to lead the hungry and badly equipped men from South Wales on a 400-mile march on the promise of shoes and clothes in the Midland and ammunition in South Yorkshire, they may have met with the reaction Bailie met at Warrington. Cromwell's speech at Gloucester helped ensure that his army would follow him on that long trek and on again into battle against an enemy superior in numbers. It was a masterful campaign, planned carefully and executed successfully by Cromwell up to Hodder Bridge when this first stage came to an end. The decision taken at Hodder Bridge to attack a larger enemy force and prevent even more forces joining the main army was bold. True, as Kitson and others point out, Hamilton and his headquarters was not as competent nor as imaginative or well informed as Cromwell, but Langdale was no fool and he was better informed, if not believed. Cromwell could not have known this, but he would have known that Langdale was a competent and experienced commander. However, the important issue was that Langdale was not conjoined with Hamilton at the point at which Cromwell chose to attack, and this probably explains why Cromwell mistakenly believed that the enemy was deliberately carefully feeding reserves on to the moors north of Preston and reacted with caution as a result. On the other hand, Cromwell had reasonable intelligence of the numbers and quality of the forces which confronted him as the battle began, and seems to have decided to launch a particularly forceful assault with a unique formation that not only ameliorated the difficult terrain but turned it to his advantage by creating a spearheaded formation to hammer at the enemy's centre. Once the hard fight in the centre was over, this spearhead was able to push into the town and fragment the enemy decisively. Cromwell by his own admission was slow to launch a thorough pursuit, but this was not his fault: the army was exhausted by the fighting, never mind by the 450 mile march which had preceded it. Moreover, he would have heard that the enemy was in chaos after the Scottish horse, which had been ordered back from Wigan, took the route via Chorley and thus missed Hamilton and the foot which was retreating southwards via the Standish road. This made the job of pursuit easier because the lack of coordination hindered Sir Thomas Middleton's ability to cover the retreat. Within days the horse had again abandoned the foot to their fate and Cromwell's reinvigorated pursuit was made much easier.

The war in the north-west became something of a policing operation as the scattered remnants of the crushed invasion force were rounded up in the North Midlands and taken into captivity.[72] The news of the momentous defeat reached Colchester and made clear to the royalist commanders in the town that there was no hope of either a rescue by Hamilton's army itself, nor of any dramatic change of fortune in the war which could induce Fairfax to call off his siege. Colchester surrendered on 27 August, three days after the news of Preston and Warrington reached the defenders. For the time being Scarborough and Pontefract held out, but the second civil war was over and switched from being a military process to a political one, in which Cromwell was intimately involved, and which would take him on a journey well beyond the limits of his previous experiences.

8

CROMWELL ALONE: IRELAND, 1648–9

Cromwell completed the Preston campaign with an advance northwards to tackle Monro's forces, leaving the mopping up operations in the Midlands to others. Scottish and other forces which had been in the rear of Hamilton's army withdrew to the Scottish border with Cromwell in pursuit. There was another development in the wake of the duke's defeat which changed the focus of Cromwell's follow-up campaign. The creation of the Engager Army had been controversial, and whilst the estates had reluctantly endorsed the Engagement the Kirk had not, with the result that although the Engager 'party' held the balance of power it was weak, and as many of its proponents had been with the invasion force it was weakened further once Hamilton crossed the border. With the defeat at Preston, the impetus for rejecting the Engagement grew, particularly in the south-west where there was a popular rising, but there was support in Edinburgh from leaders of the Kirk Party, including the Marquis of Argyll. The Mauchline rising in the south-west turned into a march on Edinburgh led by Lord Leven and David Leslie, but the Engagers were not finished yet and the marchers were confronted and defeated at Stirling: for a time this, the Whiggamore raid stalled. Meanwhile, Cromwell had been ordered to retake Carlisle and Berwick and had crossed into the north-east of England. The northern royalist cause began to implode and smaller garrisons fell to Cromwell's army. Monro refused all entreaties to stay in England and retreated to Scotland, basing his forces at Stirling. Cromwell marched via Durham, Newcastle, Morpeth and Alnwick, then crossed the border. This action was crucial in bringing about discussions between Engagers and the Kirk Party who both feared the English, and particularly what they saw as the sectarian New Model Army.[1] The discussions only really opened the way for the Engagers, once they had acknowledged that they did not rule the country, to be purged from government. Cromwell marched to Edinburgh where the Kirk Party reluctantly welcomed him. Both Carlisle and Berwick were surrendered to the English and Monro was ordered to return to Ireland.[2] Cromwell received an apparently friendly welcome in Edinburgh during early October, and he reciprocated by approving of the new regime, leaving two regiments of horse and some dragoons behind to defend the new governors whilst they set about creating an army of their own when he left the capital. Some people had misunderstood the seemingly close relationship between Cromwell, Argyll and other leading Kirk men, assuming later that they had been conspiring to remove the king.[3] This was not the case. Upon leaving Edinburgh, Cromwell returned to England and paid a second visit to the ongoing siege of Pontefract, where the Leveller colonel, Thomas Rainsborough, had been killed in what appears to have been a bungled attempt to capture him by the royalist garrison. Cromwell decided to stay. This decision has puzzled observers for over three and a half centuries, for it was during this sojourn that a revolution developed in England and Wales that would impact upon the British Isles and eventually propel Cromwell to the position of head of state.

The second civil war had been a cataclysmic event, and had consequences no one had foreseen. English and Welsh Presbyterian MPs were panicked into thinking that there was no chance of political stability, unless there could be a quick and simple agreement with the king which would head off any other internal or external threat. Therefore, despite his double defeat, the king was approached with a view to such a treaty. On the other hand, several of the New Model Army commanders, including Cromwell and his son-in-law Henry Ireton, had been appalled that they had to risk their lives and fortunes to fight again for the victory they had won in 1646. Their reaction was diametrically opposed to that of the Presbyterians. During the Putney debates a year earlier, both Cromwell and Ireton had tried to close down the more radical discussions which had both redefined the nature of the civil war and proposed a more revolutionary settlement that did not embrace a monarchy as part of the solution. The radicals had defined the king, at least himself if not the monarchy, as the source of crisis rather than the issue of balancing the powers of political institutions. To them there was little point in shuffling responsibilities: the system itself simply would not work if the monarch retained power and authority which could never be controlled by parliament.

The Engagement and second civil war had seemingly provided evidence of that truth, for the king, whilst to all intents and purposes a prisoner with his political power in abeyance, had nevertheless negotiated a treaty with Scotland and inspired if not directly commissioned the raising of forces in rebellion across the four nations. Faced with this, Ireton and others had shifted their position somewhat and were openly discussing the more radical solutions they had rejected in 1647. The death of the king, now referred to as a 'man of blood', was seen as the only means by which the blood spilt during the wars could be atoned and peace restored. Levellers petitioned for the abolition of the House of Lords, but peace negotiations were continued with the imprisoned king. Charles did not help his fortunes, for he was again confident that the situation could be turned in his favour because of an apparently optimistic situation in Ireland. This would all be shown to be nonsense, but it further underlined the inescapable truth that the king, if not the monarchy, was a liability. In all of this Cromwell appeared to play no role. Ireton proposed that the army occupy London and in the meantime began drafting a remonstrance on its behalf. The lord general's father had died earlier that year and he had assumed the title and seems to have been remained aloof from either the conservative or radical milieu around him. Ireton's *Remonstrance of the Army* proposed that parliament be purged, negotiations with the king be terminated and Charles be brought to trial. The 25,000-word document demonstrated what the radicals had argued at Putney: the king had rejected every proposal put to him since the beginning of 1642, including those recently discussed at Carisbrooke, and he had broken every agreement since the Treaty of Berwick in 1639. The remonstrance was discussed at an Army Council that Fairfax assembled at St Albans on 7 November. After four days the council found the remonstrance too radical and instead decided to approach the king directly, only to see him reject their proposals once again just as the radicals knew he would. Ireton was disappointed with the outcome and he began to talk to the Levellers, but they did not want to bring the king to trial. Fairfax, faced with the king's intransigence, turned back to the remonstrance; the council now accepted it and presented it to parliament. The Commons, frightened by its radicalism, set it aside. In response the army marched on London, and Fairfax ordered the king be brought to the city too. Parliament defied the army and declared the seizure of the king illegal. As a result of this challenge, the army plotted a purge of parliament. On 7 December, Lord Grey of Groby and Colonel Thomas Pride stood at the doors of the House of Commons and vetted the MPs as they came in: 186 were refused entry, 41 were arrested and a further 56 stayed away.

Only 154 MPs now constituted the Commons. Nevertheless, it had business to do, including establishing a High Court of Justice to try the king.[4]

All this time Cromwell remained at the siege of Pontefract, which both before and after the death of Rainsborough had been somewhat of a dilatory affair under the command of Sir Henry Cholmley, who had refused to give way to Rainsborough when he was sent by Fairfax to take charge. Cromwell took charge immediately, requesting ammunition and supplies for the siege there and at Scarborough.[5] On 9 November he sent a summons to the castle: it was refused.[6] The pay of the soldiers engaged in the siege was behind hand and Cromwell sought to get them the pay they were owed and lend the commander in the field, Colonel Charles Fairfax, £100 of his own; he also sought to retain soldiers that had been provided by Lincolnshire and Leicestershire.[7] On 15 November, Cromwell tried to impress upon Derby House the 'true state of this garrison' believing that the executive (the committee at Derby House) believed that the siege was all but won. The castle was strong and well supplied and the besieging forces needed three regiments of foot and two of horse, 500 barrels of gunpowder, match and bullets as well as a siege battery and mortars with appropriate ammunition. What it is important to note is that Cromwell, whilst directing Charles Fairfax's operations and working to try and persuade parliament to support him, was not committing any of his own regiments to the siege itself, although they were involved in the extended operation of protecting the besiegers and controlling the countryside around.[8] Cromwell was of course still the commander of all the forces in the north of England – the role he had been given when on his way north to deal with Hamilton – and still had influence in parliament. Parliament voted to provide the required resources just two days later. However, Cromwell's absence from the centre of events in the vicinity of London remains a puzzle. W.C. Abbott may have been a little harsh when he suggests that Cromwell served no purpose at Pontefract. It was true that he did not bring about the end of the siege, nor did his troops make any great contribution to it, but he was acting as commander in the north, restructuring the defences of important garrisons as well as ensuring that Charles Fairfax had the materiel he needed; the same was true over at Scarborough, where he also boosted the besieging forces. Furthermore, with the present danger of sea-born attack, Hull was strengthened, and so on. These were things which were arguably easier to do in near situ than from London. No doubt he was also waiting for the return of the regiments loaned to the Marquis of Argyll so that his army could be reassembled if necessary.

The very next day, following Pride's (and Grey's) Purge, Cromwell arrived in London. He approved of what had been done by his commander and his son-in-law during the past month. It would not be true to say that Cromwell had been fully absent from the proceedings of October and November. He had explained his position to his cousin, Robert Hammond, King Charles's scrupled 'gaoler' on the Isle of Wight; he was aware of the radical positions being taken by the soldiers under his command, and he had made his righteous anger at the seemingly hurried and craven settlement clear to Derby House. We can see his attitudes to the progress of events developing in line with those evident amongst the commanders closer to London and even with the cautious Fairfax, but what we do not know is what role he played in marshalling them. Cromwell's letters to Robert Hammond are interesting. Hammond was not likely to have been completely sympathetic and he would defy the order to send the king to London, claiming that he needed parliament's order, probably knowing that this would not come as he expected the pre-purge parliament would declare the move illegal. As a result of his scruples, Fairfax had to replace him with Colonel Ewer. Cromwell may not had realised that this was the case, however, when he wrote a loosely coded letter to Hammond on 6 November, suggesting that he was drifting closer to Leveller arguments and had rejected the Presbyterian stance on peace-making with the king. When later in the month Hammond was troubled by his conscience – he was actually about to be replaced when he had written to Cromwell (he had been recalled before the letter was sent) – Cromwell urged him to trust the lord and told him that their cause was clearly in line with God's expectations.[9] As for the army's attitude to the progress of postwar politics, Cromwell wrote to Lord Fairfax that he was aware of the 'great zeal to have impartial justice done upon Offenders; and [he wrote] I must confess, I do in all, from my heart, concur with them'. He also enclosed the petitions and letter he had received to that effect. That was on 20 November, the day the Commons received the remonstrance.[10] Cromwell was in agreement with the sentiments regarding just punishment. That very day he sent an angry letter to the Committee of Compounding which dealt with the financial aspects of fines and other impositions on parliament's enemies and had done since 1643. The spark for Cromwell's outburst was an order from the governor of Nottingham, John Hutchinson, to enable the royalist, Sir John Owen, leader of the rebellion in North Wales, to travel to London to compound for his estates. Cromwell pointed out that Owen amongst others had been a traitor who had conspired to subject England to Scottish domination: 'a more prodigious Treason than any that had been perpetrated before', and moreover 'their fault who have appeared in this summer's business is certainly double to those that were in the first [civil war], because it is the repetition of the same offence against all the witness God had borne'. He was also angry because the fines that were being imposed were only a little more severe than those imposed on the men who had surrendered Oxford at the end of the first war, when they posed little danger as opposed to Owen who nearly 'brought you to ruin'.[11] Quite simply, Cromwell and his men thought that parliament was not serious enough about bringing an end to the conflict and that radical measures were necessary.

Once back in London and Westminster, Cromwell played a full role in the developments, just as Fairfax began to bow out. Ireton concentrated on creating a new *Agreement of the People* with the Levellers and a group of other MPs; parliament itself was suspended until 12 December. Cromwell seems to have been involved in developing the plans for the king's trial. On 23 December he argued in the house that to do so normally would have made traitors of them all, but now God had brought them to this course of action. Whilst some argued that there was no constitutional precedent for such a trial, officers, Cromwell included, argued that radical action needed to be taken by such constitutional bodies as were able. In early January the proposals for the trial passed the Commons and went to the Lords which, as expected, rejected them. The radical action was taken a step further and the Commons declared itself to be the supreme representative of the people; the Lords were simply sidelined at this point and the High Court was established by the authority of the Commons alone. The king was brought to trial on 21 January, and following a series of public and private sittings found guilty of treason against the people and sentenced to death. Cromwell's name was third on the list of signatories to the death warrant following that of the court's president, John Bradshaw, and because of social precedence the only regicidal holder of an aristocratic title, Lord Grey of Groby. Charles I, King of Great Britain, was executed by the new 'acting' executive power in one of his three kingdoms on 30 January 1649.

On 31 January 1649 the new acting powers had to construct a nation. Ireland was incorporated into the new state as it was a subsidiary kingdom of the monarch from whom the new state had 'inherited'. Scotland of course was regarded as a separate nation and in theory at least able to make its own decisions regarding the monarchy; it chose to declare Prince Charles its king. Over the next weeks and months the new state consolidated the dramatic changes which the 'revolution' of November 1648–January 1649 had initiated.

The House of Lords was formally abolished on 17 March 1649, and two days later the monarchy was likewise abolished. In May the implications of the latter were confirmed when England, Wales and Ireland were proclaimed a commonwealth and free state.

Not surprisingly the revolutionary state had enemies, and the free state and commonwealth was beset by them as soon as it came into existence. Cromwell had played a prominent part in enacting the king's trial. Even if we ignore the flagrant attempts after the Restoration of the monarchy in 1660 to claim that he had forced several signatories to put their names to Charles I's death warrant, he had quelled a mini moral panic amongst the trial commissioners and had been singled out by the masked women who interrupted the trial by claiming that he was a traitor backed by less than a quarter of the people. Even though more experienced politicians crept back into Westminster after the king was dead, intent on playing a role in government if not in the act which had created that government, Cromwell was appointed the first president of the Council of State, the executive body established on 7 February 1649. The council comprised three soldiers – Fairfax, Cromwell and Skippon – five peers and 33 statesmen to govern the commonwealth. Gradually Lord General Fairfax stepped out of the limelight; indeed it had been his wife who had shouted at Cromwell during the trial, but he was to remain the commander of the army for another 16 months.

As the council grappled with what the state should be called and who should govern it, it also had to turn to the matter of the threats towards it. Essentially there were three. The first set was internal: royalists of course were vengeful, but they had recently been defeated in war and were physically, financially and morally exhausted. They might have felt that there was a sense of revulsion towards the execution of the king which could give them some popular support, and intellectually (after the publication of *Eikon Basilica*, the tract supposedly written by the king shortly before his death), there was a groundswell of sympathy. Nevertheless, the country was exhausted by war and the constant need to pay for it and the wars in Ireland, and it could not be expected that a popular rising would occur soon – after all, those rising in the south-east a year earlier had been crushed ruthlessly and some of the participants had been less than enthusiastic when the going had got tough once the New Model Army intervened. The royalists could hope for the state to collapse and leave a vacuum which they might fill, and here they might have felt more optimistic. The impetus which had brought about the revolution was not universally military, even if in the end it seemed that only the battle-hardened soldiers had the stomach for revolutionary action. Independent politicians had supported the purge of parliament, even if some balked at regicide. The Levellers too had set the groundwork for some of the political solutions and propositions and had joined the army and politicians in drafting a new constitution on the eve of the revolution. However, the leading Leveller, John Lilburne, and others rejected the notion of regicide, especially if the result was the creation of a new tyrannical regime in the form of a dictatorship of the military. Moreover, the second *Agreement of the People* had been set aside during the trial of the king, and come February neither parliament nor the Council of State was inclined to take it up again. The man who might have championed it at the Council, Henry Ireton, had been nominated to sit on it but this been not approved by parliament. Lilburne in any case declared that the *Agreement* was tainted by military influence and rejected it: and work began on a third draft. By now, however, in effect the Levellers were alienated from all elements of the army leadership and this had implications for the Levellers in the officer and other ranks who were beginning to feel as they had been left out of the revolution. There was a serious risk of mutiny in some quarters.

Secondly, there was a greater threat from external forces across the Irish Sea. Royalists might, as Charles had done late in 1648, have derived some hope from developments in the Irish situation. The Marquis of Ormond had gone back there with instructions to unite the royalists and confederate forces. A treaty had been agreed on the eve of the king's trial, although the Ulster confederate army and its general, Owen Roe O'Neill, had not agreed to the deal and would not do so for some months. Whilst Dublin and its extensive harbour at Ringsend remained in the hands of parliament's forces under Michael Jones, there were other ports such as Wexford which could act as bases for royalist ships and ports of embarkation whenever it became possible to send troops from Ireland to Britain to support or lead the royalist cause. By the middle of 1649 the allied royalist and confederate forces were on the offensive, besieging Jones in Dublin and determined to seize the Irish capital and its port.

The third threat was also foreign, but closer to home. There was a third kingdom within the British Isles with an interest in the fortunes of the royalists. Henry Guthrie had been extremely wide of the mark when he assumed that Cromwell and Argyll were plotting to overthrow the monarchy. Argyll, the Kirk Party and the Scottish political world were aghast at the presumption of the New Model Army and its murder of their monarch. Delegates of the estates had been in London during the trial trying to put a case for mediation, but they had been ignored. When the news of the king's death reached Edinburgh, Charles, Prince of Wales, was proclaimed at the Mercat Cross by St Giles' Cathedral. Negotiations with the exiled prince were opened and the estates began to discuss how they could avenge the king.

Beset by these enemies, the General Council of the Army met on 23 March 1649, two days after the surrender of Pontefract, to discuss the threats to the new free state's existence. Cromwell had been offered the command of the army for Ireland a week earlier by the Council of State but had not committed himself to an answer. At this historic meeting he not only confirmed that he would take up the post but laid out his reasons why. Although this speech laid out the state's priorities as Cromwell saw them, in effect it also laid out the course of Cromwell's remaining military career; although he knew the former, he could not have seen the latter.

Cromwell memorably said:

> I had rather be over-run by a Cavalierish interest than a Scotch interest; I had rather be over-run with a Scotch interest than an Irish interest; and I think of all, this is the most dangerous, and if they shall be able to carry on with this work they will make this the most miserable people on earth.[12]

Before coming to this point, he had indicated why he felt the Scots were an issue. Like all the other enemies the Scots had not understood the nature of the lessons God had laid before all – that the victory of parliament and the subsequent revolution were successful because they conformed to God's will. Instead they railed against the army in particular as 'an army of sectaries, which you see all their papers do declare their quarrel to be against'.[13] But more problematic was 'disunion amongst ourselves'. This would allow the royalists – what Cromwell meant by the label 'a great party', or perhaps the Levellers who were stirring up trouble within the army itself – to raise a rebellion. As for Ireland, Cromwell listed the troops ranged against the commonwealth in the three provinces where there was an important parliamentarian force: Connacht, Leinster and Ulster. As in Scotland there was a desire to have the Prince of Wales as king. Cromwell's reverse listing placed Ireland at the top of the priorities, but in reality it was to be second for the internal dissent needed to be dealt with first as it would buy time to defeat the other two enemies, which in turn would further remove hope from royalists in England and Wales by denying them external support.

The internal threats had to be tackled in several ways. Firstly there was the tidying up after the second civil war. Cromwell and others had called loudly for vengeance against the royalists and former parliamentarians who had brought about the war. Fairfax had been more direct in having Sir Charles Lucas and

Sir Gervaise Lisle shot after the siege of Colchester. There were others languishing in prisons who had to be dealt with, although Henry Hastings, Lord Loughborough, who should have been amongst these men, had managed to escape from Windsor Castle. These representatives of the 'Cavalierish interest' included principal royalists who were arraigned before the High Court of Justice in early March 1649. Following their trials, Lord Capel, the Earl of Holland the leaders of the Essex rebellion and the Duke of Hamilton, commander of the Engager Army, were executed. The Levellers were targeted too: six days after Cromwell warned about internal disunity and the day after he and colleagues were arrested by two complete regiments of foot, John Lilburne was brought before the Council of State to answer charges that they had encouraged mutiny in the army in his pamphlet, the second part of the tract *England's New Chains Discovered*, in which he and William Walwyn argued that the army had simply replaced the king as a tyrant and that the new government was as bad as that of Charles I. The Council was most concerned, not so much by the accusations in the pamphlet, but by the apparent call for parliament to prevent the army from dominating politics, which the Council of State read as an exhortation to soldiers and others to overthrow the council and parliament. Although Lilburne and Walwyn were both sent to the Tower of London, parliament was careful to ensure that they would be tried under established Common Law rather than any newly wrought authority. The council's concern was not without foundation: the next month a threatened mutiny had to be suppressed in the Strand and a soldier, Robert Lockyer, was executed. His funeral attracted massive civilian crowds bedecked in Leveller emblems. There were other stranger happenings. As Cromwell and other planned for the Irish campaign, small groups of landless people set up communes including one on St George's Common near London. These Diggers or True Levellers set up their colonies on wasteland, declaring the earth to be a common treasury with resources to be shared by all mankind. In case they could be a dangerous precedent, Lord Fairfax personally investigated the St George's colony during April only to decide they were largely harmless. Even more outlandish to some observers were the petitions drafted by women and presented to parliament on 25 April and 5 May. More threatening was the publication of a third draft of *The Agreement of the People* on 1 May. In this heady atmosphere sections of the army declared their support for the Levellers.

By this time Cromwell was assembling the army for the Irish campaign and regiments were moving towards western ports. En route some horse regiments stopped at Salisbury where they mutinied. Others mutinied at Banbury and posed a serious threat to the army's integrity. Understanding this, Cromwell and Fairfax gathered loyal regiments, and on 14 May marched towards Burford in Oxfordshire where the Leveller soldiers had established themselves. The army marched quickly, covering 50 miles in a day and catching the rebels in their beds. The commanders were in no mood to brook the demands of the rebels and would-be negotiators were swept aside. The fight was brief: Cromwell and Fairfax took control of the town quickly and the rebels surrendered. Four hundred were taken prisoner, of which four were tried and found guilty of mutiny and three of them were shot. The mutiny was effectively ended by this sharp action which also marked the beginning of the end of the power of the Levellers. Moreover, Cromwell and Fairfax's decisive stroke had, if it not ended the threat from all internal enemies, at least neutralised them for the time being. The republic could now turn its attention elsewhere and Cromwell could concentrate upon the forthcoming campaign in Ireland.

IRELAND

Cromwell had enumerated the number of units he needed to take with him to Ireland at the council meeting in March: eight regiments of foot and 3,000 horse.[14] A total of 12,000 were to be embarked. The invasion force was selected and dispatched for embarkation: four regiments of horse (Ireton's, Horton's, Scroope's and Lambert's), four of foot (Hewson's, Deane's, Cooke's and Ewer's) and five companies of the regiment of dragoons led by Major Abbott. But Scroope's regiment was one of those which mutinied en route and was disbanded. Lambert's was left in England and Colonel John Reynolds's regiment was sent instead and a new regiment was established for Cromwell. Likewise the foot regiments were reorganised and some sent ahead to reinforce Jones at Dublin.[15]

The target of Cromwell's campaign was Munster and the south of Ireland, and indeed part of the army under Henry Ireton had initially sailed to the south coast whilst Cromwell headed for Ringsend. But whilst Jones's victory at Rathmines on 2 August had rendered Ringsend a safe harbour, no such port could be found for Ireton and so he joined his father-in-law in Dublin Bay. Dublin was now safe from immediate danger, but there were still a large number of potential armies for Ormond to forge into an effective challenge, and the northern approaches to Dublin were still in the hands of the confederate/royalist alliance chiefly because they held the fortified town of

Drogheda less than 30 miles away. The garrison in the town was led by the experienced Sir Arthur Aston, who was confident that his garrison presented a challenge for any potential besieger. He had grounds for this. The town had strong walls around both the English town north of the River Boyne and the Irish town to the south of the river. Drogheda had resisted a long siege in the early days of the Irish rebellion and had remained until recently in the hands of forces loyal to parliament. Aston knew that he could buy time for Ormond to assemble his forces and deflect Cromwell from marching into southern Ireland.[16] For Cromwell, targeting Drogheda would mean that there was access from Leinster into Ulster, but it would also provide protection to the rear and supply areas when he was able to turn his attention southwards.

THE STORMING OF DROGHEDA

Cromwell was in a foreign country for only the third time in his life: the first time had been less than a year ago when he had marched to Edinburgh. Hitherto his entire life had been spent in England, where he had been born, and briefly in Wales, where his ancestry and, since the war, some of his estates lay. He set out to create a good impression with a published speech at Dublin which warned his officers and men not to 'do any wrong or violence towards Country People' and not to meddle with their goods, unless they were soldiers or office holders for the enemy.[17] Michael O'Siochru is quite right to see this an attempt to buy a form of quiescence from the wider population. Oliver Cromwell was going to be in foreign or enemy country for some time. Even if he genuinely intended to pay for everything his army consumed, slept in or fed to their horses, then he needed people to provide it and not secret it away.[18] Yet Cromwell was seen (then as now) as coming to Ireland with a sword in one hand and an English vernacular bible in the other to extirpate the Roman Catholic religion, not just as a military and political power but as a religion. Were this truly the case, then he might just have been content to be more ruthless in the collection of the necessary supplies. There were precedents on the continent. But Cromwell was trying hard to ensure that his men were paid and supplied as the campaign against Drogheda was advanced. On 1 September the march on Drogheda got under way, with Cromwell leading up to 12,000 horse and foot north. On the first night the army was at Ballygarth having moved 20 miles, where it was joined by some horse who had abandoned Ormond. As the siege artillery arrived by sea, Cromwell reached Drogheda on 2 September and immediately set up lines within musket-shot – under 300 yards – of the walls. Marshall believes that Cromwell was not a master of sieges. His record was patchy: Pembroke had taken weeks to break, Pontefract had not yielded to Cromwell at all. Even when he was not in charge, his record was not great: true, Bristol had fallen, but York had not done so until after Marston Moor and Oxford was a long, drawn-out affair. On the other hand Cromwell was good at storming garrisons. Bristol and Basing House were evidence of that; and short sieges where the enemy had little time to prepare, like Leicester, had given Cromwell experience of quick success. He was determined that Drogheda was to be an example of the latter: although Aston had prepared the already strong defences of the town, Cromwell had arranged for siege artillery to be present right at the start, and four days were spent in unloading the guns from the ships and mounting siege batteries opposite the southern section of the defences. Aston could do little to disrupt the process; he had no artillery to keep the heads of the engineers down as they laboured. A party was sent out to try and disrupt the process, but it was driven back and attempts to spy on the works were prevented when a lieutenant was captured on such a mission. Drogheda was and still is a town and port built on both the north and south banks of the River Boyne – connected by several bridges now, but by just one drawbridge in 1649. Large, somewhat dated walls, 20 feet high and six feet thick in places, surrounded both sections of the town: there were 19 towers and seven fortified gates. The south had seven towers and five gates, and it had a defended citadel at the heart of its fortifications.[19] This was the strongest part of the town's defences and was Cromwell's chief target. Although both parts of the town rise above the Boyne, the southern part with its fortified mount is higher that the northern part. If Cromwell could initially take even this part of the town its height could be used to dominate the exposed northern side. The batteries took several days to prepare, the tract *Two Letters, One from Dublin in Ireland, the Other from Liverpoole or A Bloody Fight Ireland at the Taking of Drogheda*, suggests that 6 and 7 September was taken up with this and the developing of trenches known as approaches which crept closer and closer to the town; this continued for a further two days. On 10 September the artillery, based in two batteries – one facing the south wall and the other facing the south-west wall – began to fire from less than 400 yards. Targets included the citadel on the mount, but chiefly the walls close to St Mary's Church to the south-west. Cromwell said that on the first day he destroyed the church steeple and one of the towers on the wall.[20] He had sent in a summons, and in his later letter to Lenthall said he received no satisfactory reply. In fact Aston had peremptorily rejected the call and sent out another raiding party.[21] The threat to the wall's integrity was recognised by the defenders and they constructed several earthworks within the town in preparation for an attack on the breach. Cromwell was prepared to take it slowly and enter the town piecemeal. If his men could siege St Mary's then they could hold it against a counter-attack and from there move on the mount and towards the north. The guns renewed their firing on 11 September and this time managed to finish the job of breaking down the walls.[22] At about 5.00 pm on 11 September Cromwell launched the attack: it was no mean feat, for the attackers on the south-west wall had to cross a ravine which gave the walls a natural dry moat. There were two brigaded regiments assigned to each attack. Colonel Ewer's regiment was paired with Colonel Castle's foot in the attack on the Duleek Gate, which spanned the Dublin Road's entrance into the town, and the tenalia between it and the south-west corner tower. Colonel John Hewson's regiment, with experience of successfully storming Bridgewater and Bristol, attacked the eastern walls. Moreover, both the attack on the south gate and the south-west wall had to face earthworks within. In both his letter to William Lenthall and the one to John Bradshaw, Cromwell made out that the garrison made a 'stout resistance' and disputed it 'very stiffly with us', no doubt from within the interior trenches. The tenalia and the neighbouring south-west tower were captured, but the gate into the town from the rear of the tenalia was so clogged with dead bodies it could not be used to get into the town. Colonel Castle was shot in the head and killed and the man in charge of the defences, the appropriately named Colonel Garret Wall, was also killed. Castle's men were not deterred, but Wall's men were shaken. The attackers on the east side were driven out of the walls at one point, but a brigade of two more regiments, Venables's and Farre's led by Cromwell, joined Hewson's men. It was this second attack which succeeded: Cromwell's decision to accompany Farre and Venables was crucial. Aston was ready with his horse to drive the attackers out, but the very trenches which had made it so hard to get into the town now made it impossible for the defenders to use horse against the newly entrenched parliamentarian foot which made good use of the earthworks. By this means the attackers were able to hold on to the corner of the south town and bring more and more forces into it. The next target was the citadel, which proved hard to assault, but momentum was on the parliamentarian side. Once the Mill Mount had been climbed the defenders were trapped. According to Cromwell not only was no quarter offered to the defenders, but Cromwell had ordered his men not to offer any. Quarter had been offered to defenders in the initial attack but that had been rejected, and it may have been that the hard fighting had reminded Cromwell of the arrogant attitude of Aston's rejection of his summons.[23] Whatever the case, Aston had been directing the defence in the southern town and was now cornered in the citadel on Mill Mount, where he was killed. There followed a race to the River Boyne, and in the confusion no one managed to pull up the drawbridge to the north town; Venables's regiment got there first and seized it. The chase only stopped at the town's north wall when soldiers from the garrison barricaded themselves into St Peter's Church and some of the wall towers. Cromwell claimed he had taken a hard line: 'indeed, being in the heat of the action, I forbade them to spare any that were in arms in the town'. The author of the first of the *Two Letters* was a little more specific regarding the instruction: 'putting all to the fword that were in the ftreets, and in the poftures of souldiers, But many whom they found in houfes and in found a quiet and orderly pofture they gave quarter to'.[24] Many of the victims of the killings that followed were in hot blood and occurred during the pursuit of the losers, as in any battle. On the other hand, there were some subsequent deaths even after frayed nerves had been allowed to settle a little. Cromwell summoned the soldiers trapped in St Peter's and offered mercy, but they refused: they simply may not have believed the offer was genuine. Cromwell had a bonfire of the pews built under the steeple and lit: many of the soldiers seem to have been burned to death, those that escaped were killed by the victors. The towers – the west gate and St Sunday's on the wall – were likewise summoned the next morning, but they refused too and even began to fight on. So when one finally did succumb to being starved out, the officers were clubbed to death and Cromwell turned Roman on the others, decimating the rank and file. The second tower surrendered quietly and all the soldiers were allowed to live, although all who were taken were destined to be transported to Barbados.[25] It was a bloody siege. Cromwell thought that about 2,000 had died, but the total may well be 3,500 soldiers and civilians.[26]

This was the first of the two singular events of Cromwell's career that resonate today. He was held responsible for the alleged butchery which followed the entry into the south town, which Gentles terms a 'night of terror'.[27] It started from the top. Aston was said to have been beaten to death with his own wooden leg; others including Sir Edmund Verney, son of the Sir Edmund who died at Edgehill holding the king's banner, also died. The bodies were decapitated and the heads sent to Dublin on pike staffs to be displayed. It was claimed that some officers offered quarter were killed hours or days after having surrendered. Even without these stories, the killing at Mill Mount, and at St Peter's and the north wall towers, had been brutal and prodigious and certainly after the storming was over. Cromwell was undoubtedly responsible for it; indeed we know much about the murderous aftermath because of his subsequent braggadocio letters. It colours all of our perceptions and turned Cromwell into a hate figure and bogey man in the Republic of Ireland and in other communities within the British Isles. Professor Morrill once even posed the question: was Cromwell a war-criminal? He only came to an inconclusive answer.[28] There is no doubt that he was responsible. He was in command: Drogheda fell and he destroyed an important element of Ormond's forces; experienced officers and men. He ordered that there be no quarter, but both he, his officers and some of his men ignored the order: even Aston and the officers in Mill Mount were supposed to have been offered quarter, as had been his men at the moment of entry, except in the tenalia where the fighting had been especially tough. All the soldiers in St Peter's and the two north towers were offered quarter at first, and whilst it was the following day when the towers were summoned, St Peter's had been summoned on the day of the storm. Each small stronghold may then be seen as having been given the standard offer of quarter to someone in a hopeless position, after which if they rejected it, they could expect no further offer or quarter. It does seem, however, that Aston was summoned only once and it is arguable that he was not in a hopeless position, and his blustering answer was to be expected at a first summons. On the other hand, Cromwell had placed two batteries within musket-shot of the walls. The walls were mediaeval in design and age and no match for modern artillery, and thus Aston may have been in a more hopeless position that his bluster warranted. Cromwell's strategy for attack was based on, but not the same as, those used elsewhere – the main difference being that there was no immediate back-up for the brigaded foot regiments from horse regiments. It was asserted that this was because the breaches had not been made low enough to get horse regiments into the town, and the size of the ravine was probably the reason; instead, there was a further brigade of foot regiments in support.[29] It is also clear that the scale of the victory was unexpected. Cromwell had possibly thought, as outlined above, that he would have to take the town piecemeal once through the walls: he had targeted St Mary's as an internal toehold from which to move on. However, he had commanders who could take decisions in the field, thus Venables was able to take the drawbridge without needing confirmation: a similar decision had been made earlier when there was no need to hold on to St Mary's Church as had been planned. Moreover, Cromwell demonstrated his flexibility: a commander needs to see to the overall strategy down, as Marshall suggested, to the level of selecting the brigades to lead and support the attack. However, he also knew the value of his presence on the field and when the attack on the south-east wall faltered he was prepared to lead the supporting brigade forward.[30]

With Cromwell's attack on Drogheda a success, neighbouring Trim Castle and Dundalk fell to Cromwell's army, forcing Ormond to retreat. This enabled Cromwell to concentrate on his chief targets: the south and midlands. The nature of his victory, which cleared Leinster of opponents and threw the coalition firmly on to the defensive, is usually overlooked by historians because they tackle instead the apparent slaughter of surrendered soldiers and civilians during the siege (although Kitson does call it 'faultless'[31]). This was not unusual, and the killing of members of the garrison in hot or cold blood was 'permissible' under the current 'rules' of war, for it had refused to surrender and had fallen to a storm after having done so. As for the deaths of civilians, we would now call it collateral damage, and it is clear that soldiers were aware that it should not be done, although there seems to have been an assumption that Roman Catholic clergy were classed as combatants. In any case, the period following a storm is by its nature chaotic and 'accidents' or misidentifications will happen.[32] The contemporary, Bulstrode Whitelocke, commented on the loss of 3,552 'of the enemy slain' but initially focussed a little more attention on the 64 parliamentarian deaths, including those of two colonels, Castle and Symonds, which he picked from Hugh Peters's report.[33] It is more the fact that some of the killings continued in the succeeding days which tarnishes the stunning success of Cromwell's army, both tactically at Drogheda and strategically through north Leinster.[34] By the time the Earl of Clarendon completed his history of the rebellion, he was able to write:

> they executed all manner of cruelty, and put every man that related to the garrison, and all the citizens who were Irish, man, woman, and child, to the sword; and there being three or four offices of name, and of good families, who had found some way, by the humanity of some soldiers of the enemy, to conceal them [selves] for four or five days, being afterwards discovered, [they] were butchered in cold blood.

Yet he acknowledged that the capture of Drogheda and the destruction of the forces within had destroyed Ormond's hopes of meeting Cromwell in the field.[35] Perhaps the best analysis of the evidence regarding the storming and its aftermath is that written by Micheal O'Siochru, where he takes great pains to examine the evidence for the scale of the killings and attacks on soldier and civilians and to separate what contemporaries thought of criminal acts and what we do now.[36] The conclusion is convincing and balanced, and is then used as the background to the argument that in a strategic sense it failed to deliver what Cromwell intended: a speedy resolution to the wars.

THE SIEGE OF WEXFORD

Cromwell left Drogheda after a couple of days, and Venables stayed behind to subdue the region. Following a few days in Dublin, on 27 September Cromwell led his army southwards.[37] Appreciating the value of the major ports, to himself and the enemies, the general marched on Wexford with its beautiful and useful bay into which flowed the River Slaney. Wexford, unlike Drogheda, had been a stalwart of the rebellion, providing a port facing the south of England and Wales. Several castles fell to the advancing forces: Killencarik almost immediately, then a day later Arklow was summoned and surrendered to Cromwell, and this example was followed by Ferns Castle and Enniscorthy.[38] The whole army reached the vicinity of Wexford on 2 October, but they were beset by bad weather which kept the siege guns and supplies at sea because they could not land in the storms. On 3 October, Wexford was summoned despite Cromwell's inability to open an effective siege, although Ireton had effected the capture of a fort at the entrance to the harbour, giving them control of the sea route into and out of the town, and enabling the taking of a frigate in the bay.[39] Wexford was on the southern side of the bay and linked to the north by a ferry. The town had old-fashioned mediaeval stone walls with deep earthworks erected to protect them from gunshot. Wexford Castle was outside the town, covering a good deal of the walls and dominating the town.[40] It was a few days before the guns arrived, but by 9 October they had disembarked and the batteries prepared to the south-east of the town, facing the castle: eight cannon and two mortars.[41]

The capture of Wexford was as stunning as the taking of Drogheda, but Cromwell was one of those stunned. The governor, Colonel David Sinnott, opened negotiations to buy time in the hope that Ormond could get reinforcements to him. Even though Ormond had earlier been kept at bay by Cromwell's horse, some 1,500 extra troops were sent into the town as Ormond and Sinnott tried to persuade the anxious townspeople to hold out against Cromwell.[42] Cromwell and his headquarters had discussed their approach and had decided to concentrate the batteries on the castle, and so on 11 October the artillery battered the castle walls with over a hundred missiles.[43] The walls began to crumble quite quickly and three breeches were made in two of the towers.[44] Sinnott reopened negotiations: the terms he suggested were rejected and Cromwell prepared his own counter-offer. These too were quite generous: soldiers and non-commissioned officers would be disarmed and allowed to go to their homes; officers would be allowed to live, but would be taken prisoner. The terms were still being prepared when the castle's governor, Colonel Stafford, precipitously surrendered and Cromwell's troops took over and began to turn the castle's guns on the town.[45] This was recognised as a threat to the troops on the town's walls and some deserted their posts. Before the negotiations could continue, Cromwell's regiments put their scaling ladders to the walls and got into the town too.[46] One inside they came upon some opposition, but chiefly they barged into a confusion of garrison soldiers and townspeople who, believing that the siege was at least 'on pause', had come out on to the streets. Cromwell had not issued a repeat of his notorious order to give no quarter and had of course prepared relatively generous terms, but nevertheless, no quarter was given. The soldiers rushed into the town and seem to have slaughtered anyone they encountered, between 1,700 and 3,000 according to one report. About 300 people attempting to cross the bay on the ferry and other boats were drowned as the soldiers fired on them, perhaps because it was thought that Sinnott was on one of them.[47]

This time something had gone wrong. Marshall says that 'Once more Cromwell had lost control of his army'.[48] It is arguable whether or not Cromwell had previously lost control of his army, but he certainly had not done so previously during this campaign – one of Cromwell's outstanding qualities was the loyalty he had inspired in his army and the control this gave him over the soldiers. This time he had lost control. They had stormed the town and charged through it attacking soldiers and civilians alike entirely without orders. The soldiers probably believed that they were simply following the precedent set at Drogheda a month earlier, but at Drogheda they had been acting under orders even as far as the indiscriminate killing of clergy.[49] And this time there was no hard-fought storm to justify the excesses: several days of rain and the outbreak of disease in the army were hardly the preconditions for the slaughter which followed the premature surrender of the castle. Cromwell turned to God's will as his only explanation when reporting the events to parliament. In his letter to William Lenthall, published as *A Letter from the Lord Lieutenant of Ireland*, Cromwell wrote of the soldiers: 'I could have wished that for their own good and the good of the garrison they could have been more moderate'. He was referring to plunder. However, he had already referred to the greater issue – Wexford had been ruined in the attack:

we intending better to this place than so great a ruin, hoping the town might be of more use to you and your army, yet God would not have it so; but by unexpected providence, in His righteous justice brought a just judgement upon them, causing them to become prey to the soldier, who in their piracies had made preys of so many families and made with their bloods to answer the cruelties which they had exercised upon the lives of divers poor Protestants; two of which I have been acquainted with. About seven or eight score poor Protestants were put by them into and old vessel, which being, as some say, bulged by them, the vessel sank, and they were all presently drowned in the harbour. The other was thus: they put dicers Protestants into a chapel (which since, they have used for a masshouse, and in which one or more of their priests were now killed) where they were famished to death.[50]

Even Cromwell must have had difficulty with this explanation. For a start, it meant that God had not blessed his plans (or those of his headquarters staff) as he had at Drogheda. Cromwell may well have accepted the apocryphal stories: he was a providentialist and so he may have truly seen them as God's evidence of his intentions. However, we may see a man who was fishing for an explanation of his failure, and Hugh Peters went along with it too. There is little to discuss regarding Cromwell's strategy here. The attack was well thought through, and the castle was a weak spot when using heavy artillery: its dominant position over the town would have been somewhat similar to holding the citadel at Drogheda had it needed to be taken piecemeal as Cromwell expected. That part of the strategy had worked; the castle was rapidly crumbling before a short bombardment and its dominant position was clearly recognised by the soldiers in the town who then panicked, unaware of Cromwell's relatively generous terms. But that was it. The rest was undertaken by an army out of control and Cromwell could neither direct them nor stop them.[51] Kitson, a general himself, called it 'monstrous'.[52] Marshall refers to Cromwell's peculiar mercy in allowing his soldiers two hours to destroy the valuable asset before trying to stop the violence.[53] James Scott-Wheeler, another soldier, regarded it as a double failure, whereas Gentles regards it as 'Cromwell's most inglorious victory'.[54] Such a collapse of control affects army discipline and Cromwell had tried to win the acquiescence of the wider Irish population by promising the army's maintenance of a strict disciplinary code: this, according to Ian Gentles, was an important failing.[55] Secondly, it had the opposite effect on the enemy that Drogheda promised to have; it strengthened their resolve. On the other hand, it was a major victory even if Cromwell had little to do with its completion.[56] Scott-Wheeler's belief that Wexford caused a reaction in the enemy camp is supported by O'Siochru who, whilst agreeing that gaining Wexford was a major victory which 'permanently crippled the royalist/confederate navy', saw both the strengthening of the resolve of garrisons and the emulation of Cromwell's soldiers' cruelty.[57] However, some contemporaries did not think it worth a mention: neither Whitelocke, nor Clarendon, elaborated on this victory. Those garrisons who saw the potential threat of Cromwell heading towards them may have felt differently and strengthened their defensive works, such as Galway, which continued with its modern defence building.[58] One place where Cromwell's successes were watched carefully was Edinburgh. 'all their eyes are upon Cromwell' wrote Whitelocke, adding 'that the levying of their new army did not proceed hastily'. What was probably not realised was that valuable time was being bought by Cromwell in the prospective war with Scotland.[59]

Cromwell moved from Wexford to New Ross, a crossing point on the wide River Barrow where the governor was Theobald, Lord Taaffe. Despite the surrender of several smaller outposts on the way, Taaffe appeared undaunted, but he and Ormond had agreed that if Cromwell could amass his siege guns against the garrison then he would surrender. Just a week after Wexford had fallen, Cromwell appeared outside New Ross: he had three siege guns with him and more were being shipped along the coast from Wexford and would be brought up the river. Cromwell wrote:

> Since my coming into Ireland, I have this witness for myself, that I have endeavoured to avoid the effusion of blood, having been before no place to which such terms have not beed first sent as might have turned to the good and preservation of those to whom they were offered, this being my principle, that the people and places where I come may not suffer except through their own wilfulness.

Followed with an abrupt summons, Cromwell thus addressed himself to Taaffe, who delayed sending a reply for several days. Cromwell set about placing his batteries on 18 October, and on the following day he began to fire on the town. Taaffe had been reinforced and his garrison was about 3,500 men strong, but he had decided on his options and opened negotiations despite Cromwell's refusal to stop the firing. Cromwell on the other hand was generous: the soldiers could march away with drums beating and colours flying and the townspeople could live in peace. Taaffe pushed his luck; he asked that the Roman Catholic faith be pursued in the town without let or hindrance and that he keep his artillery.

Cromwell replied in a balanced response despite having made a breach in the walls of New Ross: 'As for you carrying away any artillery or ammunition that you brought not in with you or hath not come in to you since you had the command of that place, I must deny you that.' As for the religious request:

> For that which you mention concerning liberty of conscience, I meddle not with any man's conscience. But if by liberty of conscience you mean a liberty to exercise the mass, I judge it best to use plain dealing, and to let you know, where the Parliament of England have power, that will not be allowed of.[60]

Taaffe delayed a little longer, asking for permission to send agents to negotiate and asking Cromwell to stop firing. Cromwell would only do so when Taaffe named his chosen guarantors, and so eventually the firing ceased and New Ross was handed to Cromwell. Anyone who wished to leave was allowed to do so and Taaffe could take the guns and ammunition which he had brought, leaving only those that were installed in New Ross when he took up command.[61] Some 500 of the garrison changed sides and joined Cromwell.[62]

Cromwell had a pontoon bridge constructed to allow him to move quickly south or west across the Barrow. Cromwell's military campaign continued, alongside intense diplomacy conducted by Lord Broghill, which secured the fall of Cork and Youghal into parliament's hands. As Clarendon said some years later, 'he defied fortune again; and marched so far out of the places devoted to him, and from whence he had any reasonable hope to receive supplies, that he must necessarily have been starved'.[63] Cromwell turned southwards and marched towards Waterford, the important port on the Barrow Estuary with the two significant gun batteries on the east side (Duncannon) and west side (passage Fort) of the river. Cromwell could reach Duncannon fort before the engineers had completed his pontoon and so attacked there first. Ormond had sent an experienced but unimaginative lieutenant general, the Earl of Castlehaven, to Duncannon with reinforcements and tried to continue to enhance the fort's ability to hold off Cromwell, installing Colonel Edward Wogan as governor. Wogan had formerly been a parliamentarian and faced execution if he failed to hold Cromwell out.[64] Like Ormond, Cromwell had sent his lieutenant general, Henry Ireton, to deal with the fort, but despite reinforcing him Wogan was able to hold out against the father-in-law and son-in-law team. The fort held. Unlike New Ross, Wexford, Drogheda and even Basing House, the fort had modern earthwork walls which absorbed the energy of the heavy shot fired at them by Ireton, dissipating its power and thus keeping the walls intact and an infantry assault off the cards. In turn this kept the heavier siege guns on the ships because they could not be sailed up the Barrow to be used against the great prize: Waterford. In the meantime Cromwell's forces were shrinking due to disease and the need to establish garrisons in each of his conquests. Ormond estimated that he had as few as 4,000 foot and 1,200 horse. Even so, Ormond failed to prevent a small force of reinforcements reaching Cromwell from Dublin, but on the other hand he did escape from being trapped and forced into battle near New Ross. He was able to retreat and protect the capital, Kilkenny. Whilst Cromwell concentrated on Waterford to his rear, Ormond attempted to encroach on the chain of forts protecting Cromwell, particularly Carrick, which had been captured on 19 November. However, Ormond was not a great commander and his forces comprised a coalition of soldiers who had had fought each other during the past eight years, and were now divided on strategy – divisions which Ormond unsuccessfully tried to resolve by following both, leading to a failure to rescue Waterford by defeating Cromwell in the field. Nevertheless, Ormond was able to feed experienced veteran reinforcements into the garrison several times. Despite capturing the Passage Fort, Cromwell could not storm the town or even plant his batteries on firm ground close enough to breach the defences effectively. Cromwell withdrew to winter quarters in early December. Waterford was his first setback in Ireland and left a gaping hole in his hold on the south and east of the country. Moreover, Michael Jones had died of fever and Cromwell lost a namesake and relative, Major Oliver Cromwell. It was a miserable winter.[65]

On the other hand it was welcome. Cromwell's men had been in the field since marching north from Dublin at the beginning of September: three months. The army was riven by illness – it had killed Michael Jones and debilitated Cromwell for some time. A chance to rebuild the army and resupply it was needed prior to a march northwards into the midlands. This involved getting captured veterans back by engaging in prisoner exchanges.[66] Winter was not the best time to try and ship men and supplies from England and some soldiers were lost in the attempt. However, the winter sojourn was not long: Cromwell planned to conquer the midlands with a three-pronged advance supported by Lord Broghill, and the campaign began at the end of January 1650. Scott-Wheeler has praised the campaign as audacious: even in the depths of winter it depended upon speed as much as on Cromwell's still fearsome reputation. Three fortifications fell in as many days, through the tactic of offering generous terms even when faced by veteran forces brought south from Owen Roe O'Neill's Ulster Army. On the western flank of the advance, Broghill met with similar success, but he had to employ heavy artillery at Old Castletown, and as they had resisted the six officers were shot after surrender, with the ordinary soldiers being granted quarter for their lives.[67] Cromwell had reached Fethard by 2 February, where he bluffed it out pretending he was leading an advance guard, and after a fraught night of negotiations he secured its surrender. The garrison had shot at Cromwell's trumpeter when he took the terms and seemed angry because Cromwell was attempting to parley at night. Cashel surrendered the next day without a fight.[68] After quartering in the area of Fethard and Cashel for a short while, Cromwell moved on Cahir which he attacked and took after a brief fight. By late March Cromwell had reached his chief target: the Confederation capital of Kilkenny. The governor, Sir William Butler, was defiant. Cromwell's final weeks in Ireland was destined to be bound up with two sieges, but he would soon be needed elsewhere: his political masters were about to get edgy and his commander in chief was ill at ease.

THE SIEGE OF KILKENNY

Kilkenny had been the capital of the Catholic Confederation since 1642, and was the location of the legislature and executive arms of the government. Although it had been recognised that Kilkenny might be the target of a three-pronged advance, the allied forces seemed incapable of saving it. According to Scott-Wheeler, Ormond had difficulty in getting his forces out of winter quarters to oppose the advance, despite the mild weather which had partly been responsible for enabling Cromwell to undertake the campaign – although this was intermittent, and he did report to Lenthall his problems with 'sore and tempestuous wind and rain' and 'blustering weather'.[69] The main problem for the allies was that Cromwell had faced very little opposition: potential barriers such as Fethard had crumbled before him. Scott-Wheeler thinks that Cromwell's rapid advance might also have distracted Ormond's attention and made him concentrate on Cromwell.[70] The real danger lay elsewhere: Colonel John Reynolds – who had led the foot regiments sent to strengthen Jones's Dublin Garrison the previous July and had proven himself, capturing Carrick and holding it against Ormond's counter-attack back in November – led the eastern advance. His force was small: around 900 horse in 16 undersized troops and 2,000 foot.[71] In some ways this was a masking force, using its small size to distract attention from Ireton's larger force behind it with the siege artillery in tow. On 3 February, as Cromwell reached Fethard, Reynolds attacked Callan, and when he captured the two small castles in the town he executed the garrisons because they had refused to surrender and caused Reynolds to deploy his siege guns. The third castle had, however, surrendered on terms. Cromwell joined Reynolds at Callan, but the united forces then returned to Fethard and

Cashel where there was 'good plenty both of horse and man's meat'. By the end of the month Cahir Castle and Kiltinan Castle had both been captured after a brief assault, Golden Bridge was soon in his hands and reinforcements from Dublin under Hewson arrived. Cahir's capture allowed Cromwell the opportunity for an uncustomary earthly boast: 'The castle of Cahir, very considerable, built upon a rock, and seated in an island in the midst of the Suir, was lately rendered to me. It cost the earl of Essex, as I am informed, about eight week siege with his army and artillery.'[72]

It was one of the few references to military history Cromwell made, but it suggests that he had read some. Several small garrisons had surrendered by early March and the allies' ability to collect resources and taxation – the General Applotment – declined steadily. There is no straightforward way to assess whether the Drogheda/Wexford effect was still working. Some of the garrisons, like Fethard and Cashel, surrendered without a fight, but others put up resistance. It is perhaps because Cromwell and his soldiers were inconsistent in their treatment of garrisons before and after their surrender that there was equally no consistent response. Sir Richard Butler surrendered the third castle at Callan after Reynolds shot the defenders of the other two. Cromwell spared the garrison at Cahir despite the fact that it initially defied him. Likewise the governor of Grennan Castle disputed the terms offered to him and Cromwell acquiesced and revised them.[73] One effect was that Ormond's delicately constructed alliances were falling apart. Some of the surrendering garrisons had been led by members of his own family and his half-brother Matthew Reynolds had openly defied him when summoned to explain his surrender of Cahir.[74]

On 22 March, Cromwell sent a summons to Kilkenny, having passed through Bennettsbridge. The summons was different to the others Cromwell had issued, even if brief. He referred to the wide political issue, that Kilkenny had been at the head of the attempt by Ireland to 'rend yourselves' from the 'state of England' through 'an unheard of massacre of the innocent English'. For this reason God had 'begun to judge you with his sore plague'.[75] Sir Walter Butler refused. The town was large and surrounded by walls. Like Drogheda it was divided into sections by water: the south part of the town was called High Town. In the south-east corner was the Butler family seat, the impressive castle which dominated that part of Kilkenny (and still does). High Town was the largest part of the town. North-east of the castle across the River Nore was a small suburb linked by a bridge to High Town. To the north across the smaller River Breagagh was Irish town, which was completely surrounded by walls: the east side of High Town was open to the River Nore. Sir Walter Butler was determined to resist, despite only having 400 soldiers. Survivors of the plague that had been present in the town for weeks, they could only hold High Town. The town's civil government organised the defence of Irish Town. An attempt to scare the latter failed when they defied a regiment of horse sent to face the north gate. On the other hand, at the same time Cromwell seized St Patrick's Cathedral and established a battery, which began to fire on the south walls on 25 March. One hundred cannon balls smashed a hole in the walls.

When the breach became passable, Cromwell sent Colonel Ewer with one regiment to attack Irish Town at the same time as the breach was stormed by the brigaded regiments of Colonels Hewson and Daniel Axtell to ensure that the forces there could not be fed south to counter Cromwell's attack. In any case the attack on the breach was driven off – Cromwell seems to have blamed his men who did not perform 'with the usual courage nor success, but were beaten off, with the loss of one captain, and about twenty or thirty men killed and wounded'.[76] In fact they had come across strong interior defence works, topped by palisades, facing the breach which gave the defenders the edge they needed to keep Hewson and Axtell out.[77]

Ewer's regiment had forced an entry into Irish Town defended by the part-time citizen-soldiers who, whilst not easily frightened, could be out-fought. Ewer's men then attempted to force their way into the northern end of High Town via the bridge over the Breagagh in the face of artillery fire. The attack stalled and Cromwell began to erect a second battery. At this point Butler realised that there was no hope of support from Ormond or anyone else: the Earl of Castlehaven was only 12 miles away, but his forces were depleted and unable to help. Negotiations opened but as Butler talked, on 27 March, Cromwell sent Colonel Giffard to seize the small eastern suburb, which was taken quickly. However, the eight companies Giffard led were unable to force their way into High Town across St John's Bridge. Despite the stout resistance Butler knew he was isolated and surrendered the town and castle; simultaneously the castle at Cantwell was surrendered as well.[78] Cromwell's letter reporting the catalogue of successes since the fall of Fethard listed the fall of several castles after Kilkenny, and again demanded more financial and other support from parliament in order to continue the good work.[79] The letter of 2 April also refers to the Council of State having asked him to return to England, and parliament's vote to the same effect back in January. However, the lord lieutenant pointed out that the request was somewhat late and had presumed him to be idle in winter quarters rather than in the field knocking the heart out of the confederate-royalist alliance. Moreover, the weather at sea was bad: it was not yet appropriate for him to leave Ireland.[80]

CLONMEL

The remaining stronghold in the midlands was Clonmel, held by Owen Roe O'Neill's nephew Major General Hugh O'Neill. By the end of March the alliance had more or less collapsed and royalist protestant forces had to leave Catholic territory and move northwards, with Ormond's forces shrinking further as Cromwell offered terms of surrender to the disbanded Protestant forces. By contrast, O'Neil's men were veterans from Ulster, 1,200 of them defending a town of several thousand inhabitants, which made food supply difficult. Hugh O'Neill was a veteran of the war in Europe and skilled in the defence of towns: according to Scott-Wheeler, his forces were disciplined and relationships with the town's civil administration were good despite the mutual problems of food shortages and plagues.[81] The plague had steadily reduced the garrison strength, but reinforcements arrived from the former garrisons at Cahir and Kilkenny. The town was surrounded by old-style mediaeval walls over 20 feet high and six feet thick at the base, with four large gates or bars; there was also a wide ditch outside the walls. These enclosed the north-east and west sides whilst the south was covered by the river with minimal defences. Whilst the walls were built before the widespread use of artillery, they had been improved with an escarpment built up against the inside of the walls and a counter-escarpment outside, both of which would provide a cushioning effect against gunfire.

Cromwell arrived outside Clonmel on 27 April, without the siege artillery. A decision was taken to storm the town, which may have been a mistake for the plague and hunger could have done the work for the army. There was a great deal in O'Neill's favour. Ground on two of the walled sides was soft and unsuitable for positioning a battery without a great deal of engineering work, leaving only the north wall suitable for an attack and the effectiveness of a diversionary attack muted. This meant that unlike the widely spread works of Drogheda or Kilkenny, the defenders could muster their strength at the point of attack. Three days after he arrived, Cromwell ordered the heavy artillery to be brought, but it required time and potentially hundreds of oxen to haul it. In the meantime a battery of field guns was set up to batter the north walls, but the 12-pounders could not make a large enough breach. Every evening any damage to the walls was repaired by the garrison. It is possible that there was an attempt to betray the town by the Protestant regiment within the town, but it was exposed. When one of the town's gates was opened as arranged, the parliamentarians rushed in only to be trapped and killed in large numbers.[82] It had become apparent that the siege artillery was needed, and Cromwell had to wait until the 16 May before it could arrive. However, perhaps because a battery of field guns had already been built, there was no delay in getting the 42-pounders into action against the north (St Mary's) gate. It appears that the escarpment and counter-escapement were not sufficient, perhaps because in the end they were too low to protect fully the 20-foot walls, as it took less than a day to hammer a breach into the walls which sent the stones and rubble cascading into the ditch, filling it in to an extent that it could be crossed. Cromwell had learned the geography of the town and knew that the road through St Mary's Gate, which became the town's Lough Street from the north, led directly into the town centre and could be used by horse regiments supporting the foot spearhead.

However, O'Neill was prepared. As soon as the direction of the breach and attack was known – he in effect had a fortnight's notice that the attack was focussed on the north wall even if, as is unlikely, he had not worked that out beforehand – he had earthworks built inside the breach.[83] Like those at Kilkenny and Drogheda these defences were primarily intended to keep the attackers penned into the breach area. According to Scott-Wheeler, O'Neill constructed a V-shaped killing zone to greet the attackers. However, Marshall and Gentles think that here were two parallel 80-foot-long walls constructed from the breach to Mortimer Street at an angle of roughly 90° to the external wall.[84] Whatever the shape this inner work, to the west of Lough Street, and comprising breastworks with firing platforms, artillery was placed out of sight of the breach entrance. Cromwell's plan was blunt: foot regiments would assault the breach and make their way to the north gate, which they would then open and allow Cromwell's horse troops to clatter down Lough Street into the heart of the town.

It went awry. At 8.00 am Cromwell's foot regiments, spearheaded perhaps by a brigaded pair of regiments, charged over the breach and into the trap. It appears that the men at the front realised they were trapped and tried to stop the men behind them pushing into the V-shape, to no avail. Only when the killing zone was full did the firing begin proper. Musketeers fired from the breastwork platforms and from the surrounding houses. The artillery fired chain-shot, slicing into the melee, and specially constructed 'engines' were brought into play thrusting logs into the flanks of the attackers. It was probably one of the most dramatic failures of the civil wars. There is speculation that in the few minutes it took to drive the attackers out, a thousand of Cromwell's men died in what was, it is for once appropriate to say, a bloodbath on the streets of Clonmel. Opening the north gate was simply not an option.

Cromwell tried to rally the foot to return to this breach, but they refused and so he turned to the horse regiments. The latter were so keen that they inspired some of the foot into reforming themselves for a second attempt, but not until 3.00 pm: it was a terrible mistake. Cromwell simply tried the same doomed tactic. The two regiments of horse, led by colonels Jerome Sankey and Culme, went in first – dismounted but wearing their armour, which would have offered more protection. Once again they made short work of the defenders at the breach, but in an horrific mirror of the morning's attack were trapped in the killing zone by a hail of musket-shot, cannon chain-shot and swinging logs: the townspeople joined in with the makeshift domestic and farmyard weapons available to them. This time the fighting lasted longer, as the parliamentarians desperately hung on in the zone, possibly by using their dead colleagues as protection from the murderous fire. Culme and as many as 2,000 more died. This was a loss rate of 30 per cent for Cromwell's army. After as much as three hours Cromwell called an end to the fighting and pulled his men back out of the town. It was 'the worst setback' in the army's entire history, according to Wanklyn, and certainly the worst setback of Cromwell's career according to Kitson and Gentles; Marshall is content to call it a 'severe tactical defeat for Cromwell', but he comments on Cromwell's 'noticeable' silence.[85]

It had been a splendid victory for O'Neill, but he had used all his ammunition. So in a further well-considered move, he abandoned the town by sailing his men across the River Suir during the night. Just after midnight on 10 May, the mayor, John White, opened negotiations without once mentioning that O'Neill was gone and the town effectively demilitarised. Cromwell was so relieved that he offered very generous terms, which in return for all the arms and ammunition in the town protected the townspeople from harm.[86] Only when the deal was signed and Cromwell asked after O'Neill did White let on. Cromwell was furious, naturally: a pursuit was organised, but the town was not harmed further. Defeated militarily and outwitted, Cromwell's Irish campaign came to an ignominious end. Within days he was on his way to England where his political and military masters needed him.

In the report to parliament which arrived there on 28 May, it was reported to parliament that Clonmel had been entered: it was a condensed version of the letter from W.A. published alongside an account of the execution of the Marquis of Montrose in Edinburgh on 28 May, written after the surrender had been concluded:

> This day we entered *Clonmell*, which was quit by the Enemy laft night about nine of the clock, after a teadious storme, which continued foure houres. Our men kept clofe to the breach, which they had entered, all the time, safe onlye one Accidentall Retreat in the storme We lost in this service Col *Cullum* and fome other officers, with divers private Souldiers and other wounded.

This was an astounding piece of understatement, which placed the withdrawal of O'Neill as the focus of the opening statement and completely obliterated details of the defeat and the enormous casualty rate. It ended on another conceit, returning to the issue of O'Neill now having 'stole out' of the town, but it did mention briefly the 'many great preparations' including the 'traverfe or crosse work' from which they beat 'our men off, as they entered' the breach. Two days later, Whitelocke recorded that 'in Clonmel the stoutest enemy that ever was found by the army in Ireland, and there was never seen so hot a storm of so long a continuance, and so gallantly defended in England or Ireland.[87] Just a day later Cromwell was being met on Hounslow Heath. If he had attempted to beat the bad news by getting his story in first, he had just about failed: the news was filtering in. It would be 11 June before he reported to parliament.[88]

9

THE LORD GENERAL

Cromwell returned from Ireland leaving his son-in-law, Henry Ireton, in charge in the country, although he was specifically in charge of continuing Cromwell's midlands campaign whilst others, such as Venables in the north-east and New English commander Sir Charles Coote, also prosecuted the war further north. The enemy was now primarily the Catholic Confederation's troops as the royalists, including their commanders Ormond and Inchiquin, had given up the fight. Once home, despite being commander in chief of Ireland and the Lord Lieutenant, Cromwell remained under Fairfax's command. When he returned he was greeted as a hero. Probably because news of the disaster at Clonmel had been suppressed or overtaken by the lord lieutenant himself, he was greeted as a conquering hero despite the continuation of the war. A large delegation met him at Windsor led by his wife Elizabeth, the Council of State and MPs. The same honours were repeated in London on 1 June.[1] It was a triumph. It may, on the part of the government and loyal MPs, have been desperation, because Lord Fairfax was disquieted.

For months the Scots had been sorting out their relationship with Charles I's son, Prince Charles. It had not been easy, for the question of the young man's religion was important and so was his exact role in the relationship. One of his supporters, the Marquis of Montrose, had attempted to raise northern Scotland in his name, only to be captured, tried and executed for treason by the Kirk Party government, perhaps as much as for his apostasy (he had once been a leading Covenanter general) as for his precipitous 'invasion'. Charles would, for the time being, dance to the tune of a psalm. The negotiations between Edinburgh and the 'royal court' in the United Provinces were protracted and affected the military preparations in Scotland.[2] So much so that it was ten days before the issue of the prospect of war was discussed in England. Initially it was proposed that Cromwell return to the role of lieutenant general under Lord General Fairfax, but to lead an army in the north as he had done in 1648 with Fairfax remaining in the home counties as before. This was voted down in parliament and it was recommended instead that Fairfax be ordered to prepare to lead the army in any forthcoming war.[3] Both men agreed with the order on 14 June. It was a political not a military decision. If the republic was to go to war with its former ally, the religious issues at stake needed to be addressed. Scotland had long portrayed the New Model Army and the execution of the king as being the work of the Independents, or as they referred to them in Edinburgh – sectaries. The brief alliance between Cromwell and Argyll had only been necessary to get the Kirk Party in power at the expense of Engagers and Scottish royalists. It was short-lived, and the death of Charles I had set the seal on that. Therefore, as a result of the accusations of sectarianism targeting in the Republic, it had to be made to look as there was unity of purpose crossing the religious divide between the Presbyterians and Independents: the appointment of the Presbyterian Fairfax and the Independent Cromwell would be emblematic of that unity.

Cromwell played a mediatory role in the discussions which followed; given that he was the nominee as leader of the army of one faction he was mistrusted by the others, but he continued to accept that Fairfax was the commander in chief. It is not difficult to see why there was mistrust – given that Cromwell was important in the army, the Council of State and the Irish administration he was seen as ambitious and thus watched closely. However, it was Fairfax who was the centre of attention, as it was well known that he had serious qualms about any future war with Scotland. Nevertheless, the army was being assembled in the north-east of England and a fleet was being equipped to act in concert with it. On or around 22 June, Fairfax lit the fuse: he informed the council that he was not going to accept command of the army raised for war with Scotland if the war was anything other than an defensive war. He would lead the army if it was pitched against a Scottish invasion, but he would not lead an invasion even when dressed up as a pre-emptive strike against an aggressor. This would break, he argued, the Solemn League and Covenant with the Scottish brothers in Christ. The Council of State was convinced that Scotland intended to send an army into England for the fourth time in 11 years but had resolved to strike first.[4]

Cromwell offered to join with a small committee of soldiers (John Lambert, Thomas Harrison) and politicians (Bulstrode Whitelocke, Oliver St John) to make representation to the lord general in an effort to change his mind. The meeting was held in camera in Whitehall on 24 June, and Whitelocke took notes which later made it into his diary. First, they prayed; at least, Cromwell prayed, followed by 'most of the committee'. Cromwell likewise opened the secular proceedings gently, reminding his commander that they were there 'because there seems to be some hesitation in yourself' and that the committee was to endeavour to give your excellency satisfaction in any doubts of yours which may arise concerning this affair'. Fairfax replied by thanking the committee for their efforts and acknowledging he was amongst friends, but stating firmly that he 'was not fully satisfied as to grounds or justice of our invasion upon our brethren'. Lambert asked what his qualms were. The Lord General was blunt:

> I think it doubtful whether we have a just cause to make an invasion upon Scotland. With them we are joined in the national league and covenant; and now for us, contrary thereunto, and without sufficient cause given to us by them, to enter into their country with an army, and to make war upon them, is that which I cannot see the justification of nor how we shall be able to justify the lawfulness of it before God or man.

Cromwell responded that the Scots had, in spite of the Solemn League and Covenant, invaded England in 1648, an invasion which, because it was ordered by their parliament, was a nationally sanctioned event. Furthermore, now they planned to do so again, 'joining with their king with whom they have made a full agreement without the assent or privity of this Commonwealth and are very busy at this present in raising forces and money to carry on their design'. In other words, they had invaded before and would do so again. 'Your excellency will soon determine whether it be better to have this war in the bowels of another country or of our own'. Fairfax stated his preference for a war of defence and reminded Cromwell that the estates had, since Hamilton's invasion, repudiated the Engagement and the Engagers and punished perpetrators. This was true, but Whitelocke interjected that some other perpetrators were employed in building the army 'since raised'. Fairfax was cornered at this point in the discussions, but he still maintained that the true intentions of the Scots were unknown and he maintained this in the face of Harrison's suggestion that the balance of 'human probabilities' gave them assurance of the Scots' intentions. St John and Cromwell then returned to the breaking of the Solemn League and Covenant whilst Whitelocke continued with the theme of the misery of war in their own country. The lord general responded to this onslaught by making the issue very personal: 'everyone must stand or fall by his own conscience'. Cromwell responded in kind, reminding Fairfax of the faithful servants, 'us who are officers who have served under you, and desire to serve under no other general'. He then added as an extra barb that by laying down his commission Fairfax would give a great advantage to the public enemy'. Lambert picked up on this and hammered home the point, saying he would be 'very fearful of the mischiefs which might ensue'. Whitelocke added in his diary somewhat cryptically that 'none of the committee [were] so earnest to persuade the general to continue his commission as Cromwell and the soldiers. Yet there was cause enough to believe that they did not over much desire it.'[5] Writing later, Lucy Hutchinson, certainly no friend to Cromwell, cast another light upon the discussions. She also suggested that her husband, Colonel John Hutchinson, and other officers had visited Fairfax so concerned where they that if Fairfax stepped down he would 'levell the way to Cromwell's ambitious designes'. She claimed that they were successful but that Lady Fairfax's imprecations and those of her Presbyterian chaplains changed his mind back again. Cromwell, she argued, also tried hard to dissuade Fairfax, despite her husband's fears:

> To speak the truth of Cromwell, wheras many say'd he undermined Fairfax, it was false; for in Coll Hutchinson's presence he most effectually importun'd him to keepe his commission [...] but he could by no means prevaile, allthough he labour'd it almost all the night with the most earnest endeavours.[6]

Even so, Fairfax's commission was rescinded on 26 June. Cromwell, 'by a contrivance' according to Whitelocke, was appointed captain general and commander in chief immediately, by a unanimous vote.[7] It was, according to John Grainger, the right decision. He believes that Fairfax was the wrong man for the job, especially if he was hard-hearted, but more so Cromwell had just experienced a hard campaign in Ireland and he was known for caring for his men. Fairfax, according to Grainger, was more of a 'berserker' when in battle.[8] The Council also stated that the invasion of Scotland would be, in the circumstances, legal. The command structure was soon laid out: Cromwell's relative and long-term colleague Charles Fleetwood was appointed lieutenant general; General John Lambert, who had served with Cromwell in the Preston campaign, was the major general; and another relative, Edward Whalley, was the commissary general.

Preparations on the border had been continuing whilst the discussions over leadership had been carried out at the top level. Forces to remain in England would be led by Major General Thomas Harrison. For the invasion, six regiments of horse and five regiments of foot were to be prepared. The Scots on paper had 19,000 men, but they had not been mustered. However, the day after the meeting with Fairfax at Westminster, the estates authorised the increase of the forces to 36,000 men, and just days earlier a commission had been established for investigating the religious and ideological suitability of the soldiers.[9] The commander in chief was still officially the veteran Lord Leven, whilst field command was in the hands of Cromwell's colleague from Marston Moor, David Leslie. In London, it was the size of the forces which were being mustered to oppose Cromwell that preoccupied Whitelocke. He had heard that company and troop strengths had been set at 120 and 100 respectively – at the high end of unit strengths – but were only slowly being assembled, and that they were prepared to divided each company and troop into two in order to make a total of eight regiments of horse and 12 of foot. The latter were already marching to the borders and in the direction of Berwick-upon-Tweed or Carlisle.[10] On 29 June, Cromwell left London for the north; in the meantime Prince Charles had landed in Scotland, and whilst originally a secret this had become public knowledge the day Fairfax had met the committee in Westminster. By 1 July, Whitelocke noted that parliament had heard that 10,000 foot and 27 troops, which he firstly thought was over and above the original levy (presumably the initial 19,000), had been raised. Without apparent irony, Whitelocke noted that the Scots 'resolve to invade England, if England not invade them first'.[11] Lambert was at the border and facing questions from the estates about his reasons for being there. Cromwell's arrival in York was notified to parliament on 6 July: a few days later he was at Berwick from where he sent letters to the estates giving notice of the army's view that a state of war existed, news which would now be communicated to Prince Charles who had been declared king. Only after long negotiations had the prince been accorded some of the powers accorded to a Scottish king – in the regime as it had existed for the past decade.[12] As Cromwell made a largely symbolic invasion, taking up just 200 or 300 paces, a new phenomenon was noticed. People had initially stopped coming to the border markets, but then the male inhabitants of the eastern border counties began to gather their goods, chattels and cattle and move north towards Edinburgh. Whilst Whitelocke asserted that the women left behind were supplying Cromwell's men with food and beer, the plan was that it would be other way around: the women would plead thirst and hunger and try to inveigle food from the invader, putting strain on the logistics line Cromwell would need to supply the army.[13]

The army, apart from the units detached south to keep a watching brief on or near the borders, had dug itself in on a line between Edinburgh and Leith. On the event of the actual invasion warning beacons were lit from the borders to Edinburgh and beyond: the nation once again acting together, was prepared. The invaders reached Dunbar, which had a useful port, on 26 July, but there were simply not enough supplies being landed when the army was there. A day later the army was at the market town of Haddington on the road, then as now, to Edinburgh. The city's defence works were by now so strong that Cromwell was deterred. They ran roughly along the line of present-day Leith Walk between Edinburgh to the south and the newly strengthened walled town of Leith with its harbour blocked by a boom to keep Cromwell's fleet out. Neither side would attack: Cromwell had Leith bombarded, but Leslie remained in place behind the stout earthworks and gun emplacements; it was rumoured that he had selected a potential battlefield at Gladsmore and the vanguard was stationed there when Cromwell was at Haddington. On 29 July, Cromwell advanced and faced the defences.

Cromwell's only successes were when the parliamentarian army stormed Arthur's Seat to the south of Edinburgh and also stormed a battery on St Leonard's Crags guarding the approach from the south-east.[14] There was continued fighting over Arthur's Seat on that wet day, but little else. Cromwell withdrew his drenched army the following morning. Leslie sprung from his defence lines and attacked the rearguard. His attempted pincer movement failed largely due to Hacker's regiment intervening, but he was successful in mauling the retreating forces causing Cromwell to commit several horse regiments including his own to extract the end of the line – even Lambert was wounded by a lance blow, almost reminiscent of Colonel Francis Thornhaugh's death after Preston. He was then captured briefly, before being rescued by Hacker's men.[15] As they marched back to Musselburgh, Cromwell's army found itself opposed by the townspeople who had returned from the hiding places they had used whilst Cromwell marched to Edinburgh and now tried to fortify the town. This example of the popular hostility to the sectarian invading army was soon defeated, but once in the town Cromwell was attacked by Scottish cavalry who charged into Musselburgh possibly looking for the lord general himself.[16] When he wrote to John Bradshaw, by now president of the Council of State, of the attack on the town, its repulse and the death of one of the two Scottish colonels, Colonel Archibald Strachan – the man who had defeated and captured the Marquis of Montrose, and the leader of the Musselburgh attack, Major General Robert Montgomery – he was surprisingly optimistic despite having been outfaced at Edinburgh and harassed continuously: 'Indeed this is a sweet beginning of your business, or rather the Lord's; and I believe is not very satisfactory to the enemy, especially to the Kirk's party. We did not lose any in this business, so far as I hear, but a cornet; I do not hear of four men more.'[17] The loss to the Kirk Party specifically was Strachan and Montgomery, 'two champions of the Church'. Musselburgh was too small a port to bring in the supplies Cromwell's men needed, and within a week the invaders retreated to the port of Dunbar.

THE BATTLE OF DUNBAR

It is possible that Leslie thought he had Cromwell trapped at Dunbar. He knew that Cromwell's men were suffering from disease and that he lacked supplies and pay for the soldiers, despite possessing the port at Dunbar. Ian Gentles considers that that by this point Cromwell looked as if he was out-generalled, and there was the possibility that the invasion had stalled and Cromwell might not get the army home.[18] Even English reports confirmed that Leslie by placing himself on Doon Hill: 'flanked us upon the Hills on the right hand, where they lay all night within a mile of our Army: and they sent a Party to possess the Pafs at *Copperspeth* to cut off the correspondency between us and Berwick.'[19]

The point was hammered home the next day when the two armies faced each other in battle order: 'we could not go up to meet the enemy by reason of the hills', and naturally Leslie would not come down. However, this might hold the key to the battle the next day for it would have been dangerous for either side to do otherwise, but it could be nothing other than a short-term position. Surely Leslie could not have expected Cromwell to attack directly, and even an army seemingly cornered would be unlikely to collapse quickly. Perhaps his imagination had run dry or he was waiting for Cromwell to make a mistake. In any case, a mistake was made, but not by Cromwell:

> That night it pleased the Lord to look wonderfully upon us, not only in a happy Deliverance, but a fingular and glorious Victory; a Party of ours advancing to gain the wind of the Enemy, were difcovered by a Party of theirs who came to alarm us; but not withstanding (through the Lord's great mercy) after above an hours difpute at the Pafs, upon the road-way between Dunbar and Berwick, our men obtained their end, poffeffed the Pafs whereby we might with eafe come over with our Army[20]

Cromwell had seen an opportunity and shared the information with Lambert. The two observed the Scots' position from the walled confines of Broxburn, then belonging to the Earl of Roxborough, to the north and east of the great road. They were puzzled at the Scots' intentions. Cromwell wrote: 'We could not well imagine but that the enemy intended to make an attempt upon us, or place themselves in a more exact condition of interposition'. As they watched the Scots, Cromwell told Lambert that he thought that they had presented the English with an opportunity; Lambert replied that he had just been about to say the same thing. Together they summoned Colonel George Monck and then the other colonels, and explained the situation.[21]

The battlefield presented a series of difficulties to the republican army. There was Doon Hill itself, with the remnants of an iron-age fort which had first made use of the steep sides, upon which Leslie had initially concentrated his forces. Clearly it had presented to hard a position to take and Leslie knew this – he may have undertaken the manoeuvres on the night of 2 September in order to tempt Cromwell into attacking, as the point was to defeat the invaders. The campaign had been successfully prosecuted, the attack on Edinburgh had failed and denying local supplies to the invading forces had caused problems and conditioned the retreat to Dunbar. Cromwell's army was theoretically weakened through being deprived of food and struck down by disease: some soldiers had been evacuated by sea to England. In front of Doon Hill was what was described by the author of *A Brief Narrative of the Great Victory* as a ditch, but was actually 40 or 50 feet wide and supposed to be as deep, with a stream (the Brock, or Brock's, Burn) at the bottom of it. Gentles calls it a narrow glen. It was a further massive barrier to anyone wishing to attack Doon Hill, but as the same author pointed out it would hamper anyone who attempted to cross it in either direction.[22] It was the combination of these two topographical features which enforced the stand-off on 2 September. Doon Hill did slope downwards and eastward towards a road and there was level land to the sea cliffs at its eastern end, something impossible to visualise now as years of quarrying have made it impossible to see this as Cromwell and Lambert did that night. Thus it is not possible to envisage precisely what Cromwell saw when he looked at the ground rising to Doon Hill, unlike the situation at Marston Moor.[23] Brock Burn could be crossed only at the eastern end beyond the road, at the road bridge itself and at single a point west of the road. This combination of crossing points and the gentle slope up the hill was the weak spot which Leslie needed to guard. It was also his route if he wanted to take the fight to the invaders.

It is possible that Leslie had already been hampered before the beginning of the month. Incorporating the new, young king into the Scottish political and religious world had not been a smooth ride. He and particularly his English adherents did not wish to be subsumed into a Presbyterian war effort, and on the other side many of the more radical officers in the army did not want to share their cause with the king. A month before the stand-off at Dunbar the army had been purged of 3,000 men on grounds relating to their religion or politics, not according to military needs. Having served with the Engagers, or with royalist forces at any other time, was enough to proscribe some soldiers at this juncture when about 80 experienced officers were expelled. Gentles thinks that this sapped morale in the officer corps as well as removed experienced soldiers.[24] However, it is questionable whether this made much difference. Leslie's strategy was sound up to the point where he brought his army to Dunbar and cut the invaders off from their base. As to the tactical errors which led to the Battle of Dunbar, it may be that the Kirk Party had some influence over these because it had sent representatives to accompany Leslie and the army by this point. However, at regimental level the removal of known and possibly trusted officers might have had an effect on morale when the Scottish regiments came under intense pressure and began to fall back.

Cromwell and Lambert may have been puzzled as to Leslie's intentions as they watched from the top floors of Roxborough's house, but there has been some speculation about what was happening. Wanklyn points to the argument that Leslie was in thrall to the Kirk Party representatives accompanying the army, and that they urged him to move down the eastern side of the hill to attack. This credits the Kirk representatives with the same authority as the Committee of Public Safety's representatives in revolutionary France, who accompanied the armies 140 years later.[25] Marshall also supports this theory, suggesting that they were continuing, even on the field of battle, to purge the army and urge Leslie to attack. Kitson even suggests that the Kirk representatives were citing 'inspiring, but irrelevant passages from the Old Testament'.[26] Certainly, within days of the battle Whitelocke had heard that there were such divisions, and that the soldiers had wanted 'to make rather a bridge of gold for them [Cromwell's army] to pass home but the ministers carried to a fight'.[27] The consensus of opinion largely follows what Leslie said later about not being in complete control of the army. He had little need to attack. Cromwell was evacuating the sick from Dunbar, and some of his colonels were in favour of shipping the foot out by sea and using the horse to smash a way down the Great North Road, much as the Earl of Essex had tried to do at Lostwithiel.[28]

Yet the Scottish army was exposed to the elements, which were not kindly disposed, whilst the invaders could find shelter in and around Dunbar. Holding the army together long enough for Cromwell's forces to disintegrate or evacuate might not have been practical. There would be a point at which Leslie would have to attack. His army was in good condition, Cromwell's was in decline, and the Scots could see that some troops were leaving. Leslie might simply have been shifting the blame after the event, and Grainger thinks that Leslie was 'by no means unwilling' to attack. Like Cromwell he had called a council of war with Lord Leven and six senior colonels; again, as with Cromwell, this was textbook stuff – military men only, none of the Kirk's advisors.[29] As a result of the discussions Leslie began shifting his weight, moving, in Cromwell's estimate, about two-thirds of the horse from the left wing to the right: the foot and the baggage train on the original right wing shifted eastwards towards the sea. He was now in open field battle order, with horse on each flank and foot in the centre.

Monck and the colonels all eventually agreed to attack, and preparations were put in place as night fell. Six regiments of horse and three-and-a-half regiments of foot were to form the attacking forces. The leading horse regiments were those of the three generals – Fleetwood, Lambert and Whalley – and they were to lead them in the attack; Monck was to accompany them, commanding the foot brigade.[30] The remaining regiments of horse – Twistleton's, Lilburne's and Cromwell's own – and the dragoons, with the remaining brigades of foot, led by Colonels Thomas Pride and Robert Overton, would form the reserve and protect the artillery as it moved into position. This hammer-head attack down the Great North Road, similar in some ways to the attack at Preston, was risky and the placing of the three generals in charge of the spearhead shows that Cromwell knew that his men would need some urging as they attacked. The enemy was still in a strong position: they had their artillery in place and they outnumbered the republican forces by about two to one as Cromwell claimed to believe – they were significant odds.

Getting the attack started took some time: it had been scheduled for daybreak between 4.30 and 5.00 am, but was delayed until 6.00 am, by which time it was clear daylight. The Scots had also delayed their attack: Leslie had expected the battle to be over by 7.00 am.[31] The Scots, forewarned by the later assemblage of troops, were ready and made strong resistance as Cromwell expected:

Having the advantage of their canon and Foot against our Horse before our foot could come up they made gallant resistance and there was a very hot dispute at sword point between our Horse and theirs: our first Foot after they had discharged their duty being over-powered with the enemy received some repulse[32]

Whilst the foot apparently steadied, it took the timely assistance of Cromwell's own regiment of foot to defeat the Scottish foot and the lancers which accompanied them. This second attack absorbed the rest of Monck's brigade and was supported by the reserve regiments of horse and dragoons pushing in on the eastern flank of Leslie's army, which had concentrated up to half of its strength in counter-attacking the initial assault. So complete was the republic's horse's break through the flanks of horse and foot ahead of it that there was suddenly a complete breakdown of morale in the Scottish army, which began to flee as Cromwell's forces began pushing on to the lower slopes of Doon Hill. Collapse came suddenly when the renewed attack broke the regiments facing them, and the rest of the army seemed to lose heart. Cromwell believed that the forces opposing his attack were the best that Leslie had. If that was the case, or at least recognised as such by the rest of the Scottish army, then it might be expected that their defeat would affect general morale levels. Even so, the destruction of the Scottish army was an implosion which Cromwell was able to take advantage of. As his army pushed on to Doon Hill from its gentle eastern slope a couple of regiments attempted to stem the tide, but the damage was done by the defeated horse who now careered back on to the rest of the army, causing disorder and panic. Cromwell recognised what he was seeing and dredged up a six-year-old reference: the Scots were 'made by the Lord of Hosts as stubble to our swords'.

Cromwell prefaced the second paragraph of his written account to Speaker Lenthall with the statement: 'It has now pleased God to bestow a mercy upon you, worthy of your knowledge and of the thanks and praise of all that feare and love his Name yea, the mercy is far above all praise'. To his wife he wrote that 'had been an exceeding mercy: who can tell how great it is'. The author of *A True Relation* wrote in a similar vein: 'And indeed this is the Lord of Host his own doings, and it is marvellous in our eyes'.[33] Cromwell must however be accorded the credit. He and Lambert had recognised the opportunity put before them at the eastern end of Doon Hill, as soon as Leslie shifted his axis; and Cromwell achieved what any outnumbered commander needs to do to offset the numerical disadvantage, by concentrating force against a particular point and if possible a pivotal one, the defeat of which would have massive consequences.[34] It was not just that a victory had been won, but the manner of winning which was astonishing. The attack had been carefully planned: it was risky and needed all the famous names to lead it. Although artillery had been allocated to the brigades and even to regiments, it did not play a great part, and from some accounts it seems that the Scots were the only ones to actually fire cannons during the brief fight. It was the sudden collapse of morale following the defeat at the pivotal point which caused surprise. The Scots collapsed quickly, with escaping troops making their way west and then north towards Haddington. A great number, around 10,000, were captured, about 15,000 weapons were surrendered or picked up abandoned and all 30 of Leslie's artillery pieces – from heavy guns to the leather guns – fell into Cromwell's hands. So many pikes and muskets were captured that there were simply too many to transport to England and they had to be broken up on the spot.[35] Scottish casualties were high: about 3,000 were killed, most probably during the pursuit. On 9 September parliament heard that 15,000 had been killed or taken.[36]

That the pursuit saw the Scots suffer most of their casualties is suggested by the small number of commonwealth casualties in the battle: just 40, according to *A True Relation*. Cromwell thought it was 20, as did the author of *A Brief Narrative*, who added that 'we lost none after the dispute for the Passe'. All agree that just one officer, Major Rooksby, died but according to Cromwell there was another unnamed cornet killed. Tactically it was a superb victory. A risky attack had been so successful that it had impacted upon the morale of the whole army, not just those which were engaged in the fighting at the river crossing. And it is this point which might confirm the effect of the purges. In a crisis such as the repulse of the front line, steady discipline amongst the supporting or adjacent troops is essential: it is necessary to offset the shock and fear induced by such a collapse using the trust between officers and men. This trust is often engendered over time during service in the field or training. If sufficient numbers of regimental officers had been suddenly replaced, then the Scottish regiments may not have had that bond between officers and men at company and regimental level to enable the maintenance of moral at such a crucial time, when command goes beyond the level of drill.[37]

Dunbar did not finish the war, but it severely dented the Kirk Party's hold on the army and allowed the young king to exert more control over the military.[38] Leslie had managed to assemble a force of 4,000 men at Edinburgh then left for Stirling – his men, Whitelocke recorded, 'being driven like turkeys'.[39] Cromwell was able to occupy the south-east unopposed as the government fled from the capital to the castle or on to Stirling. As the influence of the Kirk

Party waned, Charles's position got somewhat stronger, but attention was switched to the south-west where radical Presbyterians held sway and had published a remonstrance setting forth a hard-line position which opposed Charles being crowned. Whilst the Remonstrants' small force was defeated on 1 December at Hamilton, allowing the commonwealth forces to occupy the rest of lowland Scotland south of the Forth and the Clyde, Cromwell could make no headway at Stirling and pulled back from confronting Leslie there. Moderates were able to hold sway in the General Assembly and saw matters somewhat differently. Whereas the Remonstrants saw Dunbar as a sign that God was displeased with the dalliance with Charles, the moderates saw only that they needed all the support they could get. It was a question of who was to be regarded as the greatest threat to the Kirk: Charles, or the sectarian New Model Army and Cromwell. The moderates believed that it was Cromwell and his army, occupying lowland southern Scotland, which had to be dealt with first. Charles's supporters had tried to initiate a coup themselves, known as The Start, but like that of his father back in 1640 the attempt failed and Charles had no alternative but to accept that his best chance of power lay with the moderate Kirk Party members, who now included the Marquis of Argyll amongst their numbers. They too were convinced that they needed the support of the royalists in Scotland and began to work more closely with the young king, crowning him at Scone on 1 January 1651. Given command of the army, Leslie was left in place to try to hold a line between Edinburgh and Glasgow with its centre at Stirling. His strategic intention continued to be Fabian in that he denied succour to the invader by blocking access to the rich and fertile farmlands of Fife.[40] Charles and the Scots were aided in their attempts to rebuild Scotland's military forces early in the new year by Cromwell's illness, which lasted from February until May 1651 and left him, and consequently the army, largely inactive for almost five months, during which time Lambert proved unequal to the task of breaking Leslie's defence.[41] In June, Cromwell returned to his command and struck at Queensferry, forcing a crossing and making inroads into Fife. Lambert had by now also forced his way into the old kingdom after the Battle of Inverkeithing on 20 July.[42] Since his recovery, Cromwell had essentially made himself the focus of attention as he crossed and recrossed the southern lowlands, but he had been careful to leave a route to the south open for Leslie and the king whom it was suspected was more interested in marching on England than protecting Fife. So when Leslie turned on Lambert and thereby drew Cromwell to Lambert's side the route to England was open.[43]

Charles was keen on marching into England, where he hoped he would be able to raise supporters and where he could arrange to be free of Kirk Party control. There would be advantages for the Scots too: if they pushed into England then Cromwell and the main body of the army might pursue the invaders and leave Scotland free to re-establish itself. On 31 July, Leslie led the army out of Stirling to Cumbernauld. Cromwell, in the meantime, was still heading towards Perth, where over the next couple of days he was held up in a siege. The town had only been occupied a few hours before Cromwell arrived and its subsequent defence was simply a ploy to keep him occupied whilst Leslie moved towards England. By the time the great guns were ready and preparations for an assault were in place, Cromwell had heard of Leslie's march. The decoy garrison surrendered Perth, its job done.[44] Leslie had mounted his foot soldiers so they could keep up with the horse and march rapidly towards England via Lanark. On 5 August the army was on the border. By now the Scottish army was about 12,000–13,000 strong but illness, desertion and outpost duty had begun to drain Leslie's forces. Charles did not mind – despite the less than encouraging response of the garrison at Carlisle which simply slammed its doors on him, he still expected to raise enthusiastic royalists in England. One troop joined him at Penrith, but already he was shadowed. Major General Thomas Harrison with the northern English forces which had been based in Leith, having been ordered into Scotland on 18 March, now marched to Newcastle and got there the day that Leslie had reached the border.[45] Harrison was the commander of the north of England, a role similar to Cromwell's in 1648.[46] He now began to practice Fabian tactics, ordering the northern, North Midland and North Wales counties to prepare for invasion by removing food supplies and other necessities out of the way. Behind Harrison was Lambert, who on 5 August had left Fife and now set out from Leith, whilst Harrison sent out troops to find Leslie's eastern flank – by 6 August the commonwealth generals knew that Leslie was at Carlisle and going southwards towards Lancashire. Lambert moved so rapidly that he was at Penrith just a day behind the invaders. Cromwell was following up with the foot. He was concerned to be selective, leaving less-experienced regiments in Scotland. As the invaders slowed down to allow for recruitment in Lancashire the commonwealth forces began to harass them, and Lambert and Harrison joined forces in the invaders' rear with 6,000–7,000 men, to be joined by horse sent south by Cromwell. The Council of State began to mobilise the rest of the county. Cromwell's old bug-bear, Newark, was set initially as the rendezvous for the region's forces, ironically under Lord Grey of Groby, before they were redirected south to Northampton. South Midlands forces were put under the command of Charles Fleetwood to block any extensive southwards march. On 14 August, London defence forces, summoned two days earlier, assembled at Barnet.[47]

The invaders, whilst still the largest single force in England, were not getting the sort of reinforcements that they wanted. The Earl of Derby, upon whom the king had invested so much hope, brought just 300 unarmed men from his Isle of Man stronghold. Grainger thinks that the young king was alienating potential supporters by lodging with Catholic royalists on his march south.[48] Certainly few were coming to join him. On 16 August there was an attempt to block the invaders' advance as 3,000 militia were joined by Lambert and Harrison. The Scots drove off the militia from the bridge at Warrington and the commonwealth horse were unable to deploy successfully because of the tightly enclosed lands.[49] The Scots were able to hold on to the northern part of Warrington too, and Harrison and Lambert were unable to make any headway in an attack and so withdrew, letting the Scots continue southwards. Derby's recruitment campaign ended after a brief battle near Wigan, where he was worsted by Robert Lilburne's regiment. He had been successful in recent days, having assembled over a thousand men to add to his initial 300, and judging by the fact that they took on Lilburne's experienced regiment for over an hour, they must have been armed. In defeat, however, they scattered to their homes and in so doing dealt a mortal blow to Derby's recruitment campaign.[50] Debates now took place on the future direction of the invasion: North Wales and the south-west both had traditions of royalist support, and the Duke of Buckingham favoured a direct attack on London. Access to North Wales was made complicated by the defiance of the Shrewsbury governor, who pointedly referred to Charles as the commander in chief of the Scottish army.[51] Worcester, site of some of the earliest and lattermost fighting of the first civil war in England, had a long-standing royalist tradition, and moreover was sited conveniently between North Wales and the south-west – it was also somewhere from which a march on London could be launched. The invaders headed there, arriving on 22 August 1651.

THE BATTLE OF WORCESTER

Worcester had been a royalist garrison from the earliest days of the first civil war, with a ring of smaller outposts around it. It was strategically placed for trade and communications with Wales, as well as the south-west and the Midlands. Charles hoped that it would be close enough to royalists in these regions to reach him, without being too far south for the Earl of Derby and his expected recruits to reach the advancing army. Derby of course was, within three days of Charles's reaching Worcester, out of the game following the defeat at Wigan Lane on 25 August, but when Charles had reached the city he had been leading a very successful recruitment campaign in Lancashire, which might have both brought significant numbers of English royalist soldiers in itself and encouraged others across the west to join the advancing army. It might have seemed promising when the small, recently arrived parliamentarian garrison of Worcester was expelled by the council and townspeople as Charles approached; but when the north gate was opened and the mayor presented the town's keys on bended knees to Charles, the gate to the south and out of the town was left suggestively open. Almost as soon as the gates of Worcester were both reluctantly slammed with Charles and his army inside, the pursuers arrived outside. On 24 August the commonwealth's forces rendezvoused at Warwick. Lord Grey of Groby led 1,100 horse from the Midlands, and Fleetwood brought the forces from Barnet, who numbered 14,000 according to a report in parliament.[52] Cromwell awaited the arrival of his forces from the long march southwards. By 25 August the army being assembled at Warwick was greater than that in Worcester.[53] Grainger has argued that the king's campaign was more successful than it might appear. He had gained about 5,000 English royalist recruits and they were with him; and until defeated by Robert Lilburne, Derby's recruitment campaign was meeting with some success.[54] On the other hand, the invaders were facing determined opposition that looked very much like a national effort.[55] Counties had assembled their forces on command from London: the people of Lancashire, generally thought of as one of the dark places where conservatism and Catholicism had a strong hold on the people, had on the one hand provided recruits for the king, but on the other had offered little food and sustenance. Lord Fairfax had rallied to the cause and been involved in the defence of Yorkshire, his opposition to the war having been pushed aside once the Scots had invaded England.[56] The government had labelled the invaders as Scots rather than royalists. This was the fourth invasion of England in 12 years and the second to take the western route in just three. It may be that the superb organisation shown by Cromwell and the government was enacted against a backdrop of war-weariness or negative nationalism rather than being a truly united war effort, but in the end it does not matter for in the final analysis it was military strategy which counted in August and September 1651.[57] Cromwell's letter explaining his plans was read in parliament on 11 August, and he told them that he expected forces would be raised in England to try and impede the Scots' advance, and reminded his readers that the Scots had invaded before, when England was in a far less stable condition and they had still been beaten. He referred to the decision to invade as 'folly'.[58] Part of the plan Cromwell outlined was for Harrison to keep the Scots together and in effect herd them southwards. Likewise Harrison informed parliament that he had communicated with the militia committees in the counties along the Scots' line of march, and soon after that the counties themselves had reported their actions. On a daily basis parliament was receiving reports from Cromwell, Lambert and Harrison, as well as the county committees, indicating where the invaders or the Earl of Derby were and also the position of their pursuers.

On 26 August, parliament learned that Worcester's fortifications were being repaired in a letter from Fleetwood. The invaders, he reported, had 12,000 horse and foot, very few of the latter being English.[59] By 27 August it appeared that the invaders were going nowhere. There appeared to be no intention of moving towards Gloucester, they were building defence works outside Worcester and 16 carts of ladders were shipped into the city. They refortified the walls which had been demolished in recent months and rebuilt the large sconce to the east of the town outside the Sudbury Gate on the road to London, now referred to as the Fort Royal. It may be that they expected to be attacked from the north, as on the north side of the town there were four bastions with artillery mounted in them. In contrast the eastern side of the town had just one, besides that defence work built to block access to St Martin's Gate north of those linking the Fort Royal to the south-east corner of Worcester. The western side of the town was protected by the Severn, and there was just one artillery bastion constructed at the western end of the bridge that linked the city to the meadows which ran alongside the river. They also began to burn down the suburbs.[60] On the other hand, Charles's summons to men of military age had largely fallen on deaf ears, even if 2,000 men did appear at the muster. Lambert reported the situation to parliament on 1 September. On the 28 August, he had crossed the Severn at Upton, where the bridge had been damaged but not destroyed by the invaders. Repairing the bridge, Lambert made it possible for Fleetwood to cross the river. On the following day, these forces pressed forward towards Worcester and were not hindered in any way. The advance scouts, four-and-a-half miles ahead of Lambert, indeed found no one until they reached the proximity of the city itself where Cromwell, having established his headquarters at Spetchley, had already set up artillery and was firing on it. Fleetwood led his forces from Upton; Cromwell led his forces to the Hereford side of Worcester. There was no question of conducting a long siege: it might prove something of a magnet for recruitment if Charles could hold out for any length of time, and a third of the army might by this time have been English. Cromwell, with over 30,000 men, outnumbered the invaders three to one, and behind his army the major towns of Hereford, Shrewsbury and Gloucester were all defended against any breakout attempt.

Cromwell had led his forces to a line of low hills east and south-east of Worcester and about a mile away from it, with its centre on the London road as it crossed Red Hill. To supplement the possession of the bridge over the Severn at Upton, a bridge of commandeered boats was established over the river to enable approaches to the city. The Severn crossings alone did not lead directly to Worcester's western side, for the smaller but still impassable River Teme, which joined the Severn south of Worcester, protected the city from approaches from the south-west. As soon as the invaders detected movement on this flank they had set out to destroy the bridge at Powick, the scene of the first real skirmish of the civil war in England nine years earlier, but made a botched job of it leaving it repairable. To enable the linking of his army across the Teme, Cromwell had a second pontoon built over the river just west of its confluence with the Severn 'within a pistol shot' of the first, allowing access to the meadows south and west of the city from both the east of the Severn and south of the Teme, whilst keeping communications between the two wings of Cromwell's army open.[61] An assault on the more vulnerable western side of Worcester was now possible. Inside the city the options had diminished as the ring of garrisoned towns around them increased. Yet they held a strongly fortified town and they could see every move Cromwell and his generals made with telescopes or perspective glasses from the cathedral tower: enough time was thus gained to prepare for each eventuality.

On 3 September, exactly one year on from the Battle of Dunbar, the impromptu pontoons were made ready: possibly they had been constructed along the river banks and kept parallel with them until the attacking forces were ready. Cromwell's left flank, commanded by Fleetwood, advanced from Upton-on-Severn to Powick-on-Teme, starting as the sun rose that late summer's day and arriving at the Teme by between 1.00 pm and 2.00 pm.[62] The combined commonwealth forces then advanced on the city at about 2.00 pm, as each bridge was swung across the rivers with the same watchword 'the Lords of hosts' as carried at Dunbar. The advance forlorn hopes of foot – one part drawn from Fleetwood's wing, the other from Cromwell's – crossed the two rivers at the same time as Colonel Richard Deane made a noisy and distracting assault on Powick Bridge.[63] The Scots, based in the St John's suburb of Worcester and sited in the meadows west of the Severn near the bridge close to St Clement's Church, were instinctively drawn towards Deane's attack: Sir William Keith's highland regiment and the commander of this wing of the invading forces, Major General Robert Montgomery's horse, tried to repel the attack there as simultaneously some attempts were made to deal with the assault across the two pontoon bridges. Cromwell had quickly supplemented the forlorn hope on the Severn bridgehead with two foot regiments, Ingoldsby's and Fairfax's and both Hacker's and Cromwell's horse.[64] Deane's own regiment, brigaded with Goffe's foot, now crossed the Teme boat bridge. The highland regiment of Major General Pitscottie fell back on Colonel Robert Dalziel's regiment and together they used the enclosure hedges to try and hold back the advance, but they were outnumbered and driven back after what most commentators (including Robert Stapleton in his report to parliament) said was a fight which 'lasted a long time, and was very hot'.[65] As Pitscottie's men fell back, Keith's foot and Montgomery's horse at Powick had to fall back too, to prevent themselves being attacked on the flank.[66] These units were driven slowly back, through the enclosures at point of pike for much of the way: the horse of both sides were unable to manoeuvre until the meadows were reached. The author of *An Exact and Perfect Relation of Every Particular of the Fight at Worcester* seems to have expected the Scots to retreat towards Hereford or Ludlow, but instead they wheeled eastwards and got into the city via the bastioned bridge near St Clement's.[67]

At this point, about an hour into the fighting, and taking advantage of both the imbalance in the parliamentarian line caused by the dash across the river and the division of Cromwell's forces necessarily caused by the two rivers, the Duke of Hamilton and Charles launched simultaneous attacks on the north and south end of the parliamentarian forces, comprising six veteran regiments and militia forces sent from the east of England, stationed east of the city.[68] Hamilton attacked from the north or St Martin's Gate which led to Droitwich, whilst Charles debouched from the Sudbury Gate along the London Road. The plan worked, and the parliamentarians were pushed back from their positions either side of Perry Wood.[69] Cromwell's overwhelming numbers now told. With the Scots on the west bank of the Severn now retreating towards the bridge into Worcester, he could spare forces from his left wing. Cromwell himself led three regiments, perhaps including his own horse, back over the pontoons to bolster the southern wing of the commonwealth line east of the city. The Scottish and royalist momentum faded as Cromwell's numbers began to tell and the line stabilised. Exhausted and frustrated, the defenders returned to the city, but they were so closely pursued that Cromwell's men reached the gates at the same time. The large star-fort sconce, Fort Royal, was stormed by the Essex militia and its few guns were turned on Worcester.[70] In the confusion the Sudbury Gate was entered by both the fleeing royalists and Scots, as well as the fast-moving republican forces, and thus the city was entered: the last fighting took place in the city streets. Night fell quickly that late-summer day and brought an end to the fighting and any thought of a pursuit beyond the northern boundaries of the town, according to Stapleton's account.[71] Charles, Leslie, Hamilton and other mounted officers managed to get out of the north of the city through Castle Gate and Fore Gate with Leslie's brigade of horse. The rest of the invading forces, allowing for around 2,000 fatalities, surrendered; around 10,000 men became prisoners that evening and in the following days. Harrison implied that the confusion was not simply produced by nightfall on 3 September as Stapleton reported, but it lasted days. A couple of days later he wrote: 'all things were then in confusion; lords knights, and gentlemen, were then plucking out of holes by soldiers'. Moreover, 'what with the dead bodies of men and the dead horses of the enemy filling the streets, there was such nastiness that a man could hardly abide the town'.[72] The escapees fragmented between Worcester and mid-Yorkshire, surrendering in handfuls whether or not they were actually attacked. Charles Stuart, king of nowhere, began an exciting and tortuous escape that led him through the trees and priest-holes of the west Midlands and then the south-west, before heading south to Brighthelmstone in Sussex from where he took a boat to France in late October. Nine years later Charles's escape would become an adventure which saved the monarchies of England, Scotland and Ireland; but for now, in the wake of the stunning victory which secured the commonwealth, it was just the saving of a young man's life. The victory was complete in every sense. The invasion was over, the entire invading army was destroyed: captured or killed. Leslie's brigade was mopped up as it tried to make its way north. What in particular marked the victory was the level of national participation involved. This was not a victory just for the New Model Army or its successor, it was a victory for the commonwealth. Harrison praised the militia, naming those from Surrey, Norfolk and Suffolk, and said that they behaved gallantly. The author of *A True and Exact Relation* mentioned those of Essex and Surrey: it had been the former who stormed the Fort Royal outside the Sudbury Gate.[73] Marshall described the battle as Cromwell's easiest. His overwhelming numerical advantage allowed him to execute a sound plan; Wanklyn agrees to some extent, but more generously concludes that it is impossible to fault Cromwell's leadership.[74] Kitson too is generous, suggesting that the plan was unconventional and whilst Cromwell did have a preponderance of numbers the king had a strong position in the town; for J.C. Davies it was nothing less than a 'crushing victory'. It was a total victory as a result of Cromwell's tactical skill and ability: 'No more perfect instrument of military power than the New Model Army, as it was on 3 September 1651, has ever fought on English soil.'[75]

10

CROMWELL AT WAR

A CROWNING MERCY

Cromwell referred to the Battle of Worcester in awestruck terms: 'The dimensions of this mercy are above my thoughts. It is for aught I know, a crowning mercy.'[1] He saw Worcester, more than any other battle of the civil wars which had promised so much – Naseby, Preston and Dunbar included – as the final victory over the enemy. Back in 1649 he had identified three enemies of the state: the royalists, the Irish and the Scots. In the two years and six months since then he had personally defeated each and every one of them, as well as tackling mutinous soldiers and overseing campaigns led by subordinates which concluded or would shortly conclude all hostilities. There are two things one needs to bear in mind at this point. Cromwell had never seen the war as an earthly event, and nor did he believe himself or his colleagues in arms, or in parliament, as the prime movers in the dramatic events of the period 1639–52. The war was only ever about divining God's solution to the spiritually damaging impasse in government occasioned, as he and other thought, by the intractable nature of Charles I's understanding of the role of a monarch in British and Irish politics. As such, the developments or changes which Cromwell and his colleagues wanted were not simply about an earthly balance of powers within the political systems of the British Isles, they were about bringing to fruition God's plans for his chosen people in those isles, so recently, but only partially, freed from the tyranny of the Roman Church. The security of that earthly and spiritual release could only be assured by such reforms as would prevent a monarch from leading God's people back into darkness. Every victory was God's work even if apparently attained by human endeavour. However, there were complicating factors, for even if the victories were more than reasonably clear evidence of God's providence, their political and military outcome was often subsequently limited by circumstance. God's seeming victory in each of the Bishops' Wars, and the two outbreaks of war in England and Wales, had all been obfuscated subsequently by the need to deal with the king. Even with Charles dead, the latter victories in Ireland and in Scotland were still conditioned by the presence of a legitimist threat to the stability of the commonwealth. Things were beginning to change, however, and the scales were being lifted from Cromwell's eyes by the time had won at Dunbar. It can be seen from his report to parliament that he sensed the approaching complete victory:

> Thus you have the prospect of one of the most signal mercies God hath done for England and His people, this war. And now may it please you to give me the leave of a few words. It is easy to say the Lord hath done this. It would do you good to see and hear our poor foot go up and down making their boast of God. But Sir it is in your hands, and by these eminent mercies of God puts it more in your hands to give Glory to Him; to improve your power, and his blessings to His praise. We that serve you beg of you not to own us, but God alone.
>
> [...] we pray you own His people more and more; for they are the chariots and horsemen of Israel. Disown yourselves; but own your authority, and improve it to curb the proud and the insolent [...] relieve the oppressed, hear the groans of the prisoners in England [...] be pleased to reform the abuses of all professions: and if there be any one that makes many poor to make a few rich, that suits not a Commonwealth.[2]

After the Battle of Worcester he was even more confident that this victory would be unbridled. He had even told Lord Wharton a week before the battle took place:

> you have the opportunity to associate with His people in His work and to manifest your willingness and desire to serve the Lord against His and His people's enemies. Would you be blessed out of Zion and see the good of his people, and rejoice with His inheritance.[3]

When the battle had actually been fought and won he confirmed to parliament his confidence that it was now feasible to put God's plan into place:

> I am bold humbly to beg, that all thoughts may tend to the promoting of His honour who hath wrought so great salvation, and that the fatness of these continued mercies my not occasion pride and wantonness, as formerly the like hath done to a chosen nation but that the fear of the Lord, even for His mercies, may keep an authority and a people so prospered, and blessed, and witnessed unto, humble and faithful, and that justice and righteousness mercy and truth may flow from you, as a thankful return to our gracious God.[4]

Worcester was also the crown on Cromwell's military career. He journeyed to London shortly after the battle and never again fastened a sword to his side on the way to a campaign or battlefield. From this point on and for the rest of his life, Cromwell remained lord general, the captain general of the four nations' armies, but his command was now exercised through trusted lieutenants; some, like Henry Ireton, Charles Fleetwood and his own son Henry, part of his extended family, and others, such as George Monck, comrades in arms met in the heat of campaign and battle.

SWORDS INTO PLOUGHSHARES: CROMWELL THE POLITICIAN

Cromwell returned to the political world which, as I have argued elsewhere, he found was less than convinced by his confidence that the time was ripe to reform the nation's government and structures and thus not supportive of his proposals. He spent an uncomfortable 18 months growing concerned by parliament's lack of care for the men who had ventured their lives and estates to secure victory, and worried that it was becoming careless when setting out the nature of future elections. Undoubtedly important to the political world as he was, Cromwell and his allies in parliament were not able to dominate, never mind dictate, the path of commonwealth politics in the years after Worcester. When, after months of prevarication, parliament at last got around to setting up elections for its successor, Cromwell and his allies were alarmed by a series of discussions in parliament seemingly determined to pursue an intolerant approach to freedom of worship, something which was close to Cromwell's belief in the fiduciary relationship with parliament. This was thrown into high relief when parliament rejected the bill for renewing the Commission for Propagating the Gospel in Wales. For Cromwell the commission had been at the forefront of religious reform in the country, but parliament feared its exploitation by radicals like the Fifth Monarchists. By this time parliament seemed blithe towards its faithful servant and even proposed selling of the royal residence of Hampton Court, which it had only recently awarded to Cromwell. Parliamentary discussions of the plan for its own dissolution and the election of its successor had proceeded slowly, with debates each Wednesday. At the end of March 1653, MPs had decided on the property qualification for electors and upon the geographical and demographic redistribution of constituencies, but failed to press matters to their logical conclusion by setting a date for an election. On 18 and 19 April 1653, Oliver convened meetings of the Council of Officers, and also a meeting of 20 MPs and an equal number of officers, to discuss the immediate appointment of an executive committee to govern in the absence of a parliament and be charged with holding elections, which would be followed by the immediate dissolution of the house. The MPs at the meeting agreed to present the petition to the house on 20 April, and were expected to steer it through parliament that day and secure its implementation. Cromwell meanwhile met with officers and MPs to draw up plans for the proposed interim executive government. During the morning's discussions at Cromwell's house, news came from Westminster that parliament was in session. The MPs with Cromwell then left for parliament but found it not to be discussing the proposals sent to it, but instead hurriedly trying to rush through its own bill for setting up a new parliament. Cromwell gathered a squad of soldiers and marched down the road to Westminster. Leaving the soldiers outside he took his seat in the chamber. Cromwell's plan had prompted concerted opposition and the parliament was determined to complete its own bill that day and so was unusually full. Cromwell stood up and began to speak just as the bill was to be put to the vote. He praised parliament's past but attacked its recent negligence. Then came the point of his interjection: 'It is not fit that you should sit here any longer. You have sat here too long for any good you have been doing lately', before attacking some MPs personally.[5] He then got Harrison to call in soldiers to expel the MPs.[6]

Within hours an executive consisting of soldiers and MPs was established which went on to create the means of selecting a representative parliament to be drawn from across the four nations. This body – the Little Parliament, named for its size, or Barebone's Parliament, named after one of its Fifth Monarchist members, Praise-God Barebones – sat from July until December 1653, when it effectively dissolved itself and offered power directly to Cromwell. Within days of the dissolution, a completely new constitution, the Instrument of Government – very much the brainchild of General Lambert – had been approved by the council and Cromwell was named the Lord Protector, the head of state for the new Protectorate. He was also to remain in command of the armed forces. Cromwell served as Lord Protector, albeit with amended powers, from mid-1657 for the few remaining years of his life. Under his stewardship he defeated a royalist rising in 1655, ended the war with the Dutch which the commonwealth had embarked on in 1652, challenged Spanish hegemony in the West Indies and went to war as France's ally against the Spanish in the Low Countries, all without leading an army himself. The story of the Protectorate, which Cromwell led from December 1653 until his death on 3 September 1658, is a story for a different work.

THE LORD GENERAL AND THE ART OF WAR

Undoubtedly, Cromwell was a successful general. He commanded the victorious armies at the final two great battles of the civil wars, both of which combined to destroy in a comprehensive manner the republic's enemy's capacity for waging war. There were no more serious military challenges to the republic and there might never have been if Cromwell had lived longer. Cromwell's is a remarkable achievement: few commanders ever meet with so complete a success – the destruction of an enemy to such an extent that it never could mount a military challenge on such a scale again. Napoleon never achieved such success: even the Prussian army – so comprehensive destroyed at Jena–Auerstadt and in the string of pursuits and surrenders between 14 October 1806 and the defeat of the Prussian–Russian army at Friedland on 14 June 1807 – was reconstructed. Indeed, within nine years of the catastrophe of 1806 – the equivalent of the lifetime of the republic after the Battle of Worcester – a renewed Prussian army had taken part in the Russian campaign, the campaign in central Germany in 1813, the invasion of France in 1814 and the Waterloo campaign. Just 20 years before Cromwell strapped on his sword, Johann Tserclaes, Count of Tilly had defeated the forces of Frederick, King of Bohemia at the Battle of the White Mountain: a defeat so complete that Bohemia was conquered and King Frederick lost his throne, and was subsequently even driven from his Palatine Electorate. But the war did not end with Frederick's defeat: there were another 28 years of warfare in Europe to go before the Treaty of Westphalia ended what was to become known as the Thirty Years War. In the meantime the great warrior-king Gustavus Adolphus, potentially one of the contributors to the military revolution, won impressive victories at Breitenfeld and Lützen, but neither dealt a knock-out blow. Similarly the Duke of Friedland, Albrecht Wallenstein, a man who had spent 35 years obscurely farming his estates much like Cromwell before taking up the sword, also met with great military successes such as Dessau Bridge, upon which he built a strong reputation but more importantly a fortune, but he had not ended a war by doing so. In this respect Cromwell's achievement was all the more remarkable.[7] Closer to home there were few generals who could match his achievement. At no point before 1651 was a war on British and Irish soil ended even temporarily through military victory alone. The nearest equivalent was Alexander Leslie, Lord Leven. The then General Leslie achieved a surprise victory by chance in 1639 when his forces and possibly herds of cattle drove off an English army at Kelso, thus ending the First Bishop's War. Moreover, and more pointedly, his victory at

Newburn in 1640 ended the Second Bishop's War and brought to end the early Anglo-Scottish conflict. However, although no one knew it at the time, these two wars were just the start of a longer series which continued until Cromwell defeated Charles Stuart at Worcester. There is of course a list of contemporary British and Irish generals with whom Cromwell can be compared: Fairfax, David Leslie, O'Neill, Prince Rupert and Leven himself amongst them, most of whom Cromwell had fought. Of those he had not fought, Fairfax is clearly the most important. His formal military career ended in June 1650, although he did act in a less than official manner the year after during the Scottish and royalist invasion of England. Fairfax's reputation as a general is unfortunately clouded by his defensiveness about his war record after the war and a well-recognised tendency to blame others for the defeats or failures he suffered in his early career.[8] His later, successful campaigns and battles need no apology or explanation: Naseby, Langport – which he considered his finest battle – the sieges of Bristol and Oxford as well as others in the south-west, and finally his campaign in the south-east of England in 1648, proved his capacity as a general and commander. As Hopper rightly says, his appointment as commander of the New Model Army 'intensified the prosecution of the war and further hastened the royalists' defeat'.[9] But he did not see the war through in the way Cromwell did, partly as he was not so politically astute as Cromwell, but also because he could not bring himself to accept the radicalisation of the political nation any more than he could accommodate the radicalisation of the traditionally excluded elements of society energised by the Levellers and Diggers.[10] Just as convinced of providentialism as Cromwell, Fairfax could not fully believe that the death of the king and the establishment of the republic was the ultimate reason God had blessed him with victory. For this reason he decided not to fight the Scots in 1650, for they, as Cromwell less fixedly believed, were brothers in Christ who had for some of the time shared in God's victories. On campaign Fairfax was undoubtedly a sound tactician. His command at Naseby was excellent, and drawing the royalists into attacking his larger numbers when both initially held strong starting positions was masterly. His strategic vision was also good: refusing to tackle the king's defeated army in the Midlands or take on the two strongholds of Ashby-de-la-Zouch and Newark was bold. The king was able to bring together a sizeable force in the Midlands and in the end neither Ashby nor Newark would give up the fight until 1646, and both continued to deny resources and tie up parliamentarian forces for almost two years. Had they been defeated in 1645 then the parliamentarian territory in the north controlled by the Army of the Solemn League and

Covenant and the Northern Association Army could have been united with the parliamentarian south Midlands. Yet the strong royalist garrisons remained largely static, unable to provide much more than potential launching points for small campaigns and royalist pipedreams.[11] On the other hand, Lord Goring and the royalist forces in the south-west were more important. The king had banked on raising new forces in Wales and the marches to supplement his military reconstruction, but these forces did not materialise; his best chance of military recovery had always been Goring's small but veteran army which could have provided the core of a new field army. Fairfax had understood that victory lay in the destruction of field armies as a priority, rather than just attacking garrison after garrison. No matter how uncomfortable it may have been for Cromwell, who may have wanted to crush his old bug-bear Newark, turning on Goring and securing his defeat at Langport ended the possibility of the king reconstructing an experienced field army and sealed the fate of royalists in the south-west. Ultimately that bold decision ended the first civil war in England and Wales itself: but it did not end the war.

The two Leslies, Alexander and David, also possessed strong strategic vision. Subsequent to the Bishops' Wars, the ultimate expression of the elder Lord Leven's strategic vision was probably the campaign of 1644 when he invaded England. The Earl of Newcastle and Lord Forth were no mean enemies and were determined to bring Leven to battle, but for three months Leven was able to advance ever southwards, slowly but without exposing himself to being drawn into battle on foreign soil or allowing his supply lines to be compromised, until the defeat of Lord Belasyse at Selby caused Newcastle to retreat into York. David Leslie, although rarely seen holding independent command, also showed great strategic sense: his consummate campaign was that of 1650 south of Edinburgh. Cromwell was confounded in the campaign: denied vital resources and unable to edge his way into a strong enough position to attack Edinburgh. Defeat for the new lord general was a real possibility when Cromwell was forced to withdraw to Dunbar and begin evacuating his men. The point at which Leslie began to advance down Doon Hill to take on Cromwell's apparently evacuating forces was the apogee of Leslie's career. Defeat pushed him into the shadows of lesser commanders of higher social status, and the following year he played a minor and often irresolute role in the campaign in England: like Cromwell, Leslie's military career was ended by Worcester.

Of the Irish generals, Owen Roe O'Neill, the most experienced of the continental veterans, demonstrated ability in both strategy and tactics, but far too often he was in the shadow of lesser commanders who were political appointments. His greatest victory was Benburb, which was obtained when he finally got the independence and arms he needed and deserved. Yet he failed to follow up the victory because he was still not strong enough in men and materiel to tackle the Scots' Ulster garrisons, and within weeks he would be involved in internal political struggles within the Catholic Confederation.[12] O'Neill was never able to achieve complete dominance in Ulster, although he remained a potent threat until his death in 1649. His nephew Henry was the only Irish general to inflict defeat upon Cromwell and one of the few to do so in the British Isles, but this was an isolated victory, no matter how bloody and comprehensive. Even so, in the end Cromwell was able to capture Clonmel and harry O'Neill as he withdrew: within weeks the younger O'Neill was captured and killed.

The other royalist and Scottish generals Cromwell defeated included Newcastle, King Charles I, Langdale, the first Duke of Hamilton, Goring and of course Prince Rupert. Only the latter deserves direct comparison with Cromwell. Rupert was an inspiring leader who had experience of the continental wars, although much of it was theoretical because of his long period of captivity.[13] He demonstrated battlefield tactical skill at Edgehill, Marston Moor and Naseby, whilst at the same time demonstrating the limitations to his ability: such as failure to extract himself from section command and retain a battlefield-level oversight, although Kitson thinks that historians only look at this trait when Rupert was on the losing side – in other battles it helped him secure success, as at Chalgrove Field.[14] Nevertheless, Rupert was a consummate organiser of campaigns; that leading to the relief of York was his best. He also was, as Ronald Hutton has shown, an excellent logistics man: his reorganisation of the West Midlands war effort in 1644 was exemplary.[15] Undoubtedly, Rupert was an intelligent and gifted man, who later turned his hand to naval warfare and the sciences after the wars. He proved to be adept at warfare, but his campaigns were usually capped by defeat and this is very much the legacy which he left, 'swallowed up in the wreck of the royalist cause'.[16] At the tactical level too, he demonstrated insight; it is clear that at Marston Moor both he and Cromwell recognised the same possibilities in Bilton Bream, and that he sought subsequently to offset the problems presented by Cromwell's seizure of this topographical feature in an astute manner.

Of Cromwell's rivals only Fairfax, the two Leslies and Rupert, briefly, held supreme command, and at most times all of them were subject to political guidance or control. Fairfax had to break free from the Committee of Both Kingdoms on the eve of Naseby, and Leven was under the control of the revolutionary government in Edinburgh at all times, and then like Fairfax under the watchful eye of the Committee from 1645 onwards. David Leslie, as we have seen, was subject to the interference of the Kirk Party right up until the moment he committed himself to attack at Dunbar. In each case the generals' freedom of action was hampered by this oversight. Rupert was always subject to the interference of the king's political advisors. Cromwell too was hardly free of such entanglements. He was constantly in communication with Westminster, and whilst in command at Pembroke and en route to Preston he was offered 'guidance' or 'advice'. He was fortunate when in command in Ireland – as communications took so much longer to reach him he was almost completely free of parliamentarian guidance and able to control fully his own campaigns, but even then he had finally to acknowledge the summons to return to England. However, in his last campaign it was Cromwell who had the whip hand, directed Westminster's response to the invasion of England and masterminded the defeat of the invaders, commanding a government in a way that not one of his contemporaries was able to in Britain, Ireland or on the continent. However successful Cromwell was, von Clausewitz's adage still applied: 'In war the result is never final', even though he was writing of war between states. The end of the republic, however, came about after Cromwell was dead and as a result of a political implosion rather than war.[17]

CROMWELL ON THE BATTLEFIELD

J.C. Davies makes an excellent point when he argues that Cromwell's lack of experience in 1642 would not have been such a great disadvantage, as many others on all sides were in the same boat. There were several men in England and more in Scotland who had served on the continent, but they were outweighed by the amateurs who were given commissions by the king or parliament, or by colonels recruiting companies, troops and regiments on behalf of either. This amateurism extended to knowledge of logistics in warfare, although there were in terms of the horse some professions which were analogous to management of horse on the scale of a troop. Cromwell had learned his cavalry trade between summer 1642 and the spring of 1643, progressing from completely inexperienced political appointee to a colonel in a short space of time. He learned from experienced soldiers, possibly from within his network, of like-minded religious colleagues, rather than from his kin-network. But these were men whose names have not come down to us, possibly because of their initial social status: we can further only surmise that they were veterans of wars abroad, probably having fought in Protestant armies at the level of private soldiers or non-commissioned corporals and sergeants of horse. They may even have been workers from landed estate stables with the experience of managing, watering and feeding horses. Finding all of these men would not have been up to Cromwell alone – his fellow captains and officers would be working with him, piecing together a cohort of experienced soldiers and horse managers within each of their troops, so that when a regiment was being forged in 1643 the man and horse management teams were in place.

Cromwell has occasionally been described as a cavalry general. This has a great deal to support it. Cromwell brought riding a horse as his only military-related skill to his captaincy in 1642. He quickly learned the trade of troop commander and equally quickly learned the trade of a field office, leaping as he did from troop commander to regimental commander in early 1643. Although in the summer of 1642 he did in the early skirmishes around Cambridge command some foot soldiers, he probably wisely left the mechanics of infantry command to others at this stage. His first fights were cavalry affairs, notably at Belton where he used the latest techniques, adapted by Prince Rupert amongst others, to defeat a larger force than he had at his disposal. Gainsborough shows that he had mastery of cavalry actions to a very great extent. He was able to move his troops up a difficult incline and keep them together so that they assembled quickly in battle order before the enemy could attack them at a disadvantage. He was able later to rally significant numbers of his regiment's troops to enable an attack on the royalist reserve when it became apparent that it had the potential to overturn the victory won at the outset. His major contributions at Marston Moor, Naseby and Langport were as lieutenant general of horse, and it was his superb control of this wing (and, it must be said of Marston Moor, David Leslie's) which enabled victory. However, even here there are caveats to the assumption. At Gainsborough and Naseby, as well as to a lesser extent Marston Moor, we need to include dragoons into the equation, for Cromwell made extensive use of them or directed their actions in these battles. Although 150 years later, dragoons would be classed in France as medium/heavy cavalry and in Britain they would be firmly seen as heavy cavalry unless designated specifically as light dragoons, in the mid-seventeenth century dragoons were classed as infantry. They fought on foot, using carbines or flintlock muskets, and rode second-rate horses in order to move rapidly from place to place. Colonel Okey's use of them as mounted troops during the closing stages of Naseby remains remarkable even if not truly exceptional. In other words, even when serving in the role of a cavalry commander Cromwell demonstrated that he could make use of other arms in combination with horse.

By the time Cromwell had to command foot regiments the work of creating, recruiting, training and leading them had been done by their colonels and majors. Cromwell left no writings suggesting what he understood of contemporary debates on the number of files musketeers should fight in, or indeed whether he gave it a thought or just left it to the colonels and the major generals of foot.[18] David Blackmore has asserted that indeed there is no record of any such discussions at all following the demonstration at Edgehill that fire by introduction and alternate-rank firing was insufficient to force a conclusion.[19] Blackmore, using firsthand witness accounts, is able to surmise that in certain armies, such as Waller's at Cheriton, Gustavus Adolphus's Swedish method of having three ranks fire simultaneously was being used with more effect than single-rank firing, and that this was done at close range with devastating effect. It is likely that this system was used by foot regiments serving under Cromwell at Preston and Dunbar, and it is probably what he meant by 'close firing' in his letter about the former. Cromwell did by 1649 have a foot regiment of his own – he succeeded to the command of Colonel Richard Deane's regiment for the Irish campaign, and though there is no firm evidence of his leadership of the regiment at field officer level, it would be surprising if he were not as assiduous at coming to terms with the work of a foot regiment as he had been as a captain of horse back in 1642 in learning that trade. He may well have depended on the lieutenant colonel, Henry Bowen, and the major, Lewis Audley.[20] However, whatever his ability as a regimental commander there is little doubt that he developed the ability to command foot at brigade level and beyond, once he had detached command during 1645 in the south-west, and there is little doubt that he was by 1648 at least inspiring confidence in foot soldiers as well as he could with horse regiments. He was personally to be found on foot at Drogheda, and with combined arms at Worcester when he drove back the attackers after recrossing the boat bridge over the Severn.

As a regimental officer, a field officer and a staff officer, Cromwell had a fairly consistent record. He participated in few defeats on the battlefield, and only one stands out: the second Battle of Newbury where, although he was very firmly in a secondary role, his own performance matched the lacklustre display shown by those who were in charge (Waller and Manchester). Unlike Marston

Moor, where the three commanders were truly dismal, Cromwell did not offset their mistakes. On the other hand, in the other great battles of the civil war where he was involved (Marston Moor, Naseby, Langport, Preston, Dunbar and Worcester), as well as the minor battlefield triumphs (Gainsborough and Winceby), Cromwell's performance was never lacking. His actions on the field, whether commanded or in command, won the day at all of them. Fairfax truly directed Langport and remained justifiably proud of it, but the hammer blow itself was Cromwell's; an early example of his all-arms grasp of battlefield tactics. At Marston Moor, Dunbar and probably at Worcester, he had won the day before a shot was fired. At Preston and Dunbar it was his instinctive use of a sharp all-arms spearhead which weighted the scales against his opponent early in the fighting.

The main element in Cromwell's success seems to have been agency. Where he had some direct or crucial indirect input into battles or skirmishes, they met with victory; his role at Newbury was relatively constrained.

On the battlefield, Cromwell made use of what was at hand. At both Marston Moor and Dunbar, Cromwell could see the way that the high ground sloped down in ways that gave an attacker the possibility of reaching the flank of the force on the hill. He was clearly able to see this from both angles, as an attacker and defender needed to, although in both cases he took the role of attacker. At Marston Moor he could see that if Rupert held Bilton Bream he could force his way up on to the ridge, whereas at Doon Hill it was Cromwell who could see how he could barge his way on to the hill. He could also see how unpropitious terrain could be used, if not to an advantage, at least to offset the disadvantage it offered. At Preston the presence of a sunken road running in the proposed direction of attack could have fatally divided an attacking force. By creating a kind of combined arms fist, with horse in the lane and foot on either side, Cromwell created a unique attacking force to work as a hammer blow on the enemy foot. In general the use of combined arms was advocated by Monck, who certainly must have advised this at Dunbar when he was called upon for advice by Cromwell and Lambert as they planned the attack on the lows slopes of Doon Hill.[21] Monck was in Ireland when Cromwell assembled his hammer blow at Preston, yet the ratios he used – two divisions of foot to one of horse in the front line (where the word division is not used as a precise or immutable definition) – match Monck's advice and even the diagrams in his treatise to some extent. Gentles believes that Cromwell's genius lay in forging 'a military instrument that was fit to carry out his policy of aggressively seeking out and destroying the enemy'.[22] There is a good deal of truth in this, but it has to be seen very broadly. In terms of creating the original regiment this is certainly the case. It could be seen not only as Cromwell's training ground but as a school for men who would go on to lead their own regiments, much the same as some others, such as perhaps the royalist Lord Loughborough's horse. But this cannot be taken to extremes; the New Model Army could have provided an extension of this policy, but even in Cromwell's wing the horse was by no means homogenous, created as it was from regiments raised by others. From then on Cromwell's relationship with his own regiments was diluted at best; he lost command of the original one, and as general would have much less direct contact with the new ones named for him later, both horse and foot. When he first constructed his own army in 1649 for Ireland, that would have presented an excellent opportunity for forging an arm in his own (regiment's) image, but in the wake of the mutinies of that spring, some of the regiments were given to new commanders, whilst some were newly forged on the eve of the campaign. When he went to Scotland, the army had been assembling long before he was even appointed commander. At Worcester he absorbed a range of forces into his command and led them adroitly. To fully develop Gentles's claim, we have to acknowledge that Cromwell could create his force on the hoof: in days leading up to an attack on an enemy position as at Worcester, in the hours before a battle as at Dunbar, or even in seconds and minutes before launching an attack as at Marston Moor. Cromwell could create just the right force imaginatively as at Preston and Dunbar or by the book as at Belton to suit his needs. His flexibility of mind must have been impressive and we can only guess at its working out. He had no Alexandre Berthier to transcribe his thought into written orders, thus depriving us of an opportunity to study how his mind sifted options, but we need to surmise that he must have been 'of outstanding intellect'.[23]

GETTING TO THE BATTLEFIELD

General Sir Frank Kitson believes that Cromwell's three independent campaigns were notable for the level of planning he undertook to ensure success. He spent a long time before leaving Wales for Ireland in 1649, and England for Scotland a year later, ensuring that all requirements were provided. Whilst one might agree with the general assessment and the specific points that Kitson makes about using sea-borne transport for supplies and heavy artillery, it must be remembered that this failed to work in Scotland, and that the sea had proved a reluctant ally during the siege of Pembroke. General

Kitson draws an interesting analogy between the Worcester campaign and Napoleon's Ulm campaign in 1805, when both generals brought disparate and differing forces together so quickly that the enemy was trapped in its bases before they could react sufficiently to the situation facing them. Whilst the Ulm campaign was on a much grander scale and the distances covered much greater, Kitson is right: the effect of the attacker's movements were in both cases almost mesmeric. Neither Charles Stuart and the 'unfortunate' Mack could understand the speed of the process by which they were being encircled, leaving neither to attempt a breakout before it was too late.[24]

Cromwell understood the five things Sun Tzu had laid out as crucial to strategy: the way, the weather, the terrain, the leadership and discipline. Cromwell's way was to have the confidence of his men and confidence in their understanding of the cause: in this case God's cause – the 'knows what he fight for and loves what he knows' part of his definition of a good trooper. Cromwell could no more control the weather than any man and he was sometimes hampered by it as he was at Pembroke. As we have seen, Cromwell was the master of terrain, using it where he could to influence decisions on the field and adapting to it imaginatively when needs be. He was a convincing leader, caring for his men's well-being because he knew that they were risking lives and estate for the cause and sharing danger with them. He also understood that good logistical support enabled the maintenance of discipline in the army as much as having a clear chain of command.[25] Cromwell showed his grasp of strategy early on: his view of Newark's importance back in 1643 shows this on a grand scale, and that he seems not to have demurred in 1645, when presented with the possibility of an attack on the stronghold after Naseby, from his commander's decision to turn the south-west, demonstrates that he always understood the larger considerations of strategy. He was able to take risks and demonstrate caution by turn. He showed too much of the latter at Pembroke, but ample of the former when he crossed the Pennines to attack Hamilton a few weeks later.[26]

Thus it is clear that Cromwell had developed a sound strategic sense by 1651: the Worcester campaign was consummate whether or not Cromwell had engineered the situation to such an extent that he ensured Charles would march into England. In the final analysis it is unlikely that he had: Charles had ample reasons for invading England, not least the belief that he may free himself from the controlling hand of the Kirk Party. This aim was clearly unpopular with David Leslie and many Scots, but popular with English veterans who had been likewise sidelined by the Scots. There was little need for

Cromwell to prompt an invasion and it is stretching it too far to suggest it was all engineered; in any event Cromwell was busy taking control of Fife. The ensuing campaign in England was slick and carried out with great skill, but Cromwell had learned from the campaign in 1648, having defeated an invasion using the same route. It must not be forgotten that excellent though his last campaign was, he was not an infallible strategist: he had failed to out-manoeuvre Leslie just a year before, and although he had led a successful campaign in Ireland, it was not perfect in its execution during the months between Wexford and the advance from Youghal.

SIEGE WARFARE

One of the chief components of the military revolution consisted of siege warfare, both defence and attack. Siege warfare in the British Isles was not on a continental scale or level of sophistication. There were few complete modern fortifications in Britain or Ireland, although engineers such as Bernard de Gomme did build fortifications to supplement the defensive works of garrisons using continental design methods: Newark had some examples of these in its later works and several Irish garrisons incorporated modern methods too. The south-coast fortifications built by Henry VIII were almost obsolete as soon as they were topped out, whilst the more modern fortifications at Berwick were rarely put to the test. The largest sieges – of the towns York, Newark, Oxford and Bristol, or major houses like Basing – were, by the standards of true *trace Italienne*, amateur. Although they all borrowed something from continental works, star forts, earthworks, scarps and counter-scarps, they were selective or partial rather than complete systems. Cromwell participated in some long sieges, and York and Pembroke are examples of mediaeval structures he tackled. At the first he was not in charge and was detached with roaming cavalry for much of the time, whilst at the second he delayed his departure because he was waiting for the siege artillery to arrive. In most cases – Basing, Pembroke and Bristol – Cromwell preferred to storm a town after a bombardment with heavy artillery, rather than pursue a protracted siege. This was the case at Basing, Pembroke eventually, and Drogheda; it would have been the case at Wexford too. Pembroke – the exception – was protracted simply because he was waiting for the guns to arrive. Clonmel failed simply because O'Neill had witnessed continental sieges at firsthand. Cromwell's presence at Pontefract was political rather than military and whilst he ensured that the logistical elements were in place for the siege he contributed little else. Indeed, Padraig Lenihan's assessment is blunter: 'Cromwellian siege tactics were crude. Cromwell himself [...] launched assaults with a minimum of preparation. This bull-headed approach paid off at Drogheda but proved a costly failure at Clonmel'.[27]

MILITARY REVOLUTION

There are two questions which become relevant with regard to Cromwell's generalship and the military revolution. Firstly, how do the civil wars relate to the supposed military revolution: do they confirm its existence and was there any evidence of a revolution in military thought and practice in the civil wars of Britain and Ireland? Secondly, how does Cromwell relate to the supposed military revolution: do his actions confirm its existence and is there any evidence of a revolution in his military thought and practice? If for a moment we decide that there was a revolution and that the fairly rapid transmission of ideas through the printing press (and circulated manuscript) was part of the revolution, then Cromwell was born as a propitious time. Firstly, during the past century there had been a growth in the circulation of both printed and manuscript manuals of instruction for soldiers. Secondly, there was a significant number of veterans of the ongoing continental wars who had been exposed to elements of the 'military revolution', thus his 'education' would have been two-fold.[28] In 1642, Cromwell was very much a virgin or amateur soldier, appointed to a captaincy for the wrong reasons and without the personal means in terms of estate and income to create a troop of managed horse from his own resources. The availability of locally printed military manuals would certainly, in his terms, have been a 'God-send'. If this is indeed revolutionary, as writers as diverse as Parker and Scannell claim, then Cromwell was a child if not a progenitor of that revolution.[29] Again we do not have any direct evidence from his own writings or the observations of others that Cromwell read the textbooks available to him, as an inexperienced captain of horse or later, and so we have to infer this from what he did. There are a few snippets of circumstantial evidence: he blatantly and perhaps unknowingly refers to his text-book learning in his earliest accounts, such as the clear statement that he consulted his fellow officers before charging the royalist horse at Belton, and much later he lets us know that he and his fellow generals watched and discussed Leslie's movements the evening before Dunbar, and that he credited Lambert with having the exact same thought about the opportunity it presented, when there was no need to do so.

To that he added his own contribution; he substituted the large staffed stable with a kin and religious kindred network, from which he was able to select his first officers and men and which he expanded, through personal contact, throughout the ensuing years.

One of the apparent contradictions about Cromwell is his attitude to his ordinary soldiers. His concerns for their welfare could be considered as simply the essentials of generalship: without pay and other necessities his soldiers – if you like, his source of real authority – simply could not and would not fight, and they may not have hung around either. Yet this is to assume that Cromwell had little real care for his men, which is to forget that he had brought them together without having had a prior fiduciary relationship with any of them: the bonds of wage-slavery were not in place when they first volunteered their lives in his service. That they did not desert in huge numbers when the association neglected their welfare demonstrates that a level of trust was in place which could for some time overcome hunger and dissatisfaction in the vast majority of his men. He repaid that by haranguing the paymasters on their behalf. Cromwell was prepared to listen to his men too. When the soldiers demanded three things in 1646–7 – back pay, indemnity and pensions for widows and orphans – he listened and took their side against the parsimony and thoughtlessness of parliament. Furthermore, he and Fairfax personally undertook potentially traitorous actions in order to defend and assert their soldiers' rights and needs, by marching on London and challenging parliament's power. He even listened to the soldiers on the field of conflict. He took notice of the foot soldiers' grumblings before Clonmel when they complained that the horse regiments were not always involved in front-line action during the sieges which marked warfare in Ireland. Cromwell, like Clausewitz after him, understood the need to be seen to share the dangers of the fighting 'when the inertia of the whole [army] gradually comes to rest on the commander alone', and used his personal presence to great effect at Preston, Drogheda and Dunbar. Perhaps the most clear example was once again Worcester, where he led the brigades across the boat bridges and then back again to deal with Charles's counter-attack.[30] There were limits: he could not force his men into situations where they could be uselessly slaughtered, and at Clonmel they refused to enter the breach after hours of murderous but otherwise pointless fighting.

This may seem to contrast with the way Cromwell blocked the calls for democratic progress at Putney and Corkbush. Yet there are two things which explain this. In specific terms the Corkbush Fields rendezvous was a direct challenge to the generals' authority: it was both in defiance of direct orders not to meet whilst at the same time being an alternative command structure issuing orders to the soldiers. The subsequent mutinies of 1649 – on the Strand, en route for embarkation points for the Irish campaign and at Burford – were examples of the same defiance of existing structures and the establishment of a rival command structure. This simply could not be allowed within an armed force, especially in an age of deference. Such confusion could lead to chaos, division and defeat: the war was not yet over and the royalists would take advantage of division. Moreover, to a certain extent Cromwell believed (as did King Charles I) that subjects, commanders and kings were clearly different. He would thus listen to soldiers when the matters were military or conditions of service, but not when it was about politics. The exception to this would be officers, especially generals, whatever their social origins. Cromwell acknowledged Ireton's right to hold political views even when these became radicalised in late 1648. He also accepted that Lambert could draft a political constitution in 1653, but he could not accept that common soldiers and Leveller allies could do likewise.

ARMY SIZE AND SHAPE

There is no record of Cromwell discussing the nature of an army, the ratios of horse to foot or the ratios of pike to shot, or the number of ranks in which the foot regiments should fight. Other generals did and so we should expect that Cromwell gave thought to such issues. We do know how he put together his armies on the field, the brigading of regiments and the combination of arms which he assembled for various tasks. We are left, however, with the impression that he was a man with his sleeves rolled up intent on thought only so long as it led directly to action. This cannot be true. As indicated above, Cromwell was not merely a horse general: he excelled at combined arms attacks and he could handle foot as a staff officer, as at Worcester, and in the role of a field officer, as in the second wave attack at Drogheda. His thought was flexible and he could use unusual combinations of units, as at Preston where he capitalised on the potential problem of having a sunken lane running in his direction of attack. The scale of warfare in the British Isles is usually seen to be on the small side, and some of the battles were indeed little more than skirmishes when compared with war on the continent. The Battle of the White Mountain saw 43,000 men engaged – 21,000 under Ferdinand and 22,000 under Tilly – whilst Breitenfeld involved 76,000: 39,000 Swedes and Saxons versus 37,000 imperialists. On the other hand, Lützen was fought by just 27,500 men – 16,200 Swedes and allies, versus 11,300 under Wallenstein – a battle well within the numbers range of a civil war battle.[31] Lützen was somewhat smaller than the Battle of Marston Moor, which involved over 35,000 in total, and was a similar scale to the Battle of Naseby with little more than 24,000 men on both sides. Cromwell's armies were often small; he only had about 11,200 at Preston and somewhat fewer at Dunbar. In other words the development of larger and larger armies and the logistical support necessary to maintain them seem at first glance not to be reflected fully in Britain and Ireland during the wars themselves. However this is not wholly true. The forces under Cromwell's command at Worcester numbered up to 35,000 men, which whilst on the one hand represented the majority of forces available in England and Wales, and thus did not match the numbers of forces available to other nations, it did represent an army in the field in the same category as Breitenfeld. Also it must be noted that this army was raised in England and Wales alone and did not represent the sort of multinational conglomerate led in the field by Gustavus Adolphus or Wallenstein; thus it represented, in England and Wales at least, an increasing capacity to mobilise manpower for war. There were of course other forces still fighting in Scotland and Ireland when Cromwell led the attack on the invaders at Worcester, adding several thousand more men to Britain and Ireland's capacity for war. It has been estimated that England by the 1650s match Sweden in military manpower, even if it could not compete with the larger nations such as Spain and France, although in terms of numbers they were both in decline by then.[32]

More remarkable was that this army, whilst bringing together several distinct components – veterans, what might be termed professional soldiers with less experience and part-time militia – was directly under the command of one man rather than a commander who was judged to be in command on the day on grounds of experience, or more riskily seniority (e.g., Leven at Marston Moor). Cromwell, in Ireland (perhaps by circumstance) and at Worcester as lord general, had unreserved command – the other generals, who had raised and led the components, served as trusted lieutenants with specific roles to play in battles but throughout the campaign were subordinate to him.

The royalist and parliamentarian taxation systems in England and Wales set in place during the civil wars were, theoretically at least, a more effective means of exploiting the resources of the nation than anything that had come before. When run effectively, something which the circumstances of civil war naturally made more difficult, the rival systems could support the armed forces reasonably well. Royalists called their regular tax 'contribution', while parliament chose the name 'weekly tax' and then later 'monthly pay'. They were collected somewhat imaginatively, in both cash, which was used to pay wages and buy weapons or raw materials, and in the form of goods such as food and beer, which could be used to sustain the men and horses.

Both the royalist and parliamentarian collections made use of the soldiers as tax collectors. However, both could break down in the face of enemy action and even the weather and sometimes soldiers were left without pay and supplies. This was true even of the enhanced system put in place to support the New Model Army, which was initially a far more realistic approach to collections, being based only on counties from which parliament knew it could collect tax at the beginning of 1645. Even so, in the early years of the war Cromwell had to chivvy the county committees of East Anglia into maintaining regular financial support for his men, and in 1646–7 he found himself allying with his men's demands for payment of their arrears. In both cases his men could depend on him to stand up for their due rewards.

Oliver Cromwell is one of the most remarkable people in British and Irish history, and probably in European history too. It would not be true to say that he was instrumental in the military revolution, but he was a child of the revolution, in the same way as Cromwell was, in a social and political sense, born of the English or British revolution. Unlike the popular history version of Cromwell, he was not instrumental in bringing about the war against Charles I and nor was he at the forefront of the radicalism which would see him end up as the head of state; yet in war and politics Cromwell's fate was decided by these two revolutions. He had to adapt to both in order to retain his equilibrium. It was the military surge which hit him first, forcing him into an unfamiliar world wherein he had been entrusted to participate as, at first, a minor leader of men. The tide of military writing and the returning waves of veterans from the great experiment of war on the continent made it possible for Cromwell to learn the new trade quickly. This is not to say that Cromwell made no impact; there were other men on both sides with the same opportunities – command, readily available textbooks, experienced colleagues and the confidence of those with more authority – who did not rise to such prominence or the fortune to have books dedicated to them. Cromwell absorbed the ideas from books, conversations and experience to make him a general. He created no lasting tactics or strategy even within his own arm, where the changing formations of horse tactics were devised on the continent. This is not a criticism. Napoleon is often said to have created no major new tactic or strategy and is reckoned to be one of the world's greatest generals; even his claim to have invented 'Ordre Mixte' is questioned. Wellington, likewise one of Europe's greatest military leaders, invented nothing in the way of strategy or tactics other than sensibly having his men take cover; as David Blackmore has amply shown, devastating short-range firepower, followed by a rapid, controlled charge was something which Wellington could employ 'off the shelf', and the successful use of reverse slopes, which was likewise incredibly effective, was used by Fairfax at Naseby. This lack of originality does not undermine any of these generals' claim to greatness. Thus Cromwell was no Maurice, nor even a Gustavus Adolphus, but then he was more successful than either of them as he alone brought about the end of a war through devastating victory. Cromwell learned his trade in middle-age and showed remarkable aptitude for it. He could adapt his armed forces as needs required, being as adroit in combined arms fighting as he was at cavalry tactics. He understood logistics from the point of view of a man at the pivot of the relationship between payer and paid: pleading for his regiment's wages in 1643 and again for his army's in 1646–7 and on campaign. In 1649 and 1650–1 he had more ability to ensure regular pay and plan ahead: his experience of hand-to-mouth supply and his tangential relationships to the collection of cash-and-kind local levies gave him unique insight into the needs and process. Cromwell absorbed the parts of the military revolution which impinged upon his situation and regurgitated them on the battlefields of Britain and Ireland to devastating effect. He was a general of national and international importance: a master of strategy, tactics and logistics and more importantly an imaginative fast learner and adaptor.

NOTES

1 CROMWELL THE MAN

1. Wilber Cortez Abbott, *The Writings and Speeches of Oliver Cromwell* (Harvard University Press, Cambridge, four volumes, 1937–47), Vol. III, p. 453; Ivan Roots, ed., *Speeches of Oliver Cromwell* (London, Dent, 1989), p. 42.
2. Huntingdonshire County Record Office (henceforth HRO), 3870/1, Huntingdon St John Composite Register 1588–1682, np, under 1599.
3. HRO, 3870/1, Huntingdon St John Composite Register passim, entries for 1593–1605.
4. Peter Gaunt, *Oliver Cromwell* (Oxford, Blackwell, 1996), pp. 31–2.
5. HRO, 3870/1, Huntingdon St John Composite Register 1588–1682, np, under 1599.
6. HRO, HB26/14, Survey of Huntingdon, 1572.
7. Gaunt, *Cromwell*, p. 30.
8. John Morrill, ed., *Oliver Cromwell and the English Revolution* (London, Longman, 1990), see Chapter 1. See also Gaunt, *Oliver Cromwell*, p. 32.
9. Ian Gentles, *Oliver Cromwell* (London, Palgrave MacMillan, 2011), p. 2.
10. J. Colin Davies, *Oliver Cromwell* (London, Arnold, 2001), p. 15.
11. Robert S. Paul, *The Lord Protector* (Grand Rapids, Michigan, William B. Eerdmans Publishing Company, 1955), p. 31.
12. W.B. Patterson, *King James VI ad I and the Reunion of Christendom* (Cambridge, Cambridge University Press, 1997), p. 269.
13. Abbott, *Writings*, Vol. 1, p. 27.
14. Patterson, *King James*, p. 269.
15. Davies, *Oliver Cromwell*, calls it a 'mystery'; Gentles, *Oliver Cromwell*, believed he definitely moved to London, p. 2; Gaunt, *Oliver Cromwell*, thinks that he helped his mother with the estate and may have gained legal training, p. 32.
16. Wilfred Prest, *The Inns of Court under Elizabeth I and the Early Stuarts* (London, Longman, 1972), p. 37.
17. Abbott, *Writings*, Vol. 1, p. 33.
18. Prest, *The Inns of Court*, p. 15.
19. *Perfect Politician*, p. 8 and John Heath, *Flagellum*, pp. 9–10 as cited by Abbott, *Writings*, Vol. I, pp. 32–3.
20. Davies, *Oliver Cromwell*, p. 15.

21. Martyn Bennett, *Oliver Cromwell* (London, Routledge, 2006), p. 17.
22. Antonia Fraser, *Cromwell Our Chief of Men* (London, Weidenfeld and Nicholson, 2008), pp. 31–2.
23. Gaunt, *Oliver Cromwell*, p. 33; Davies, *Oliver Cromwell*, pp. 15–16; Gentles, *Oliver Cromwell*, p. 3.
24. HRO, H Charter 17, also to be found in A.P. Wood, *The History of Huntingdon from the Earliest to the Present Times* (Huntingdon, 1824), p. 339.
25. Richard Cust, *The Forced Loan and English Politics, 1626–1628* (Oxford, Oxford University Press, 1987), p. 324.
26. Abbott, *Writings*, Vol. 1, pp. 61–2.
27. Conrad Russell, *The Crisis of Parliaments: English History, 1509–1660* (Oxford, Oxford University Press, 1971), pp. 308–10.
28. Morrill, *Oliver Cromwell*, pp. 27, 29; Simon Healy, '1636: The Unmaking of Oliver Cromwell?', in Patrick Little, ed., *Oliver Cromwell: New Perspectives* (London, Palgrave, 2009), p. 25; Bennett, *Oliver Cromwell*, p. 25.
29. Morrill, *Oliver Cromwell*, pp. 30–1.
30. Cited in Abbott, *Writings*, Vol. I, p. 68.
31. Ibid., p. 68.
32. Healy, 'The Unmaking', p. 25.
33. Gentles, *Oliver Cromwell*, p. 4; Gaunt, *Oliver Cromwell*, p. 33.
34. Morrill, *Oliver Cromwell*, pp. 33–5; Healy, 'The Unmaking', pp. 25–6.
35. HRO, Vol/I/15 St Ives Manor Court 1632–1661, np, entry for 3/10/1634; M. Carter, ed., *Edward Pettis's Survey of St Ives, 1728* (Cambridge, Cambridge Record Society, 16, 2002), pp. 9–10.
36. Carter, *Edward Pettis's*, pp. 14–16.
37. HRO, St Ives Vestry Book, 1626–1724, np, entry for 22 April 1633 and 7 April 1634.
38. W. Page, ed., *Victoria County History of Huntingdonshire* (London, St Catherine's Press, 1932), Vol. II, p. 218.
39. Morrill, *Oliver Cromwell*, p. 22; Page, *History of Huntingdonshire*, p. 219.
40. Gaunt, *Oliver Cromwell*, p. 34, suggests that he had slipped from the gentry. Davies, *Oliver Cromwell*, p. 16, calls his status 'ambiguous'; Gentles, *Oliver Cromwell*, p. 4, calls him a 'yeoman'.
41. Healy, 'The Unmaking', pp. 29–30.

2 CROMWELL AND THE COMING OF WAR

1. John S. Morrill, ed., *Oliver Cromwell and the English Revolution* (London, Longman, 1991), p. 36; see also Gaunt, *Davies and Gentles on the Cromwells' Social Standing*, as referred to in Chapter 1.
2. Simon Healy, '1636: The Unmaking of Oliver Cromwell?', in Patrick Little, ed., *Oliver Cromwell: New Perspectives* (London, Palgrave, 2009), p. 24; Morrill, *Oliver Cromwell*, p. 33.
3. Peter Gaunt, *Oliver Cromwell* (Oxford, Blackwell, 1996), p. 34.
4. Healy, 'The Unmaking', p. 26.
5. Ibid., p. 26.
6. See Healy's exploration of this in ibid., pp. 28–30.

7. M. Bennett, *The Civil Wars in Britain and Ireland* (Oxford, Blackwell, 1997), pp. 35–7.
8. Brian Quintrell, 'Oliver Cromwell and the Distraint of Knighthood', *Bulletin of the Institute of Historical Research* 57 (1984), passim. Bennett, *Oliver Cromwell*, pp. 27–8.
9. C. Hill, *God's Englishman: Oliver Cromwell and the English Revolution* (Harmondsworth, Pelican, 1979), p. 47.
10. Morrill, *Oliver Cromwell*, p. 36.
11. Bennett, *The Civil Wars*, pp. 38–40.
12. British Library, Sloane Ms 2069, f96v.
13. Healy, 'The Unmaking', pp. 33–4; Gaunt, *Oliver Cromwell*, p. 35.
14. Morrill, *Oliver Cromwell*, p. 34; J.C. Davis, *Oliver Cromwell* (London, Arnold, 2001), p. 17.
15. Ian Gentles, *Oliver Cromwell God's Warrior and the English Revolution* (London, Palgrave Macmillan, 2011), p. 5.
16. M. Lee, *The Road to Revolution: Scotland under Charles I* (Chicago, University of Illinois Press, 1985), pp. 4–5; Peter Donald, *An Uncounselled King: Charles I and the Scottish Troubles, 1637–1641* (Cambridge, Cambridge University Press, 1990), p. 17.
17. J.S. Morrill, *The Nature of the English Revolution* (London, Longman, 1993), pp. 92–3.
18. Archibald Johnston of Wariston (edited by G.H. Paul, D.H. Fleming and J.D. Ogilvy) *Diary of Archibald Johnston of Wariston* (Edinburgh, Scottish History Society, 1911), pp. 265–6.
19. D.H. Fleming, ed., 'Scotland's Supplication and Complaint against the Book of Common Prayer (otherwise Laud's Liturgy), the Book of Canons and the Prelates, 18 October 1637', *Proceedings of the Society of Antiquaries of Scotland* LX (1825–6); D. Stevenson, *The Covenanters: The National Covenant and Scotland* (Edinburgh, Saltire Society, 1981).
20. Bennett, *The Civil Wars*, pp. 52–3.
21. Gaunt, *Oliver Cromwell*, p. 34.
22. Morrill, *Oliver Cromwell*, p. 37.
23. Gaunt, *Oliver Cromwell*, p. 36; Gentles, *Oliver Cromwell*, p. 7.
24. Wilber Cortez Abbott, *The Writings and Speeches of Oliver Cromwell* (Cambridge, MA, Harvard University Press, four volumes, 1937–47), Vol. I, p. 97.
25. Gaunt, *Oliver Cromwell*, pp. 37–8.
26. Abbott, *Writings*, Vol. I, p. 109.
27. Morrill, *Oliver Cromwell*, p. 45.
28. Abbott, *Writings*, Vol. 1, pp. 109–10.
29. Antonia Fraser, *Cromwell: Our Chief of Men* (London, Weidenfeld and Nicholson, 2008, originally published 1973), pp. 72–3.
30. J. Heath, *Flagellum* (London, 1663), p. 23.
31. Charles Firth, *Oliver Cromwell and the Rule of the Puritans in England* (Oxford, Oxford University Press, 1966, originally 1900), p. 43.
32. Gentles, *Oliver Cromwell*, p. 8.
33. Abbott, *Writings*, Vol. I, p. 109.
34. Esther S. Cope and William H. Coates, eds, *Proceedings of the Short Parliament of 1640* (London, Royal Historical Society, 1977), pp. 134–40.
35. Cope and Coates, *Proceedings*, pp. 70, 178.
36. Bennett, *The Civil Wars*, pp. 64–6.

37. Mark Fissell, *The Bishops' Wars: Charles I's Campaigns against Scotland, 1638–1640* (Cambridge, Cambridge University Press, 1994), pp. 209–10.
38. Fissell, *The Bishops' Wars*, p. 52.
39. Ibid., pp. 50–9.
40. Bennett, *The Civil Wars*, pp. 67–9.
41. David Brunton and David H. Pennington, *Members of the Long Parliament* (Cambridge, MA, Harvard University Press, 1958), p. 112.
42. Stephen K. Roberts, 'The Early Parliamentary Career of Oliver Cromwell', in Little, *New Perspectives*, pp. 40–1; J.S.A. Adamson, 'Oliver Cromwell and the Long Parliament' in Morrill, *Oliver Cromwell*, p. 46.
43. Abbott, *Writings*, Vol. I, p. 121.
44. Morrill, *Oliver Cromwell*, pp. 45–7 and Adamson in the same, pp. 51–3.
45. Roberts, 'The Early Parliamentary Career', pp. 58–9.
46. Bennett, *Oliver Cromwell*, pp. 43–4.
47. According to Ashley, it was his chief concern; Maurice Ashley, *Oliver Cromwell and the Puritan Revolution* (London, The English Universities Press, 1958), p. 46.
48. Bennett, *Oliver Cromwell*, p. 47.
49. Abbott, *Writings*, Vol. I, p. 133.
50. Marija Jansson, ed., *Two Diaries of the Long Parliament* (Stroud, Alan Sutton St Martin's Press, 1984), p. 49, from William Drake's notebook.
51. Abbott, *Writings*, Vol. I, p. 142; Morrill, *Oliver Cromwell*, p. 47.
52. Ibid., p. 141.
53. Bennett, *The Civil Wars*, pp. 90–101.
54. S.R. Gardiner, ed., *Constitutional Documents of the Puritan Revolution* (Oxford, Clarendon Press, 1979), pp. 202–32.
55. Gardiner, *Constitutional Documents*, pp. 254–7.
56. Ibid., pp. 258–61.
57. Bennett, *The Civil Wars*, pp. 120–2.
58. Abbott, *Writings*, Vol. I, pp. 187–9; Bennett, *The Civil Wars*, pp. 131–3.

3 CAPTAIN CROMWELL: THE MAKING OF THE SOLDIER

1. John Cruso, *Instructions for the Cavallrie* (Cambridge, University of Cambridge, 1632), p. 9.
2. Cruso, *Instructions*, pp. 3, 5, 7.
3. Ibid., pp. 7–8.
4. Wilber Cortez Abbott, ed., *The Writing and Speeches of Oliver Cromwell* (Cambridge, MA, Harvard University Press, 1937), Vol. I, p. 208.
5. Keith Roberts, *Pike and Shot Tactics* (Oxford, Osprey, 2010), p. 32.
6. Cruso, *Instructions*, p. 30.
7. William Barriff, *Military Discipline or the Young Artillery Man* (London, 1635), p. 62.
8. D. Blackmore, *Arms and Armour of the English Civil War* (London, Royal Armouries, 1990), p. 9.
9. Blackmore, *Arms and Armour*, pp. 14, 24, 50.
10. Alan Marshall, *Oliver Cromwell, Soldier: The Military History of a Revolutionary at War* (London, Brassey's, 2004), p. 59.

11. Abbott, *Writings*, Vol. I, p. 200; Frank Kitson, *Old Ironsides: The Military Biography of Oliver Cromwell* (London, Weidenfeld and Nicholson, 2004), p. 37.

12. Nathaniel Fiennes's account, *A Most True and Exact Relation of Both the Battles Fought by his Excellency and his Forces Against the Bloudy Cavaliers* (London, Joseph Hunscroft, 1642), p. 3, which in the letter to Lord Saye and Sele, Fiennes's father, makes it clear that Cromwell's troops arrived at Kineton after four o'clock.

13. Abbott, *Writings*, Vol. I, p. 204.

14. Cruso, *Instructions*, p. 10.

15. Ibid., p. 14.

16. Abbott, *Writings*, Vol. I, p. 225.

17. Ibid., pp. 248–9; Kitson, *Old Ironsides*, p. 50.

18. Abbott, *Writings*, Vol. I, pp. 261–2.

19. Geoffrey Mortimer, *Wallenstein: The Enigma of the Thirty Years War* (London, Palgrave, 2010), pp. 25, 30.

20. Peter Wilson, *Europe's Tragedy: A New History of the Thirty Years War* (London, Penguin, 2009), p. 94.

21. Abbott, *Writings*, Vol. I, p. 204: Oliver Cromwell's speech, 13 April 1657.

22. Ibid., p. 216.

23. Bulstrode Whitelocke, *Memorials of the English Affairs* (Oxford, Oxford University Press, 1853), Vol. 1, p. 72.

24. Abbott, *Writings*, Vol. I, p. 205.

25. Ibid., p. 256.

26. M. Bennett, *Oliver Cromwell* (London, Routledge, 2006), pp. 58–60.

27. Abbott, *Writings*, Vol. I, p. 256.

28. Ibid., p. 258.

29. Ibid., p. 199.

30. Mortimer, *Wallenstein*, pp. 30–1, 33–4.

31. In the 1980s Stephen Porter argued that *brandschatzung* was common in England during the civil wars, but the arguments did not fully convince some. Stephen Porter, 'The Fire Raid in the English Civil War', *War and Society* 2/2 (1984); M. Bennett, 'Contribution and Assessment: Financial Exactions in the English Civil War', *War and Society* 5/1 (1986).

32. Abbott, *Writings*, Vol. I, p. 218.

33. Ibid., p. 232.

34. Ibid., p. 247.

35. Ibid., pp. 252–3.

36. Ibid., pp. 258–9.

37. Cruso, *Instructions*, pp. 8–10.

38. Abbott, *Writings*, Vol, I, p. 221.

39. Cruso, *Instructions*, p. 34.

40. Barriff, *Military Discipline*, pp. 55–6, 60.

41. Cruso, *Instructions*, p. 16.

42. Ibid., pp. 43–4.

43. Ibid., pp. 47–55.

44. Ibid., p. 65.

4 CROMWELL THE TACTICIAN: EDGEHILL TO WINCEBY

1. Malcolm Wanklyn, *Warrior Generals Winning the British Civil Wars* (New Haven and London, Yale University Press, 2010), pp. 22–3.
2. The work of Peter Young, *Edgehill, 1642: The Campaign and the Battle* (Kineton, Windrush Press, 1967), still holds sway, although recent archaeological work suggests that the traditional layout of the fight is erroneous. Currently Malcolm Wanklyn's brief account of the battle is convincing; Wanklyn, *Warrior Generals*, pp. 26–31.
3. Wanklyn, *Warrior Generals*, p. 30.
4. Bennett, *The Civil Wars*, p. 136.
5. Frank Kitson, *Old Ironsides: The Military Biography of Oliver Cromwell* (London, Weidenfeld and Nicholson, 2004), p. 42.
6. Wilbur Cortez Abbott, ed., *The Writing and Speeches of Oliver Cromwell* (Cambridge, MA, Harvard University Press, 1937), Vol. I, p. 204.
7. Ibid., p. 208.
8. Ibid., pp. 209–10.
9. Ibid., p. 211.
10. Martyn Bennett, 'The Royalist War Effort in the North Midlands, 1642–1646' (unpublished PhD thesis, Loughborough University of Technology, 1986), p. 182.
11. *Perfect Diurnal*, 6 March, cited in Abbott, *Writings*, Vol. 1, p. 215.
12. John Vernon, *The Young Horfe-man, or the Honeft Plain-dealing Cavalier* (London, Andrew Coe, 1644), p. 3.
13. Clive Holmes, *Seventeenth-Century Lincolnshire* (Lincoln, History of Lincoln Committee, 1980), p. 166.
14. HMC, *Report on the Papers of Reginald Rawdon Hastings* (London, HMSO, 1930), pp. 98–9; Eliot Warburton, ed., *Memoirs of Prince Rupert and the Cavaliers, Including their Private Correspondence* (London, 1849), p. 189.
15. Abbott, *Writings*, Vol. I, pp. 230–2.
16. Vernon, *The Young Horfe-man*, p. 3.
17. Samuel Rawson Gardiner, *History of the Great Civil War* (Gloucestershire, Windrush Press, 1991), Vol. 1, p. 143; Charles H. Firth, *Oliver Cromwell and the Rule of the Puritans in England* (Oxford, Oxford University Press, 1966), p. 98; Ian Gentles, *Oliver Cromwell: God's Warrior and the English Revolution* (London, Palgrave Macmillan, 2011), p. 27.
18. John Gell, 'A True Relation of What Service Hath been Done by Colonel John Gell', unpublished tract, in Stephen Glover, *The History, Directory and Gazetteer of Derbyshire* (Derby, 1829), p. 62.
19. Lucy Hutchinson, *Memoirs of the Life of Colonel Hutchinson* (Longman, Orme and Rees, London, 1806), pp. 74–6; British Library, Thomason Tracts, E92/3, *Certain Informations*, 20 February–6 March, 1642–3, British Library Thomason Tracts E86/41, *Mercurius Aulicus* 9th week, 1643, np.
20. Clive Holmes, *The Eastern Association in the English Civil War* (Cambridge, Cambridge University Press, 1974), pp. 69–70.
21. Robert Bell., ed., *Memorials of the Civil War Comprising the Correspondence of the Fairfax Family, with the Most Distinguished Personages Engaged in that Memorable Contest*

(London, Richard Bentley, 1849), Vol. I, p. 45, letter from John Hotham to Lord Fairfax, 24 May 1643.

22. Bennett, 'The Royalist War Effort', p. 191.
23. Bell, *Fairfax*, Vol. I, p. 46, Hotham, Cromwell, Miles Hobart and Lord Grey to Lord Fairfax, 2 June 1643.
24. HMC *Rawdon*-Hastings, Vol. II, Letter, Queen Henrietta Maria to Hastings, 1 June 1643, pp. 102–3.
25. Abbott, *Writings*, Vol. I., pp. 234–5.
26. Ibid., p. 237.
27. Ibid., p. 236.
28. *A True Relation of Colonel Cromwells Proceedings against the Cavaliers* (London, Benjamin Allen, 1643), p. 2; C. Davies, *Stamford in the Civil War* (Stamford, Paul Watkins, 1992); Holmes, *Seventeenth-Century Lincolnshire*, p. 168.
29. Vernon, *The Young Horfe-man*, p. 42.
30. John West, *Oliver Cromwell and the Battle of Gainsborough* (Boston, Richard Key, 1992), p. 10.
31. Eric Gruber von Arni and Andrew Hoppe, curators, 'Battle Scarred: Surgery, Medicine and Military Welfare during the British Civil Wars', exhibition at the National Civil War Centre (Leicester, University of Leicester, 2016), p. 10.
32. Abbott, *Writings*, Vol. I, p. 245.
33. Ibid., p. 11; John Aubrey, *Brief Lives* (Harmondsworth, Penguin Classics, 1987), p. 157.
34. Abbott, *Writings*, Vol. I., pp. 240–1; Holmes, *Seventeenth-Century Lincolnshire*, p. 169.
35. Abbott, *Writings*, Vol. I., p. 243.
36. Peter Gaunt, 'The Battle of Gainsborough, 28 July, 1643', *Cromwelliana* (1998), pp. 8–11.
37. Abbott, *Writings*, Vol. I, pp. 239, 241. Cromwell's account refers to 50, the equivalent of five full regiments of foot, but the joint account suggests that there were 19 in Newcastle's regiment alone which would have made that almost a double-regiment, which was the second one in the line of march. West, *Gainsborough*, p. 12.
38. Abbott, *Writings*, Vol. 1, pp. 250–1; Holmes, *Seventeenth-Century Lincolnshire*, p. 169; A.A. Garner, *Boston and the Great Civil War* (Richard Kay, Boston, 1972), p. 7.
39. Holmes, *Eastern Association*, p. 87.
40. Bell, *Fairfax*, p. 58.
41. Abbott, *Writings*, Vol., I, pp. 255–6.
42. Ibid., p. 259.
43. Holmes, *Seventeenth-Century Lincolnshire*, p. 170; Garner, *Boston*, pp. 9, 12.
44. Holmes, *Seventeenth-Century Lincolnshire*, p. 170.
45. Garner, *Boston*, p. 13; Clive Holmes, 'Colonel King and Lincolnshire Politics' *The Historical Journal* 16/3 (1973), p. 458.
46. Holmes, *Colonel King*, pp. 456–8.
47. Gentles, *Oliver Cromwell*, p. 30.
48. Abbott, *Writings*, Vol. I, p. 265; Bell, *Fairfax*, Vol. I, p. 64.
49. Ibid., pp. 63–5.
50. Alan Marshall, *Oliver Cromwell Soldier: The Military History of a Revolutionary at War* (London, Brassy's, 2004), pp. 99–100; Frank Kitson, *Old Ironsides*, p. 66–7.

51. Garner, *Boston*, pp. 10–11; Holmes, *Seventeenth-Century Lincolnshire*, p. 183.
52. Abbott, *Writings*, Vol. I, p. 270. The gentle if not subtle suggestion was ignored and the troopers effected their reformation as predicted.
53. Holmes, *Seventeenth-Century Lincolnshire*, p. 183.
54. Ibid., pp. 271–3; Holmes, *Seventeenth-Century Lincolnshire*, p. 184.
55. Malcolm Wanklyn, *The Warrior Generals: Winning the British Civil Wars* (London, Yale University Press, 2010), pp. 8–9.
56. Abbott, *Writings*, Vol. I, p. 272.
57. John Cruso, *Instructions for the Cavallrie* (Cambridge, University of Cambridge, 1632), p. 5.
58. Ibid., pp. 6–7.

5   CROMWELL THE GENERAL, 1644

1. Martyn Bennett, *The Civil War in Britain and Ireland, 1637–1651* (Oxford, Blackwell, 1997), pp. 158–9.
2. Samuel Rawson Gardiner, *History of the Great Civil War* (Adelstrop, Windrush, 1991), Vol. I, pp. 125–6, 127.
3. R. Ashton, *The English Civil War: Conservatism and Reaction* (London, Arnold, 1978), p. 200; J.P. Kenyon, *The Civil Wars of England* (London, Weidenfeld and Nicholson, 1989), p. 91.
4. Wilbur Cortez Abbott, *The Writings and Speeches of Oliver Cromwell* (Cambridge, MA, Harvard University Press, four volumes, 1937–47), Vol. I, p. 275. Cromwell signed on 5 February 1644.
5. Peter R. Newman, *The Battle of Marston Moor* (Chichester, John Byrd, 1981), pp. 14–15.
6. Gardiner, *History*, Vol. I, pp. 259, 300; Kenyon, *Civil Wars of England*, p. 95; Martyn Bennett, 'The Royalist War Effort in the North Midlands, 1642–1646' (unpublished PhD thesis, Loughborough University of Technology, 1986), p. 220.
7. Hutton, R., *The Royalist War Effort* (London, Longman, 1980), pp. 122–3.
8. Abbott, *Writings*, Vol. I, pp. 274–5.
9. Ibid., pp. 278–80.
10. Bennett, *The Civil Wars*, p. 206.
11. John Rushworth, ed., *Historical Collections* (London, seven volumes, 1657–1701), Vol. III, p. 304; John Gell, 'A True Relation of What Service Hath been Done by Colonel John Gell', unpublished tract, in Steven Glover, *The History, Directory and Gazetteer of Derbyshire* (Derby, 1829), p. 64.
12. *Report on the Papers of Reginald Rawdon Hastings* (London, HMSO, 1930), Vol. II, pp. 123, 124; Robert Bell, ed., *Memorials of the Civil War Comprising the Correspondence of the Fairfax Family, with the Most Distinguished Personages Engaged in that Memorable Contest* (London, Richard Bentley, 1849), pp. 82–4; Alfred. C. Wood, *Nottinghamshire in the Civil War* (Wakefield, S.R. Publishing, 1971), p. 74.
13. Bennett, 'Royalist War Effort', pp. 205–7.
14. Peter Young, 'Royalist Army at the Relief of Newark' *Journal of the Society for Army Historical Research*, 30/124 (1953).
15. *Calendar of State Papers: Domestic (CSPD) Charles I* (Liechtenstein, Kraus Reprint, 1967), 1644, p. 77; Abbott, *Writings*, Vol. I, p. 282.

16. G. Parker, *The Military Revolution* (Cambridge, Cambridge University Press, 1996, second edition), p. 28.

17. Peter Wenham, *The Great and Close Siege of York* (Kineton, Roundwood Press, 1970), chapter nine discusses the known earthworks and their postwar survival.

18. Royal Commission on Historical Monuments (RCHM), *The City of York* (HMSO, London, 1971), Vol. II, p. 22.

19. RCHM, *York*, p. 24.

20. Wenham, *Great and Close*, pp. 41–2.

21. Bennett, 'The Royalist War Effort', pp. 224–6.

22. David Cooke, *The Road to Marston Moor* (Barnsley, Pen and Sword, 2007), p. 81; Peter R. Newman and Peter R. Roberts, *Marston Moor 1644: The Battle of the Five Armies* (Pickering, Blackthorn Press, 2003), p. 30; Frankl Kitson, *Prince Rupert Portrait of a Soldier* (London, Constable, 1994), p. 182.

23. Bennett, 'The Royalist War Effort', p. 225.

24. Abbott, *Writings*, Vol. I, p. 284.

25. Newman and Roberts, *Marston Moor*, pp. 29–30.

26. Peter Young, *Marston Moor 1644: The Campaign and the Battle* (Kineton, Windrush Press, 1970); Peter Newman, *The Battle of Marston Moor* (Chichester, John Byrd, 1981); Newman and Roberts, *Marston Moor*; Stuart Reid, *All the King's Armies* (Staplehurst, Spelmount Publishers, 2007), passim; Cooke, *Road to Marston Moor*, all contain differing dispositions.

27. Newman and Roberts, *Marston Moor*, p. 36.

28. Captain Stewart, *A Full relation of the Victory Obtained through God's Providence by the forces commanded* by *General Leslie* (Edinburgh, Evan Tyler, 1644), p. 4.

29. W.H., *A Relation of the Great Success of the Parliaments Forces under the Command of General Lesley, the Earl of Manchester and the Lord Fairfax* (W.F., 1644), np.

30. Lionel Watson, *A More Exact Relation of the Battel near York* (London, M. Simmons for H. Overton, 1644), p. 4.

31. Newman and Roberts, *Marston Moor*, pp. 50–1.

32. Stephen Bull, *The Furie of The Ordnance: Artillery in the English Civil Wars* (Woodbridge, The Boydell Press, 2008), discussed the battle and the numbers of guns on both sides but does not discuss the Bilton Bream incident in any detail. See Chapter 6.

33. Peter Newman, *Marston Moor, 2 July 1644: The Sources and the Site* (York, Borthwick Institute, 1978), p. 21. The local information supplied to me came from my brother-in-law, Paul Hawksby, who was born in New Row opposite Bilton Bream and whose family has lived in Tockwith for decades, as we walked the western end of the battlefield.

34. Stewart, *A Full Relation*, pp. 7–8; *The Glorious and Miraculous Battle at York* (Edinburgh, James Lindsey, 1644). W.H., *A Relation*, p. 4.

35. *Pers com* via email, in July 2015 Andrew Hopper responded to a direct question about Fairfax's commission: 'Essex commissioned Ferdinando Fairfax commander in chief of the northern counties of York, Lincoln, Notts, Derbyshire, Staffordshire, Lancashire, Cheshire, Durham, Northumberland, Cumberland and Westmorland on 24 November 1642. His letter did not mention a rank. – perhaps the issue was ducked? See TNA SP 28/3A/195. Ferdinando received this on 3 December (Lord Journals, v, 494) But Ferdinando submitted a pay claim as

General in 1646 that went back to Nov 1642: TNA, SP 23/3/214Ferdinando was required by Essex (seeking to mediate in the quarrel between the Fairfaxes and Hothams) to appoint the younger John Hotham as Lieutenant General (not Sir Thomas Fairfax) on 1 Feb 1643: BL, Add MS 34195, fo. 35. Therefore I have not found Sir Thomas held a commission from Essex as lieutenant-general in 1642/ early 1643 (although he probably did at some point later – perhaps after the Hothams' arrest). I expect it would be found somewhere in SP 28. Until then he acted as his father's cavalry commander, but by Essex's letter of 24 Nov 1642 Ferdinando was technically only permitted to commission to ranks of colonel and below.'

36. Watson, *A More Exact Relation*, p. 4.
37. Ibid.; Major General Sir James Lumsden's account, Young, *Marston Moor*, p. 267; Newman and Roberts, *Marston Moor*, p. 56.
38. *A Letter from Lord Leven, the Earl of Manchester and Lord Fairfax ... Concerning the Great Victory* (Edinburgh, Evan Tyler, 1644), p. 10.
39. Watson, *A More Exact Relation*, pp. 6–7.
40. Abbott, *Writings*, Vol. I, p. 287; W.H., *A Relation*, p. 3.
41. Stewart, *A Full Relation*, p. 6.
42. Abbott, *Writings*, Vol. I, pp. 287–8; Newman and Roberts, *Marston Moor*, pp. 98–9; Duchess of Newcastle, *The Life of William Cavendish, Duke of Newcastle* (London, 1886).
43. Watson, *A More Exact Relation*, p. 6.
44. Newman and Roberts, *Marston Moor*, p. 100; Cooke, *Road to Marston Moor*, p. 131. Young, *Marston Moor*, p. 134, thought that Manchester remained on the field longer than either Lord Leven or Lord Fairfax.
45. *The Glorious and Miraculous Battle at York*, p. 1.
46. Newman and Roberts, *Marston Moor*, p. 101.
47. Stewart, *A Full Relation*, pp. 7–8.
48. Watson, *A More Exact Relation*, p. 6.
49. Young, *Marston Moor*, pp. 243–4, citing Fairfax's own account.
50. Watson, *A More Exact Relation*, p. 6.
51. Stewart, *A Full Relation*, p. 10.
52. Newman and Roberts, *Marston Moor*, pp. 118–24.
53. Wanklyn, *Warrior Generals Winning the British Civil Wars* (London, Yale, 2010), p. 108. Malcolm Wanklyn, *Decisive Battles of the English Civil War* (Barnsley, Pen and Sword, 2006), pp. 132–5.
54. CSPD, 1644, p. 191.
55. Newcastle, *Life of William Cavendish*, p. 164; Rushworth, *Historical Collections*, Vol. III, Part 2, p. 644; A.S. Turberville, *A History of Welbeck Abbey and its Owners* (London, Faber and Faber, 1937), p. 112.
56. Newcastle, *Life of William Cavendish*, p. 164; Rushworth, *Historical Collections*, Vol III, Part 2, p. 664; Derbyshire Record Office, D803/M29 Gresley Copybook, f91, letter: Lord Fairfax to the Derby Committee, 7 August 1644; Alfred C. Wood, ed., *Memorials of the Holles Family* (London, Camden Society, 1937), p. 161.
57. Malcolm Wanklyn, *Decisive Battles*, p. 137.
58. Ibid., p. 149.

6 THE POLITICS OF WAR, 1644–7

1. Wilbur Cortez Abbott, *The Writings and Speeches of Oliver Cromwell* (Cambridge, MA, Harvard University Press, four volumes, 1937–47), Vol. I, pp. 287–8.
2. British Library, Harleian Mss166, f87; *W.H., A Relation of the Great Success of the Parliaments forces under the command of General Lesley, the Earl of Manchester and the Lord Fairfax* (W.F., 1644), and Lionel Watson, *A More Exact Relation of the Late Battell Near York* (London, M. Simmons for H. Overton, 1644). Both made the point that Cromwell was central to the victory. Even those with a Scottish perspective generally gave Cromwell credit, even if they would also credit David Leslie.
3. Abbott, *Writings*, Vol. I, p. 240.
4. Ibid., pp. 277–8.
5. Ibid., p. 302.
6. Ian Gentles, *The New Model Army in England, Ireland and Scotland, 1645–1653* (Oxford: Blackwell, 1992), p. 4.
7. Bulstrode Whitelocke, *Memorials of the English Affairs* (Oxford, Oxford University Press, 1853), Vol. I, p. 343.
8. Gentles, *New Model Army*, pp. 4–5.
9. HRO, 3343/M80, ff. 9, 11.
10. HRO, 3343/M80, ff. 9, 11; Gentles, *New Model Army*, p. 3.
11. Whitelocke, *Memorials*, Vol. II, p. 344.
12. Ibid.
13. Ibid., pp. 346–8.
14. Gentles, *New Model Army*, p. 5.
15. Abbott, *Writings*, Vol. I, p. 302.
16. Ibid., pp. 303–4.
17. Ibid., p. 305.
18. Ibid., pp. 306–7.
19. Ibid., p. 310.
20. Ibid.
21. Ibid., pp. 314–15.
22. Ibid.; Gentles, *New Model Army*, p. 6.
23. Martyn Bennett, *Oliver Cromwell* (London, Routledge, 2006), pp. 96–8.
24. Gentles, *New Model Army*, p. 10.
25. Ibid., pp. 10–11.
26. Malcolm Wanklyn, *Reconstructing the New Model Army* (Solihull, Helion and Co., 2015), p. 23.
27. Peter Young, *Naseby, 1645: The Campaign and the Battle* (London, Century Publishing, 1985), pp. 135–9, 144–8; Wanklyn, *Reconstructing*, pp. 50–1, 53, 55, 63.
28. Ibid., p. 25.
29. Ibid., pp. 24–5.
30. Young, *Naseby*, pp. 119–90, 195–200; Wanklyn, *Reconstructing*, p. 25.
31. Abbott, *Writings*, Vol. I, p. 334.
32. Ibid., pp. 339–41.
33. Gentles, *New Model Army*, p. 25.
34. Abbott, *Writings*, Vol. I, pp. 352–3.
35. Ibid., p. 355.

36. Gentles, *New Model Army*, pp. 26–7.
37. Glenn Foard, *Naseby: The Decisive Campaign* (Barnsley, Pen and Sword, 2004); Malcolm Wanklyn, *The Warrior Generals: Winning the British Civil Wars* (London, Yale University Press, 2010); Martin Marix Evans, *Naseby 1645: Triumph of the New Model Army* (Oxford, Osprey, 2007).
38. Suffolk Record Office, Purcell-Fitzgerald Collection, Acc. No. 2803, Estate Map of Naseby; Austin Woolrych, *The Battles of the English Civil War* (London, Batsford, 1960).
39. Martyn Bennett, 'The Royalist War Effort in the North Midlands, 1642–1646' (unpublished PhD thesis, Loughborough University of Technology, 1986), pp. 240–3.
40. W.G., *A Just Apology for an Abused Army* (London, H. Overton, 1647), p. 5; *Three Letters from the Right Honourable Sir Thomas Fairfax, Lieutenant General Cromwell* (London, 1645); Foard, *Naseby*, p. 191.
41. W.G., *A Just Apology*, p. 5.
42. Joshua Sprigge, *Anglia Rediviva*, cited in Young, *Naseby*, p. 348.
43. Foard, *Naseby*, p. 232, estimates this to be about 480 yards.
44. Austin Woolrych, *Battles of the English Civil War: Marston Moor, Naseby, Preston* (London, Phoenix Press, 2000), p. 126; Young, *Naseby*, p. 4.
45. Gentles, *New Model Army*, p. 55.
46. Foard, *Naseby*, pp. 197–201.
47. Marix Evans, *Naseby*, pp. 30–2; D. Blackmore, 'Counting the New Model Army', *Civil War Times* 5 (2003), p. 8; now available at: https://djblackmore.wordpress.com/home/articles-2/counting-the-new-model-army-2/.
48. H.G. Tibbet, ed., *The Letterbook of Colonel John Okey, 1606–1662* (Bedford, Bedford Historical Record Society, 1963), pp. 10–11; *Anglia Rediviva*, cited in Young, *Naseby*, pp. 338, 348.
49. The initial close can be discerned on the 1630 map, see note 38.
50. Marix Evans, *Naseby*, p. 62; Foard, *Naseby*, p. 246.
51. Ibid., pp. 252–3.
52. *Anglia Rediviva*, reprinted in Young, *Naseby*, pp. 350–1.
53. Foard, *Naseby*, p. 255.
54. *Anglia Rediviva*, reprinted in Young, *Naseby*, p. 350.
55. The Diary of Sir Henry Slingsby of Scriven, reprinted in Young, *Naseby*, p. 318.
56. Wanklyn, *Reconstructing*, p. 53.
57. Slingsby, as cited in Ibid., p. 318.
58. Not as John Lord Belasyse declared 'without any handsome dispute', cited in Young, *Naseby*, p. 321.
59. *Anglia Rediviva* makes it clear that the royalists marched forward, fired and then fell on with the sword, before being beaten by Whalley. It is also clear that they were rallied behind the royalist reserve. Young, *Naseby*, p. 349.
60. Cited in Young, *Naseby*, p. 349.
61. Marix Evans, *Naseby*, p. 74.
62. *Three Letters from the Right Honourable Sir Thomas Fairfax*, p. 3; Abbott, *Writings*, Vol. I, p. 300.
63. H.G. Tibbet, *Colonel John Okey, 1606–1662* (Bedford, Bedford Historical Record Society, XXXV), p. 11.

64. *Anglia Rediviva*, cited in Young, *Naseby*, p. 357.

65. *Three Letters from the Right Honourable Sir Thomas Fairfax*, p. 3 and Abbott, *Writings*, Vol. I, p. 300.

66. There has in recent years been something of a debate about the action at Wadborough, with Foard and, more concertedly perhaps, Marix Evans suggesting that the royalist reserves and other forces formed up to face their pursuers, and finds of bullets suggest that something of a firefight took place there with the New Model Army, which formed up in battle formation to confront the royalists. Wanklyn suggests that the evidence is too weak to suggest anything like a stand-off between two battalia and that it is more likely that this was simply a firefight between two moving forces, one retreating and one pursuing. In either case the outcome was the same; the royalists were pursued to Leicester and beyond.

67. *Moderate Intelligencer*, 19–26 June 1645, np; *Parliaments Post*, 24 June – 1 July 1645, np.; J. Rushworth, *Historical Collections*, Vol. IV, Part 1, p. 50; Bennett, 'The Royalist War Effort', p. 227.

68. Malcolm Wanklyn, 'The Royalist Campaign in Somerset in July 1645 Reconsidered', *Journey of the Society of Army Historical Research* 46/186 (1968), pp. 71–3.

69. Wanklyn, *Reconstructing*, pp. 50–1, 53.

70. Abbott, *Writings*, Vol. I, p. 365.

71. Ibid., p. 364.

72. Ibid., p. 365.

7 CROMWELL IN COMMAND

1. Ian Gentles, *The New Model Army in England, Ireland and Scotland, 1645–1653* (Oxford, Blackwell, 1992), p. 70.

2. Ibid.

3. *A Full Relation of the Taking of Bath* (London, Barnard Alsop, 1645), p. 1.

4. Ibid., p. 2; *A Fuller Relation of the Taking of Bath* (London, Thomas Bates, 1645), p. 3.

5. *A Full Relation of the Taking of Bath*, p. 3; *A Fuller Relation of the Taking of Bath*, p. 3; J. Wroughton, *A Community at War: The Civil War in Bath and North Somerset, 1642–1650* (Bath, The Lansdown Press, 1992), pp. 123–4.

6. *Two Letters to the Honourable William Lenthall Esquire Speaker of the House of Commons Concerning the Siege of Bristol* (London, Edward Husband, 1645), p. 3.

7. Ibid.

8. Gentles, *New Model Army*, p. 71.

9. Wroughton, *Community at War*, pp. 127–8; Bennett, *The Civil War in Britain and Ireland, 1637–1651* (Oxford, Blackwell, 1997), pp. 221–3.

10. Samuel R. Gardiner, *History of the Great Civil War* (Gloucestershire, Windrush Press, 1991), Vol. III, p. 305.

11. *Two Letters*, pp. 5–6.

12. Peter Young, *Naseby 1645: The Campaign and the Battle* (London, Century, 1985), pp. 135–6.

13. *Two Letters*, pp. 6–7.

14. Ian Gentles, *Oliver Cromwell God's Warrior and the English Revolution* (London, Palgrave Macmillan, 2011), p. 49.

15. *A Declaration of his Highness Prince Rupert* (London, 1645), p. 6.

16. J. Birch and T.W. Webb, ed., *Military Memoirs of Colonel John Birch* (London, Camden Society, 1873), p. 3.
17. *A Declaration*, p. 7.
18. Patrick McGrath, *Bristol and the Civil War* (Stroud, Bristol Historical Association and Alan Sutton, 1981), pp. 36–7.
19. Wilbur Cortez Abbott, *The Writings and Speeches of Oliver Cromwell* (Cambridge, MA, Harvard University Press, four volumes, 1937–47), Vol. I, p. 374.
20. *A Declaration*, p. 10.
21. *Lieut. Generall Cromwell's Letter* (London, Edward Husband, 1645), p. 4.
22. Abbott, *Writings*, Vol. I, p. 375.
23. *A True Relation of the Taking of Bristol* (London, Edward Husband, 1645), p. 16.
24. Ibid., p. 17.
25. Abbott, *Writings*, Vol. I, p. 375.
26. *A True Relation of the Taking of Bristol*, pp. 18–19; *A Declaration*, p. 10.
27. *A True Relation of the Taking of Bristol*, p. 19; *A True Relation of the Taking of Bristol by Sir Thomas Fairfax* (London, Richard Bishop, 1645), p. 3; Abbott, *Writings*, Vol. I., p. 375.
28. *A Declaration*, p. 28.
29. Abbott, *Writings*, Vol. I, p. 375.
30. *A True Relation of the Taking of Bristol by Sir Thomas Fairfax*, p. 3.
31. *A True Relation of the Taking of Bristol*, pp. 19–20.
32. Abbott, *Writings*, Vol. I, p. 375.
33. Ibid., p. 376.
34. *A Declaration*, p. 28.
35. Abbott, *Writings*, Vol. I, p. 377.
36. Ibid., p. 377.
37. Ibid., pp. 377–8.
38. Ibid., pp. 381–2.
39. H. Peters, *The Full and Last Relation of All Things Concerning Basing House* (London, Jane Coe, 1645), p. 1.
40. Martyn Bennett, 'Roman Catholic Officers in the North Midlands: 1642–1646', *Journal of Military and Strategic Studies* 6 (Winter 2003–Spring 2004), p. 15.
41. W. Beech, *More Sulfure for Basing* (London, John Wright, 1645), p. 14.
42. Peters, *The Full and Last Relation*, pp. 1–2, 3, 4.
43. David Farr, *Major General Thomas Harrison: Millenarianism, Fifth Monarchism and the English Revolution, 1616–1660* (Farnham, Ashgate, 2015), pp. 61–2.
44. Peters, *The Full and Last Relation*, p. 2.
45. *A Bloody Slaughter at Pembroke Castle in Wales* (London, Gilbert Mabbott, 1648), pp. 1–3, 4–6.
46. Bennett, *Civil Wars*, pp. 298–303.
47. Abbott, *Writings*, Vol. I, p. 606; *Colonell Poyers Forces in Wales Totally Routed* (London, BA, 1648), p. 1.
48. *Colonell Poyers Forces in Wales*, pp. 5–6.
49. Abbott, *Writings*, Vol. I, p. 609.
50. Ibid., pp. 611–12.
51. *A Dangerous Fight at Pembroke Castle* (London, RG, 1648), p. 6. Despite this pamphlet's title, the section on Pembroke is confined to the last half-page. It is dated 19 June, five days after Cromwell's letter to the committee at Derby House. There is a

brief reference to the failure of the attempted storm in *The Articles of Agreement between the Lord General and the Kentishmen* (London, BA, 1648), pp. 5–6, which mentions its failure.

52. Abbott, *Writings*, Vol. I., p. 613.
53. Ibid., p. 619.
54. Ibid., p. 621.
55. Alan Marshall, *Oliver Cromwell Soldier: The Military History of a Revolutionary at War* (London, Brassy's, 2004), pp. 174, 177; Frank Kitson, *Old Ironsides: The Military Biography of Oliver Cromwell* (London, Weidenfeld and Nicholson, 2004), p. 148, 151–2; Gentles, *New Model Army*, p. 258 and *Oliver Cromwell*, pp. 67–8.
56. Abbott, *Writings*, Vol. I, p. 606.
57. Ibid., p. 626.
58. *A Full Relation of the Great Victory of the Parliament's Forces led by Lievt Gen Cromwel* (London, John Wright, 1648), p. 1.
59. Stephen Bull and Mike Seed, *Bloody Preston: The Battle of Preston, 1648* (Lancaster, Carnegie Publications, 1998), pp. 60–1.
60. *A Full Relation of the Great Victory*, p. 1.
61. Ibid., p. 2; *A Letter Written by Lieutenant General Crumwell* (London, I.M., 1648), p. 33.
62. Bull and Seed, *Bloody Preston*, pp. 104–9.
63. *A Full Relation of the Great Victory*, pp. 3, 4.
64. *A Letter from Holland being a True Relation of all the Proceedings of the Northern Armies* (London, 12 October, 1648), p. 4.
65. *A Letter from Holland*, p. 5; Malcolm Wanklyn, *Decisive Battles of the English Civil War* (Barnsley, Pen and Sword, 2006), p. 195.
66. *A Letter from Holland*, p. 5.
67. *A Full Relation of the Great Victory*, pp. 3–4.
68. Ibid., p. 4.
69. *Three Letters Concerning the Surrender of Many Scottish Lords* (London, John Wright, 23 August 1648), pp. 1, 2.
70. Marshall, *Oliver Cromwell*, p. 187; Kitson, *Old Ironsides*, p. 158.
71. Kitson, *Old Ironsides*, p. 159; Marshall, *Oliver Cromwell*, pp. 187–8.
72. Wanklyn, *Decisive Battles*, p. 197.

8   CROMWELL ALONE: IRELAND, 1648–9

1. Wilbur Cortez Abbott, *The Writings and Speeches of Oliver Cromwell* (Cambridge, MA, Harvard University Press, four volumes, 1937–47), Vol. I, p. 650.
2. Ibid., p. 670.
3. 'Diary of Henry Guthrie', in J.G. Fyffe, ed., *Scottish Diaries and Memoirs 1550–1746* (Stirling, Enea's MacKay, 1928), pp. 152–3.
4. Martyn Bennett, *The Civil War in Britain and Ireland, 1637–1651* (Oxford, Blackwell, 1997), pp. 310–12.
5. Abbott, *Writings*, Vol. I, p. 674.
6. Ibid., p. 681.
7. Ibid., pp. 680–1.
8. Ibid., pp. 683–4.

9. Ibid., pp. 676–8, 696–9.

10. Ibid., pp. 690–1.

11. Ibid., pp. 691–2.

12. Abbott, *Writings*, Vol. II, p. 38.

13. Ibid., pp. 37, 38; Ivan Roots, *The Speeches of Oliver Cromwell* (London, Dent, 1989), p. 7.

14. Abbott, *Writings*, Vol. II, p. 36.

15. Alan Marshall, *Oliver Cromwell, Soldier: The Military History of a Revolutionary at War* (London, Brassy's, 2004), pp. 204–5.

16. Marshall, *Oliver Cromwell*, pp. 209–10; James Scott-Wheeler, *Cromwell in Ireland* (London, St Martin's Press, 1999), p. 83; Micheal O'Siochru, *God's Executioner: Oliver Cromwell and the Conquest of Ireland* (London, Faber and Faber, 2008), pp. 81–2; Malcolm Wanklyn, *The Warrior Generals: Winning the British Civil Wars* (London, Yale University Press, 2010), p. 210; Frank Kitson, *Old Ironsides: The Military Biography of Oliver Cromwell* (London, Weidenfeld and Nicholson, 2004), pp. 171–3.

17. Abbott, *Writings*, Vol. II, p. 111.

18. Siochru, *God's Executioner*, pp. 79–80.

19. Marshall, *Oliver Cromwell*, p. 208.

20. *Two Letters, One from Dublin in Ireland and the Other from Liverpoole, or A Bloody Fight in Ireland* (London, Robert Ibbotson, 1649), p. 5; Abbott, *Writings*, Vol. II, p. 125.

21. Marshall, *Oliver Cromwell*, p. 213.

22. Abbott, *Writings*, Vol. II, p. 126.

23. Ibid., p. 126; *Two Letters*, p. 2.

24. Ibid., p. 2; Abbott, *Writings*, Vol. II, p. 126.

25. Abbott, Vol. II, pp. 126–7.

26. Ian Gentles, *The New Model Army in England, Ireland and Scotland, 1645–1653* (Oxford, Blackwell, 1992), p. 361; Peter Gaunt, *Oliver Cromwell* (Oxford Blackwell, 1996), p. 119.

27. Gentles, *New Model Army*, p. 361.

28. John Morrill, 'Was Oliver Cromwell a War Criminal?', *BBC History* 1/1 (2001).

29. Bulstrode Whitelocke, *Memorials of the English Affairs during the Reign of Charles I* (Oxford, Oxford University Press, 1853), Vol. III, p. 111.

30. Marshall, *Oliver Cromwell*, p. 216.

31. Kitson, *Old Ironsides*, p. 176

32. Charles H. Firth, *Oliver Cromwell and the Rule of the Puritans in England* (Oxford, Oxford University Press, 1966), p. 255; J.C. Davis, *Oliver Cromwell* (London, Arnold, 2001), p. 108; Ian Gentles, *Oliver Cromwell: God's Warrior and the English Revolution* (London, Palgrave Macmillan, 2011), p. 113.

33. Whitelocke, *Memorials*, Vol. III, p. 110.

34. Scott-Wheeler, *Cromwell in Ireland*, pp. 86–8; Marshall, *Oliver Cromwell*, pp. 219–20; Wanklyn, *The Warrior Generals*, p. 211; Kitson, *Old Ironsides*, pp. 175–6.

35. Earl of Clarendon (edited by W. Mackay), *History of the Rebellion and Civil Wars in England* (Oxford, Oxford University Press, 1888, republished 1992), Vol. V, p. 102.

36. O'Siochru, *God's Executioner*, pp. 84–93.

37. *A Perfect and Particular Relation of the several marched and proceedings of the Armie in Ireland* (London, Francis Leach, 1649), p. 3; *A Letter From the Lord Lieutenant of Ireland* (London, Edward Husband, 1649), p. 1.

38. *A Perfect and Particular Relation*, p. 3; *A Letter from the Lord Lieutenant*, p. 1.

39. *A Perfect and Particular Relation*, p. 4; *A Letter from the Lord Lieutenant*, pp. 4–5.

40. *The Taking of Wexford* (London, Francis Leech, 1649), pp. 3–4.

41. *A Perfect and Particular Relation*, p. 7.

42. Marshall, *Oliver Cromwell*, pp. 222.

43. *A Letter from the Lord Lieutenant*, p. 5.

44. *A Perfect and Particular Relation*, p. 7.

45. Ibid.

46. *The Taking of Wexford*, p. 3; *A Letter from the Lord Lieutenant*, pp. 6–7.

47. *The Taking of Wexford*, pp. 3–4.

48. Marshall, *Oliver Cromwell*, p. 223.

49. This appears to be Gentles's view, Gentles, *New Model Army*, p. 367.

50. *A Letter from the Lord Lieutenant*, pp. 6–7. The capitalisation in this quotation is that in Abbott, *Writings*, Vol. II, p. 142.

51. Davies, *Oliver Cromwell*, p. 109; Gaunt, *Oliver Cromwell*, p. 119.

52. Kitson, *Old Ironsides*, p. 178.

53. Marshall, *Oliver Cromwell*, p. 224.

54. Gentles, *Oliver Cromwell*, p. 115.

55. Ibid.

56. Scott-Wheeler, *Cromwell in Ireland*, pp. 98–9.

57. O'Siochru, *God's Executioner*, pp. 97–8.

58. Padraig Lenihan, *Confederate Catholics at War, 1641–48* (Cork, Cork University Press, 2001), pp. 153–4.

59. Whitelocke, *Memorials*, p. 108.

60. *A Letter from the Right Honourable The Lord Lieutenant of Ireland Concerning the Surrender of the Town of Ross* (London, Edward Husband, 1650), pp. 8–9; Abbott, *Writings*, Vol. II, pp. 145–6.

61. Abbott, *Writings*, Vol. II, pp. 146–7.

62. *A Letter from the Right Honourable The Lord Lieutenant of Ireland*, pp. 10–11; Abbott, *Writings*, Vol. II, p. 148; Scott-Wheeler, *Cromwell in Ireland*, p. 102; Gentles, *Oliver Cromwell*, p. 116.

63. Clarendon, *History of the Rebellion*, Vol. V, p. 103.

64. Scott-Wheeler, *Cromwell in Ireland*, p. 108.

65. Abbott, *Writings*, Vol. II, pp. 176–7; Scott-Wheeler, *Cromwell in Ireland*, pp. 113–14; Kitson, *Old Ironsides*, pp. 180–1; Marshall, *Oliver Cromwell*, p. 226; O'Siochru, *God's Executioner*, pp. 103–4.

66. Abbott, *Writings*, Vol. II, pp. 192–3, 206.

67. Ibid., p. 213.

68. Ibid., pp. 212–13.

69. Ibid., pp. 213–14; Scott-Wheeler, *Cromwell in Ireland*, p. 128; O'Siochru, *God's Executioner*, p. 119.

70. Scott-Wheeler, *Cromwell in Ireland*, p. 129.

71. Sixteen troops should have been at least 1,480 and perhaps as many as 1,600 men, suggesting that on average the troops were half-size.

72. Abbott, *Writings*, Vol. II, pp. 217–18.

73. Ibid., pp. 217–19.

74. O'Siochru and Scott-Wheeler have different interpretations of this: the former thinks that Reynolds, backed by his and Ormond's mother, refused to obey the summons;

Scott-Wheeler seems to imply that he did and explained the weaknesses of the aged fortifications. O'Siochru, *God's Executioner*, p. 120; Scott-Wheeler, *Cromwell in Ireland*, p. 131.

75. Abbott, *Writings*, Vol. II, p. 224.
76. Ibid., p. 233.
77. Marshall, *Oliver Cromwell*, pp. 228–9.
78. Gentles, *New Model Army*, pp. 372–3; Gentles, *Oliver Cromwell*, p. 118.
79. *A Letter from the Lord Lieutenant of Ireland* (London, Edward Husband and John Field, 1650), passim; Kitson, *Old Ironsides*, p. 182
80. Whitelocke, *Memorials*, Vol. III, p. 178; Abbott, *Writings*, Vol. II, pp. 234–5.
81. Scott-Wheeler, *Cromwell in Ireland*, p. 151; O'Siochru, *God's Executioner*, pp. 124–5.
82. Marshall, *Oliver Cromwell*, p. 230; Scott-Wheeler, *Cromwell in Ireland*, p. 152; Abbott, *Writings*, Vol. II, p. 246.
83. Marshall, *Oliver Cromwell*, p. 230; Scott-Wheeler, *Cromwell in Ireland*, p. 152; Abbott, *Writings*, Vol. II, p. 246.
84. Marshall, *Oliver Cromwell*, p. 231; Scott-Wheeler, *Cromwell in Ireland*, p. 154; Gentles, *Oliver Cromwell*, p. 118.
85. Malcolm Wanklyn, *The Warrior Generals: Winning the British Civil Wars* (London, Yale University Press, 2010), p. 211; Kitson, *Old Ironsides*, p. 183; Gentles, *New Model Army*, p. 373; Marshall, *Oliver Cromwell*, p. 232; Gaunt, *Oliver Cromwell*, p. 121.
86. Abbott, *Writings*, Vol. II, p. 252.
87. *A Relation of the Execution of Iames Graham* (London, E. Griffin, 28 May, 1650), last page; Whitelocke, *Memorials*, Vol. III, p. 196.
88. Ibid., pp. 199, 201.

9   THE LORD GENERAL

1. Wilbur Cortez Abbott, *The Writings and Speeches of Oliver Cromwell* (Cambridge, MA, Harvard University Press, four volumes, 1937–47), Vol. II, p. 261.
2. Martyn Bennett, *The Civil War in Britain and Ireland, 1637–1651* (Oxford, Blackwell, 1997), pp. 339–41.
3. Abbott, *Writings*, Vol. II, pp. 262–3.
4. Bulstrode Whitelocke, *Memorials of English Affairs from the Beginning of the Reign of Charles I to the Restoration of Charles II* (Oxford, 1853), Vol. III, p. 206.
5. Whitelocke's coverage of the discussion appears to be verbatim, but it does not cover the whole meeting and stops part way through, before winding up by saying that 'Much other discourse passed [...] to the same purpose'. Whitelocke, *Memorials*, Vol. III, pp. 207–11.
6. Lucy Hutchinson, *Memoirs of the Life of Colonel Hutchinson* (London, Longman, Orme, Rees and Brown, 1806), pp. 311–12.
7. Whitelocke, *Memorials*, Vol. III, p. 211. Gentles suspects that Cromwell was tempted by the chance to be commander in chief and sought only to limit the damage Fairfax's standing down would have on the cause. Ian Gentles, *The New Model Army in England, Ireland and Scotland, 1645–1653* (Oxford, Blackwell, 1992), p. 386.
8. J.D. Grainger, *Cromwell Against the Scots: The Last Anglo-Scottish War, 1650–1652* (East Linton, Tuckwell Press, 1997), p. 12.

9. Grainger, *Cromwell Against the Scots*, pp. 16–17.
10. Whitelocke, *Memorials*, Vol. III, p. 212.
11. Ibid., p. 213.
12. Abbott, *Writings*, Vol. II, pp. 283–8; Whitelocke, *Memorials*, Vol. III, p. 222; Grainger, *Cromwell Against the Scots*, pp. 17–18.
13. Whitelocke, *Memorials*, Vol. III, p. 222; Gentles, *New Model Army*, p. 388.
14. Abbott, *Writings*, Vol. II, p. 298; Grainger, *Cromwell Against the Scots*, pp. 25–6.
15. Abbott, *Writings*, Vol. II, p. 300.
16. Ibid., p. 300; Grainger, *Cromwell Against the Scots*, p. 27.
17. Abbott, *Writings*, Vol. II, pp. 300–1.
18. Gentles, *New Model Army*, p. 391.
19. *A True Relation of the Routing of the Scottish Army* (London, John Rushworth, 9 September, 1650), p. 4.
20. Ibid., p. 4.
21. *A Letter from the Lord General Cromwell* (Cork, 1650), p. 5.
22. *A Brief Narrative of the Great Victory* (London, William Du Gard, 1650), p. 2; Gentles, *New Model Army*, p. 392.
23. *Scotland's Historic Fields of Conflict: Dunbar II*, Gazetteer, p. 3; http//www.battlefieldstrust.commedia600.pdf.
24. Gentles, *New Model Army*, p. 390.
25. Malcolm Wanklyn, *The Warrior Generals: Winning the British Civil Wars* (London: Yale University Press, 2010), p. 218.
26. Marshall, *Oliver Cromwell*, p. 246; Kitson, *Old Ironsides*, p. 196.
27. Whitelocke, *Memorials*, Vol. III, p. 238.
28. Gentles, *New Model Army*, p. 394.
29. Grainger, *Cromwell Against the Scots*, p. 42.
30. *A Letter from the Lord General*, p. 4; *A Brief Narrative of the Great Victory*, p. 2, says that there were only two regiments of foot and this was recorded by Whitelocke; Whitelocke, *Memorials*, Vol. III, p. 237.
31. Grainger, *Cromwell Against the Scots*, p. 45.
32. *A Letter from the Lord General*, p. 4.
33. Ibid., p. 2; Abbott, *Writings*, Vol. II, p. 329; *A True Relation of the Routing*, p. 4.
34. J.C. Davis, *Oliver Cromwell* (London, Arnold, 2001), p. 105; Peter Gaunt, *Oliver Cromwell* (Oxford Blackwell, 1996), p. 128.
35. Whitelocke, *Memorials*, Vol. III, p. 239.
36. Ibid., p. 238; Abbott, *Writings*, Vol. II, pp. 329–30.
37. Gentles, *New Model Army*, p. 394, hinted at this possibility, but unlike his assertion that Cromwell may have been outgeneralled by September, he does not repeat it in his biography of Cromwell. Ian Gentles, *Oliver Cromwell God's Warrior and the English Revolution* (London, Palgrave Macmillan, 2011), pp. 125–6.
38. Christopher Hill once suggested that Dunbar may have strengthened Charles Stuart's hand by weakening the Kirk Party. He certainly was able to take a more central role after the battle. Christopher Hill, *God's Englishman: Oliver Cromwell and the English Revolution* (Harmondsworth, Penguin, 1972), p. 120.
39. Whitelocke, *Memorials*, Vol. III, p. 239.
40. Keith Brown, *Kingdom or Province: Scotland and the Regal Union* (London, Palgrave Macmillan, 1992), p. 135.

41. News of Cromwell's illness seems to have reached parliament on 17 February 1651, but was reported in past tense by Whitelocke, On 10 March it was reported that he 'was sick'. Whitelocke, *Memorials*, Vol. III, pp. 289, 294.

42. Ibid., p. 323; Gaunt, *Oliver Cromwell*, p. 131.

43. Bennett, *Oliver Cromwell* (London, Routledge, 2006), pp. 192–3. Gaunt, *Oliver Cromwell*, p. 132, thinks that this was a deliberate act, basing his belief on the letter Cromwell had written to Speaker Lenthall on 4 August (Abbot, *Writings*, Vol. II, p. 444), suggesting that an invasions of England would allow the commonwealth a victory which would end the war before the winter.

44. Whitelocke reports this as a siege at St Johnstone, Perth's alternative name, Whitelocke, *Memorials*, Vol. III, pp. 326–7, as did Cromwell in his summons, Abbott, *Writings*, Vol. II, pp. 440, 442–3.

45. Whitelocke, *Memorials*, Vol. III, p. 295.

46. Abbott, *Writings*, Vol. III, p. 444; Whitelocke, *Memorials*, Vol. III, p. 329.

47. Ibid.

48. Grainger, *Cromwell Against the Scots*, p. 121.

49. Whitelocke, *Memorials*, Vol. III, pp. 331–2.

50. Ibid., pp. 338–9.

51. Ibid., p. 335.

52. Ibid.

53. Ibid., p. 336.

54. Grainger, *Cromwell Against the Scots*, pp. 126–7.

55. Colin Davies is one of those who suggests that it might all have been pre-planned, Davies, *Oliver Cromwell*, p. 106. But it must be remembered that this had happened before, just three years earlier, and some elements of the campaign such as the shadowing of the Scottish advance had been in place then. Moreover, many of the generals leading the campaign had been involved in defeating the 1648 invasion: rather than a real pre-planned campaign, it was a very skilful response enhanced by experience.

56. Whitelocke, *Memorials*, Vol. III, p. 338; Gentles, *New Model Army*, p. 405; Hill, *God's Englishman*, p. 124.

57. Davies thinks it unified the people and its new government. Davies, *Oliver Cromwell*, p. 106; Gentles, *Oliver Cromwell*, p. 127.

58. Whitelocke, *Memorials*, Vol. III, p. 328.

59. Ibid., p. 336.

60. There is a birds-eye view of the city, *An Exact Ground-Plot of ye City of Worcester as it stood fortifyd 3 Sept. 1651*, engraved in 1662. British library, http://collection.britishm useum.org/id/object/PPA171968, which shows the city surrounded by the fighting on 3 September 1651; it purports to show the newly constructed works as they were that day; Gentles, *New Model Army*, p. 406.

61. *A Letter from the Lord General Cromwell Touching the Great Victory Obtained Near Worcester* (London, John Field, 1651), p. 3.

62. Gentles, *New Model Army*, p. 408.

63. *A Letter from the Lord General*, p. 4; *An Exact and Perfect Relation of Every Particular of the Fight at Worcester* (London, Francis Leach, 1651), p. 1; Whitelocke, *Memorials*, Vol. III, p. 345.

64. *An Exact and Perfect Relation*, p. 1.

65. *A Letter from the Lord General*, p. 4; *An Exact and Perfect Relation*, p. 1; Whitelocke, *Memorials*, Vol. III, p. 345. Maurice Ashley, *Oliver Cromwell and the Puritan Revolution* (London, The English Universities Press, 1958), p. 61.

66. *An Exact and Perfect Relation*, p. 1.

67. Ibid., p. 2.

68. Gentles, *New Model Army*, p. 409.

69. Whitelocke, *Memorials*, Vol. III, p. 346

70. *A Letter from the Lord General*, p. 4; Whitelocke, *Memorials*, Vol. III, p. 346.

71. Ibid.

72. Ibid., p. 348.

73. Ibid.; *A True and Exact Relation*, p. 2.

74. Alan Marshall, *Oliver Cromwell, Soldier: The Military History of a Revolutionary at War* (London, Brassy's, 2004), pp. 262–3; Wanklyn, *Warrior Generals*, p. 226.

75. Kitson, *Old Ironsides*, p. 213; Davies, *Oliver Cromwell*, p. 106.

10 CROMWELL AT WAR

1. Wilbur Cortez Abbott, *The Writings and Speeches of Oliver Cromwell* (Cambridge, MA, Harvard University Press, four volumes, 1937–47), p. 463.

2. Ibid., p. 325.

3. Ibid., p. 453.

4. Ibid., p. 463.

5. Ibid., pp. 641–4.

6. Martyn Bennett, *Oliver Cromwell* (London, Routledge, 2006), pp. 206–7.

7. G. Parker, 'The Military Revolution 1560–1660: A Myth', *Journal of Modern History* 48/2 (1976), p. 205.

8. Andrew Hopper, *Black Tom: Sir Thomas Fairfax and the English Revolution* (Manchester, Manchester University Press, 2007), pp. 229–30.

9. Hopper, *Black Tom*, p. 234.

10. Ian Gentles, *Oliver Cromwell: God's Warrior and the English Revolution* (London, Palgrave Macmillan, 2011), p. 134.

11. Martyn Bennett, 'The Royalist War Effort in the North Midlands, 1642–1646' (unpublished PhD thesis, Loughborough University of Technology, 1986), Chapter 6.

12. Martyn Bennett, *The Civil War in Britain and Ireland, 1637–1651* (Oxford, Blackwell, 1997), pp. 253–4.

13. Frank Kitson, *Prince Rupert: Portrait of a Soldier* (London, Weidenfeld and Nicholson, 1996), p. 274.

14. Kitson, *Prince Rupert*, p. 279.

15. Ronald Hutton, *The Royalist War Effort* (London, Longman, 1981), pp. 138–42.

16. Kitson, *Prince Rupert*, p. 284.

17. Carl Von Clausewitz, *On War* (Oxford, Oxford University Press, 2008), p. 19.

18. D. Blackmore, *Destructive and Formidable: British Infantry Firepower 1642–1765* (Barnsley, Frontline, 2014), p. 23.

19. Ibid., pp. 16–17. George Monck in his treatise on war does not mention it despite writing, according to Maurice Ashley, the treatise in the middle of the civil war, although it was not published until 1671. George Monck, Duke of Albemarle,

Observations on Military and Political Affairs (London, Henry Mortlocke, 1671); Maurice Ashley, *Cromwell's Generals* (London, Jonathan Cape, 1954), pp. 199–200.

20. Malcolm Wanklyn, *Reconstructing the New Model Army* (Solihull, Helion and Co., 2015), pp. 100–1.
21. Monck, *Observations*, p. 45.
22. Gentles, *Oliver Cromwell*, p. 134.
23. Von Clausewitz, *On War*, p. 57.
24. Frank Kitson, *Old Ironsides: The Military Biography of Oliver Cromwell* (London, Weidenfeld and Nicholson, 2004), pp. 220–1.
25. Sun Tzu, *The Art of War* (London, Shambhala, 2005), pp. 1–7.
26. Kitson, *Old Ironsides*, p. 221.
27. Padraig Lenihan, *Confederate Catholics at War 1641–1649* (Cork, Cork University Press, 2001), p. 155.
28. Paul Scannell, *Conflict and Soldiers' Literature in Early Modern Europe: The Reality of War* (London, Bloomsbury, 2015), p. 10.
29. Ibid., pp. 147–9.
30. Von Clausewitz, *On War*, p. 50.
31. Peter Wilson, *Europe's Tragedy: A New History of the Thirty Years War* (London, Penguin, 2009), pp. 303–6, 472–5, 507–11.
32. Parker, 'Military Revolution', pp. 206–7.

BIBLIOGRAPHY

PRIMARY MANUSCRIPT SOURCES

British Library
Harleian Mss166.
Sloane Ms 2069.
An Exact Ground-Plot of ye City of Worcester as it stood fortifyd 3 September 1651, engraved in 1662 according to the British library, http://collection.british museum.org/id/object/PPA171968.

Derbyshire Record Office
D803/M29 Gresley Copybook.

Huntingdonshire County Record Office
3343/M80.
3870/1, Huntingdon St John Composite Register 1588–1682.
3870/1. Huntingdon St John Composite Register.
H Charter 17.
HB26/14 Survey of Huntingdon, 1572.
Vol/I/15 St Ives Manor Court 1632–61.
St Ives Vestry Book, 1626–1724.

Suffolk Record Office
Purcell-Fitzgerald Collection, Acc No. 2803. Estate Map of Naseby.

PRIMARY SOURCES: CONTEMPORARY NEWSBOOKS AND PUBLICATIONS

The Articles of Agreement between the Lord General and the Kentishmen (London, B.A., 1648).

Barriff, William, *Military Discipline or the Young Artillery Man* (London, 1635).

Beech, W., *More Sulfure for Basing* (London, John Wright, 1645).

Bloody Slaughter at Pembroke Castle in Wales (London, Gilbert Mabbott, 1648).

Brief Narrative of the Great Victory (London, William Du Gard, 1650).

Certain Informations, 20 February–6 March (1642–3).

Colonell Poyers Forces in Wales Totally Routed (London, B.A., 1648).

Cruso, John, *Instructions for the Cavallrie* (Cambridge, University of Cambridge, 1632).

A Dangerous Fight at Pembroke Castle (London, R.G., 1648).

A Declaration of His Highness Prince Rupert (London, 1645).

An Exact and Perfect Relation of Every Particular of the Fight at Worcester (London, Francis Leach, 1651).

A Full Relation of the Great Victory of the Parliament's Forces led by Lievt Gen Cromwel (London, John Wright, 1648).

A Full Relation of the Taking of Bath (London, Barnard Alsop, 1645).

A Fuller Relation of the Taking of Bath (London, Thomas Bates, 1645).

The Glorious and Miraculous Battle at York (Edinburgh, James Lindley, 1644).

Heath, J., *Flagellum* (London, 1663).

A Letter from Holland being a True Relation of all the Proceedings of the Northern Armies (12 October 1648).

A Letter from Lord Leven, the Earl of Manchester and Lord Fairfax… Concerning the Great Victory (Edinburgh, Evan Tyler, 1644).

A Letter from the Lord General Cromwell (Cork, 1650).

A Letter from the Lord General Cromwell Touching the Great Victory Obtained Near Worcester (London, John Field, 1651).

A Letter from the Lord Lieutenant of Ireland (London, Edward Husband, 1649).

A Letter from the Lord Lieutenant of Ireland (London, Edward Husband and John Field, 1650).

A Letter from the Right Honourable The Lord Lieutenant of Ireland Concerning the Surrender of the Town of Ross (London, Edward Husband, 1650).

A Letter Written by Lieutenant General Crumwell (I.M., August, 1648).

Lieut. Generall Cromwell's Letter (London, Edward Husband, 1645).

Mercurius Aulicus, 9th week (1643).

Moderate Intelligencer, 19–26 June (1645).

Monck, George, *Observations on Military and Political Affaires* (London, Henry Mortlocke, 1671).

Parliaments Post, 24 June–1 July (1645).

Peters, H., *The Full and Last Relation of All Things Concerning Basing House* (Jane Coe, London, 1645).

A Perfect and Particular Relation of the Several Marches and Proceedings of the Armie in Ireland (London, Francis Leach, 1649).

A Relation of the Execution of Iames Graham (E. Griffin, London, 28 May 1650).

Stewart, Captain, *A Full Relation of the Victory Obtained through God's Providence by the Forces Commanded by General Leslie* (Edinburgh, Evan Tyler, 1644).

The Taking of Wexford (London, Francis Leech, 1649).

Three Letters from the Right Honourable Sir Thomas Fairfax, Lieutenant General Cromwell (London, 16 June 1645).

Three Letters Concerning the Surrender of Many Scottish Lords (London, John Wright, 1648).

A True Relation of Colonel Cromwells Proceedings against the Cavaliers (London, Benjamin Allen, 1643).

A True Relation of the Routing of the Scottish Army (London, John Rushworth, 9 September 1650).

A True Relation of the Taking of Bristol (London, Edward Husband, 1645).

A True Relation of the Taking of Bristol by Sir Thomas Fairfax (London, Richard Bishop, 1645).

Two Letters, One from Dublin in Ireland and the Other from Liverpoole, or A Bloody Fight in Ireland (London, Robert Ibbotson, 1649).

Two Letters to the Honorable William Lenthal Esquire Speaker of the House of Commons Concerning the Siege of Bristol (London, Edward Husband, 1645).

Vernon, John, *The Young Horfe-man, or the Honeft Plain-dealing Cavalier* (London, Andrew Coe, 1644).

Watson, Lionel, *A More Exact Relation of the Late Battell Near York* (London, M. Simmons for H. Overton, 1644).

W.G., *A Just Apology for an Abused Army* (London, H. Overton, 1647).

W.H., *A Relation of the Great Success of the Parliaments Forces under the Command of General Lesley, the Earl of Manchester and the Lord Fairfax* (W.F., 1644).

PRINTED PRIMARY SOURCES

Abbott, Wilbur Cortez, *The Writings and Speeches of Oliver Cromwell* (Cambridge, MA, Harvard University Press, four volumes, 1937–47).

Ashburnham, John, *A Narrative of His Attendance on King Charles* (London, Payne and Foss, 1830).

Aubrey, John, *Brief Lives* (Harmondsworth, Penguin Classics, 1987).

Baillie, Robert (ed. D. Laing), *The Letters and Journals of Robert Baillie, 1637–1662* (Edinburgh, Bannatyne Club, three volumes, 1841–2).

Baker, W.T., ed., *Records of the Borough of Nottingham 1625–1702* (Nottingham, Nottingham Corporation, 1900).

Baxter, Richard (ed. N.H. Keeble), *The Autobiography of Richard Baxter* (London, Dent, 1985).

Bell, Robert, ed., *Memorials of the Civil War Comprising the Correspondence of the Fairfax Family, with the Most Distinguished Personages Engaged in that Memorable Contest* (London, Richard Bentley, 1849).

Birch, John (eds J. and T.W. Webb), *Military Memoirs of Colonel John Birch* (London, Camden Society, 1873).

Calendar of State Papers: Domestic, Charles I (Liechtenstein, Kraus Reprint, 1967).

Calendar of State Papers Relating to Ireland in the Reign of Charles I, 1633–47 (London, HMSO, 1901).

Calendar of State Papers Relating to Ireland in the Reign of Charles I, 1647–60 (London, HMSO, 1903).

Caulfield, R., ed., *The Council Book of the Corporation of Youghal* (Guilford, 1878).

Charles, B.J., ed., *Calendar of the Records of the Borough of Haverfordwest, 1539–1660* (Cardiff, University of Wales Press, 1967).

Clanricarde, Earl of (ed. J. Lowe), *Letter-Book of the Earl of Clanricarde 1642–47* (Dublin, Irish Manuscripts Commission, 1983).

Clarendon, Earl of (ed. W.H. Mackay), *The History of the Rebellion and Civil Wars in England* (Oxford, Clarendon Press, 1888).

Coates, W.H., H. Wilson, A.S. Young and V.F. Snow, eds, *The Private Journals of the Long Parliament* (New York, Yale University Press, 1982).

Cope, Esther S. and W.H. Coates, eds, *Proceedings of the Short Parliament of 1640* (London, Royal Historical Society, 1977).

Cranford, J. (printer), *The Souldiers Catechisme Composed for the Parliaments Army*, 1644 (London, Cresset Press, n.d.).

Cromwell, Oliver (ed. T. Carlyle), *Oliver Cromwell's Letters and Speeches*, 3rd edition (London, Ward Lock and Co., n.d.).

Erickson, J. ed., *The Journal of the House of Commons, 1547–1900* (New York, Readex Microprint, 1964).

Everitt-Green, Mary Ann, ed., *Calendar of the Committee for Compounding* (Liechtenstein, Kraus Reprint, 1967).

——, ed., *Calendar of the Committee for the Advance of Money* (Liechtenstein, Kraus Reprint, 1967).

Firth, Charles H., ed., 'Journal of Prince Rupert's Marches', *English Historical Review* 13 (1899).

Firth, Charles H. and R.S. Rait, eds, *Acts and Ordinances of the Interregnum* (London, HMSO, 1911).

Fleming, D.H., ed., 'Scotland's Supplication and Complaint against the Book of Common Prayer (otherwise Laud's Liturgy), the Book of Canons and the Prelates, 18 October 1637', *Proceedings of the Society of Antiquaries of Scotland* 60 (1825–6).

Fyffe, J.G., ed., *Scottish Diaries and Memoirs 1550–1746* (Stirling, Eneas MacKay, 1928).

Gardiner, Samuel R., ed., *The Constitutional Documents of the Puritan Revolution* (Oxford, Clarendon Press, 1889).

Gell, John, 'A True Relation of What Service Hath been Done by Colonel John Gell', unpublished tract, in Steven Glover, *The History, Directory and Gazetteer of Derbyshire* (Derby, 1829).

Historical Manuscripts Commission Volumes, *Report on the Manuscripts of the Marquis of Ormonde* (London, HMSO, 1899); *Report on the Manuscripts of the Marquis of Ormonde*, new series (London: HMSO, 1902); *Report on the Papers of Reginald Rawdon Hastings* (London: HMSO, 1930).

Hutchinson, Lucy, *Memoirs of the Life of Colonel Hutchinson* (London, Longman, Orme, Rees and Brown, 1806).

Jansson, Marija, ed., *Two Diaries of the Long Parliament* (Stroud, Sutton, 1984).

Johnston of Wariston, Archibald (eds G.H. Paul, D.H. Fleming and J.D. Ogilvie), *Diary of Sir Archibald Johnston of Wariston* (three volumes, Edinburgh, Scottish History Society Publications, LXI, 1911, Second Series, XVIII, 1919, Third Series, XXIV, 1940).

Luke, Samuel (ed. G. Phillips), *Journal of Sir Samuel Luke* (three volumes, Oxford, Oxfordshire Record Society, 1950–3).

Margaret, Duchess of Newcastle (ed. C.H. Firth), *Memoirs of William Cavendish Duke of Newcastle and Margaret His Wife* (London, Routledge, n.d.).

Morton, A.L., *Freedom in Arms: A Selection of Leveller Writings* (London, Lawrence and Wishart, 1975).

Razzell, Edward and Peter Razzell, eds, *The English Civil War: A Contemporary Account. The Papers of the Venetian Ambassadors, 1625–1675* (five volumes, London, Caliban, 1996).

Roots, Ivan, *The Speeches of Oliver Cromwell* (London, Dent, 1989).

Roy, Ian, ed., *The Royalist Ordinance Papers* (Oxford, Oxfordshire Record Society, 1964).

Rushworth, John, ed., *Historical Collections* (seven volumes, London, 1657–1701).

Sun Tzu (trans. Thomas Cleary), *The Art of War* (Boston, USA, Shambhala, 2005).

Symonds, Richard (ed. C.E. Long), *Diary of the Marches of the Royal Army* (London, Camden Society, 1859).

Terry, C.S., ed., *Papers Relating to the Army of the Solemn League and Covenant: 1643–7* (two volumes, Edinburgh, Edinburgh University Press, 1917).

Tibbet, H.G., *The Letter Book of Colonel John Okey, 1606–1662* (Bedford, Bedford Historical Record Society, XXXV, 1963).

Von Clausewitz, Carl, *On War* (Oxford, Oxford University Press, 2008).

Warburton, Eliot, ed., *Memoirs of Prince Rupert and the Cavaliers, Including their Private Correspondence* (London, 1849).

Whitelocke, Bulstrode, *Memorials of English Affairs from the Beginning of the Reign of Charles I to the Restoration of Charles II* (Oxford, 1853).

Wood, Alfred C., ed., *Memorials of the Holles Family* (London, Camden Society, 1937).

SECONDARY SOURCES

Anderson, Matthew S., *War and Society in Europe of the Old Regime, 1618–1789* (Leicester, Leicester University Press, 1988).

Ashley, Maurice, *Cromwell's Generals* (London, Jonathan Cape, 1954).

——, *Oliver Cromwell and the Puritan Revolution* (London, The English Universities Press, 1958).

——, *The Battle of Naseby and the Fall of King Charles I* (Stroud, Sutton, 1992).

Ashton, Robert, *The English Civil War: Conservatism and Reaction* (London, Arnold, 1978).

Barratt, John, *Sieges of the English Civil Wars* (Barnsley, Pen and Sword, 2009).

Bennett, Martyn, 'Contribution and Assessment: Financial Exactions in the English Civil War', *War and Society* 5/1 (1986).

——, 'The Royalist War Effort in the North Midlands, 1642–1646' (unpublished PhD thesis, Loughborough University of Technology, 1986).

——, *Travellers' Guide to the Battlefields of the English Civil War* (Exeter, Webb and Bower, 1990).

——, *The Civil War in Britain and Ireland, 1637–1651* (Oxford, Blackwell, 1997).

——, 'Roman Catholic Officers in the North Midlands: 1642–1646', *Journal of Military and Strategic Studies* 6 (Winter 2003–Spring 2004).

——, *Oliver Cromwell* (London, Routledge, 2006).

Black, Jeremy, *A Military Revolution? Military Change and European Society 1550–1800* (Basingstoke, Macmillan, 1991).

——, 'Was there a Military Revolution in Early Modern Europe?', *History Today* 58/7 (2008).

Blackmore, David, *Arms and Armour of the English Civil War* (London, Royal Armouries, 1990).

——, 'Counting the New Model Army', *Civil War Times* 5 (2003), available at https://djblackmore.wordpress.com/home/articles-2/counting-the-new-model-army-2/.

——, 'Destructive and Formidable: British Infantry Firepower 1642–1765' (unpublished PhD thesis, Nottingham Trent University, 2012).

——, *Destructive and Formidable: British Infantry Firepower 1642–1765* (Barnsley, Frontline, 2014).

Brown, Keith, *Kingdom or Province? Scotland and the Regal Union* (London, Palgrave Macmillan, 1992).

Brunton, David and D.H. Pennington, *Members of the Long Parliament* (Cambridge, MA, Harvard University Press, 1958).

Bull, Stephen, *The 'Furie' of the Ordnance* (Woodbridge, Boydell, 2008).

Bull, Stephen and Mike Seed, *Bloody Preston: The Battle of Preston, 1648* (Lancaster, Carnegie Publications, 1998).

Capp, Bernard, *Cromwell's Navy* (Oxford, Clarendon Press, 1989).

Carlton, Charles, *Going to the Wars: The Experience of the British Civil Wars, 1638–1651* (London, Routledge, 1992).

Carter, M., ed., *Edward Pettis's Survey of St Ives, 1728* (Cambridge, Cambridge Record Society, 16, 2002).

Casaway, Jerold I., *Owen Roe O'Neill and the Struggle for Catholic Ireland* (Philadelphia, University of Pennsylvania Press, 1984).

Cooke, David, *The Road to Marston Moor* (Barnsley, Pen and Sword, 2007).

Coward, Barry, *Oliver Cromwell* (London, Longman, 1991).

Cust, Richard, *The Forced Loan and English Politics, 1626–1628* (Oxford, Oxford University Press, 1987).

Davies, C., *Stamford in the Civil War* (Stamford, Paul Watkins, 1992).

Davis, J.C., *Oliver Cromwell* (London, Arnold, 2001).

Day, Jon, *Gloucester and Newbury: The Turning Point of the Civil War* (Barnsley, Pen and Sword, 2007).

Donagan, Barbara, *War in England, 1642–1649* (Oxford, Oxford University Press, 2008).

Donald, Peter, *An Uncouncelled King Charles I and the Scottish Troubles, 1637–1641* (Cambridge, Cambridge University Press, 1990).

Durston, Christopher, *Cromwell's Major-Generals: Godly Government during the English Revolution* (Manchester, Manchester University Press, 2001).

Edwards, David, Padraig Lenihan and Clodagh Tait, eds, *Age of Atrocity: Violence and Political Context in Early Modern Ireland* (Dublin, Four Courts, 2007).

Farr, David, *Major General Thomas Harrison, Millenarianism, Fifth Monarchism and the English Revolution, 1616–1660* (Farnham, Ashgate, 2015).

Firth, Charles H., *Oliver Cromwell and the Rule of the Puritans in England* (Oxford, Oxford University Press, 1966, originally published in 1900).

——, *Cromwell's Army* (London, Greenhill, 1992, originally published 1902).

Fissell, Mark, *The Bishops' Wars: Charles I's Campaigns Against Scotland, 1638–1640* (Cambridge, Cambridge University Press, 1994).

Foard, Glenn, *Naseby: The Decisive Campaign* (Barnsley, Pen and Sword, 2004).

Fraser, Antonia, *Cromwell: Our Chief of Men* (London, Weidenfeld and Nicholson, 2008, originally published 1973).

Gardiner, Samuel R., *History of the Great Civil War* (Gloucestershire, Windrush Press, 1991).

Garner, A.-A., *Boston and the Great Civil War* (Boston, Richard Kay, 1972).

Gaunt, Peter, *Oliver Cromwell* (Oxford, Blackwell, 1996).

———, 'The Battle of Gainsborough, 28 July, 1643', *Cromwelliana* (1998).

———, *The English Civil War: A Military History* (London, I.B.Tauris, 2014).

Gentles, Ian, *The New Model Army in England, Ireland and Scotland, 1645–1653* (Oxford, Blackwell, 1992).

———, *Oliver Cromwell: God's Warrior and the English Revolution* (London, Palgrave Macmillan, 2011).

Grainger, John D., *Cromwell Against the Scots: The Last Anglo-Scottish War, 1650–1652* (East Linton, Tuckewell Press, 1997).

Gruber von Arni, Eric and Andrew Hopper, curators, 'Battle Scarred: Surgery, Medicine and Military Welfare during the British Civil Wars', exhibition at the National Civil War Centre (Leicester, University of Leicester, 2016).

Hill, Christopher, *God's Englishman: Oliver Cromwell and the English Revolution* (Harmondsworth, Pelican, 1979).

Holmes, Clive, *The Eastern Association in the English Civil War* (Cambridge, Cambridge University Press, 1974).

———, *Seventeenth-Century Lincolnshire* (Lincoln, History of Lincoln Committee, 1980).

Hopper, Andrew, *Black Tom: Sir Thomas Fairfax and the English Revolution* (Manchester, Manchester University Press, 2007).

Hutton, Ronald E., *The Royalist War Effort* (London, Longman, 1982).

Kenyon, John P., *The Civil Wars of England* (London, Weidenfeld and Nicholson, 1989).

Kingra, Mahinder S., 'The *Trace Italienne* and the Military Revolution during the Eighty Years' War 1567–1648', *The Journal of Military History* 57 (1973).

Kitson, Frank, *Prince Rupert: Portrait of a Soldier* (London, Constable, 1994).

———, *Old Ironsides: The Military Biography of Oliver Cromwell* (London, Weidenfeld and Nicholson, 2004).

Lee, Maurice, *The Road to Revolution: Scotland under Charles I* (Chicago, University of Illinois Press, 1985).

Little, Patrick, ed., *Oliver Cromwell: New Perspectives* (London, Palgrave, 2009).

McGrath, P., *Bristol and the Civil War* (Stroud, Bristol Historical Association and Alan Sutton, 1981).

Malcolm, Joyce L., 'A King in Search of Soldiers: Charles I in 1642', *Historical Journal* 21/2 (1978).

Marshall, Alan, *Oliver Cromwell, Soldier: The Military History of a Revolutionary at War* (London, Brassey's, 2004).

Matrix Evans, Martin, *Naseby 1645: Triumph of the New Model Army* (Oxford, Osprey, 2007).

Morrill, John S., ed., *Oliver Cromwell and the English Revolution* (London, Longman, 1991).

———, *The Nature of the English Revolution* (London, Longman, 1993).

———, 'Was Oliver Cromwell a War Criminal?', *BBC History*, 1/1 (2001).

Mortimer, Geoffrey, *Wallenstein: The Enigma of the Thirty Years War* (London, Palgrave, 2010).

Newman, Peter R., *Marston Moor, 2 July 1644: The Sources and the Site* (York, Borthwick Institute, 1978).

———, *The Battle of Marston Moor* (Chichester, Anthony Bird, 1981).

————, *Royalist Officers in England and Wales, 1642–60* (New York, Garland, 1981).

————, *The Old Service: Royalist Regimental Colonels and the Civil War, 1642–46* (Manchester, Manchester University Press, 1993).

Newman, Peter R. and Peter R. Rogers, *Marston Moor 1644: The Battle of Five Armies* (Pickering, Blackthorne Press, 2003).

O'Siochru, Micheál, *God's Executioner* (London, Faber, 2008).

Page, W., *Victoria County History of Huntingdonshire* (London, St Catherine's Press, 1932).

Parker, Geoffrey, *The Military Revolution*, 2nd edition (Cambridge, Cambridge University Press, 1996).

Patterson, W.B., *King James VI ad I and the Reunion of Christendom* (Cambridge, Cambridge University Press, 1997).

Paul, Robert S., *The Lord Protector* (Grand Rapids, Michigan, William B. Eerdmans Publishing Company, 1955).

Porter, Stephen, 'The Fire Raid in the English Civil War', *War and Society* 2/2 (1984).

Prest, Wilfred, *The Inns of Court under Elizabeth I and the Early Stuarts* (London, Longman, 1972).

Quintrell, Brian, 'Oliver Cromwell and the Distraint of Knighthood', *Bulletin of the Institute of Historical Research* 57 (1984).

Reid, Stuart, *All the King's Armies* (Staplehurst, Spelmount Publishers, 2007).

Reilly, Tom, *Cromwell: An Honourable Enemy* (Dublin, Brandon Books, 1999).

Roberts, Keith, *Pike and Shot Tactics* (Oxford, Osprey, 2010).

Rogers, Clifford J., *The Military Revolution Debate: Readings on the Military Transformation of Early Modern Europe* (Boulder, Westview Press, 1995).

Royal Commission on Historical Monuments, *The City of York* (London, HMSO, 1971).

Russell, Conrad, *The Crisis of Parliaments: English History, 1509–1660* (Oxford, Oxford University Press, 1971).

Scotland's Historic Fields of Conflict: Dunbar II, Gazetteer, http//www.battlefieldstrust. commedia600.pdf.

Scott-Wheeler, James, *Cromwell in Ireland* (Dublin, Gill and Macmillan, 1999).

————, *The Irish and British Wars 1637–1654* (London, Routledge, 2002).

Seel, G.E., *The Civil Wars and Republic* (London, Longman, 1999).

Smith, David I., *Cromwell and the Interregnum* (Oxford, Blackwell, 2003).

Stevenson, David, *The Covenanters: The National Covenant and Scotland* (Edinburgh, Saltire Society, 1981).

————, *The Scottish Revolution 1637–1644* (Edinburgh, John Donald, 2003, originally published 1973).

————, *Revolution and Counter Revolution in Scotland, 1644–51* (Edinburgh, John Donald, 2003, originally published 1977).

Stoyle, Mark, *Loyalty and Locality: Popular Allegiance in the English Civil War* (Exeter, Exeter University Press, 1994).

————, *From Deliverance to Destruction: Rebellion and Civil War in an English City* (Exeter, Exeter University Press, 1996).

————, *The Black Legend of Prince Rupert's Dog: Witchcraft and Propaganda in the English Civil War* (Exeter, University of Exeter, 2011).

Turberville, A.S., *A History of Welbeck Abbey and its Owners* (London, Faber and Faber, 1937).

Wanklyn, Malcolm, 'The Royalist Campaign in Somerset in July 1645 Reconsidered', *Journey of the Society of Army Historical Research* 47/186 (1968).

———, *Decisive Battles of the English Civil War* (Barnsley, Pen and Sword, 2006).

———, *The Warrior Generals: Winning the British Civil Wars* (London, Yale University Press, 2010).

———, *Reconstructing the New Model Army* (Solihull, Helion and Co., 2015).

Wanklyn, Malcolm and Peter Young, 'A King in Search of Soldiers: Charles I in 1642: A Rejoinder', *Historical Journal* 24/1 (1981).

Wenham, Peter, *The Great and Close Siege of York* (Kineton, Roundwood Press, 1970).

West, J., *Oliver Cromwell and the Battle of Gainsborough* (Boston, Richard Key, 1992).

Wilson, Peter, *Europe's Tragedy: A New History of the Thirty Years War* (London, Penguin, 2009).

Wood, Alfred C., *Nottinghamshire in the Civil War* (Wakefield, S.R. Publishing, 1971).

Wood, A.P., *The History of Huntingdon from the Earliest to the Present Times* (Huntingdon, 1824).

Woolrych, Austin, *Battles of the English Civil War* (London, Pan, 1966).

———, *Battles of the English Civil War: Marston Moor, Naseby, Preston* (London, Phoenix Press, 2000).

———, *Britain in Revolution* (Oxford, Oxford University Press, 2002).

Worden, Blair, *Roundhead Reputations: The English Civil War and the Passions of Posterity* (Harmondsworth, Penguin, 2001).

Wroughton, John, *A Community at War: The Civil War in Bath and North Somerset 1642–1650* (Bath, The Lansdown Press, 1992).

Young, Peter, 'The Royalist Army at the Relief of Newark', *Journal of the Society for Army Historical Research* 30/124 (1953).

———, *Edgehill 1642: The Campaign and the Battle* (Kineton, Roundway Press, 1967).

———, *Marston Moor 1644: The Campaign and the Battle* (Kineton, Roundway Press, 1970).

———, *Naseby 1645: The Campaign and the Battle* (London, Century, 1985).

Young, Peter, ed., *Newark upon Trent: The Civil War Siegeworks* (London, HMSO, 1964).

INDEX